Ray Tracing: A Tool for All

Jon Peddie

Ray Tracing: A Tool for All

Jon Peddie
Jon Peddie Research
Belvedere Tiburon, CA, USA

ISBN 978-3-030-17489-7   ISBN 978-3-030-17490-3   (eBook)
https://doi.org/10.1007/978-3-030-17490-3

This Springer imprint is published by the registered company Springer Nature Switzerland AG
The registered company address is: Gewerbestrasse 11, 6330 Cham, Switzerland

Foreword I

Shaded rendering has been one of the central topics of computer graphics research since the 1960s. Over the following decades, researchers have developed rendering techniques that evolved step-by-step from smooth shading to realistic reflections and ultimately to a level of realism that allows us to ignore the fact that the rendered images are not real.

Back in the early 1980s, Jon Peddie and I met for breakfast one weekend morning to discuss ways to commercialize realistic rendering. At the time, the idea seemed far-fetched. Today, it has become commonplace and it has found applications we had not imagined.

Making use of realistic rendering, whether for Hollywood special effects, video games, or redecorating your living room still requires an understanding of what it is and how it works. Papers, journals, books, and courses dive into the topic and open up the world of rendering to the average programmer. But what if you are not a programmer? Today, most of us want to use the technology without programming it from scratch. Regardless, a sophisticated graphics system requires some understanding of the technology in order to get the most use from it. That's where Jon Peddie's text comes into play.

Somewhere between the ten thousand foot overview and the vast collection of GPU code hiding beneath the surface is a level of explanation and understanding that provides a prospective user with enough background to get started. This book covers that range in detail, but in a manner that can be understood without reviewing graduate-level mathematics. It does a particularly good job of identifying both hardware and software resources to enable a beginning practitioner to get up and running.

To me personally, the most compelling sections of the book are the ones that fall into the category labeled "I didn't know that!" The number of contributors and the diversity of approaches that have brought realistic rendering to its current state are remarkable. Rather than attempting to condense this all into a summary, Jon has opted for completeness and has given the reader a full view of the topic.

In essence, this book is a story. It explains the technology, the applications, and the products, while also providing a history. You, the reader, don't need to spend 40 years writing and reviewing technical papers on rendering and ray tracing. Just read the book.

Chapel Hill, North Carolina   Turner Whitted

Foreword II

Ray tracing is a topic that has inspired many engineers, artists, and storytellers. For some, it is a computer graphics course; for others, it is a degree; and for many—an entire career.

I count myself as one of those people so inspired. One day strolling through the engineering library, I browsed through a book entitled simply "Introduction to Ray Tracing." It instantly captured my imagination. The images were strikingly beautiful (compared to the state of the art the time), the math was approachable, and it only took a few hours to produce a single image! I soon learned that I was not alone—that other students and researchers were exploring the frontiers "photorealism," or the idea that a computer-generated image could be indistinguishable from a photograph.

For me, this inspiration launched a career. I am now a Vice President at Nvidia where I lead a team of dedicated engineers who are striving to make ray tracing fast enough to be used in real-time computer graphics. The goal is to bring the techniques that have brought advancements in visual effects and animation to gaming and design. Many in the industry share that goal.

It was this role that introduced me to Jon Peddie and his vast sphere of influence. I quickly learned that he travels the world in pursuit of technology, especially computer graphics, and ray tracing in particular. He is always learning, asking questions, probing technology, and getting all sides of a story. Along with Kathleen Maher, Jon integrates this information into some of the most influential reports in the computer graphics industry, including TechWatch and the JPR Workstation report. In addition, Jon gives countless lectures, serves on advisory boards, and has been recognized by ACM and CAAD for his efforts.

That is why I was intrigued when he told me of his plan to write a book on ray tracing. Many technical books have covered this topic in great depth, and Jon mentions many of them herein. However, "Ray Tracing: A Tool for All" brings an entirely fresh perspective to the topic. While he covers the technology and business in great depth, it is approachable by technical and non-technical readers alike.

Ray tracing has roots in medieval times, but received first attention for computer graphics via a paper by Turner Whitted at SIGGRAPH 1979. Ray tracing operates by simulating the physics of light as particles that interact with various surfaces, using very few simplifying assumptions. Because the human visual system is highly attuned to lighting in the physical world, subtle details can make the difference between an object looking "realistic" and "fake." Ray tracing can capture these effects, such as global illumination, soft shadows and accurate materials. Consequently, ray tracing is nearly ubiquitous in computer animation and visual effects industry. It is also rapidly becoming the standard in product design, marketing, and even real-time gaming.

A ray tracing program can be simple enough to fit on a business card, but turning it into a fully functional system (or renderer) results in very large sophisticated software. The results can be undeniably beautiful, and this book highlights many of these examples.

What Jon has done is take all of this technical excitement—the passions of inventors, the curiosity of a student or researcher, the creativity of the artists—and mapped it to the ecosystem and companies in the modern world. He covers the businesses around ray tracing, the interplay between the technology and the companies, and he speculates on what the future will bring to the industry. True to Jon's reputation, the book is filled with facts, data, and unique insight. It discusses the history, the workflows, the research papers, the hardware, the start-ups, and the primary technical challenges being tackled in the industry today.

Behind the technology and businesses, the primary goal of computer graphics is to use a visual I illusion to tell a story. Whether used for entertainment, a product introduction, or to gain insight—ray tracing has found application in a broad set of industries. Jon outlines these applications and ecosystems in a clear manner.

I learned a lot from reading "Ray Tracing: A Tool for All." It collects the under-documented aspects of computer graphics and paints a portrait that blends both technology and business. I expect that it will help inspire even more people to join in the quest of photorealistic rendering.

Dr. Steven G. Parker
Vice President
Professional Graphics, Nvidia
Chapel Hill, North Carolina

Acknowledgements

How could anyone write a book like this without having too many friends? I've met so many people over the years, starting with Turner Whited in 1979, who have made incredible discoveries and inventions. And then, demonstrating their extraordinary grace and charity, they took the time to edit (and mostly correct) the material I sent to them—I am truly blessed.

I know I'm missing someone or two in this list, and to you, should you read this, I am truly sorry—call me, I'll make amends.

My benefactors and mentors—the folks who really know what ray tracing is about, this book really would not exist without these people.

Helen Desmond, my patient and supportive editor at Springer
Alexander Keller, Nvidia—great comments and polite nudges
Alexandra Constantine, Autodesk
Ankit Patel, Nvidia
Brian Savery, AMD
Colin McLaughlin, Chaos—invaluable resource
Daniel Pohl, Intel—brilliant developer
David Harold, Imagination Technologies
David Laur, Pixar
David McGavran, Maxon
David Tracy, Chaos
Frederic Servant, Autodesk—a real pro
Glen Matthews, AMD
Henrik Edstrom, Autodesk
Igor Zanic, Houdini
Jama Jurabaev, Lucas Arts
John Hart, University Illinois
Joseph Taraborrelli, Sony
Josh Mings, Luxion
Katrina Felicano-Stoddard, Intel
Lon Grohs, Chaos

Ludwig von Reiche, Nvidia
Lynette Clee, Chaos
Oliver Meiseberg, Maxon
Phillip Miller, Chaos
Rolf Herken, ViewMagic
Sean Morrison, BRL-CAD
Steven Parker, Nvidia—who didn't sign up to be my editor and ended up reading every word
Tom Svilans, 3D modeler
Ton Roosendaal, Blender
Turner Whited, Nvidia (ret)—a big debt

My colleagues and collaborators

Kathleen Maher—encouraged me to see it through
Ruchike Saini
Jaydeep Bhattacharjee
Robert Dow
Peter McGuinness

Contents

List of Figures

List of Tables

Chapter 1
Preface

Abstract The goal of this book is to explain the many methods of rendering a digital image in a computer and what is ray tracing. Ray tracing is one part of the continuum of rendering solutions on the path to a perfect photorealistic image. Ray tracing has several cousins with a similar name such as Path Tracing and ray casting, which sometimes get used interchangeably; that is not correct and can be confusing. One of the objectives of this book is to establish clear delineation between those other technologies whose only common element is a word, but not the technology, algorithm, or result. Ray tracing holds the promise of providing us with the most cost-effective photorealistic images possible. The process has been criticized for being such an enormous consumer of computer resources, but new developments in hardware and algorithms are changing that and making real-time ray tracing not only possible but practical.

The ambition of artists, film producers, product designers, and engineers has been to simulate an image of a scene, a story, a product or a building before it was ever actually constructed. Architects have built scale models of buildings, as have car designers to convey the ideas they are trying to express. Film and game producers and directors have used storyboards to try and convey the sense of the movie or the game. And advertisers want to create perfect renditions of their product in the best possible light. In addition, product and machinery designers want to find the weaknesses in a design before it is ever built. Likewise, movie directors want to see what the final imager will look like before the arduous task of postproduction or to create a whole new world that does not actually exist. And marketers want to show potential customers what a product will look like to stimulate demand for it. At the same time, all these desires are also used for testing ideas. Should a character in a movie have green skin, have long hair or no hair? Will the light reflect from the windows of the proposed building blind its neighbors, or perhaps cast such a shadow the neighbors will never see sunlight again? The testing of such ideas is called virtual prototyping in manufacturing and pre-viz (previsualization) in the movie and TV industry.

© Springer Nature Switzerland AG 2019   1
J. Peddie, *Ray Tracing: A Tool for All*,
https://doi.org/10.1007/978-3-030-17490-3_1

All of those people, who are in various stages of the pipeline to bring the consumer or customer the final product need photorealistic images to tell their story, sell their project or sell their product. And they need those images, or video, in a cost-effective and timely manner. Ray tracing can, and does do that, and as things go faster, ray tracing will be called on more, by more people to do it more often.

There are two concepts presented in this book about visual perception. One is the concept of a pipeline: proposal and presentation to sell the idea, design of the proposed thing, manufacturing of the thing, and marketing of it. That last stage, marketing of it, often runs in parallel with the manufacturing stage, so the prospective customer is ready and hopefully anxious to see of getting the thing. Think of how far in advance movie previews are now, or how far in advance a skyscraper or bridge design is from the time it is built.

The other concept objective of the book is to explain that as good as ray tracing is, and it is not the end point. It is but one step on the path to computer-generated images that are so realistic, or fantastic that one can't distinguish them from the real or the imagined thing. The human visual system and supporting senses are the most amazing detectors in the universe and can detect in a fraction of a section the slightest mistake, this is sometimes referred to as the uncanny valley, but it goes beyond that. Photorealistic, physically accurate ray-traced images are almost perfect, and yet, a trained eye can still spot the discrepancies, so we will continue down the continuum in pursuit of the perfect image (Fig. 1.1).

Fig. 1.1 Saya. *Source* Teruyuki and Yuki Ishikawa

Teruyuki and Yuki Ishikawa are a husband-and-wife team of freelance 3D computer graphics artists from Tokyo. One of their recent creations is a character named Saya, and she is the star in the movie they are self-producing. According to the artists, the hardest part was achieving the moist, soft, and translucent skin of girls this age. However, the hair is not (yet) up to their expectations.

Every non-diagram image in this book is a ray-traced image, and it was difficult to not just fill the book with beautiful illustrations.

This book will provide insight for technologists, marketing and management people, educators, academics, and the public who are interested in photorealistic concepts, history, and practice, and the visual and sensory science behind the improvements in advanced display systems. From the explanation of the concepts of rendering issues, through the detailing of visual display and informational access systems, this book provides the reader an understanding of the issues related to defining, building, and using (with respect to our senses), our perception of what is represented, and ultimately, how we assimilate and react to this information.

The following chapters get a little technical but do not delve into the esoteric and abstract mathematics of ray-tracing algorithms. This is not a math book.

Finally, there is a discussion on some of the suppliers, take note—there are too many, over 70, to list and discuss them all. However, so many of the suppliers have such fantastic software with such clever tricks they simply had to be included. My apologies to those left out and to the customers and fans of those left out.

Ray tracing will touch all parts of our lives, our society, and if it is done right, we will never be aware of it, the images will be so perfect, so natural we won't even think about them. In the case of fantasy, the images will be so beautiful we will fall in love with them or scared out of our shoes. If fantasy images are so scary that we suspend disbelief about how the image was constructed and instead see it as a magical and scary monster, the artists can pat each other on the back and go have a beer.

Studying ray tracing is like spiraling down a Mandelbrot that reveals progressively ever-finer recursive detail. Down and down I go into the never-ending rabbit hole, finding one thing, only to learn about three others and on and on it goes—*Jon Peddie.*

1.1 About the Cover

The cover image is of the World Trade Center in New Your city and was created by Ferran Traité born in Spain and now located and living in New Jersey.

In 2018, I took a picture of the World Trade Center building, and the two of them are shown together in Fig. 1.2.

For many readers, if I hadn't pointed out that the image on the left was computer generated, it would have been assumed to be a photograph.

Fig. 1.2 Rendered and photograph of the World Trade Center

1.2 Terminology and Definitions

I have tried to avoid technobabble and geek-talk, and (hopefully) all acronyms are explained the first time they are used. There is an extensive glossary in the appendix which I encourage you to refer to if you encounter a word that is not familiar or ambiguous to you. One of the difficulties of writing a book on a technical subject is to make it as easy as possible for any reader, but not so laborious in explanations it would bore a more sophisticated or technical reader. I'll let you decide how well I did.

One of the most commonly used words, which is not a technical term but used as a modifier for technical descriptions is mapping or mapped.

Mapped A term that is used often in computer graphics, which loosely means to be fitted to something. One maps to a spatial distribution of (something). A texture map is a 2D image of something, bricks, or wood paneling for example.

Texture mapping is the electronic equivalent of applying wallpaper, paint, or veneer to a virtual computer graphics object—where a 2D surface (the texture map) is wrapped around (fitted to) a 3D object. Then, the 3D object acquires a surface texture (appearance) of the 2D surface. So the texture was "mapped."

Mapped is also used in the term, bitmapped. That is a way of describing a surface, such as a computer screen (display) as having several bits or points that can be individually illuminated, and at various levels of intensity. A bitmapped 4K monitor would have over 8-million bits or pixels.

Bump-mapped is a technique for creating the appearance of depth from a 2D image or texture map. Bump mapping gives the illusion of depth by adding surface detail by responding to light direction—it assumes brighter parts are closer to the viewer. It was developed by Jim Blinn and is based on Lambertian reflectance which postulates the apparent brightness of a Lambertian surface to an observer is the same regardless of the observer's angle of view.

Normal maps can be referred to as a newer, better type of bump map. A normal map creates the illusion of depth detail on the surface of a model, but it does it differently than a bump map that uses grayscale values to provide either up or down information. It is a technique used for faking the lighting of bumps and dents—an implementation of bump mapping. It is used to add details without using more polygons.

MIP-mapped. A mipmap is one of a series of different versions of the same texture, each at a different resolution. The one closest to the viewing image is chosen, which saves computation time.

Chapter 2
Introduction

Abstract Ray tracing isn't new, nor is it the end-point in realistic, physically accurate rendering. In fact, it is a subset of global illumination, and partner with ray-casting, path-rendering, and other techniques. Ray tracing can be traced back to the 1950s, and even further, but it came into its own in the 1980s with the development of faster computers, more of them, and new algorithms and discoveries. As with many technologies, it got its start due to military research.

Ray tracing is the most essential general-purpose rendering technique available. It is not the only rendering technique, nor is it the fastest, but it can be the most accurate and can be the most photorealistic. It is one method within a continuum of methods of rendering a computer-generated image, but it has revolutionized rendering for art, gaming, engineering, and architecture.

Written for anyone who wants to learn about the ray-tracing market, this book discusses the suppliers, the programs, and the technology. This book is not intended as a tutorial on ray-tracing mathematics or physics, or how to use ray-tracing software. It includes information on the many suppliers in the field who will affect the way the rendering market will develop in the future. And, it includes some historical backgrounding to explain how the technology has gotten to this point of being a core piece of the rendering process and as a basis for our predictions of the future of rendering.

Ray tracing isn't just about shiny surfaces; there are all types of uses for and styles of ray tracing; one researcher likens it to writing because it can accommodate a wealth of different styles

Also, ray tracing, and rendering, in general, is used in all stages of a project or product from concept selling/proposal, through manufacturing/production, to marketing. Ray tracing gets used in every step of the pipeline.

© Springer Nature Switzerland AG 2019
J. Peddie, *Ray Tracing: A Tool for All*,
https://doi.org/10.1007/978-3-030-17490-3_2

2.1   Who Needs It?

For certain types of design, ray tracing is not desirable but demanded. For example, in the design of optical systems (lens, mirrors, and other components), jewelry design, lighting fixtures, and lamp design. In addition to such physical designs, there is a field of ray tracing for wave and field design in radio and acoustics. In these examples, the design, and resultant images and data must be absolutely physically accurate and depending upon the consumer of the data and images, photorealistic.

Designers of almost any product need a physically accurate representation of a design, both for the concept and production. From automotive, architecture, and aerospace, to fashion, film, and furniture, from games, TV, and consumer products, to packaging and medical diagnostics.

In the design of products from airplanes to jewels an engineer and some cases also a scientist is involved. In advertising, film, TV, games and product packaging, a 3D artist, CG artist, and a CG supervisor are involved, and a marketing people and directors are looking over their shoulders making suggestions and asking questions—lots of players get into the act in the pursuit of a beautiful image.

In the past 20 years or more in the film industry, a 3D render pipeline was designed to deliver frames split up in layers or passes for the compositing department. In the compositing stage, the passes then allowed artists and directors to *tweak* (adjust) the lighting and looks of environments and layering of images to allow or create effects like depth-of-field (DOF) and motion-blur to be applied efficiently.

In the case of movies and TV, a beautiful picture doesn't always mean it is physically accurate or obeys the laws of physics other than light. A crazy-shaped car, house, or airplane may defy gravity and credibility, but regardless, light has to be reflected or absorbed physically correctly; so, viewers can buy into the fantasy.

For 3D animation and film, the main pipeline change thanks to affordable ray tracing is that lighting artists and designers now can visualize and prepare shots with high-quality light simulation and camera effects such as DOF and motion-blur (Mblur) from suppliers like OTOY. That eliminates for a large part the need for compositing—traditionally, the largest department in film production where everything comes together. The concepts for M-blur in ray tracing are rooted in interactive distribution ray tracing, which in turn trace their origin to Cook's 1986 distributed ray-tracing paper.[1]

The animation film Piper (2017) made by Pixar was one of the first using this technique.[2] Blender did the same in some of their shorts such as Operation Barbershop (2017).[3] That means that most renders are, or will become single-pass

---

[1]Cook (1986).

[2]https://RenderMan.pixar.com/stories/piper.

[3]https://www.youtube.com/watch?v=mN0zPOpADL4.

renders, with only some extra buffers saved for special effect compositing and color grading. That will save time, the programs are easier to sue, and the costs of the software are or will be less as well.

2.2 Ray Tracing Isn't New

Ray tracing programs first appeared in 1979 with the (Army's) Ballistic Research Laboratories' BRL CAD program developed by the US Army Research Laboratory in at Aberdeen Proving Ground, Md.[4]

Part of BRL-CAD was lib—the library that contained the geometry support, including data representations for the primitives, support for raytracing, and binary I/O support for CSG geometric descriptions (Fig. 2.1).

The first public release BRL-CAD as a package was in 1984. BRL CAD became an open-source project in December 2004. The foundation for BRL-CAD dates to the MAGIC system and Appel's work in the late 1960s (see Sect. 2.2). BRL-CAD is still in use and available as an open-source software program (Fig. 2.2).

BRL was disestablished in 1992 and its mission, personnel, and facilities were incorporated into the newly created US Army Research Laboratory (ARL). BRL-CAD ray tracing has been steadily developed and now includes advanced features such as global illumination.

The first commercially available ray-tracing program was Mental Images' mental ray program in late 1987 based on a patented deterministic quasi-Monte Carlo sampling methodology which many think is superior to the stochastic-based Monte Carlo methodology. Mental Images were founded in April 1986. Pixar incorporated in February 1986, spinning off an existing group from Lucasfilm. RenderMan became a public specification in 1988 and a commercial product shortly thereafter.

From the video-side of the industry, LightWave 3D was an early 3D modeling, animation, and rendering tool introduced by NewTek as part of its Video Toaster product. LightWave 3D transformed TV graphics. The precursor to LightWave 3D was Videoscape[5] written by Allen Hastings and the 3D Modeler written by Stuart Ferguson. Both programs were sold by Aegis Software. In 1987, Videoscape 3D had "now with fast ray tracing like results" on the box. In 1990, Aegis Videoscape for the Amiga, and Modeler, written by Stuart Ferguson and designed to work with Videoscape, were integrated into the NewTek's Video Toaster and rebranded LightWave 3D. So, from the standpoint of LightWave 3D, ray tracing was always in the product.

---

[4]BRL-CAD Overview https://brlcad.org/wiki/Overview.

[5]VideoScape3D, Personal Computer Museum, https://pcmuseum.ca/details.asp?id=37761&type=software.

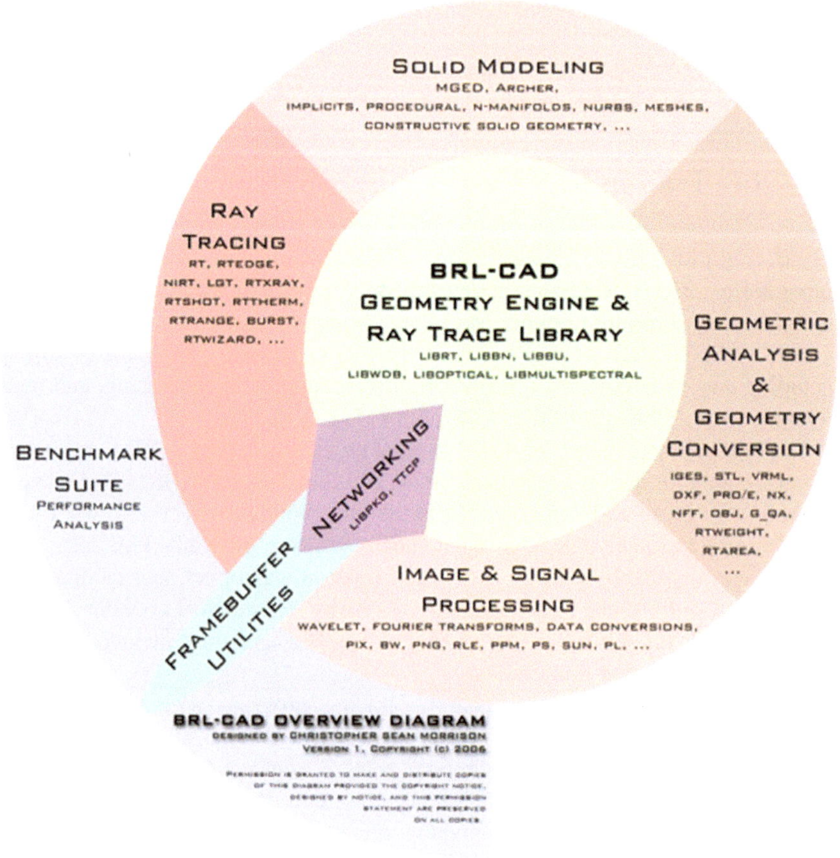

Fig. 2.1 BRL-CAD overview

Fig. 2.2 Famous SGI cube
logo was created using
BRL-CAD ray-tracing
program. *Credit* Sean
Morrison

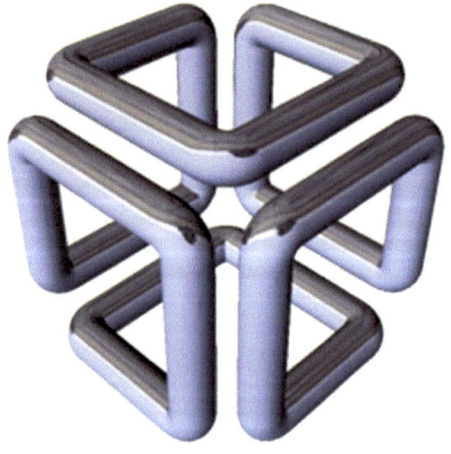

2.3   A Little History

Undoubtedly, the rendering market is one of the more glamorous segments of the computer industry. Rendering is the technology that underlies beautiful computer graphics images, including TV and movie special effects, animations, games, architectural renderings, design visualizations, scientific visuals, advertisements, medical, and more. I like to say I follow the pixel. In the case of rendering, ray tracing is the technology that polishes the pixels.

Rendering is a well-understood technology that benefits from continuous fine-tuning and improvement. For more than 40 years, rendering has mainly been limited by the hardware capabilities of computers and associated processors. In the meantime, many good renderers have been developed. The trick has been to develop and maintain software that works with the major content creation programs (i.e., CAD, media and entertainment, etc.) while continuing to take advantage of new technology (hardware and algorithms) as it is incorporated into such content creation programs and people's workflows.

Rendering has become the subject of renewed interest as dramatic performance improvements have come from the hardware industry. Not only are processors becoming more powerful, new programming methods are being developed to more efficiently unlock the capabilities of parallel processors for repetitive jobs. The arrival of multi-core processors and application program interfaces for graphics processing units processing has opened the doors for increased interest in ray-tracing technology. The basic technology isn't new, but the combination of clever programming and powerful hardware is bringing advanced rendering into the mainstream. There have also been dedicated hardware ray-tracing processors introduced into the market (APIs, GPU).

There are two primary types of rendering: rasterization (also known as scanline or polygon rendering) and ray tracing. Both work with the same basic geometric models. There are several companies offering ray-tracing software and hardware, often with clever and unique procedures that differentiate based on performance, speed, and rendering accuracy. All major programs for CAD and 3D modeling have a built-in rasterization capability, and the suppliers are adding ray tracing. Many application software suppliers also work with independent ray-tracing options. Rasterization is well understood and considered the basic or primary technique. The fundamental rasterization algorithms do not accurately display shadows, material effects, and lighting in order to provide fast rendering of the image. Baked-in effects are often used in game development to save compute time. Rasterization techniques may be used in conjunction with ray tracing where they can add a pleasing quality and/or save on rendering time.

Ray tracing is a rich, robust, and highly competitive market and is a subsegment of other markets. No single ray-tracing program, whether independent or integrated, is capable of serving all the application needs for ray tracing because of limitations in material libraries and possible integration of global illumination and voxels.

Therefore, the supplier(s) of ray-tracing software have to carefully pick and choose their target markets to avoid wasting precious resources learning the hard way.

This book will not go into any of the mathematical basics for ray tracing or any code (program) examples. History will only be discussed when necessary to make a point, such as how long computer-based ray tracing has existed and how it may have evolved.

2.4 Ray Tracing not New

As mentioned above, general credit for the first published use of ray-casting for visualization is given to Arthur Appel for the work described in his paper, "Some techniques for shading machine renderings of solids," in May 1968, if anyone did it before him, they did not publish their work (Fig. 2.3).[6]

And, the earliest recorded reference to ray-tracing system is the computerized ray tracer used at the Ballistic Research Laboratory (BRL) for ballistic analysis developed by Mathematical Applications Group, Inc. (MAGI).

The original MAGIC program (Mathematical Applications Group, Inc., code) is described as, "A Geometric Description Technique Suitable for Computer Analysis

Fig. 2.3 Appel projected light at a 3D computer model and displayed the results on a plotter using a form of tone mapping to create light and dark areas. *Source* Arthur Appel

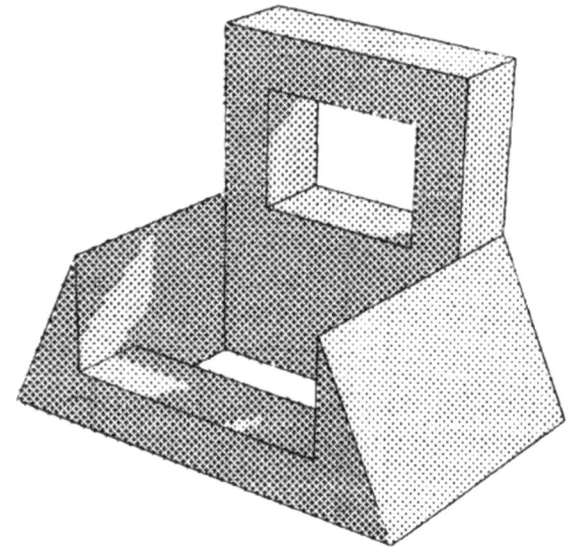

---

[6]Appel (1968).

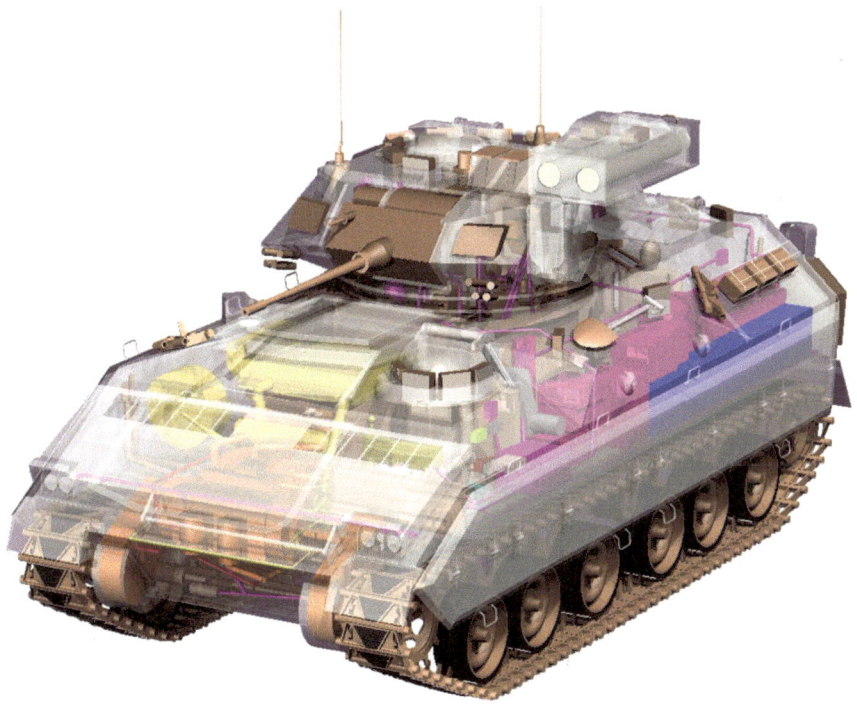

Fig. 2.4 Translucent Bradley fighting vehicle rendered in BRL-CAD. *Source* Sean Morrison (2002)

of Both the Nuclear and Conventional Vulnerability of Armored Military Vehicles" published in August 1967 (Walter et al.).[7] MAGI adapted MAGIC for visualization and thus played an important role in the commercial development of using tracing for visualization of combinatorial solid geometry in computer graphics (CGI) (Fig. 2.4).

However, it should be pointed out Walter et al., were not trying to generate a photorealistic image, but rather were trying to demonstrate the application of computer analysis of both the nuclear and conventional vulnerability of armored military vehicles, and the rays they were concerned with were gamma rays.

The Army's Ballistic Research Laboratory continued its work and developed the Geometric Information for Targets (GIFT). While developing the algorithms, observers acknowledged that the techniques could be prohibitively expensive in the required computing time.

---

[7]Walter et al. (1968). Corporate Author: Mathematical Applications Group Inc White Plains NY, Work Performed Under Contract No. DAAD05-67-C-0041 for the Department of the Army Ballistic Research Laboratories, Aberdeen Proving Ground, Maryland.

In addition computational ray tracing is used for optical design, radio signals, electromagnetic effects, survivability, and to avoid the computational complexities of Maxwell's equations in 1962.[8] It is probable that manual ray tracing (starting at a point and drawing lines to simulate some a physical effect) began in the art community to understand perspective.[9]

It is interesting and relevant to note that the initial application of ray-casting algorithms were for visualizing difficult mathematical calculations because now that computers have become fast enough to make the techniques practical, ray tracing is being explored for scientific visualization and analysis once again (Refer to the Continuum for brief explanation of the difference between ray casting and ray tracing, Sect. 4.3.1.5).

In 1979, Turner Whitted would elaborate on the ray-casting algorithms developed in the 60s to introduce recursive ray tracing.[10] Whitted followed the path of a ray beyond the initial surface it hits. He said after a ray hits an object, it generates three new rays, a reflection, refraction, and shadow, which can also be traced to greatly improve realism. Whitted's paper can mark the beginning of the pursuit to use a computer to generate photorealistic and physically accurate renditions of 3D objects in 3D space.

2.4.1   From Humble Beginnings

The Commodore Amiga microcomputer was introduced in 1985 and as it was developed it became an ideal platform for graphics and animation with an expansion port for video devices—the video slot. The Amiga supported Newtek's Video Toaster, one of the first all-in-one graphics and video editing packages. Video Toaster and the Amiga gave people working on TV a low cost, computer-based alternative for television graphics. The later addition of the Video Flyer by Newtek made possible the first nonlinear video editing program for the Amiga.

The Amiga made 3D ray-tracing graphics available for the masses with Sculpt 3D. Before the Amiga, ray tracing was only available for dedicated graphic systems such as Ramtek, Jupiter Systems, and IBM (5080).

One of the earliest ray-tracing demos on the Amiga was Eric and Cathryn Graham's program "The Juggler." Eric rendered the frames in a ray tracer he wrote called ssg, a Sculpt precursor. The rendered images were encoded in the Amiga's

---

[8]https://en.wikipedia.org/wiki/Ray_tracing_(physics).

[9]Massironi, Manfredo, "The Psychology of Graphic Images: Seeing, Drawing, Communicating" (Volume in the University of Alberta, Department of Psychology, Distinguished Scholar Lecture), pp 79–83.

[10]Whitted (1980).

HAM display mode and then assembled into a single data file using a lossless delta compression scheme similar to the method that would later be adopted as the standard in the Amiga's ANIM file format.[11]

The Amiga brought 3D raytracing graphics to the masses for the first time—Jeff Atwood

The juggler may seem primitive by today's standards. Maybe it is, but it was revelatory back in 1986.

2.5   Realism, Accuracy, and Functionality

There are no definitions or metrics of functional realism in computer graphics, or the relationship between accuracy and fidelity in computer graphics images. Accuracy refers to the correctness of the image with respect to some physically measurable property of the scene such as radiance. Fidelity, on the other hand, means: does the image tell the truth? Does it allow the observer to perceive important properties of the scene with the same certainty that they could in the real world? Although it is possible to measure accuracy with instruments, the only way to measure fidelity is to see how well observers are able to perform meaningful visual tasks using different kinds of images.

But, what about fantasy? What about animations that use ray tracing for global illumination, shadows, reflections, and ambience? What about *Cars*? The *Cars* films, the studio's REYES (Render Everything You've Ever Seen) algorithm (see Sect. 8.1.20), mixed with some ray-tracing techniques, had been used to deal with shiny car surfaces in 2006.[12] In 2013, Walt Disney Animation Studios revealed its Hyperion path-tracing Renderer at Eurograph (Fig. 2.5).[13]

Fig. 2.5 Lightning McQueen in Cars 2—circa 2011. *Source* Wikipedia

[11]https://blog.codinghorror.com/real-time-raytracing/.

[12]Christensen et al. (2006).

[13]Eisenacher et al. (2013).

The point being that although ray tracing is often presented as being the best physically accurate means of producing a photorealistic image, in the case of animations, games, and some advertisements, the rendered objects are not physically accurate; however, the way light is reflected from them is physically accurate.

2.5.1   Three Types of Realism in Computer Graphics

Margaret Hagen[14] introduced the concept that there are different methods of portraying realism in which certain properties of a scene are accurately represented, and others are approximated, abstracted, or omitted (*Varieties of Realism,* Cambridge Press, 1986).

The point of this idea is that pictures can be realistic in some respects and not in others. For example, Dürer's "A Young Hare (see Appendix: Sect. A.2.1) is extremely realistic, but not photoaccurate. However, the iconic Utah teapot is geometrically accurate. Rendering methods can make its rendering photoaccurate but not necessarily realistic (Fig. 2.6).

Although Hagen focused primarily on how the geometric aspects of scenes are represented by images (see Appendix: Sect. A.2.2), her basic concept has been expanded to three varieties of realism in computer graphics, which are:

- Physical realism—in which the image provides the same visual stimulation as the scene;

Fig. 2.6 A hare versus a variation of the Utah teapot. *Source* Wikipedia

---

[14]Hagen (1986).

- Photorealism—in which the image produces the same visual response as the scene; and
- Functional realism—in which the image provides the same visual information as the scene.

Each of these descriptions uses different criteria to determine if an image is realistic, and therefore each one places different demands on the image generation process. Together, they provide an evaluation criterion that can be used to appraise the realism of a computer graphics rendering.

Physical realism is accomplished with ray tracing. Ray tracing is accurate and realistic. Rasterization (also known as scanline rendering) can be pseudo-realistic. Ray tracing takes time to compute and render, rasterization can be done in milliseconds and at high resolution with lots of colors.

Examples of realistic, but not accurate images are those found in simulators and games, animations, and special effects. Realism is defined as the fidelity of the information the image provides.

Functional realism is defined as having to provide the same visual information as the actual scene. Information in this sense means knowledge about the meaningful properties in a scene, such as their shapes, sizes, positions, motions, and materials that allow the observer to make reliable visual judgments (Fig. 2.7).

An image is a visual representation of a scene; in that it represents selected properties of the scene to the viewer with varying degrees of realism or accuracy. No single rendering solution will satisfy all users' needs, nor is there on single "right" solution. Most of the interesting extensions for nearly any renderer will be to its material library.

Correct material modeling plays a vital role in a virtual prototype or simulation; however, finding the appropriate abstractions and mathematical models to describe light interaction is a difficult task. As the famous British statistician, George E. P. Box (October 18, 1919–March 28, 2013) noted: "Since all models are wrong the scientist cannot obtain a 'correct' one by excessive elaboration".[15]

Many common materials show a complex behavior, being partly diffuse, partly specular, reflecting, or emissive. A material may additionally exhibit transparency, both in a diffuse and/or specular way. On passing through transparent media, light refraction, absorption, and scattering occur.

These effects can be described with a bi-directional, reflection, and transmission distribution function (BRDF or BRTF) that produces reflection and transmission dependent on both incidence and outgoing light direction. Employing such detailed methods is only needed for special tasks such as simulation light-redirection elements in daylight design. The use of BRDF, BRTF is mandatory in Path Tracing, a stochastic Monte Carlo method of rendering 3D images and scenes such that the global illumination is faithful to reality. The concept stochastic sampling was introduced to computer graphics by Robert Cook in 1984.[16]

---

[15]Box (1976).
[16]Cook (1986).

Fig. 2.7 In animation you want perfect reflections and shadows, but the objects may be pure fantasy: Toy Story. *Source* Pixar Wiki

2.5.1.1 Monte Carlo

Monte Carlo is an umbrella term for various stochastic algorithms because they get used in several different ways. If for example, one has a large and complicated system that you are trying to model and analyze, and it has a large set of elements, one can count up every point of data and draw a statistical conclusions (known as the brute force way), or one can randomly select a few elements of the data set that are representative of the whole. A common example is a randomized medical test of a few thousand patients. One uses a smaller set of values (samples), and although it won't give the exact data that could be obtained by checking every patient of interest, the sampling is a very close approximation when the results are analyzed. The critical step is to make sure that one picks well distributed samples, so each class is representative of a wide range of patients. The result is one gets essentially the same result with a lot less work gathering and processing data. That's the basic concept of the Monte Carlo method (e.g., George E. P. Box's quote above).

Tied to that, the other main part of the stochastic analysis is some randomization —that is, the generation of sample **noise**. Noise is important because it breaks up (disturbs) regular patterns in whatever one is sampling. If one samples something that changes with a frequency similar to the sampling frequency, then the results can become homogeneous, and details missed in-between. Monte Carlo sampling helps prevent that. So, noise is employed to break up aliasing artifacts.

For the most common cases of practical simulations, a set of straightforward algorithms exists that treats each of the above-mentioned aspects separately. Material description then can be done with a few parameters for diffuse reflection, specularity, transparency, etc.

As mentioned, certain illumination algorithms and reflective or translucent materials may require more rays to be recast into the scene. Material definitions may also provide an emission function—i.e., radiation not just reflection or refraction of light.

One place where stochastic sampling is employed is for hair where there are more fine strands than one would like to calculate the geometry of, and which are too small for individual pixels. It is used in image sampling techniques like shadow filtering to generate the penumbra across multiple frames. Also, in screen-space reflections, which is the form of 2D ray tracing.

So yes, a major focus of the renderer has been shifted to being more selective in where to perform major and complex calculations, and a large amount of frame time for filtering, denoising, and de-aliasing the in final image. And, this comes with the benefit of allowing those calculations done less frequently, to be much more sophisticated.

As CPU and GPU computing power increases, interactive ray tracing will be able to provide higher visual quality. However, for that to be realized, interactive and offline systems must have an identical description of materials.

2.5.2 Stylistic Versus Photorealistic

One of the main points about ray tracing is that ray-tracing produces physically accurate images and that they can be photorealistic depending upon the desires of the artist and producer. For example, BMW wants a perfectly accurate image that is photorealistic. However, Pixar wants a physically accurate image (for the reflections off of their cars) and do not want it to be photorealistic, but rather stylistic.

Stylistic is possibly more challenging because if the image is not physically accurate (to the fantasied model), then the results creep into the uncanny valley, the illusion is broken, and disbelief sets in—the death of storytelling and immersiveness.

Physically accurate means the light behaves correctly on the objects in a scene—it doesn't mean the scene is necessarily physically accurate. In an animation, or special effects driven scenes, the laws of physics, especially gravity, may be completely wrong. People and animals don't walk on air for a few steps before failing. Their bodies don't stretch as a chasm opens up beneath them, and trucks don't flip up into the air.

2.5.2.1 Sometimes You Can't See It

Jama Jurabaev the renowned artist from Tajikistan, and now at Lucas Arts, did a series of treatments using 3D modeling assets from Terminator 6 (yes—six). The images used Blender for the 3D modeling and Otoy's GPU-enabled ray-tracing program. Take a look—no reflections, but the light in the scene is physically accurate, and the image is stylistic (Fig. 2.8).

You can see more of Jama's work here: https://tinyurl.com/y7dskr5t. And in one of his dark moody cuts, you can see shiny on a robot (Fig. 2.9).

However, what most people think of when the subject of ray tracing comes up is either shiny spheres or a dazzling automobile. The options are actually much broader.

Fig. 2.8 Ray tracing used in stylistic fantasy film, "Terminator 6". *Source* Jama Jurabaev

Fig. 2.9 Ray-traced robot before (left) and after environmental layering (right). *Source* Jama Jurabaev

Fig. 2.10 Car design is one of the most popular and demanding ray-tracing applications (Soviet Moskvich 412—1974, Daniartist90)

2.5.2.2   The Payoff of Ray Tracing

Ray tracing saves the automotive industry millions of dollars by avoiding photo-shoots—the sheet metal and plastic panels that make a Mercedes look like a Mercedes and not a Cadillac or Volvo, and vice versa.

The ability to create completely realistic content with ray tracing has forever changed advertising allowing digital models to be used even before the real cars comes off the assembly lines, putting cars in impossible situations, multiplying them, anything the imagination demands. Cars are the most obvious example, but the revolution is evident throughout advertising (Fig. 2.10).

Automobiles are perfect specimens for ray tracing because they do not have any flat surfaces. Also, many automobiles have multi-layered paint which adds to the complexity of creating a physically accurate representation of the vehicle.

2.5.2.3   The Need for Ray Tracing

In the movies, the FX scenes couldn't be done without ray tracing. The animations couldn't be done. That is not to say animations aren't done without ray tracing, just that the big box office titles need and use ray tracing extensively.

Almost no consumer product is proposed, designed, virtually prototyped, manufactured, or marketed without ray tracing.

Fig. 2.11 Ray-tracing programs

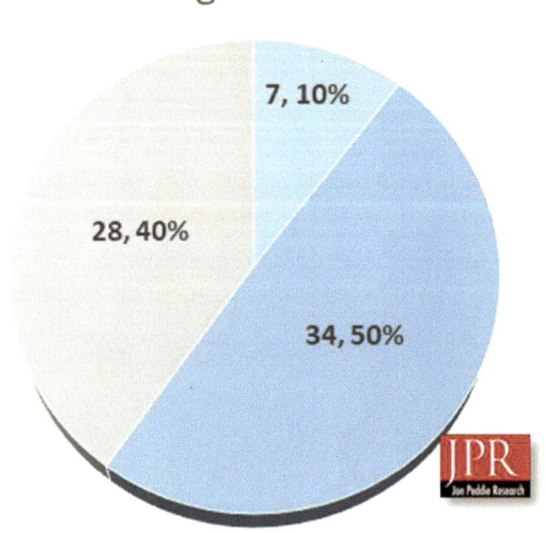

Programs = 69

7, 10%

28, 40%

34, 50%

▪ Integrated   ▪ Stand-alone   ▪ Plug-in

There are over 69 ray-tracing programs. That leads to two conclusions:

1. There are too many suppliers and there will be consolidation—picking a winner could be tricky.
2. The average age of the supplier companies is 18, not a start-up industry, so there must be plenty of demand (Fig. 2.11).

Another point of view is there is no single answer, each program has some feature (that the others don't) and is valued. And, that is really the correct conclusion. Many organizations, especially the film, TV, and advertising industries use multiple ray-tracing programs in their productions. A scene, whether for a movie, TV advertisement, or show, or an advertisement in a magazine, will have multiple layers of effects. A layer for water, one for smoke, one for character's skins and another for their hair or eyes, and layers for the important objects in the scene. Each item will have a different look and feel, and make use of a particular, and often unique material, maybe one that isn't from this planet. And no single ray-tracing program has or will ever be able to get that span of elements, or materials. So, several ray tracers get used for a single image, scene, or frame. There are ray-tracing programs that are used exclusively for gems, some just for clothing and fashion, a couple just for leather, and a couple for layered automotive paint as examples. Furthermore, new ray-tracing techniques continue to be invented, with new academic publications appearing in multiple industry conferences each year. These ideas help spur innovation and competition in the industry.

The uniqueness of many of the programs ensures their survival, but at the same time establishes the limit to their total available market and growth prospects. The purveyors of ray-tracing software—and their users—are artisans. They are not, nor will they ever be, mass producers like Microsoft, SAS, or Sales Force. That is the charm, and the limitation of the segment—may it never change.

2.6 Technical Papers and Books

More papers, patents, and Ph.D.'s have been written and awarded on ray tracing than any other computer graphic technique. I have identified 8 books and 786 papers that have been written on ray tracing since 1982 (see Appendix). The number of papers peaked in 2007 (56), and the curve falls off in 2018, because I stopped collecting data in late-2018. With the advent hardware, ray-tracing accelerators introduced I expect the paper submittals to increase (Fig. 2.12).

Ray tracing is a subset of the rendering market. The rendering market is a subset of software for larger markets including Media and Entertainment (M&E), Architecture, Engineering and Construction (AEC), computer-aided design (CAD), scientific, entertainment content creation, and simulation-visualization. Not all users who have rendering capabilities in their products use it. At the same time, some products have been developed solely as rendering tools, and there are products that include 3D modeling and animation and rendering capabilities, and they may be used primarily for rendering, primarily for modeling, or primarily for animation.

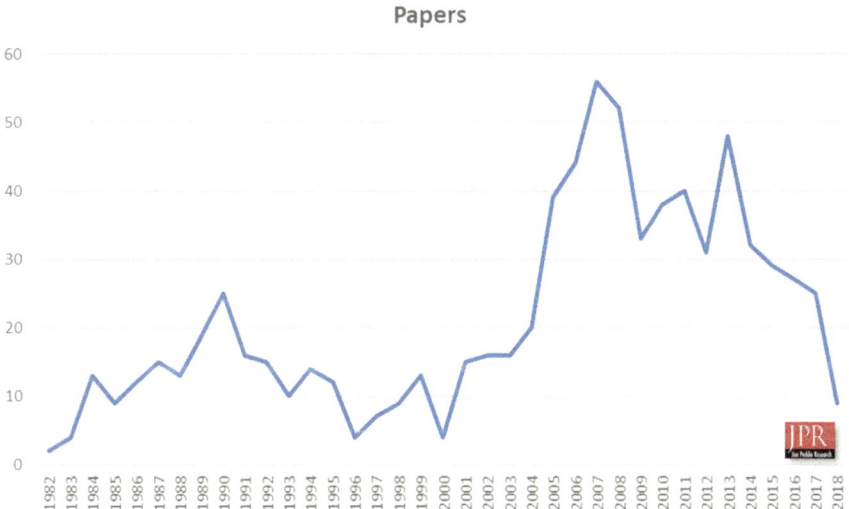

Fig. 2.12 Papers on ray tracing published in academic journals since 1982

Because ray tracing is so vital, and at the same time computationally burdensome, researchers and organizations have spent years and millions of dollars trying to speed it up. A typical ray-traced scene on just an old-fashioned HD screen can tax a CPU so heavily the image can only be updated maybe every second or two—certainly not the 33 ms seconds needed for real-time rendering.

It used to be that GPUs couldn't help much because one of the characteristics of ray tracing is it has no memory, and every frame is a new frame, so the computational load is immutable. Also, the branching that occurs in ray tracing defeats the power of a GPU's similar-instruction, multi-data (SIMD) architecture. Things have changed.

It's not just about making things look better, but about communicating more effectively

This book is about geometry-based ray tracing and does not embrace field, optical, audio, simulation, or other non-3D (virtual or real) ray-tracing applications or software.

Ray tracing does occur during the simulation process in programs like Nvidia's OptiX. OptiX allows one to control which rays are traced, just not how they are traced. Such programs are not by nature a modeling software, but a simulation program where 2D patterns get rendered in the 3D plane. While one can import and export 3D objects from the program, it is not like the modeling capabilities in SolidWorks, Rhino, Maya, and others.

2.7 Material Libraries Critical

Before 2015, all ray tracer engines came with their own materials libraries. Cataloging the characteristics of all the types of materials in the world is beyond the resources of any company's ability to develop and support. Moreover, the lack of standards has held back any cooperative development in the industry; however, a few companies have agreed to work together and share their libraries (Fig. 2.13).

I believe existing libraries will become more open and the most ray-tracing engines will be able to avail themselves of a large library of materials. Some of the methods and sources of material libraries are discussed further at Sect. 5.2.

2.8 Rendering Becomes a Function of Price

I expect to see 3D rendering become a capability offered as an online service. It is not altogether clear what effect this will have on the market; however, I believe it will result in increased use of ray tracing and lower the cost to an as-needed basis. It also offers the promise of being able to apply vast quantities of processing power limited only by the amount of money the user is willing to pay. Ray tracing will become time (to render a scene) divided by cost.

Fig. 2.13 An example of various materials applied to the same object. *Source* Epic

That will, and is today, bringing down the time to generate a ray-traced frame for an animation for example, but not quite to real-time ray tracing at 4K or beyond just yet—however, real-time is within our grasp today.

2.9 Shortcuts and Semiconductors—The Need for Speed

Who cares about ray tracing and whether it is fast or slow?

One of the main points about ray tracing is that ray tracing produces physically accurate images and that they can be photorealistic depending upon the desires of the artist and producer. For example, BMW wants a perfectly accurate image that is photorealistic. However, Pixar wants a physically accurate image (for the reflections off of their cars) and do not want it to be photorealistic, but rather stylistic.

Stylistic is possibly more challenging because if the image is not physically accurate (to the fantasied model) then the results creep into the uncanny valley, the illusion is broken, and disbelief sets in—the death of storytelling and immersiveness.

Physically accurate means the light behaves correctly on the objects in a scene—it doesn't mean the scene is necessarily physically accurate. In an animation, or special effects driven scene the laws of physics, especially gravity, may be completely wrong.

The Cost of Ray Tracing But, when comparing the computational and hardware costs of ray tracing, some people have said, that using ray tracing simply to achieve shininess is unnecessary given the excellent quality that precomputed "baked-in" lighting techniques can produce.

However, baked-in lighting does not move, it is static, it is only used for distance shading or games where the time of day does not change.

One can also use environment probes which renders the environment from a specific point in space. They are used to write the results to a texture map for an overlay of reflective surfaces, like water or windows, but again it is static. If one has a line of trees next to a body of water the fake reflections (of the tress and sky) only line up from a very specific angle, if you move away from the scenery moves but the reflection doesn't.

The Payoff of Ray Tracing The advantage is for content creators. Not having to create art with baked lighting and fake reflections, and workarounds for effects saves a lot of time that can be dedicated elsewhere, thus improving the graphics in other areas as well as giving us more accurate reflections and lighting.

Investigations to find clever ways to reduce the computational load by using intelligent algorithms to examine a scene and deterministically allocate what objects are visible, and which surfaces need rendering will continue.

Hybrid techniques are being improved and evolved where only certain portions of a scene are ray traced. Objects in the distance, for example, don't need to be ray traced; flat, dull-colored objects don't need it (Fig. 2.14).

Semiconductors are being developed that specifically accelerate ray tracing. Imagination technologies has a ray-tracing engine that when combined with the advanced techniques just described can render an HD scene with partial ray-traced elements several times a second. Also, Nvidia has introduced ways to optimize a standard GPU for ray tracing.

Fig. 2.14 Use of variance-based adaptive sampling on this model of Christmas cookies from Autodesk 3ds Max provided a better final image in record time. *Source* Chaos Group

All these ideas and developments will converge in the very near future, and real-time, easy to use ray tracing will be realized.

2.10 Challenges

If carried out to the extreme ray tracing produces a perfect, physically accurate, image, but it might take days or even weeks. One of the desires heard from users of ray tracing is the need for ease of use. Smart, adaptive settings based on what the artist is trying to do, or the available rendering resources can do, are being investigated.

Another major inhibitor for ray tracing is the difficulty of creating 3D models suitable for rendering in the first place. New approaches to modeling using photogrammetric techniques and also building libraries of models are helping make modeling and rendering more accessible. Some software tools are easier than others and that is a continuously evolving front.

References

Appel A (1968) Some techniques for shading machine renderings of solids. In: AFIPS '68 (Spring) proceedings of the April 30–May 2, 1968, spring joint computer conference, Atlantic City, New Jersey, 30 Apr–02 May 1968, pp 37–45

Box GEP (1976) Science and statistics. J Am Stat Assoc 71:791–799. https://doi.org/10.1080/01621459.1976.10480949

Christensen PH et al (2006) Ray tracing for the movie 'Cars'. Pixar Animation Studios

Cook RL (1986) Stochastic sampling in computer graphics. ACM Trans Graph 5(1):51–72

Eisenacher C et al (2013) Sorted deferred shading for production path tracing. In: Eurographics symposium on rendering 2013, vol 32, no 4

Hagen MA (1986) Varieties of realism: geometries of representational art. Cambridge University Press, 31 May 1986

Walter et al (1968) A geometric description technique suitable for computer analysis of both the nuclear and conventional vulnerability of armored military vehicles

Whitted T (1980) An improved illumination model for shaded display. Commun ACM 3(6):343–349

Chapter 3
The Rendering Industry

Abstract The rending industry, and ray tracing specifically is an enigma in that it looks like a start-up industry with dozens of supplies making it ripe for consolidation, and yet it's been in existence since the mid-1980s—hardly a start-up situation. That is partially due to the relative ease of generating a ray tracing program—the math is very straight forward and easy to understand and code. But more so because of the quest for efficiency and the unending demand for material libraries. One of the reasons there are so many ray tracing programs available is because of the industry-specific material libraries each program has. Big companies with CAD and 3D modeling main-line programs will have two to four in-house ray tracing programs of their own, plus a half dozen plug-ins that work with the main program. It's not uncommon for a studio for example to employ four to six different ray tracing programs in the production of the movie, using each one for a particular look.

A land of enchantment and danger

The ray tracing rendering industry is well understood and venerable. It's also wide open and chaotic. In fact, it is one of the few industries that show all the characteristics of a young, start-up market and also of a very stable, low growth mature market. It's not likely that the situation will settle out any time soon.

It's obvious why the ray tracing industry has all the characteristics of a mature market—it is mature at least when talking about production renderers used in filmmaking and integrated renderers used with the leading 3D modeling and animation tools such as 3ds Max, Maya, Cinema 4D, Modo, Lightwave, and Blender. The major markets for these tools are movies/TV/video and visualization for CAD, medicine, and scientific exploration. There are strong products in each market, and they all have their loyal customers who like the look they get and the ease with which the tools fit into their workflow pipeline. The traditional rendering industry has been defined by the expensive cost of rendering in terms of hardware resources. As a result, expert programmers have developed software tricks that to produce realistic (and fantastical) results while being able to lessen the load on rendering resources as much as possible. For much of the history of rendering—the hardware requirements have been astronomic, and rendering has been a trade-off between money and time.

It's also obvious why the rendering industry can feel like a start-up industry segment. It has seen several major inflection points that have completely changed the nature of the industry. These inflection points have hit the market in three waves as Moore's Law has changed the equations and democratized rendering.

- Between 2002 and 2010, Moore's Law had done its job sufficiently well that ray tracing was no longer out of reach for 3D artists working in small companies or even individuals. New companies appeared to challenge the incumbents including Chaos Group, Solid Angle, and Cebas.
- In 2000, software prices for the leading modeling and animation products plummeted. The effect has been to shove smaller companies out of business and centralize the industry around a few leaders. Today Autodesk leads, followed by The Foundry, Maxon, and Lightwave. A consumerist/low-end market struggles to arrive.
- GPU compute has enabled the development of rendering programs that take advantage of GPU cores—with the potential of turning even modest systems into render farms.
- A complementary technology evolution has enabled cloud-based technologies, which have the potential to transform the rendering industry in time.

Characteristics of the leading rendering companies in the movie business

- The leading companies providing rendering tools for TV/movies are augmenting the rendering revenues with particle-based effect tools and physics.
- The leading companies work closely with their customers to define R&D goals.
- The majority of the work done on rendering is done in-house by studios that are perfecting their own looks and developing their own shaders.
- The field of suppliers for rendering tools is narrow.

3.1   Leading Companies Rendering in AEC and Product Design

Companies providing 3D visualization services in the CAD fields frequently work with the leading modelers including 3ds Max, Maya, Cinema 4D, Modo, and Rhino. They frequently rebuild models from scratch or find themselves reducing CAD models to base geometry to remove difficult-to-render objects or reduce model complexity.

Visualizations often combine several elements—stylized drawings, floor plans, walk-throughs, light studies, etc. It's not all about rendering.

There is a lot of opportunity opening up for visualization for design and AEC. SketchUp has spurred numerous rendering start-ups and cloud-based rendering services. However, there is a bit of a race to the bottom. People who are using the free version of SketchUp are not likely to spend a lot of money for a renderer.

As is the case with all visualization tools, interactive performance for ray tracing is essential. Inexperienced customers will suffer frustration with cloud-based rendering that doesn't offer tools for prerendering, test renders, etc. Even then, many customers will be reluctant to try cloud-based rendering if they're not sure what the end result will be. It's important to offer value-add tools to stand out above the crowd.

As an aside, one of the companies that were interesting was ThinkBox (acquired by Amazon in 2017). The company builds tools for the movie and video industry, including particle effects generators. Amazon is doing very well with the portal feature Deadline, a render job scheduling tool. The company is also looking at building tools for the AEC market, with its first product being Sequoia for creating models from 3D scans. Another rising company is Cl3VER, which enables online architectural walk-throughs with very stylish templates. The company introduced a VR creation tool and partnerships with Chaos Group, Archvision, and IrisVR.

3.2 The Future

Some companies have survived on the basis of their breadth of services, including training and support. They're supporting all the major tools. Some are also supporting several shaders and material libraries.

Material libraries offer an opportunity and a threat. The leading companies are offering material library tools and formats and thus have a way to lock-in their customers. Nvidia hopes to use its leverage with GPUs and marketing power to widely disseminate their materials and tie customers to their libraries (and thus, their hardware) through its MDL program; however, MDL is not specific to GPUs.

The successful companies will be those who can offer:

- Ease of use, including test images and production run progress monitoring
- Some guarantee of success
- Tweaks that enhance ray tracer performance. In general, physics-based optical fidelity is not as valuable as "looks right."
- Service and support

There is a shake-up coming in the rendering industry and those companies that offer ray tracing and not much else will be the first to go. Some which can't support the costs of continuing R&D will just disappear as customers move on to the latest ray tracing program. Others with interesting and novel capabilities, but insufficient marketing skills or budgets will be acquired. The industry is evolving in a traditional way, consolidating and favoring the larger firms.

Chapter 4
The Continuum

Abstract The use of a computer to generate a simulated image can be traced back to the first games and CAD programs in the late 1970s. Simulations of weather maps, circuit boards, mechanical drawing of automobiles (actually dating back to the early 1960s) show the interest and unending quest for a faithful representation of a physical thing, or a fantasy thing. Over the decades, brilliant computer scientists from various disciplines as diverse as geographical information systems to movie animations, and CAD drawings for giant buildings, bridges, and space ships came up with clever ways to create amazing looking images—but they were for the most part trickery, and not faithful to the physics of light. The difference between a physically accurate photorealistic image and a clever approximation in terms of computing workload is 100–10000 times. It is almost a law that as soon as new more accurate rendering technique is developed, the workload to use it goes up by orders of magnitude. Then, other clever researchers figure out ways to do it more efficiently and the process becomes affordable in time and hardware and is adopted for everyday use. That process is a continuum and doesn't indicate any end point.

The rendering of images generated in or by a computer to obtain realistic and accurate representations is a significant discussion and effort in computer graphics, and probably will always be.

The quest has always been to obtain the most realistic looking image, in the shortest amount of time at the highest resolution possible.

In the earliest days of computer graphics, the displays were vector scopes that could only generate outlined images. The first computer graphics application was computer-aided design—CAD, which was the use of a computer to create 2D, three-view, and mechanical drawings.

© Springer Nature Switzerland AG 2019   33
J. Peddie, *Ray Tracing: A Tool for All*,
https://doi.org/10.1007/978-3-030-17490-3_4

Raster graphics or scanline graphics were introduced in the early 1970s when A. Michael Noll adopted TV displays for computer image generation while at Bell Labs in the late 1960s.[1]

A raster graphics or bitmap image is a dot matrix data structure that represents a generally rectangular grid of pixels (points of color) for creating characters. The early microcomputers like the popular consumer computers such as the Commodore PET 2001, and RadioShack TRS-80 used modified TV displays when introduced, as did the Altair 8800, the creation of Albuquerque, N.M.'s Micro Instrumentation and Telemetry Systems (MITS) that got Bill Gates and Paul Allen so excited. Because of limited memory and processing power, the early machines only generated dot matrix characters. However, clever ways were developed to turn them into graphic images.

Memory got less expensive, faster, and more dense. Processors followed Moore's law, and by the late 1970s, we had 512×512 bitmapped raster-scan computer graphics systems. That marked the beginning of the computer graphics industry, and ACM—the American Computer Machinery organization's Special Interest Group on Computer Graphics—SIGGRAPH was formed in 1974. With it, computer scientists from universities, the government, and few fledgling companies began developing machines and software with the goal of making realistic images or pictures. Over the 45 years, we saw new, clever techniques for trying to obtain the holy grail of a synthesized image that was indistinguishable from the real thing. Ray tracing was the best approach and was demonstrated by Turner Whitted at Bell Labs in 1979. However, ray tracing was not the end, and equally smart techniques were developed at Cornell University such as radiosity in the early 1980s. In the mid-1990s, the concepts of light-field rendering were developed by Levoy[2] and Gotler[3]. By presenting a light field using technology that maps each sample to the appropriate ray in physical space, one obtains an autostereoscopic visual effect akin to seeing the original scene, and similar in viewing to a hologram.

These developments lead to the conclusion or awareness of a continuum of image processing in the pursuit of a perfect synthesized image or picture, in real time, on the highest resolution screen with the highest color reproduction capabilities possible.

It all has to do with the understanding how light behaves and then mapping that to limited capabilities of a computer.

---

[1]Noll (1971).

[2]Levoy and Hanrahan (1996).

[3]Gotler et al. (1996).

4.1   The Rendering Equation

In computer graphics, the rendering equation is an integral equation in which the equilibrium radiance leaving a point is the sum of emitted plus reflected radiance under a geometric optics approximation. There are various realistic rendering techniques in computer graphics that attempt to solve this equations (Fig. 4.1).

The rendering equation describes the total amount of light emitted from a point x along a particular viewing direction, given a function for incoming light and a bidirectional reflectance distribution function (BRDF, see Glossary),

Where

x is   the location in space

w_o is   the direction of the outgoing light

Ω is   the unit hemisphere centered around $\{n\}$ containing all possible values for w_i

w_i is   the weakening factor of outward irradiance due to the incident angle, as the light flux spreads across a surface whose area is larger than the projected area perpendicular to the ray, written usually as cos θ i

The BRDF is a fundamental radiometric concept and accordingly is used in computer graphics for photorealistic rendering of synthetic scenes.

Solving the rendering equation for any given scene is the primary challenge in realistic rendering. One approach to solving the equation is based on finite element

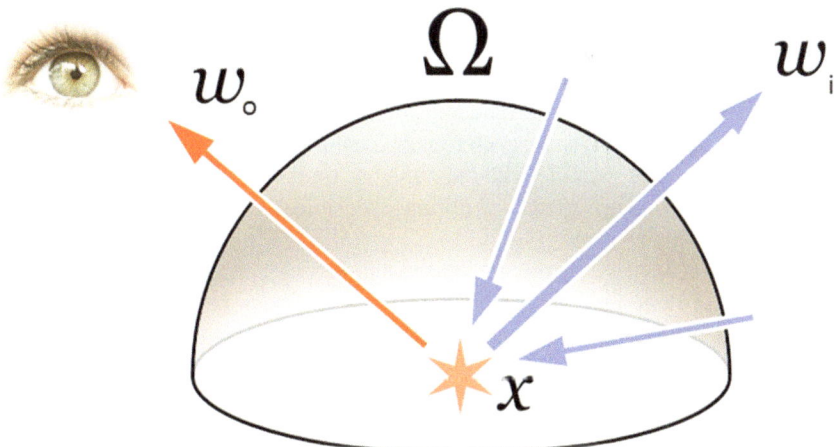

Fig. 4.1 The rendering equation describes how light behaves

methods, leading to the radiosity algorithm. Another approach using Monte Carlo methods has led to many different algorithms including Path Tracing, photon mapping, and Metropolis light transport, among others.[4]

Monte Carlo ray tracing requires a highly detailed and physically based scene description as input. The algorithm applies the laws of physics to simulate the propagation of light through the scene, rather than ad hoc approximations of visual phenomena. This type of simulation requires extremely detailed geometric models (engineering models, for example, are typically accurate to a fraction of a millimeter). Because ray tracing is less performance sensitive to geometric complexity, all surfaces can be finely tessellated. In addition to high geometric detail, photorealistic rendering requires that the physical properties of the material's surface appearance are modeled correctly. In contrast to rasterization, where shaders are used to achieve certain visual effects, the materials in a photorealistic ray tracer describe how light is scattered when striking a surface. A BRDF represents this information. Their physical emission properties also describe light sources. A common representation is the high dynamic range (HDR) environment light. It models the lighting conditions of a real location in a single HDR image. This image is considered as a light source in the rendering system. Virtual objects illuminated by this light appear as if they were in the actual location.

4.2 Scanline Rendering

Scanline rendering is an algorithm for visible surface determination, in 3D computer graphics, that works on a row-by-row basis rather than a polygon-by-polygon or pixel-by-pixel basis.

All of the polygons to be rendered are sorted first by the top y-coordinate at which they first appear. Then, each row or scanline of the image is computed using the intersection of a scanline with the polygons on the front of the sorted list, while the sorted list is updated to discard no-longer-visible polygons as the active scanline advances down the image (Fig. 4.2).

The main advantage of this method is that sorting vertices along the normal of the scanning plane reduces the number of comparisons between edges. Another advantage is that it is not necessary to translate the coordinates of all vertices from the main memory into the working memory—only vertices defining edges that intersect the current scanline need to be in active memory, and only once is each vertex read in. The main memory is often very slow compared to the link between the central processing unit and cache memory, and thus, avoiding re-accessing vertices in main memory can provide a substantial speedup.

---

[4]Kajiya (1986).

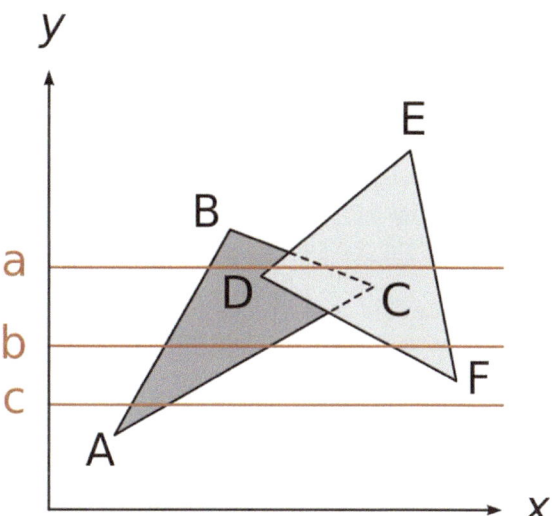

Fig. 4.2 Scanline algorithm example

The main advantage of scanline rendering over z-buffering is that the processing visible pixels is kept to the absolute minimum which is always one time if there are no transparency effects used—a benefit for the case of high-resolution or expensive shading computations.

Through rough front-to-back sorting (approaching the "reverse painter's algorithm") used in modern z-buffer systems, one can realize similar benefits. Early z-reject (in conjunction with hierarchical z) and less common deferred rendering techniques are possible on programmable GPUs.

Scanline techniques, working on the raster, have the drawback that overload can occure if not handled gracefully.

4.2.1   Z-Buffering

In computer graphics, z-buffering, also known as depth buffering, is the management of image depth coordinates in 3D graphics, usually done in hardware, sometimes in software. It is one solution to the visibility problem, which is the problem of deciding which elements of a rendered scene are visible.

When projecting an object on the screen with a 3D-rendering engine, the depth (z-value) of a generated pixel in the projected screen image gets stored in a buffer (the z-buffer or depth buffer). A z-value is the measure of the perpendicular distance from a pixel on the projection plane to its corresponding 3D-coordinate on a polygon in world space.

The z-buffer has the same internal data structure as an image, namely a 2D-array, with the only difference being that it stores a z-value for each screen pixel instead of pixel data. It has the same dimensions as the screen buffer, except when multiple

Z-buffers are used, such as in split-screen rendering. It operates in screen space and takes as its input a projected image that originates from a projection of an object to the screen.

Initial visibility tests (such as back-face culling) are completed before creating a projection from world-space to screen-space conversion. Secondary visibility tests (such as overlap checks and screen clipping) on objects' vertices get conducted before passing an image to the z-buffer. Primary and secondary visibility tests do not require the checking of individual pixels, so the z-buffer is relieved of some work.

When viewing an image containing partially or fully overlapping opaque objects or surfaces, it is not possible to fully see those objects that are furthest away from the viewer and behind other objects (i.e., some surfaces hidden behind others). The identification and removal of these surfaces are called the hidden surface problem. To improve rendering time, the hidden surfaces are removed before a projected image of the surfaces is being passed to the z-buffer. The z-buffer calculates the z-value of a pixel corresponding to the first object and compares it with the z-value at the same pixel location in the z-buffer corresponding to the object that is known to be closest to the viewer to check for overlap. If the calculated z-value is smaller than the z-value already in the z-buffer, then the current z-value in the z-buffer is replaced with the calculated value. That doesn't necessarily mean that the first object as a whole is closer to the viewer than the closest known object, but it does mean that the z-values corresponding to 3D-point on the first object's surface in world space are closer to the viewer. In other words, the objects are intersecting, and at least some part of the first object is closer and thus visible to the viewer. In the end, the z-buffer allows correct reproduction of the general depth perception: A close object hides one further away. That is called z-culling. z-buffering was first described in 1974 by Wolfgang Straßer.[5]

The painter's algorithm is another common solution which, though less efficient, can also handle non-opaque scene elements. The z-buffer uses the image space method for hidden surface detection. A z-buffer can refer to a data structure or to the method used to perform operations on that structure.

4.2.2   Painter's Algorithm

The painter's algorithm, also known as a priority fill, is one of the most straight-forward solutions to the visibility problem in 3D computer graphics. When projecting a 3D scene onto a 2D plane, it is necessary at some point to decide which polygons are visible.

The name "painter's algorithm" refers to the technique employed by many painters for painting distant parts of a scene before parts which are nearer, thereby

---

[5]Straßer (1974).

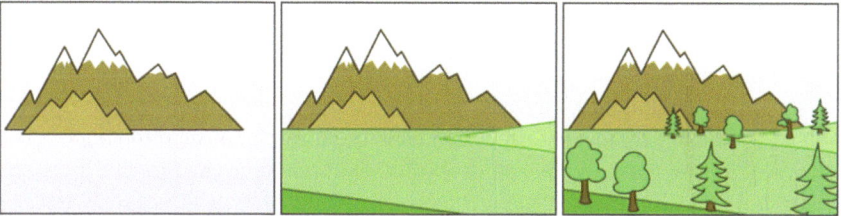

Fig. 4.3 Example of the painter's algorithm

covering some areas of distant parts. The painter's algorithm sorts all the polygons in a scene by their depth and then paints them in this order, farthest to closest. It paints over the parts that are not visible—thus solving the visibility problem—at the cost of having painted invisible areas of distant objects. The ordering used by the algorithm is called a depth order and does not have to respect the numerical distances to the parts of the scene: The essential property of this ordering is that if one object obscures a part of another, then the first object is painted after the object that it obscures. Thus, valid ordering is described as a topological ordering of a directed acyclic graph representing occlusion between objects (Fig. 4.3).

The distant mountains are painted first, followed by the closer meadows; finally, the trees are painted. Although some trees are more distant from the viewpoint than some parts of the meadows, the ordering (mountains, meadows, trees) forms a valid depth order, because no object in the ordering obscures any part of an object painted later.

A reverse painter's algorithm may also be used, in which objects nearest to the viewer are painted first—with the rule that one must never apply paint to parts of the image that are already painted (unless they are partially transparent). In a computer graphic system, this can be very efficient, since it is not necessary to calculate the colors (using lighting, texturing and such) for parts of a much distant scene that are hidden by nearby objects. However, the reverse algorithm suffers from many of the same problems as the standard version.

4.3   Ray Tracing

Who uses photorealistic rendering? A wide range of applications use photorealistic rendering. Designers and engineers use the technology to visualize virtual proto-types. This usage reduces time to market and development cost by reducing the number of physical prototypes required. In recent years, the quality of computer-generated images has reached a level of realism, where renderings are indistinguishable from photographs. That made it possible to replace photographs by computer-generated pictures for marketing purposes. In the same way, architects use rendering technology to visualize new buildings for their customers, and they use similar methods to model the interior lighting accurately. Photorealistic rendering is also used extensively for visual effects and animated feature films by the movie industry.

In computer graphics, ray tracing is a rendering technique for generating an image by tracing the path of light as pixels in an image plane and simulating the effects of its encounters with virtual objects. The technique can produce a very high degree of visual realism, usually higher than that of typical scanline rendering methods, but at a higher computational cost.

Advanced shading effects can make visualizations more effective. The advantage, opportunity, and goal of ray tracing are to provide additional visual cues à better convey 3D shape—it is not about looking better, but about more effective communications.

There are at least four types of rays involved in ray tracing:

- Eye rays originate at the eye as depicted in Fig. 4.4.
- Shadow rays: from surface point toward light source
- Reflection rays: from surface point in mirror direction
- Transmission rays: from surface point in refracted direction

The ray-tracing algorithm calculates the ray from the viewer's eye through each pixel, computes the point of the closest intersection with a scene surface, then shades that point by computing shadow rays, and spawns reflected and refracted rays—repeats for the object(s) of interest, or the entire scene.

Recursive ray tracing simulates specular reflection and shadows through and off of transparent surfaces (transmission with refraction). It can use or employ indirect

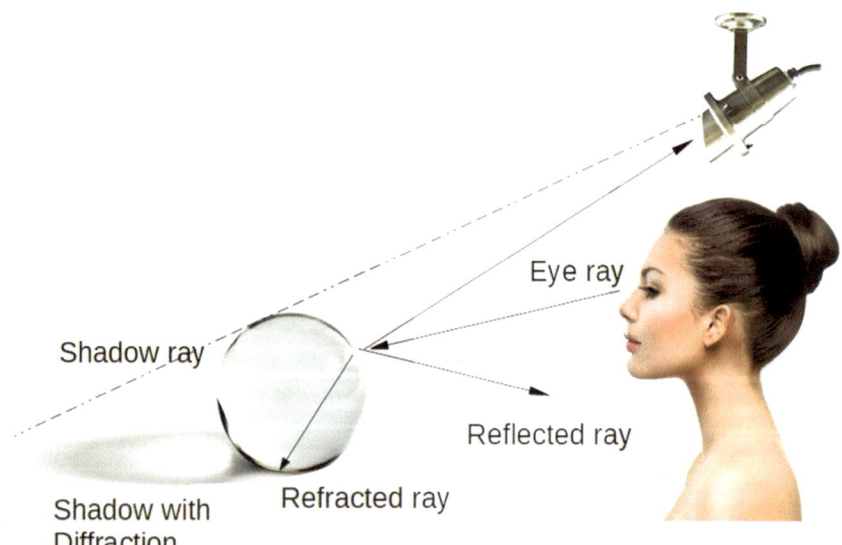

Fig. 4.4 Rays in ray tracing

illumination (a.k.a. global illumination), sometimes area light sources, and sometimes fog or other caustic influences.

As mentioned previously, Arthur Appel is given credit for being one, if not the first one, to use ray casting for visualization.

Appel wrote at the time, "Some applications of computer graphics require a vivid illusion of reality... If techniques for the automatic determination of chiaroscuro with good resolution should prove to be competitive with line drawings, and this is a possibility, machine-generated photographs might replace line drawings as the principal mode of graphical communication in engineering and architecture."

The Army's Ballistic Research Laboratory continued its work and developed the Geometric Information for Targets (GIFT). While developing the algorithms, observers acknowledged that the techniques could be prohibitively expensive in the required computing time.

Ray tracing creates accurate reflections, refractions, shadows, and other features that can make a scene look great (Fig. 4.5).

It is interesting and relevant to note that the initial application of ray-casting algorithms was for visualizing difficult mathematical calculations because now that computers have become fast enough to make the techniques practical, ray tracing is being explored for scientific visualization and analysis once again. (Refer to the appendix for a brief explanation of the difference between ray casting and ray tracing, see Chap. 7).

Ray tracing, broadly speaking, can be segmented into three general categories:

1. Off-line
2. Interactive
3. Real-time

Fig. 4.5 Still life with RenderMan 20. *Source* Dylan Sisson RenderMan community

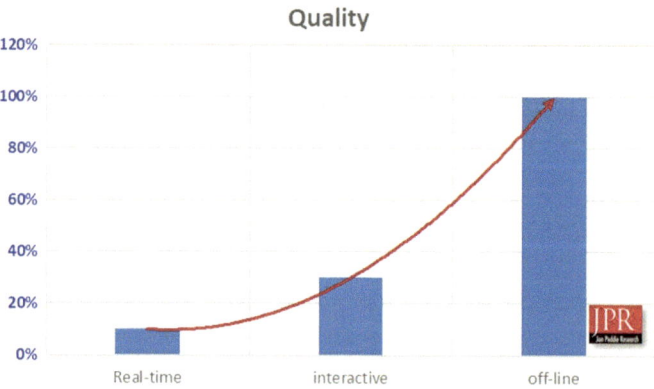

Fig. 4.6 Relative performance versus quality in various modes of ray tracing

Off-line is used extensively by the cinema, ad-agencies, and in design studios. It is the highest quality.

Interactive ray tracing reduces the number of rays and bounces in a compromise to get a good-looking picture and still offers the user the ability to manipulate the model.

Real-time ray tracing can be accomplished, with certain restrictions, and as of March 2018, the assistance of a small supercomputer. I expect that requirement to be relaxed due to clever software and processor improvements due to Moore's law (Fig. 4.6).

One of the tricks of ray tracing is to only ray trace certain elements or objects within an image, for example, the fenders of a car, but not the tires, or maybe headlamps. Although ray tracing, if done correctly, gives you a physically correct image, it is dependent on the material library used. If, using the car example again, you place the vehicle on a road with leaves or stones on it, that portion of the scene will not benefit in realism if accurately ray traced and so it can be a simple texture map.

In the image below, the background isn't ray traced, nor does it need to be, but the floor might be depending on what material the director wants to use (Fig. 4.7).

Ray tracing is capable of simulating a wide variety of optical effects, such as reflection and refraction, scattering, and dispersion phenomena (such as chromatic aberration).

The realism of all rendering methods can be evaluated as an approximation to the equation. Ray tracing, if it is limited to Whitted's algorithm, is not necessarily the most realistic. Methods that trace rays, but include additional techniques (photon mapping, Path Tracing), give a far more accurate simulation of real-world lighting. Radiosity and light-field rendering may be the ultimate for realism.

Not perfect: Ray tracing by itself is not perfect. Basic ray-traced images are very clean, so the alignment of objects and sampling can lead to unintended patterns known as moiré patterns and aliasing.

Fig. 4.7 Star Wars stormtroopers rendered in real time with ray tracing (Nvidia)

Ray tracing gives a color for every possible point in the image. However, a square pixel contains an infinite number of points and those points may not all have the same color. Sampling is used where a color of one point (typically center of pixel) is chosen. But regular special sampling leads to aliasing, what is known as jaggies, which can produce moiré patterns. Aliasing is one frequency (high) masquerading as another (low). An example is the strange effect of a wagon wheel appearing to be rotating backward (aptly known as the wagon-wheel effect). The problem is partially solved by **super-sampling**, firing more than one ray for each pixel (**subsampling** the pixel) and then averaging the results. All that adds to the computational load of ray tracing. A more sophisticated technique is to use adaptive super-sampling (ASS). ASS sparsely samples areas with fairly constant appearance and heavily samples areas with lots of variability. Even more sophisticated techniques involve stochastic sampling—instead of a regular grid, the algorithm subsamples pixels randomly and then adaptively subsamples them.

The **global illumination** algorithm based on photon maps is a two-pass method. The first pass builds the photon map by emitting photons from the light sources into the scene and storing them in a photon map when they hit non-specular objects. The second pass, the rendering pass, uses statistical techniques on the photon map to

Fig. 4.8 Crytek Sponza scene—a common scene for showcasing global illumination (model from McGuire Graphics Data)

extract information about incoming flux and reflected radiance at any point in the scene. The photon map is decoupled from the geometric representation of the scene. This is a key feature of the algorithm, making it capable of simulating global illumination in complex scenes containing millions of triangles, instanced geometry, and complex procedurally defined objects (Fig. 4.8).

Compared with **finite element radiosity**, photon maps have the advantage that no meshes are required. The radiosity algorithm is faster for simple diffuse scenes but as the complexity of the scene increases, photon maps tend to scale better. Also, the photon map method handles non-diffuse surfaces and caustics.[6]

Monte Carlo ray-tracing methods such as **Path Tracing**, bidirectional Path Tracing, and Metropolis light transport (MLT) can simulate all global illumination effects in complex scenes with very little memory overhead. A photon map has a benefit compared with these methods of efficiency but needs extra memory to store the photons. For most scenes, the photon map algorithm is significantly faster, and the result looks better since the error in the photon map method is of low frequency which is less noticeable than the high-frequency noise of general Monte Carlo methods.[7]

The recent work in ray tracing has largely focused on minimizing the total number of rays needed to render a high-fidelity image, or on improving the average performance of traced rays (Glassner 1989; Havran 2000; Wald 2004).

Metropolis light transport, a variant of the Monte Carlo method, is the perturbing of previously found paths in order to increase performance for difficult scenes, which was introduced in 1997 by Eric Veach and Leonidas J. Guibas.[8]

---

[6]https://graphics.pixar.com/library/HQRenderingCourse/paper.pdf.

[7]Jensen (2001).

[8]Veach and Guibas (1997).

Normal Path Tracing is slowed or confounded by optical phenomena such as bright caustics, chromatic aberration, fluorescence, or iridescence. MLT works very well on some of these shots, while being very complex to implement which is why few people have tried it.

MLT can also be very fast on complex shots and yet more expensive to render on others. For example, its approach of nodally mapping paths bidirectionally helps it focus on the problem of light just coming through a keyhole in a door to a darkened room or to produce very accurate caustics. But a full MLT can be slower than other algorithms when rendering simple scenes. The power of Metropolis is in exploring difficult occurrences, and its strongest point is sometimes its weakest point when dealing with simple scenes.

Sometimes with an MLT, one cannot use the same sampling techniques used with a Path Tracing system, at least not everywhere in the code. One cannot use quasi-Monte Carlo, for example, in many places.

Distributed ray tracing, also called as stochastic ray tracing, is a refinement of ray tracing that allows for the rendering of "soft" phenomena. It is a term originally coined by Robert Cook[9] in his 1984 paper. Cook's observation was that in order to perform anti-aliasing in a ray tracer, the renderer needs to perform spatial upsampling—that is, to take more samples (i.e., shoot more rays) than the number of pixels in the image and combine their results. One way to do this is to shoot multiple rays within a pixel and average their color values. However, if the renderer is already tracing multiple rays per pixel anyway to obtain an anti-aliased image, then these rays can also be distributed among additional dimensions than just the pixel position to sample effects that could not be captured by a single ray. This comes without any additional computational cost on top of spatial upsampling. If, for example, one is shooting multiple rays within a pixel to compute an anti-aliased result, then one can get motion blur for free by using a different time value for each ray (or soft shadows if they connect to a different point on the light source, or depth of field if they use a different starting point on the aperture, etc.).

Monte Carlo ray tracing is a term that is slightly ambiguous. In most cases, it refers to rendering techniques that solve the rendering equation, introduced by Jim Kajiya in 1986, using Monte Carlo integration.

Practically, all modern rendering techniques that solve the rendering equation, such as Path Tracing, bidirectional Path Tracing, progressive photon mapping, and VCM, can be classified as Monte Carlo ray-tracing techniques. The idea of Monte Carlo integration is that we can compute the integral of any function by randomly choosing points in the integration domain and averaging the value of the function at these points. At a high level, in Monte Carlo ray tracing, we can use this technique to integrate the amount of light arriving at the camera within a pixel in order to compute the pixel value. For example, a path tracer does this by randomly picking a point within the pixel to shoot the first ray and then continues to randomly pick a direction to continue to the surface it lands on, and so forth. We could also

---

[9]Cook (1984).

randomly pick a position on the time axis if we want to do motion blur, or randomly pick a point on the aperture if we want to do depth of field, or a random point on a light source for soft shadows.

If this sounds very similar to distributed ray tracing, that's because it is. We can think of distributed ray tracing as a very informal description of a Monte Carlo algorithm that samples certain effects like soft shadows. Cook's paper lacks the mathematical framework to really reason about it properly, but one could implement distributed ray tracing using a simple Monte Carlo renderer. It is worth noting that distributed ray tracing lacks any description of global illumination effects, which are naturally modeled in the rendering equation (it should be mentioned that Kajiya's paper was published two years after Cook's paper).

You can think of Monte Carlo ray tracing as being a more general version of distributed ray tracing. Monte Carlo ray tracing contains a general mathematical framework that allows you to handle practically any effect, including those mentioned in the distributed ray-tracing paper.

Distributed ray tracing is not a term that is used to refer to the original algorithm. More often, one will hear it in conjunction with distribution effects, which are simply effects such as motion blur, depth of field, or soft shadows that cannot be handled with a single-sample ray tracer.

In distributed ray tracing, one stochastically samples many rays in many directions which may or may not be preferred by the BRDF, whereas in Monte Carlo ray tracing or simply Path Tracing, one samples only one ray in a direction preferred by the BRDF. So, there are two obvious advantages Path Tracing would have:

Computationally less expensive: With the same computing power, one has the freedom of calculating over more object hits as compared to distributed ray tracing where there are multiple rays.

Less noise: Distributed ray tracing samples rays in directions that might not be preferred by the BRDF, therefore introducing unwanted artifacts.

And so, Path Tracing would give one better results.

4.3.1   Path Tracing

Path Tracing is an extension of the ray-tracing algorithm. It simulates many light paths per pixel and takes the average value to calculate the final color of each pixel. Whenever a ray hits a surface, a new ray is traced from that hit point in a random direction until the maximum path depth is reached or until a Russian roulette-like mechanism kills the ray. As a result, Path Tracing can produce effects like diffuse color bleeding, glossy (blurry) reflections, soft shadows, real area lights, true depth of field.

Path Tracing uses random sampling (i.e., "Monte Carlo"—*Russian roulette*) to incrementally compute a final image. The random sampling process makes it possible to render some complex phenomena which are not handled in regular ray tracing, but it generally takes a longer time to produce a high-quality path-traced image.

The random sampling in Path Tracing causes noise to appear in the rendered image. The noise is removed by letting the algorithm generate more samples, i.e., color values resulting from a single ray. A more in-depth explanation of the Path Tracing algorithm is given below.

Path Tracing should probably be attributed to Jim Kajiya in his 1986 paper, *The Rendering Equation*.[10] It uses some of the same mechanisms as Whitted's style ray tracing, but Path Tracing can be used to solve more complex lighting situations (with diffuse interreflection or caustics) through the use of Monte Carlo integration to solve an integral equation which represents light transport within a scene. It represents a more disciplined approach to image generation, capable of reproducing a richer set of light/surface interactions.

4.3.2   The Difference Between Path Tracing and Ray Tracing

Path Tracing is physically based simulation of light that allows highly realistic rendering. It is an elegant algorithm that can simulate many of the complex ways that light travels and scatters in virtual scenes. Path Tracing uses ray tracing in order to determine the visibility in-between scattering events. Ray tracing is a basic operation that can be used for many things. Therefore, ray tracing alone does not automatically produce realistic images. Light transport algorithms like Path Tracing can be used for that. However, while elegant and very powerful, naive Path Tracing is very costly and takes a long time to produce stable images. Adaptive filters have been proposed that reuse as much information as possible across many frames and pixels in order to produce robust and stable images.

4.3.3   Noise in Ray Tracing

Real-time GPU renderers use rasterization or what is known as scanline rendering. GPUs have been great at doing rasterization for over twenty years and can accomplish real-time rendering. To deliver real-time rendering, game engines and other renderers use clever techniques, but they are fakes and approximations. Anyone who uses such tools knows immediately what those limitations are and the extra work that is needed to try and approximate the desired effects.

Real-time rasterization rendering can't do real reflections, refractions, or light bounces. To generate such lighting effects, the rendering programs have to approximate/fake those effects. Ray tracing accomplishes the correct handling of the lighting of them, but it takes time to accomplish. As a result, only off-line renderers used ray tracing.

---

[10]Kajiya (1986).

Instead of tracing hundreds to thousands of rays per pixel, researchers developed a technique known as **denoising** to save time. The concept is to trace a few rays and then denoise the image; typically done in the past, but developments have moved ray tracing more toward real time.

There are two methods of denoising: temporal and spatial.

Temporal denoising renders a few rays every frame; they are different, and over time, they average out to give one a smooth result—a lot like how temporal anti-aliasing works. For a still image, temporal denoising works well. For a moving image, there are problems with ghosting.

Temporal denoising combines the results of multiple frames and accomplishes iterative refining. For a still image, the refined image is as good as if one had used hundreds of rays per pixel. For a moving image, it creates ghosts which have to be culled using motion information and that leaves noise where culling occurs.

Spatial denoising is applied to the noisy areas and uses a smoothing filter on them such as an edge blur. It doesn't work well with animation, and it creates moving splotches. It also removes the sharpness from objects that should be sharp. Therefore, only in certain areas does spatial denoising get used.

Spatial denoising combines the results of multiple neighboring pixels like a blur filter. However, it creates shimmering on moving images—splotches of blurred, moving noise.

The problem with overblurring is that sampling over boundaries of objects makes sharp things look blurry. Therefore, spatial denoising is used to fix problems of temporal denoising where temporal denoise fails (Fig. 4.9).

Increasing the rays per pixel increases the rendering time proportionally. Using ten rays per pixel takes ten times as long or render, yielding one-tenth of the

Fig. 4.9 This scene renders at about 30–40 fps using just one ray per pixel. It is noisy but one can get a good sense of what the image looks like. *Source* Notch

frames-per-second, and the image still has noise in it. Applying temporal denoising to that (10 rays per pixel) image is the finishing touch for a high-quality image—as long as the camera doesn't move. As soon as it does, temporal smears appear in the image.

In some areas, such as flat open spaces, the technique works well, but any vertical or occulted parts suffer from smearing. To fix that problem, another filter is employed which is called temporal ghost suppression. That results with noise appearing around the vertical surfaces. If one uses spatial denoising, the places where the vertical surfaces meet the floor are blurry. As a result, practitioners have figured out how to use temporal and spatial denoising at the same time which for most situations gives a really good result.

Denoising limitations: Denoising relies heavily on temporal refinement succeeding. It has problems with moving lights and some problems with moving objects. It takes a long time to refine very glossy reflections and diffuse surfaces.

Denoising is not a magic or silver bullet. Any time anything in the scene is moved, lights, objects, or the camera, it causes temporal denoising to fail. The glossier a surface is or the more diffused it is, the noisier it will be and it will take longer to refine or resolve to a satisfactory image quality.

Nonetheless, denoising is important and will influence how real-time workflows with ray tracing are going to change, how and what one creates, and how one's image looks.

4.3.4   Global Illumination

Radiosity, ray tracing, beam tracing, cone tracing, Path Tracing, Metropolis light transport, ambient occlusion, photon mapping, and image-based lighting are examples of algorithms used in global illumination, some of which may be used together to yield results that are not fast, but accurate.

Images rendered using global illumination algorithms often appear more photo-realistic than images rendered using only direct illumination algorithms. However, such images are computationally more expensive and consequently much slower to generate. One common approach is to compute the global illumination of a scene and store that information with the geometry, e.g., radiosity. That stored data can then be used to generate images from different viewpoints for generating walk-throughs of a scene without having to go through expensive lighting calculations repeatedly.

4.3.5   The Difference Between Ray Tracing and Ray Casting

Like ray casting, ray tracing "determines the visibility of surfaces by tracing imaginary rays of light from viewer's eye to the object in the scene" (Foley 701[11]).

---

[11]Foley, "Computer Graphics: Principles and Practice," p701

Fig. 4.10 Iconic Wolfenstein 3D screenshot. *Source* Wikipedia

Ray casting is faster than ray tracing.

Ray casting is faster because in its world it is limited by one or more geometric constraints (simple geometric shapes); a ray-tracing world can be almost any shape. Ray casting was developed in the early 1980s and was successfully exploited by John Carmack in his groundbreaking 3D shooter, *Wolfenstein 3D* (id Software), in 1992[12]. Ray casting is a technique that transforms a limited form of data (a very simplified map or floor plan) into a 3D projection by tracing rays from the viewpoint into the viewing volume (Fig. 4.10).

The term ray casting was first used in computer graphics in a 1982 paper by Scott Roth[13] to describe a method for rendering constructive solid geometry models.

Ray casting is considered the most basic of computer graphics rendering algorithms and uses the geometric algorithm of ray tracing. The first ray-casting algorithm used for rendering was presented by Arthur Appel in 1968[14].

As mentioned above, ray casting is much faster than ray tracing. The speed and simplicity of ray casting come from computing the color of the light without recursively tracing additional rays that sample the radiance incident on the point that the ray hits. That eliminates accurately rendering reflections, refractions, or the natural falloff of shadows; however, all of these elements can be faked to a degree, by the use of texture maps or other methods creatively, sometimes referred to as hand baking. The high speed of calculation made ray casting a well-used rendering tool in early real-time 3D video games.

Ray-tracing-based rendering algorithms operate in image order to render three-dimensional scenes to two-dimensional images. Geometric rays are traced from the eye of the observer to sample the light (radiance) traveling toward the observer from the ray direction (Fig. 4.11).

---

[12]https://en.wikipedia.org/wiki/Wolfenstein_3D.

[13]Roth (1982).

[14]"Ray tracing and other Rendering Approaches" (PDF), lecture notes, MSc Computer Animation and Visual Effects, Jon Macey, University of Bournemouth

Fig. 4.11 Ray-traced image of glasses showing the perfect reflections and refractions, as well as shadows. *Source* Gilles Tran

Ray tracing can generate a very high degree of visual realism, higher than that of typical scanline rendering methods, but it uses a lot more computing cycles. Therefore, ray tracing has been relegated to applications where the image can be rendered slowly ahead of time and where highly accurate reflections and shadows are needed. Ray tracing can be used for still images and film and television visual effects and recently in real-time applications like video games where speed is critical. Ray tracing is capable of simulating a wide variety of optical effects, such as reflection and refraction, scattering, and dispersion phenomena (such as chromatic aberration).

Ray-tracing technology provides at least two principal operations: Tracing rays to determine the first point seen from the origin of a ray into its direction, and determining the mutual visibility of two points in space (a.k.a. shadow rays).

This is an oversimplified view of the things, but it is the principle. Ray tracing per se deals with the geometry of things (only).

From there, one can build everything else. Simulating global illumination comprises of sampling light transport paths that connect light sources and pixels and sum up their contributions. One such algorithm is Path Tracing, which tries to generate the paths starting from the camera. This is done by tracing one ray after another. And then, the complication (or the art) starts: How efficient one's renderer is, is very much dependent on selecting whether to trace a ray scattered of a surface (or in a volume) or whether to trace a shadow ray to connect to a light source.

Similarly, ray tracing can be used to create images that are super-sampled and/or anti-aliasing.

The strength of ray tracing as compared to rasterization is that it is independent of the screen resolution and/or the number of light sources in a scene. So, one can work adaptively. This is not very feasible with rasterization.

Images rendered using global illumination algorithms often appear more photorealistic than images rendered using only direct illumination algorithms. However, such images are computationally more expensive and consequently much slower to generate. One common approach is to compute the global illumination of a scene and store that information with the geometry, e.g., radiosity. That stored data can then be used to generate images from different viewpoints for generating walk-throughs of a scene without having to go through expensive lighting calculations repeatedly.

One paradigm to face this challenge in rasterization is to do sparse shading, i.e., sharing shading computations across pixels. In early ray casting, it has been shaded micropolygons (the Pixar REYES architecture). This principle survived until the Manuka rendering technology by Weta was introduced.[15] Instead of colors per micropolygon, one stores bidirectional scattering distribution function (BSDF) parameters per vertex of a micropolygon grid.

This is the principle of decoupling shading from anti-aliasing and thus from resolution. The efficiency of this approach varies. If one has high details, then it does not buy you much; however, in regions of low detail, it helps a lot. That is why level of detail (LOD) is important. Again, this is simple in rasterization, but unsolved in ray tracing (unless one goes really conservative and such as the Manuka system).

4.3.6 Recursive Ray Tracing

The next major advancement with ray tracing was that of recursive ray tracing. Older algorithms lacked realism because they didn't account for reflections, refractions, and shadows. This is because these older algorithms would simply calculate the color upon hitting an object. Once that was accomplished, the tracing process ended then and there. Turner Whitted, in 1979, decided to let the ray continue even after hitting an object. Except now, the ray had three options. It could generate up to three new types of rays, one for reflection, one for refraction, and one for shadows. Reflection rays would travel back from an object. A refraction ray could travel through an object but at an angle to mimic the refractive index of the material. Lastly, a shadow ray would be traced toward the light source until it

---

[15]https://www.wetafx.co.nz/research-and-tech/technology/manuka/.

Fig. 4.12 Coffee room rendering using OneRender ray tracer. *Source* OneRender

collided with an opaque object. This way, the iterative method of tracing and then breaking down the rays into the three categories allowed for a lot more realism to be added to the rendered image.

Ray-tracing-based rendering algorithms operate in image order (from the screen or viewer to the light source) to render three-dimensional scenes to two-dimensional images. Geometric rays are traced from the eye of the observer to sample the light (radiance) traveling toward the observer from the ray direction (Fig. 4.12).

Because ray tracing uses more computing cycles to generate a very high degree of visual realism, it has been consigned to situation where the image can be rendered slowly, that is, changing with the advent of specialized ray-tracing accelerators and artificial reality (AI) techniques.

4.4   Photon Mapping

Ray tracing and photon mapping provide a practical way of efficiently simulating global illumination including interreflections, caustics, color bleeding, participating media, and subsurface scattering in scenes with complicated geometry and advanced material models.

Ray tracing is one of the most popular and powerful techniques in the image synthesis repertoire: It is simple, elegant, and easily implemented. [However], there are some aspects of the real world that ray tracing doesn't handle very well (or at all!) as of this writing. Perhaps the most important omissions are diffuse interreflections (e.g., the "bleeding" of colored light from a dull red file cabinet onto a white carpet, giving the carpet a pink tint), and caustics (focused light, like the shimmering waves at the bottom of a swimming pool).

At the time of the development of the photon map algorithm in 1993, these problems were still not addressed efficiently by any ray-tracing algorithm. The photon map method offers a solution to both problems. The photon map algorithm was developed in 1993–1994 and is a versatile algorithm capable of simulating global illumination including caustics, diffuse interreflections, and participating media in complex scenes. It provides the same flexibility as general Monte Carlo ray-tracing methods using only a fraction of the computation time.

Among the techniques mentioned above, photon mapping is the only one that works similarly to how lighting works in real life; i.e., it shoots photons from the lights. All the other techniques work the reverse way: They shoot rays out of the camera, bounce them around, and eventually hit a light.

When these camera rays hit an object, the primary GI engine is used. If GI requires multiple bounces, the secondary GI engine is used for these bounces. The figures below show how this happens when you enable "brute force" for both primary and secondary GI engines.

Zero GI bounces: Camera shoots a ray and hits the wall (point "A"). The primary GI engine is used and shoots another ray which is shown in red. This way, direct lighting on the floor (point "B") affects point "A" (Fig. 4.13).

One GI Bounce: The processing now goes a bit further. Point "B" uses the secondary GI engine to gather illumination from the sphere by shooting a single ray (shown in blue). This way, the direct lighting of the floor (point "B") and the sphere (point "C") affects point "A" (Fig. 4.14).

Shooting photons from the lights or shooting rays from our eyes is, in some ways, equivalent. If you flip the direction of all the arrows above, it is as if lighting came from the light source, bounced off the sphere, floor, and wall, and then reached the camera!

So why have separate primary and secondary GI engines? The results of primary GI lighting are directly visible to the camera, so it needs to be as high quality as

Fig. 4.13 Zero GI bounces
with photon mapping

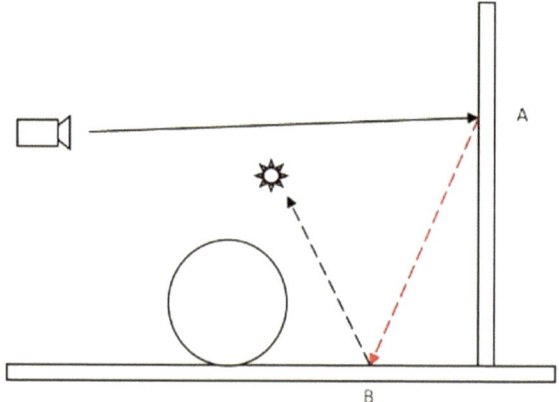

Fig. 4.14 Multiple and
secondary GI bounces with
photon mapping

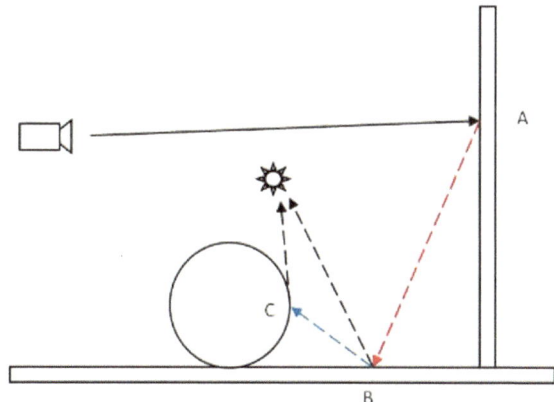

possible. Secondary GI lighting, on the other hand, often represents the smallest
part of the final lighting so it can afford to be of somewhat lower quality (think
"blurrier" or "noisier") without introducing significant visual artifacts.
Approximating secondary GI like that has significant performance and, sometimes,
quality advantages.

This technique works similarly to how light behaves in real life. In one stage, it
shoots photons from light sources, bounces them around the scene, and stores them
on surfaces. Then, on the second stage, the renderer uses these photons to render the
final image. The technique provides a very good degree of control, and for reasonable numbers of photons, it renders fast.

However, it is considered an outdated technique. Photons have to be stored in
GPU memory, so too many photons can be prohibitive in terms of memory usage.
There are a few settings to tweak, and some experimentation might be needed to get
a clean result, and processing time and storage may be wasted for photons that will
not end up being visible to the camera.

4.5   Brute Force

Brute force works the opposite way to photon mapping. Instead of shooting photons
from the light, it shoots several rays from each surface and bounces the rays around.
It can be very accurate, there is no flickering in animations, and it is easy as it only
has one setting to tweak ("Num Rays"). Also, it does not require any storage, so the
final image resolution and scene detail do not matter.

However, it is the slowest technique. And unless many rays are shot per pixel, it
can produce grainy images—especially in difficult lighting situations.

4.6   Radiosity

In 3D computer graphics, radiosity is an application of the finite element method to solving the rendering equation for scenes with surfaces that reflect light diffusely. Unlike rendering methods that use Monte Carlo algorithms (such as Path Tracing and ray tracing), which handle all types of light paths, typical radiosity only accounts for paths which leave a light source and are reflected diffusely some number of times before hitting the eye.

Radiosity is a global illumination algorithm in the sense that the illumination arriving on a surface comes not just directly from the light sources, but also from other surfaces reflecting light. Radiosity is viewpoint independent, which increases the calculations involved, but makes them useful for all viewpoints (Fig. 4.15).

A general radiosity method accounting for all interreflections of light between diffuse and non-diffuse surfaces in complex environments was introduced in 1986 by David Immel, Michael Cohen, and Donald Greenberg, at Cornell University [16].

Fig. 4.15 Scene rendered with radiosity renderer and visualizer (By David Bařina, Kamil Dudka, Jakub Filák, Lukáš)

---

[16]Immel et al. (1986).

As contrasted with previous radiosity methods, surfaces are no longer required to be perfectly diffuse reflectors and emitters. A complete, viewer-independent description of the light leaving each surface in each direction is computed, allowing dynamic sequences of images to be rendered with little additional computation per image. Phenomena such as "reflection tracking" and reflections following a moving observer across a specular surface are produced. Secondary light sources, such as the light from a spotlight reflecting off a mirror onto a wall, are also accounted for. The inclusion of radiosity calculations in the rendering process often lends an added element of realism to the finished scene, because of the way it mimics real-world phenomena.

Notable commercial radiosity engines are Enlighten by Geomerics (used for games including Battlefield 3 and Need for Speed: The Run); 3ds Max; formZ; LightWave 3D; and the Electric Image Animation System.

4.7 Light-Field Rendering

Light-field rendering is a method for generating new views from arbitrary camera positions without depth information or feature matching, simply by combining and resampling the available images.

Light-field rendering: By extracting appropriate 2D slices from the 4D light field of a scene, one can produce novel views of the scene. Depending on the parameterization of the light field and slices, these views might be perspective, orthographic, crossed-slit (Zomet 2003), general linear cameras (Yu and McMillan 2004), multi-perspective (Rademacher 1998), or another type of projection. Light-field rendering is one form of image-based rendering (Fig. 4.16).

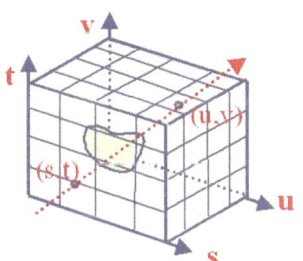

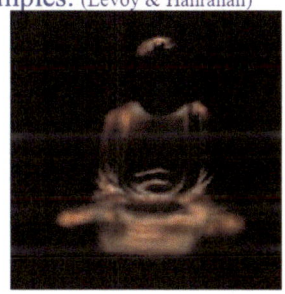

Fig. 4.16 Light-field rendering (IEEE VR 2003 tutorial)

Light-field rendering in itself is not a new technique and has actually been around for more than 20 years but has only recently become a viable rendering technique. The first paper was released at SIGGRAPH 1996, and the method has since been incrementally improved by others.[17]

In mid-2017, Google announced that "Seurat," a novel surface light-field rendering technology which would enable "real-time cinema-quality, photorealistic graphics" on mobile VR devices, developed in collaboration with ILMxLAB.[18] The technology captures all light rays in a scene by prerendering it from many different viewpoints. During runtime, entirely new viewpoints are created by interpolating those viewpoints on the fly, resulting in photoreal reflections and lighting in real time.

Disney also released a paper called "Real-time rendering with compressed animated light fields," demonstrating the feasibility of rendering a Pixar quality 3D movie in real time where the viewer can actually be part of the scene and walk in between scene elements or characters (according to a predetermined camera path).

One of the first movies that showed a practical use for light fields is *The Matrix* from 1999, where an array of cameras firing at the same time (or in rapid succession) made it possible to pan around an actor to create a super slow-motion effect ("bullet time").

Rendering a light field is actually surprisingly easy with Blender's Cycles and doesn't require much technical expertise (besides knowing how to build the plug-ins).[19]

Special effects studio Otoy, has been a proponent of light-field rendering, and likens it to holographic techniques. Holographic, virtual reality has been part of popular culture ever since Gene Roddenberry introduced the Holodeck in *Star Trek: The Next Generation*, in 1987. (The Holodeck was not in the Original Star Trek Series it was first introduced in, *Star Trek: The Animated Series*, as Uhura, Sulu, and McCoy get trapped in it in the animated episode, The Practical Joker.[20])

Holographic video, or holographic light-field rendering as it is technically known, produces stunningly realistic images that can be viewed from any vantage point. Because of its computational complexity, commercial holographic video and VFX have not been commercially viable. Otoy introduced a more affordable light-field stage using GPU technology that they call the OctaneRender.

---

[17]Levoy and Hanrahan (1996).

[18]http://www.roadtovr.com/googles-seurat-surface-light-field-tech-graphical-breakthrough-mobile-vr/.

[19]http://raytracey.blogspot.com/2017/05/practical-light-field-rendering.html.

[20]Peddie (2013).

4.7.1 Voxels

A voxel represents a value on a regular grid in three-dimensional space. As with pixels in a bitmap, voxels themselves do not typically have their position (their coordinates) explicitly encoded along with their values.

Voxels are frequently used in the visualization and analysis of medical and scientific data. Some volumetric displays use voxels to describe their resolution. For example, a display might be able to show $512 \times 512 \times 512$ voxels.

The word voxel originated by analogy with the word "pixel," with vo representing "volume" and el representing "element"; similar formations with el for "element" include the words "pixel" and "texel" (a texture element).

Another technique for voxels involves raster graphics where one simply ray traces every pixel of the display into the scene, tracking an error term to determine when to step. A voxel represents a single sample, or data point, on a regularly spaced, three-dimensional grid.

The planes of a light field can be the indices for the generation of voxels. Light-field acquisition devices allow capturing scenes with unmatched post-processing possibilities. However, the huge amount of high-dimensional data poses challenging problems to light-field processing in interactive time. In order to enable light-field processing with a tractable complexity, the concept of super-ray has been introduced, which is a grouping of rays within and across views, as a key component of a light-field processing pipeline (Fig. 4.17).

Fig. 4.17 Field of voxel-rendered oranges was rendered and shown in real time (25–40 fps at 768 lines) in 2009. *Source* Unlimited detail

Fig. 4.18 Point-to-voxels surfacing example. *Source* Nvidia

The easiest way to think of a voxel is as a 3D pixel—a cube. As a cube, it has six times as many surfaces to process than a simple pixel. Now, true that all six sides can't be seen, at least two of them can't, and usually only three of them can.

If ray casting takes one unit of time (to render a given image), ray tracing would take 10–100 units of time. And a voxel rendering (done honestly) would take 1000 or more. Researchers have employed various tricks to make voxel rendering look as if it was rendering faster. But like ray casting, they were tricks that brought with them artifacts and inaccuracy. And usually, they were not even very attractive (Fig. 4.18).

Voxels can be used for rendering clouds of smoke, ocean waves, and other ultra-dynamic and usually non-predictive flows. They are also used for medical imaging. Voxels are used to build the digital slices that make up tomograms and magnetic resonance imaging (MRI).

In modern computer graphics, all three techniques can be used and often are especially in cinema. The computer graphics toolbox is full of clever and useful tools, and like any good mechanic or carpenter, one doesn't try and use one tool for all problems. So, the difference between ray casting, ray tracing, and voxels is speed versus accuracy, and quality of the image. And just as Ray Charles would mess up his music if he tried to play it at the wrong tempo, a computer image will be messed up if the wrong tool is used in the name of speed. One must find the right tempo for a given image.

4.8   Problems Ray Tracing Doesn't Solve

People get excited about modern hardware bringing us closer to the magical holy grail of real-time ray tracing (RTRT). Some people think once we have RTRT, we can fully simulate entire digital worlds, everything will be photorealistic, and graphics will become a "solved problem". This simply is not true and in fact highlights several fundamental misconceptions about the problems faced by modern games and other interactive media.

Because most of the rays don't actually hit the camera and are simply wasted, a brute-force method is incredibly inefficient; therefore, many complex algorithms (such as photon mapping and Metropolis light transport) have been developed to yield approximations that make ray tracing vastly more efficient. These techniques are almost always focused on attempting to find paths from the light source to the camera, so rays can be cast in the reverse direction. Some early approximations actually cast rays out from the camera until they hit an object and then calculated the lighting information from the distance and angle, disregarding other objects in the scene. While highly efficient, this method produced extremely inaccurate results.

It is with a certain irony that ray tracing is touted as being a precise, super-accurate rendering method when all ray tracing is actually done via approximations in the first place. Pixar uses photon mapping for its movies. Most ray tracers operate on stochastic sampling approximations. We can do RTRT with reasonable hardware if we allow approximations (biases); however, it is limited. However, graphic development doesn't stop when someone develops RTRT, because there will always be a room for a better approximation and/or quality.

In computer graphics, too much is not enough—Jon Peddie, 1981.

4.8.1   Photorealism

The meaning of photorealism is difficult to define because the term is subjective.

Defining photorealism as rendering a virtual scene such that it is indistinguishable from a photograph of a similar scene has been the goal. This, however, raises the issue of just how indistinguishable it needs to be. This is because there are different degrees of "indistinguishable" due to the differences between people's observational capacities and the use case at hand. Many people will never notice a slightly misaligned shadow or a reflection that is slightly too bright. For others, they will stand out and completely destroy their suspension of disbelief (the goal of CG).

The human visual system spans a very large range of light levels. This gives rise to high dynamic range (HDR) challenges in photography and image generation in computers. Computer games, for example, will change the brightness of the entire scene (called the gamma), instead of combining the brightness of multiple exposures to brighten some areas and darken others in the same image (called gamut).

Therefore, creating a photorealistic image is not just a matter of being mathematically physically accurate, but also one of being able to faithfully produce an accurate color and luminesce range image—with most of today's limited (i.e., 8-bit) display systems, it simply is not possible. However, with the advent of 4k screens (UHD), and 10-bit Rec. 2020 or BT.2020 standards, the color fidelity of displays will vastly improve and more fully exploit the benefits of physically accurate ray tracing.

4.8.2   Surface Complexity

Ray tracing is often cited as allowing an order of magnitude in more detail in models by being able to efficiently process many more polygons. That is true in that ray tracing is not subject to the same computational constraints that rasterization is. Rasterization must render every single triangle in the scene, whereas ray tracing is only interested in whether or not a ray hits a triangle. Unfortunately, it still has to navigate through the scene representation. Even if a ray tracer could handle a scene with a billion polygons efficiently, this raises completely unrelated problems involving RAM access times and cache pollution that suddenly become actual performance bottlenecks instead of micro-optimizations.

Ray-tracing approximation algorithms can take advantage of rays that degrade quickly with few bounces before becoming immaterial such as in a city or a forest. However, in an environment with highly reflective materials such as a kitchen, or an automobile, the highly reflective materials slow down the ray tracer, because now rays are bouncing hundreds of times off a myriad of surfaces instead of just a few.

4.8.3   Scale

As the depth of a scene increases from the viewer, the need and value of ray tracing diminish. It is similar to tessellation of polygons—up close you want as many polygons as possible to represent smooth and complex surfaces; in the distance, you don't need as many, your eye simply can't resolve them. Ray tracing a star field, for example, would be insidious and ridiculously time-consuming.

Therefore, user intervention is needed to maintain meaningful precision when faced with astronomical scales, and that impacts the rendering pipeline and throughput. These are problems that arise in any rendering pipeline, regardless of what techniques it uses, due to fundamental limitations in our representations of numbers.

4.9   Summary

From the 2D painter's algorithm to scanline rendering and the z-buffer, computer graphics made tremendous improvements in image quality. Due to limited computing power, various clever shading tricks, texture-mapping schemes, and shadow-mapping projections were used with scanline rendering that created real-time life-like images that could easily fool most casual observers. However, it became well understood in the 1980s that ray tracing was what had to be done for physically accurate, synthesized images to look realistic (Fig. 4.19).

Ray tracing was employed but was (and still is) computationally burdensome. For users who had the computing and time budget, beautiful images were created using ray tracing on high-resolution screens. As processors got faster and not much more expensive thanks to Moore's law, it became possible to render ray-traced images in real time (i.e., at 30 fps) on a HD (1920 × 1080) 30-bit deep screen.

Computer scientist, however, didn't stop with ray tracing and went on to develop images that employed global illumination techniques that are known as radiosity. At the turn of the century, volumetric techniques were being explored.

The quest for the perfect picture will go on. In 2018, real-time ray tracing on a PC was realized at HD resolution; in years to come, it will be possible on a 4K and then an 8K screen. Suspension of disbelief will be a foregone conclusion.

Ray tracing can be found in other application areas such as optical design, acoustic design, and radio-frequency design and analysis. According to Friedrich Kittler's Optical Media[21], optical media faced their end with the emergence of computer graphic techniques such as ray tracing and radiosity.

For the purpose of this book, I will concentrate on ray tracing as applied to computer graphics.

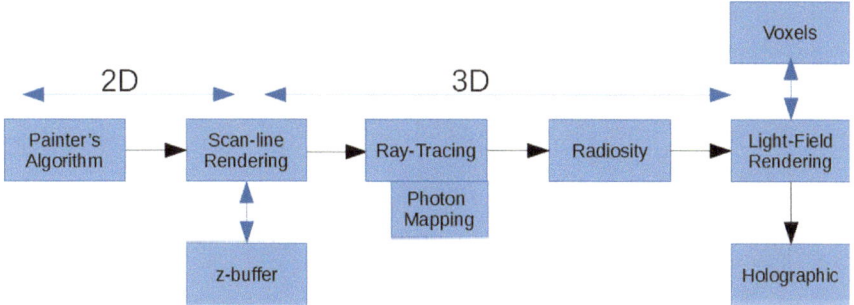

Fig. 4.19 Continuum of rendering

---

[21]Kittler and Ogger (2001). The article is based on a talk he gave in 1998.

References

Cook R (1984) Distributed ray tracing, In: Proceedings of the 11th annual conference on SIGGRAP'84 computer graphics and interactive techniques, ACM New York, NY, USA, pp 137–145

Glassner A (1989) An introduction to ray tracing. Morgan Kaufmann

Gotler S, Grzeszczuk R, Szelinski R, Cohen M (1996) The lumigraph. In: Proceeding computer graphics, ACM, 1996, pp 43–54

Havran V (2000) Heuristic ray shooting algorithms. Ph.D. thesis, Department of Computer Science and Engineering, Faculty of Electrical Engineering, Czech Technical University in Prague

Immel DS, Cohen MF, Greenberg DP (1986) A radiosity method for non-diffuse environments (PDF). In: SIGGRAPH 1986, p 133. https://doi.org/10.1145/15922.15901, ISBN 0-89791-196-2

Jensen HW (2001) Realistic image synthesis using photon mapping, AK Peters

Kajiya TJ (1986) The rendering equation (PDF). In: SIGGRAPH 1986, p 143. https://doi.org/10.1145/15922.15902, ISBN 0-89791-196-2

Kittler F, Ogger S (2001) Computer graphics: a semi-technical introduction. Grey Room 02, pp 30–45

Levoy M, Hanrahan P (1996) Light-field rendering. In: SIGGRAPH 1996. https://graphics.stanford.edu/papers/light/light-lores-corrected.pdf

Noll AM (1971) Scanned-display computer graphics. Commun ACM 14(3):143–150. https://doi.org/10.1145/362566.362567

Peddie J (2013) The history of visual magic in computers. Springer, London. https://doi.org/10.1007/978-1-4471-4932-3

Roth SD (1982) Ray casting for modeling solids. Comput Graph Image Process 18(2):109–144. https://doi.org/10.1016/0146-664X(82)90169-1

Straßer W (1974) Schnelle Kurven- und Flächendarstellung auf grafischen Sichtgeräten (PDF). Berlin

Veach E, Guibas LJ (1997) Metropolis light transport. Computer Science Department, Stanford University

Wald I (2004) Real-time ray tracing and interactive global illumination. Ph.D. thesis, Saarland University

Chapter 5
Work Flow and Material Standards

Abstract Although the basic ray racing algorithm is relatively straight forward, the supporting components to produce a high-quality ray traced image are formidable. How long an image is allowed to take to resolve brings into question the degree of accuracy and fidelity desired, or acceptable. If a rendering is halted before it is fully resolved, some practitioners says such a compromise results in a biased image. Standards in libraries, APIs, shading languages and colors to mention a few have to be taken into consideration. And finally, the quality of the display and/or printing device to show the ray traced results. In an attempt to create an open workflow and interchangeable files companies have promoted the idea of an open materials library and a standard file format. Progress has been made in that effort, but there are certain proprietary looks, that represent important product differentiation that companies will never share.

Rendering is the process of generating an image from a 3D model using computer graphics. This manner of visual communication aids customers, colleagues, and suppliers in understanding one's design or product. Rendering is usually thought of as being at the end of a product design pipeline; however, with new high-speed rendering capabilities, and interactivity, rendering has become a parallel operation and even a leading function as visualization of the product is essential feedback to the design. In film production, it is known as Pre-vis (pre-visualization).

5.1 Biased Versus Unbiased

As fast as modern ray tracing has become, simple shading is still useful for quick looks at the product being designed. To speed up the rendering, some accuracy may be compromised. Less accurate rendering is known as biased.

There are many potential sources of bias. A rendering algorithm is usually biased because it ignores some type of lighting effect, it misrepresents the contributions of various lighting effects to the image, or it simply computes some quantity of light

© Springer Nature Switzerland AG 2019
J. Peddie, *Ray Tracing: A Tool for All*,
https://doi.org/10.1007/978-3-030-17490-3_5

inaccurately. Most methods are biased because they ignore certain classes of light paths (e.g., light which bounces of mirrors or is focused through glass). In this case, the result is darker than the correct image and may lack important visual cues. Real-time methods often skip visibility calculations required for correct shadowing, yielding a result which is too bright. Other methods introduce bias by interpolating among a sparse set of sample values, ignoring high-frequency features and giving the image a blurry appearance. Geometric aliasing (e.g., approximating a smooth surface with triangles) may also appear to be a source of bias.

One of the most challenging things for an unbiased renderer is subsurface scattering (SSS). Many solutions are point-based. That is one of the biggest challenges for a ray tracer, trying to make something accurate and at the same time fast enough to be used in real-life production. Most approaches are point-based.

5.1.1   Biased Versus Consistent

People often confuse the term unbiased with the term consistent; for example, you may hear someone say (incorrectly), "photon mapping is unbiased since it converges to the correct solution." These two terms have two precise and different meanings, and it is important to understand the difference. Consistency is easy to understand: if an approximation approaches the correct solution as computation time increases, then the method is consistent. However, merely knowing that a method is consistent tells you very little. For instance, it does not tell you how quickly the method converges to the correct solution, nor does it give any bound on the error.

In other words, as more samples are taken the probability of the error is greater than some fixed value # approaches zero. Most often, "**consistent**" just means # = 0, i.e., the estimator approaches the exact answer.

Bias is slightly subtler: a method is unbiased if it produces the correct answer on average. An easy way to think about bias in rendering is to ask, "if I rendered the same image millions of times using different random numbers, would averaging the results give me the right answer?" If the answer is "no", you probably have a biased algorithm.

5.1.2   Radiosity

Standard radiosity considers only paths of light bounced diffusely from one surface to another until it hits the eye. Additionally, irradiance is computed over a coarse grid which does not properly capture occlusion (shadows). Although the latter source of error disappears as grid resolution increases, radiosity will always neglect certain types of light paths. Therefore, it is not consistent.

Table 5.1 Biased versus unbiased in different rendering schemes

	Biased	Consistent
Radiosity	Y	N
Rasterization	Y	N
Ray tracing	N	Y
Photon mapping	N	Y

5.1.3   Rasterization

Most real-time rendering is done using an API such as Metal, DirectX, OpenGL, or Vulkan which performs all shading based on the information passed to each triangle by a rasterizer. Traditionally, this framework was limited to integration of paths which bounce of a single diffuse surface before hitting the eye. Most images produced via rasterization will not produce the correct solution, regardless of the level of quality (Table 5.1).

Modern real-time APIs are a mutant example of the tradeoff between speed and robustness: nearly any effect can be achieved in real-time, at the cost of highly special-purpose algorithms.

5.2   Importance of Material Library

When a scene is created using ray tracing, it involves producing an image that faithfully represents the way light behaves. People refer to ray tracing as being physically accurate, However, to be physically accurate does not just mean the geometry of the scene is accurate, but that the way light behaves correctly, accurately, when encountering the various surfaces in the scene. The surfaces may be anything one can imagine from water to leather, to skin, to bricks, and everyone's favorite chrome and glass. Those surfaces are referred to as materials (Fig. 5.1).

Ray-tracing software providers have material libraries as part of their program, regardless if it is a plug-in, an integrated, or a stand-alone ray-tracing program. The extensiveness of that library is a qualifying function for whether a particular ray tracer is used or not, and it is not uncommon for high-end ray tracer users like movies studios to use several ray tracers for just that reason—to get the material they desire for a scene or object in it.

Because of the expansion of use and interest in ray tracing, there has been a movement by the ray tracer suppliers to incorporate material libraries from other sources and supplier, because no single supplier could ever have every material imaginable in their library. In this section, I list a few of the most popular or well-known libraries and suppliers (Fig. 5.2).

Believability is a big part of making great looking scenes or images. And, materials are a significant part of whether the final rendered image looks realistic or not. This goes beyond just photorealism. It applies equally to stylized cartoony images.

Fig. 5.1 Light's interaction with materials determines the image's believability

Fig. 5.2 Materials are used in photorealistic and fantasy images. *Source* Blender.org

Typically, when a company shows its material library, it will use a small ball, usually on a little stand or platform, to show some of the materials available and their surfaces, as illustrated in Fig. 5.3. The balls are often embossed with the company's logo or some other geometric form.

They are called shader balls and is designed to scrutinize the material under various lighting conditions such as:

Fig. 5.3 Blender's Cycles' material library. *Source* Blender.org

- direct versus indirect
- concave versus convex
- the silhouette of the object (important for things like velvet)
- Parts of different thicknesses

It is not certain when it started in rendering, but automotive paint companies do something similar—painting a sample with convex and concave regions.

5.2.1 Standards (USPs, OSL, Etc.)

Open Shading Language (OSL) is an open-source shader system was developed by Sony Pictures Imageworks (SPI). They developed it for their in-house renderer (which is a modified version of Arnold), and it was the exclusive shading system for big VFX films.

The real strength of OSL is the ability to write one's own shaders. One can create materials, lights, displacement, or patterns in the OSL language itself. OSL's surface and volume shaders define how surfaces or volumes scatter light in a way that allows for importance sampling; thus, it is well suited for physically based renderers that support ray tracing and global illumination.

It is used in Blender's Cycles ray-tracing program and Otoy's OctaneRender. OSL is available under the "New BSD" license and can be integrated into commercial and free software applications. The source code is available on github. There is also a good course from SIGGRAPH, on practical physically based shading.[1]

The **Unified Shader Model** (known in Direct3D 10 as "Shader Model 4.0") refers to a form of shader hardware in a graphical processing unit (GPU) where all of the shader stages in the rendering pipeline (geometry, vertex, pixel, etc.) have the same capabilities.[2]

A shader is a piece of code that is executed on the graphics processing unit (GPU), usually found on a graphics card, to manipulate an image before it is drawn to the screen. Shaders allow for various kinds of rendering effect, ranging from adding an X-ray view to adding cartoony outlines to rendering output.[3]

The history of shaders starts at LucasFilm in the early 1980s.[4] LucasFilm hired graphics programmers to computerize the special effects industry. This proved a success for the film/rendering industry, especially at Pixar's Toy Story movie launch in 1995. RenderMan introduced the notion of Shaders;

> The RenderMan Shading Language allows material definitions of surfaces to be described in not only a simple manner but also highly complex and custom manner using a C-like language. Using this method as opposed to a predefined set of materials allows for complex procedural textures, new shading models and programmable lighting. Another thing that sets the renderers based on the RenderMan Interface Specification, or RISpec apart from many other renderers, is the ability to output arbitrary variables as an image—surface normals, separate lighting passes and pretty much anything else can be output from the renderer in one pass.

The term shader was first only used to refer to "pixel shaders," but soon enough new uses of shaders such as vertex and geometry shaders were introduced, making the term shaders more general. Shaders have forced some important movements in the video(card) hardware which will be further examined in the following sections.

---

[1]SIGGRAPH 2012 Course: "Practical Physically Based Shading in Film and Game Production": https://blog.selfshadow.com/publications/s2012-shading-course/.

[2]"Common Shader Core (DirectX HLSL)". Microsoft. Retrieved 2008-08-17.

[3]Hergaarden (2011).

[4]"RenderMan shader history," 2006. http://wiki.cgsociety.org/index.php/RenderMan.

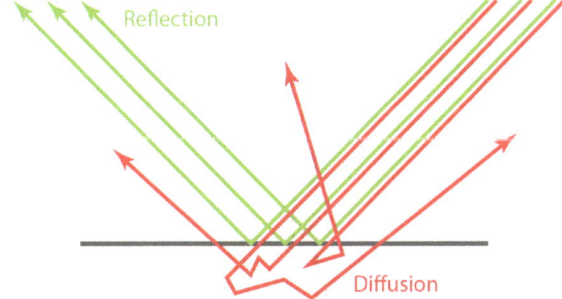

Fig. 5.4 Diffusion and reflections

5.2.2   Physically Based Rendering

Physically Based Rendering (PBR) means that materials reflect or absorb light like how they would (approximately) in real life. A PBR object's shading approximately resembles what it would look like in the real world[5] (Fig. 5.4).

The different properties that make a type of material are called material channels. For instance, one type of material channel will determine the color of the material, and another will determine how rough it is.

5.2.2.1   Physically Accurate?

Using a PBR shader does not mean one's artwork is physically accurate. A PBR system is a combination of physically accurate lighting, shading, and properly calibrated art content.

5.2.2.2   Free PBR Sources

One can build a material's library from PBR textures. Such textures are made procedurally and from scans and contain information on both color and roughness channels.

There are several sources of free PBR textures, a few are listed here (Fig. 5.5).

5.2.2.3   CC0 Textures

Physically based rendering allows for incredibly realistic surfaces, but generating a good PBR texture is not easy: One must wait for good lighting conditions, go outside and shoot the textures, stitch the images together and create all the maps.

---

[5]Russell (2015).

Fig. 5.5 Free PBR where you can download 100% free PBR materials and texture files. *Source* FreePBR.com

That is why texture sites exist, allowing one to quickly get all the textures one needs. But most of the time there is a catch. One can't simply redistribute these textures from other sites as files. You can simply take all the textures on this site, include them in your project and distribute it, however, you like. You don't even need to give credit https://cc0textures.com/.

5.2.2.4   Cgbookcase

All of the 250+ textures on Dorian Zgraggen's cgbookcase.com come with all the different map types needed to create a beautiful material: Ambient Occlusion, Base Color, Height, Metallic, Normal, Roughness, etc. One can use the textures to commercial as well as non-commercial projects, one can publish and sell them as part of a 3D model on TurboSquid or even resell the textures on their own. One can also share them with one's friends. One can literally do anything with them. Plus, one doesn't have to give credit. One can also request textures on https://www.cgbookcase.com/request-a-texture/.

5.2.2.5   Free PBR

At Free PBR, one can download free PBR materials and texture files. FreePBR.com is a site dedicated to the video game development and 3D community who are looking for materials and texture maps to use in a PBR workflow. It was developed and created by Brian Huebert to support indie game developers and 3D artists with free content for their video games and projects. He uses a mix of photographs and procedural workflows, depending on the material. I use Photoshop, Substance Designer, Bitmap2Material, Quixel, and Marmoset Toolbag. Free PBR, or physically based rendering materials offer the metalness/roughness as well as the metallic/smoothness workflow. The 2K texture maps can be used in Unreal Engine, Unity, Blender, and more. There are 260 textures available for free with six new textures being added every week. These PBR textures map sets are free to use in one's games with 3D with no cost involved. Even if one makes money off the video game, the author's only requirement is that you may not redistribute these PBR file sets on other sites, file sharing sites, email, and so on https://freepbr.com/.

5.2.2.6 Khronos

API and middleware provider Khronos offer a physically based material resource in glTF 2.0. It includes core support for materials that could be used for physically based shading. Part of this process involved choosing technically accurate, yet user-friendly, parameters for which developers and artists could use intuitively. This resulted in the introduction of the metallic roughness material to glTF. These parameters can be provided to the material in two ways. Either the parameters can be given constant values, which would dictate the shading of an entire mesh uniformly, or textures can be provided that map varying values over a mesh. More information can be found about glTF at its GitHub page.

5.2.2.7 Textures.Com

Founded in 2005 as CGTextures.com, Textures.com is a website that offers digital pictures of all sorts of materials. The site has pictures of fabrics, wood, metal, bricks, plastic, and many more. The images are textures and can be used for graphic design, visual effects, in computer games and any other situation where one needs a nice pattern or background image. One can download up to 15 images for free every day. If one needs more or bigger images, one can purchase a credit pack or a subscription. The How it works page has more information about download quotas https://www.textures.com/about.

5.2.3 Allegorithmic's Substance Designer

Clermont-Ferrand, France-based Allegorithmic has been involved with the process of texture creation since 2003 and claims over 95% of AAA game studios use Substance in their production pipelines.

In November 2016, Allegorithmic introduced **Substance Source**, a physically based material library, featuring customizable assets that range from fully procedural to fully scanned. It enabled artists to build off premade, curated content, using or customizing materials to fit any creative vision. Substance Source is available to Substance Live users at no extra charge. There are over 1500 PRB materials in the library.

Physically based rendering is a method of shading and rendering that provides a more accurate representation of how light interacts with surfaces. It can be referred to as physically based rendering or physically based shading (PBS). One Substance

Fig. 5.6 An example of materials from Allegorthmic's substance source library (image Raphael Rau)

file contains outputs needed for most workflows: Classic, PBR Metallic, Roughness, Specular and Gloss. The company says one can export materials at any resolution and up to 8k to use in any situation or platform (Fig. 5.6).

According to Allegorithmic, one can create materials with full control and infinite variations. A user can edit complete texture sets instantly and produce Substance textures and MDL materials that will be directly handled in one's renderer or game engine. The company offers an excellent guide on physically based rendering and shading.[6]

Substance Designer is a 3D material authoring and scan processing tool. It has become popular in the entertainment industry for physically based rendering material authoring.

Substance designer can accept scan processing. It can process scans through filters and tools in an adapted to photogrammetry workflow. Substance Designer has a set of software tools and filters including: Crop Tool, Color Equalizer Tool, Extract Channels filters (Multi-angle to Albedo, Multi-angle to Normal, Normal to Height), Smart Patch Clone Tool, Smart Auto Tile Tool.

---

[6]"The Theory of Physically Based Rendering And Shading," https://www.allegorithmic.com/pbr-guide.

5.2.4   Everyday Material Collection

Greyscalegorilla offers the Everyday Material Collection for Arnold, Octane, and Redshift, Cinema 4D and other applications. Over 350 drag-and-drop materials for Cinema 4D. According to the company, it is a simple material workflow to use (Fig. 5.7).

The library contains over 362 materials delivered as .lib4d presets. There are 4K tileable textures organized into folders by Material Name. There is also a Bitmap-based shader library with Drag-and-drop use via C4D Content Browser.

The Everyday Material Collection was built for use in Cinema 4D R18+ using either Arnold, Octane, or Redshift. (Physical and Standard renderers are not supported.)

For advanced Houdini, Maya, or 3ds Max users, you are able to build PBR materials using the EMC texture maps, but they do not offer technical support to non-C4D users.

Fig. 5.7 Greyscalegorilla material collection includes 12 different categories of in-demand textures and shaders

Fig. 5.8 MaterialX has been used Lucas films (© and ™ 2017 Lucasfilm Ltd. all rights reserved)

5.2.5   MaterialX

MaterialX is an open standard for the transfer of rich material and look-development content between applications and renderers. Originated at Lucasfilm in 2012, MaterialX has been used by Industrial Light and Magic in feature films such as *Star Wars: The Force Awakens* and *Rogue One: A Star Wars Story*, and by ILMxLAB in real-time experiences such as *Trials on Tatooine* (Fig. 5.8).

Lucasfilm says MaterialX addresses the current lack of a common, open standard for representing the data values and relationships required to transfer the complete look of a computer graphics model from one application or rendering platform to another, including shading networks, patterns and texturing, complex nested materials and geometric assignments. To further encourage interchangeable CG look setups, MaterialX also defines a complete set of data creation and processing nodes with a precise mechanism for functional extensibility.

The MaterialX library, now at release v1.36.0, is an open-source project released under a modified Apache license.

5.2.6   Nvidia's MDL

Until 2015, all ray tracers had their own material libraries, a few programs could use libraries from other ray tracers. When the ray hits an object, the material properties of that object are evaluated to determine if it is reflective or diffuse, and what color it is. The library of such objects is vast; it is the world, everything from shiny automobile fenders to wisps of smoke, from rough wood to a baby's skin. The characteristics of all those materials are beyond the resources of any company to develop and support. And, the lack of standards has held back any cooperative development in the industry. Some companies have agreed to work together and share their libraries.

Fig. 5.9 Several different materials (Nvidia)

The primary reason why materials have traditionally been locked to renderers, and even to specific products, has mostly to do how materials have always referenced shaders. Shaders usually included the rendering algorithm and were renderer-specific. To get materials into another renderer, or even another product, meant that you needed to port the shader—which is a large task, that requires the shader source, someone intimate with the target renderer, and has to be done for each shader in turn—only to find that what the shader was doing may be incompatible with the target renderer. This occurred now and then, but rarely, even when all the source was within the same company (Fig. 5.9).

Material libraries are vast and vary from industry to industry. The libraries of materials used in designing the painted surfaces of automobiles are drastically different from the materials used in creating a human's face or hair, which is totally different from the materials used for clothing, etc. It is close to impossible for one firm to have robust libraries in all segments ray tracing might be used. Therefore, a ray-tracing supplier has to specialize to a certain degree, and that partially explains why there are so many suppliers.

Nvidia is trying to change that with the introduction of their materials definition language (MDL), which allows a ray-tracing program to share materials and lights between different applications. They hope to establish a standard to describe digital materials. They now claim to have over 100 materials in their library and are offering MDL for free. This not only will improve performance, productivity, and throughput but will also put these capabilities in the hands of millions of users.

The Nvidia Material Definition Language (MDL) offers one the ability to share physically based materials and lights between supporting applications. For example, one can create an MDL material in an application like Allegorithmic Substance Designer, save it to one's library, then use it in Nvidia's Iray or Chaos Group's V-Ray, or any other supporting application. Once a material is created, one can be confident it will maintain its appearance as one moves it into any compatible applications in the workflow. Such interchangeability is a valuable method to save time and effort. Company's products compatible with Nvidia's MDL include Siemen's NX, Daz3d, ESI Group's IC.IDO, Algorithmic, Chaos, and others.

Unlike a shading language that produces programs for a particular renderer, Nvidia says materials in their MDL define the behavior of light at a high level. Different renderers and tools may then interpret the light behavior and create the best possible image, whether it is an OpenGL-based application or physically based renderer like Iray.

Material definitions are constructed from physically based elements and functions that may be layered to achieve a robust continuum of materials without the need to program or compile. Output from leading measurement devices, like those from X-Rite, can also be used as elements and customized with layers and functions to greatly extend their usage range.

While MDL materials and lights can move easily between supporting applications, they require the MDL Material Exchange package or the Nvidia vMaterials library[7] to be installed for proper operation. Guides and tips on exchanging materials are available in the Materials section of the Nvidia Advanced Rendering Forum.[8]

Nvidia has established an MDL Advisory Board, consisting of partners developing applications with MDL guides and manages the development of the MDL specification.

MDL was originally developed by Nvidia for its Iray ray-tracing program. MDL defines the properties of materials for all rendering modes of Iray. Material properties range from the color of surfaces, to their reflection or refraction properties, light emission of surfaces, scattering and absorption properties of volumes, and even to additional geometric properties of surfaces, such as cutouts, displacements, or bump maps, which are commonly not modeled in the primary geometric description.

MDL changes the problem of porting by not including the rendering algorithm and instead of defining only the materials with physically based building blocks. Most any PBR renderer uses a similar approach and can thus match what is being described in the MDL. And although each renderer's building blocks will vary, they will be very close and will result in a material that fits within that renderer's "world" so to speak. A renderer then adds MDL support by adding this translator/compiler once, after which they can read any MDL written.

---

[7]Nvidia's Materials library: https://www.nvidia.com/en-us/design-visualization/technologies/vmaterials/.

[8]Nvidia's advanced rendering forum: https://forum.nvidia-arc.com/.

MDL's physically based hierarchical layered material model relies, at its core, on the following:

- Bidirectional Scattering Distribution Functions (BSDF)[9] (see Glossary)
- Emissive Distribution Functions (EDF)
- Volume Distribution Functions (VDF)

MDL describes what should be computed and the renderer, in turn, uses this information to decide how to compute the image depending on the geometry, lighting and camera settings.

Note that procedurals/functions (which are often part of materials) do include their algorithm within them but that this is relatively easy to support as they define a "map" that is fed to the renderer and isn't part of the actual rendering algorithm (how light is reflected, etc.). An interesting aspect is that these custom MDL functions are pretty easy to write, and they can stay GPU accelerated without the author doing anything extra.

In late 2015, Nvidia decided to make MDL an open software development kit (SDK) and free. More information can be found here: http://www.nvidia-arc.com/fileadmin/user_upload/iray_documentation/nvidia_mdl_introduction.140512.A4.pdf.

If MDL is adopted by users and other ray-tracing suppliers, the breadth and spectrum of materials available will greatly increase and help expand the use of ray tracing in more situations.

5.2.7 X-Rite's AxF

Grand Rapids, MI-based X-Rite's AxF is the foundational component of the company's Total Appearance Capture (TAC) Ecosystem. Founded in 1958, the company says AxF files are used to capture, store, edit, and communicate material characteristics throughout the digital design workflow.

Capturing material appearance data in a single, editable, portable file format is an obstacle in the virtualization of products, especially when different formats are used in parallel. This poses an issue when consistency in appearance must be achieved. X-Rite claims AxF is a format designed for system-independent of communication digital appearance.

X-Rite says AxF can deliver a standardized format for communicating material appearance data. It has been used with a variety of CAD, PLM, 3D rendering solutions. It has been used in product design, development, manufacturing, sales, and marketing. The company says it reduces cycle time, control cost and ensure consistency in color and appearance. X-Rite says AxF is a vendor-neutral

---

[9]Bartell et al. (1980).

appearance format, is scalable, and extensible. Extensions can be defined without harming existing support in third-party applications.

Capture

Capturing exact appearance characteristics is vital to improving quality and speeding up time to market for products, factories, transport, and infrastructure. X-Rite says their TAC7 Scanner can make physically accurate measurements so that the virtual material has the same optical properties of its physical counterpart under any lighting condition and in any scenario. This also allows reuse of materials across multiple projects.

An AxF file made with a TAC7 has the exact same optical characteristics as the real material. With more accurate material capture, key decisions about color and material can be made earlier in the design process.

Communicate

X-Rite offers a viewer, the Pantora AxF Viewer. With it, says the company, one can visualize and swap 3D materials in a controlled scene with real-time rendering. The viewer has drag-and-drop capability of materials. It also supports Changes to the lighting to see how a material would look under different conditions. Pantora acts as a controlling hub among X-Rite TAC components, connecting digital material input sources with output destinations such as X-Rite's Virtual Light Booth, third-party rendering software and PLM systems.

Visualize and Compare

The Virtual Light Booth provides the capability to accurately compare physical and digital material samples under the same perceptual conditions—from illumination to contextual to observational factors which allows a designer to make a more informed material selection. That can reduce approval times, improve product quality, and accelerate time to market.

5.3 Quality Issues

There are several reasons why people choose to use ray tracing: realistic reflections, sharp or soft shadows, diffused reflections, and ambient occlusion. Ray tracing's popularity stems from its basis in a realistic simulation of lighting over other rendering methods. Effects such as reflections and shadows, which are difficult to simulate using other algorithms, are a natural result of the ray-tracing algorithm.

Ambient occlusion is widely used in movie production since it gives a good indication of creases on surfaces and spatial proximity of objects and is a computational easier (but crude) approximation of global illumination.

There are multiple layers of complexity in ray tracing. Methods that trace rays, but include additional techniques (photon mapping, Path Tracing), give the far more accurate simulation of real-world lighting. And they take longer to render, so it is always a tradeoff.

Using ray tracing for faces requires subsurface scattering materials for the skin, which add still more complexity and compute time.

5.3.1 Skin and Subsurface Scattering

Nvidia has improved its subsurface scattering (SSS) in Iray last year and will be doing more going forward now that they have the likes of DAZ using Iray (Fig. 5.10).

Bidirectional scattering-surface reflectance distribution function or B surface scattering RDF (BSSRDF), describes the relation between outgoing radiance and the incident flux, including the phenomena like subsurface scattering (SSS). The BSSRDF describes how light is transported between any two rays that hit a surface. It performs subsurface scattering, gives a softer visual effect than bidirectional scattering distribution function (BRDF), which works on the surface of objects. The academic research using BSSRDF delivers beautiful results (e.g., on marvel statues), but as far as I know, it is not practical yet for commercial rendering. The Directional Pole model gets them closer to become practical (Fig. 5.11).

Fig. 5.10 Realistic skin is rendered using subsurface scattering and specific materials. *Source* Nvidia

Fig. 5.11 Comparison of
BRDF to BSSRDF
reflections. *Source* Mike
Seymour

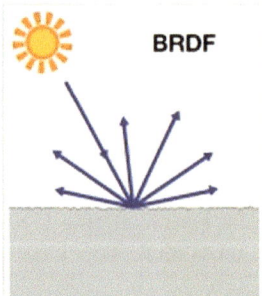 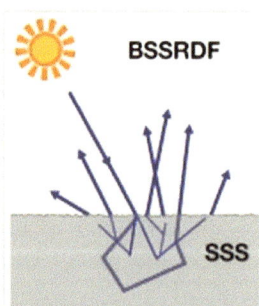

Fig. 5.12 Translucent
grapes. *Source* Pixar

Subsurface scattering is an important effect for realistic rendering of translucent materials such as skin, flesh, fat, fruits, milk, marble, and many others. (Fig. 5.12).

Subsurface scattering is responsible for effects like color bleeding inside materials, or the diffusion of light across shadow boundaries. The photograph below shows an example of translucent objects.

Fig. 5.13 Chaos Group says the use of variance-based adaptive sampling on this model of Christmas cookies from Autodesk 3ds Max provided a better final image in record time. *Source* Chaos Group

5.3.2 Variance-Based Adaptive Sampling

Chaos Group has developed an acceleration technique for its V-Ray add-in rendering toolkit for Autodesk 3ds Max which the company claims provide 20–50% faster rendering for most scenes. Described as a variance-based adaptive sampler (VBAS) it provides a more uniform noise distribution, faster setup, and improved imagery for VR, VFX, and architectural visualization workflows (Fig. 5.13).

VBAS provides:

- Better sampling of dark areas and faster sampling of over bright areas
- More consistent noise detection
- Final image quality is less dependent on materials and lights settings
- Improved alpha channel sampling, especially in scenes with depth of field and motion blur
- Works in bucket and progressive rendering modes

The company says it will provide automatic sampling of lights and materials—removing the need to set subdivisions manually.

5.3.3 Hybrid

The mixing of ray tracing and scan-line rasterization is being employed by several users. If a problem can be solved efficiently by rasterization one doesn't need to solve it with ray tracing unless it is proved that it would work out much better that way.

However, how many users really only using scan-line? Very few (maybe no) products offer only pure scan-line rendering. Many seem to be hybrid, where the scan-line renders the majority of scene while utilizing selective ray tracing for those features that need it (reflections/refractions, soft shadows, etc.). In some standard renderers, the user can select the ray cast number. With a ray cast of 1, it is using scan-line. Turn up the rays cast number or turn on refraction or glass index and now the renderer is ray tracing.

3ds Max, for example, has a reflection setting in its scan-line dialog with a "number of bounces" setting. Since scan-line by definition does not technically bounce, turning up the number of reflective bounces means it is tapping into selective ray tracing.

Hybrid complicates the problem because if it is hybrid, then how do we (they) account for the RT portion since it will obviously take the majority of render time.

5.3.4 Summary

The market for ray-tracing engines is vast and complex. Because of the range of materials, and the differences in approximations and tricks, no single ray-tracing engine can satisfy all users. Even so, there are too many suppliers for such a market regardless of the unusual numbers of niches that exist. Therefore, I believe there will be a consolidation, which can already be seen with some of the acquisitions.

Given the entrenched position of the big players, newer developers of ray trace engines and libraries, will have to find niches where they can stand out. These niches might be an application area/industry, or a method of acceleration of ray tracing for specific users. It could be possible to find success by defining a new niche based on some specific area of expertise.

As mentioned throughout the book and in the appendix, the demand and burden of a broad, accurate material library can't be overstated. Look at how best to support materials (including emerging standards). The established companies have done extensive work on this front, competitors will be obliged to have some kind of answer.

Companies developing ray-tracing software independently from the content creation software companies have the option of:

- licensing their software to the content creation software companies,
- licensing it directly to the users of content creation software, and

- licensing it to service agencies who generate ray-traced images for content creators who don't have the skills or time to generate the desired ray-traced images.

The successful companies will be those who can offer:

- Ease of use, including test images and production run progress monitoring
- Some guarantee of success
- Tweaks that enhance ray tracer performance. In general, physics-based optical fidelity is not as valuable as "looks right"
- Service and support

And last but not least be on the lookout for custom hardware implementations for ray-tracing acceleration. Moore's Law will continue to offer opportunities to clever designers in terms of computing density and the reduction in the cost of transistors.

Prospective users/buyers of ray-tracing software are advised to:

- Consider materials and their support by the renderers (including possibly emerging material standards)
- Support for non-Intel HW platforms (GPUs, ARM)
- Consider total cost of ownership (TOC), including SW license cost—but also (and probably more important) availability of skills, materials, performance (including on GPUs, if so available), HW cost, support of the RT software by (cloud) render services for incremental demands (at least for peak demand that your projects are likely to require)

The idea of real-time ray tracing is, of course, desirable, but not fundamental. As has been demonstrated, rendering time is simply a function of economics—how many processor cycles can you afford to apply to the problem. Remember Blinn's law, and Peddie's axiom, rendering always takes the same amount of time, and in computer graphics, too much is not enough.

5.4 Importance of HDR Monitors

High dynamic range (HDR) displays deliver better contrast and color accuracy, as well as more vibrant colors, compared to standard dynamic range (SDR) displays. As a result, HDR is gaining interest for a wide range of applications, including movie viewing, gaming, and creation of photograph and videograph content.

HDR displays are a wonderful technology, but not something that ray tracing itself is concerned with, but rather, the digital content creation (DCC) tool, which must color manage the imagery being displayed.

Prior to HDR monitors and TV screens, tone mapping was used. Tone mapping is a technique used in image processing and computer graphics to map one set of colors to another to approximate the appearance of high-dynamic-range images in a medium that has a more limited dynamic range. If a scene or product was created in 30- or 36-bit color (10 or 12 bits per primary RGB channel) it will exceed the display capability of a conventional 24-bit display. Typically, a simple (default) tone mapping algorithm will compress the top (bright) one or two bits and the lower (dark) one or two bits to fit the HDR image into a 24-bit device. Most of the time it looks OK. Sometimes, however, the artist may want to accentuate the brighter (or darker) shades or tones. Software exists (e.g., Photoshop) that will allow adjusting the Gamut (tonal range) of the print on-screen and make further adjustments to make sure that all the tones fit within the desires of the presenter. HDR and professional color-grading monitors eliminate this process.

Computer monitors are starting to support high dynamic range (HDR), which means they can handle more detail in the brightest and darkest parts of an image, along with a wide color gamut. HDR has proven a revolution among HDTVs, and every high-end television now supports it. While it still has issues with Windows, it is definitely a feature people are looking for in high-end monitors today.

In mid-2017 that HDR monitors like Dell's UltraSharp 27 4K started to appear. Things changed (for the better) when VESA introduced a new standard, DisplayHDR, which set a baseline for PC HDR displays.[10] DisplayHDR is the high-performance monitor and display specification that defines the display industry's open standard specifying HDR quality, including luminance, color gamut, bit depth, and rise time.

The first release of the new specification, DisplayHDR version 1.0, focuses on liquid crystal displays (LCDs), establishing three distinct levels of HDR system performance to facilitate adoption of HDR throughout the PC market: DisplayHDR 400, DisplayHDR 600, and DisplayHDR 1000. The number ("400", "600", etc.) refers to the brightness level and is expressed in candela per square meter (cd/m^2) is the derived SI unit of luminance, also referred to as Nits. Additional tiers are expected to be added later to support continuous innovations and improvements in display performance. All tiers require support of the industry standard HDR-10 format. The "-10" refers to 10 bits per primary (RGB). Most monitors in use today are 8 bits per primary (or channel) which yields 16.7 million possible colors. A 10-bit monitor can produce 1.07 billion possible colors.

Such monitors are calibrated on AdobeRGB and sRGB to an accuracy of Delta-E less than 2, using, for example, Portrait Display's CalMAN display calibration software. CalMAN is the industry-leading solution used by nearly every professional video calibrator, and by most users in broadcast, production, post-production, and is the most popular solution for home video enthusiasts.[11]

Obviously if one wants to see a realistic ray-traced rendering of an image, then one has to have the best display possible. Film and TV studios have professional video monitors for on-set, editing, color grading, OB, studio and live production. In Full HD, 4K and HDR.

---

[10]VESA DisplayHDR Specifications: https://displayhdr.org/

[11]CalMAN: https://calman.spectracal.com/feature-matrix.html

Dell has introduced a 10-bit 8K monitor (7680 × 4320) at 60 Hz with 400 cd/m^2 (Nits) brightness and although they don't promote it as an HDR monitor, it in fact is. Dell also has a Custom Color mode, the SDKi or the optional (Dell) X-rite iDisplay Pro colorimeter.

Color standards vary depending upon who is quoting them. The most commonly quoted color space is CIE 1931.

CIE colorimetry isn't even half the story of color science, it is a tiny piece of the huge puzzle of human perception and engineering that is color science. Don't confuse understanding it with understanding color perception. Colorimetry is essentially algebra; human perception is much more complex.

CIE 1931 is a Color Matching System. Color matching does not attempt to describe how colors appear to humans, color matching tells us how to numerically specify a measured color, and then later accurately reproduce that measured color (e.g., in print or digital displays) (Fig. 5.14).

The diagram shows the Rec. 2020 (UHDTV) color space in the triangle and the location of the primary colors. Rec. 2020 uses Illuminant D65 for the white point. Rec. 2020 defines a bit depth of either 10 bits per sample or 12 bits per sample (Fig. 5.15).

Monitors for mastering HDR content need to support multiple gamma curves. The most prevalent is the SMPTE 2084 standard called the Perceptual Quantizer or PQ curve developed by Dolby. The chart below shows digital code values versus luminance for several gamma curves.

Fig. 5.14 CIE 1931 chromaticity diagram (Wikipedia)

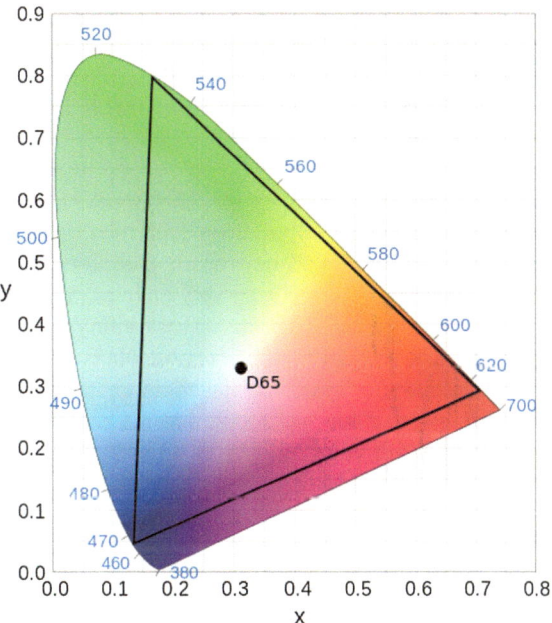

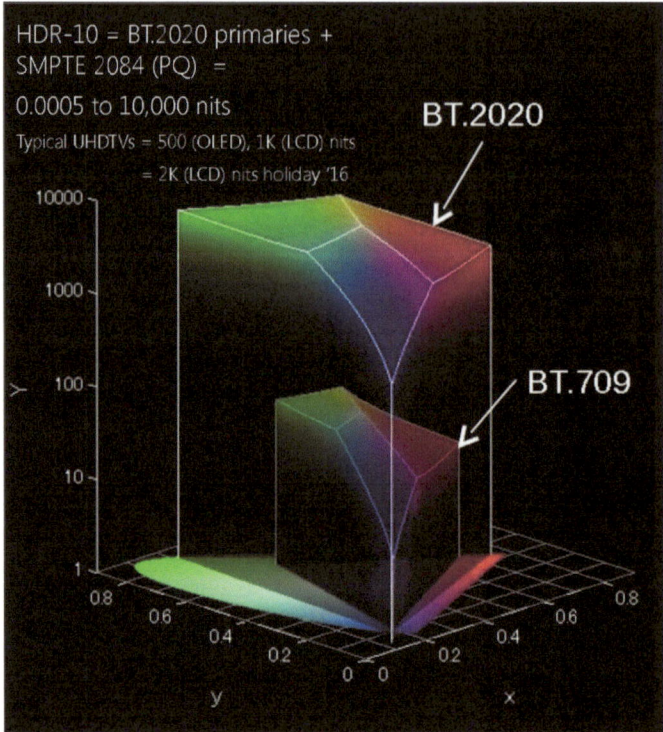

Fig. 5.15 Color/luminance volume: BT.2020 (10,000 nits) versus BT.709 (100 nits); Yxy. *Source* Sony

The PQ curve not only covers a much large range of luminance values, but the code values are locked to certain luminance values. That means a pixel that is supposed to be at 100 nits will have a specific code value. That is not the case with the other gamma curves where the code values can have different luminances depending upon the range of the particular display (Fig. 5.16).

"We have developed new charts that allow you to visually evaluate how close the monitor is to the PQ curve," claimed SpectraCal President, L.A. Heberlein. These can be shown in linear or logarithmic units.

CalMAN v5.6 with HDR support offers a direct-load 3D Look-Up Table (3D LUT) calibration functions. Heberlein explained that LUTs were originally developed to create a certain "look" that the colorist wanted. But it has evolved since then to be much more. "Instead of adjusting the monitor, we adjust the video stream so that the final result is correct. This takes into account the whole delivery system including coupling errors so that you always see a calibrated image. Such 3D LUTs used to take hours and hours to set up, but now we can do it in 10 min," explained Heberlein.

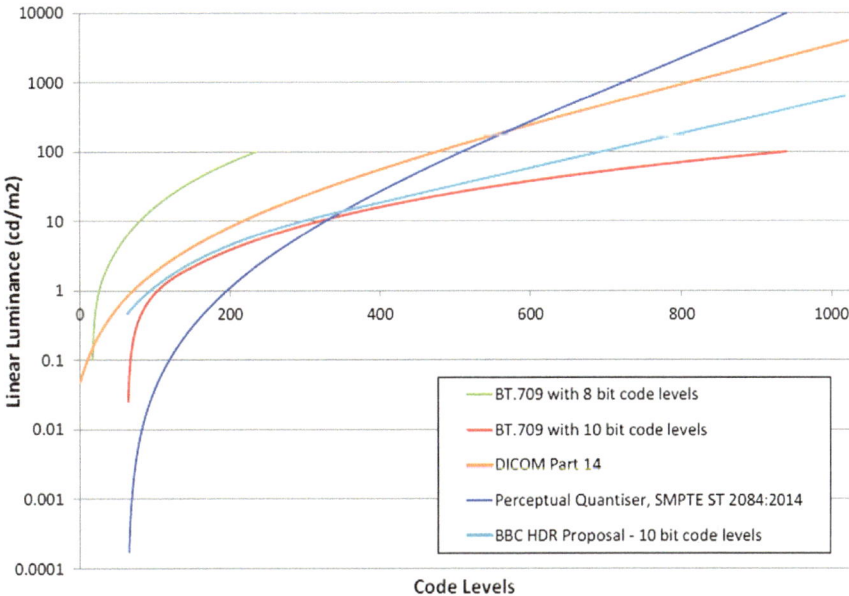

Fig. 5.16 Various gamma curves (Insight Media)

CalMAN v5.6 also offers Color Primary reference points for more than 20 color gamuts, including both DCI P3 and Rec BT.2020, with different white points and gamma curves to match commercial DCI, Dolby Vision, or HDR 10 formats.

Dolby Vision represents the most encompassing approach to HDR with lots of capabilities and room for growth but less powerful versions are also going to come to market as well. Here, the leading approach is called HDR10

As ray tracing becomes more popular and prevalent, the demand for HDR monitors will increase with it. That includes not just the professional markets, but gamers as well.

5.5 Importance of Full-Color Printers

Advertisers, public relation and marketing agencies, architects, and product designers use printed materials to display and sell their products, projects, and proposals. When the images are ray-traced rendering a full-color printer is used. Full-color printers are often large, expensive, and difficult to operate and maintain. Also, they are not used too frequently by a single company or department. Therefore, they are usually owned and operated by service organizations, like Kinkos.

Fig. 5.17 The colors of
CMYK

Full color is the printer industry means more than 10 million different colors, which is somewhere between 5.7 bits per primary and 6 bits per primary.

Terms like 4/4, 4/1, 4/0, etc. are a sort of printing industry shorthand to express how many ink colors are applied to each side of a printed piece (Fig. 5.17).

4/4 is pronounced "four over four" and means there are four ink colors applied to the front of the piece and four ink colors applied to the back. These four colors are not just random colors—they are Cyan, Magenta, Yellow, and black, also known collectively as CMYK. CMYK printing is also called four-color process or four-color printing and is used to generate what we know as full-color printing. So, a printed piece designated as 4/4 has the four CMYK ink colors applied to it on both sides.

Adobe PostScript device-independent color, Apple ColorSync, CIE International color standards, ICC

Color printers will have a print resolution of 600 × 600 dpi to as high as 9600 × 2400 dpi

References

Bartell FO, Dereniak EL, Wolfe WL (1980) The theory and measurement of bidirectional reflectance distribution function (BRDF) and bidirectional transmittance distribution function (BTDF). In: Proceedings of SPIE, Radiation scattering in optical systems, vol 257, pp 154–160. https://doi.org/10.1117/12.959611. Retrieved 14 July 2014

Hergaarden M (2011) Graphics shaders. VU Amsterdam. http://files.m2h.nl/Literaturestudy Shaders.pdf

Russell J (2015) Basic theory of physically-based rendering. Adv Tutor. https://marmoset.co/posts/basic-theory-of-physically-based-rendering/

Chapter 6
Applications of Ray Tracing

Abstract Ray tracing has been traditionally used with applications for media and entertainment (3D animation, rendering), product development (CAD/CAM/CAE), life sciences (medical, molecular), energy, and other operations. The ray-tracing programs are used by engineers and artist proposing a project concept or new product design, by designers who bring the first renditions of the project or product for evaluation, by manufacturing people who build and test the project, or product virtually in the computer. And then when everything is proven and acceptable, marketing people use ray tracing to create images to sell the product. Ray tracing is used in all four stages from project concept to fulfillment. The concept of virtual prototyping and in the film industry pre-viz has been embraced by most industries and has saved millions of dollars by eliminating redos and expensive after-sales repairs.

Ray tracing can be used in almost every industry, government agency, academic institution, and even private parties. There are ray-tracing programs from over a hundred sources, many of them are free, and new hardware and software developments have made the rendering time shorter than ever.

Ray tracing is used to design systems and to represent the data generated by those systems, and it is used to conceptualize a product and then to sell the product. It is used to create simulations of real-world situations and imaginary worlds. It is used to model and visualize proteins and molecules and to design new compounds that do not yet exist, and then, if created and manufactured, it is used to display the pill, and the package it comes in, the store it is sold in, the trucks that deliver it, the road the truck travels on, and all the components within all those elements. Ray tracing is like electricity and air; it is used everywhere and can be found in everything. How then does one categorize a ray-tracing application?

Some of the other applications for ray tracing are:

- Product design and virtual prototyping
- Engineering and architecture
- Advertising (print to video)
- Optical engineering and design
- Audio engineering and design

© Springer Nature Switzerland AG 2019
J. Peddie, *Ray Tracing: A Tool for All*,
https://doi.org/10.1007/978-3-030-17490-3_6

- Geophysical modeling and presentation
- Medical and scientific
- Entertainment (games to movies and TV)
- Simulations and visualizations
- Interference and design checking
- New media—e.g., VR.

This is not an exhaustive list, and the applications for ray tracing have steadily increased over the years as techniques and processors have improved.

6.1 The Pipeline

I have approached it by visualizing a four-stage pipeline, starting with conceptualization, into design, then manufacturing, and finally marketing.

And please note, by a product I mean, and include anything from a washing machine to a movie, from a surgical training scenario to an analysis of a body scan, from an airplane or car design to the simulation of the airplane flying or the car crashing. Physically accurate modeling, virtual prototyping, and data analysis are absolutely essential for product satisfaction, safety, reproducibility, and reliability.

When one has a target customer in mind, there is nothing better than presenting in a virtual environment that allows the prospective customer or user to understand how the product would fit in the real world. Ray tracing accomplishes this relatively quickly and inexpensively, enriching design reviews and helping stakeholders connect with the design.

The ability to show a physically accurate (or fantasy imagined) image, possibly with animation, conveys the designer's, the imaginer's, and the support's message to levels not possible before. The famous saying—a picture is worth 1000 words—is truly realized with a perfectly rendered image. And, unlike story boards, or artists renditions, the customer or investor, gets what he or she bought—*what you see is what you get*.

Since the design, the model, has been developed in a 3D domain, the renderings of it are accurate to the design. That enables two benefits to the developers. First it leads directly to virtual prototyping which is a genuine try it (fly it) before you buy it. Virtual prototyping allows the developer or director to make tweaks, adjustments, to realize their visualization, the thing they saw in their mind's eye.

Production can take longer than expected, and even if it is done on time, the marketing team needs as much lead time as possible to generate interest, excitement, and ultimately the demand for the new product or movie. Therefore, taking advantage of the digital model, final marketing material can be produced prior to final products. That way consumers are primed and ready to buy when the product is available. It is estimated 95% of the automobile commercials are simulations and the cars they are showing haven't been built at the time of the viewing. The same is true of outtakes of movies and games, and other consumer products. This is certainly true of all space ventures and projects.

In the following sections of this chapter, I will describe the use of ray tracing in the stages of development of a product in the four stages of the pipeline from idea to consumer.

Later in this book, I discuss cloud-based visualization (CBV). Cloud-based visualization can be used at the conception/proposal stage and the presentation (selling) stage.

6.1.1   Conception—STAGE ONE

Ray tracing is used in the proposal and planning stage to visualize what the final product should look like. This is often referred to virtual prototyping, and in the movie industry as pre-vis (also known as pre-viz). Architects, automobile and aerospace firms, consumer goods and clothing designers, and industrial machinery designers to name a few use ray tracing to create concepts to sell the idea or product to management, prospective customers or patients, and government agencies. In some cases, in the very early brainstorming concept creation sessions, rasterization rending is used in the interest of time. In the TV and movie industry, that is known as storyboarding.

The concept starts with the construction of a 3D model. The model may not (usually doesn't) represent the final product and usually lacks detailed aspects needed for manufacturing, testing, and certification. A building or car, for example, will simply be a shell with none of the important parts underneath it.

The following are some of the popular examples of using ray tracing in the concept stage.

6.1.1.1   Simulations of Things that Don't Exist

Ray tracing is used for showing how a product might look. Buildings, airplanes, automobiles, and even clothes are simulated and then rendered with ray tracing to see how potential buyers will react. Almost all automobile ads, printed models, and TV are computer-produced with ray tracing. Cars that aren't built yet are shown to dealers and as a teaser to TV viewers. The cost and delays associated with photographing a car are so great, and they are almost never used anymore. Obviously, the skyscrapers being proposed couldn't be built first. The use of scale models is declining and is often replaced by 3D virtual and/or printed models. Ray-traced models are being to show city planners and adjacent property owners how the building will create shadows and reflect light over a 24-h period, and at various seasons all are done using ray tracing.

Ray tracing is used to create models of simulations and of products or designs not (yet) actually built.

The following examples show some examples of things that were designed, but not built, and yet the images are photorealistic and totally believable—not too unlike the fantastic worlds that are created for special effects in the movies (Figs. 6.1, 6.2, 6.3 and 6.4).

Fig. 6.1 This is an example of a Boeing 797 blended wing concept airplane that was never built - realistic looking isn't it. *Source* Wikipedia—Popular Science magazine

Fig. 6.2 The Ford GT90 was never built. *Source* Ford

Fig. 6.3 241-floor, 3162-ft-high structure would be named "The Bride" and sit in the middle of Basra, Iraq. Courtesy of AMBS architects

Fig. 6.4 Proposed Airbus A390. *Source* Airbus

Virtual prototyping is a method in the process of product development. It involves using computer-aided design (CAD), computer-automated design (CAutoD), and computer-aided engineering (CAE) software to validate a design before committing to making a physical prototype. This is done by creating (usually 3D) computer-generated geometrical shapes (parts) and either combining them into an "assembly" and testing different mechanical motions, fit and function. The assembly or individual parts could be opened in CAE software to simulate the behavior of the product in the real world.

Typically, virtual prototype models are actual CAD models, and when it comes to rendering, the models are rebuilt in design products such as 3ds Max, Maya, Modo, and Cinema 4D. Increasingly, the leading CAD programs have been developing features that enable easier simplification of models for the purposes of rendering (and analysis), but I believe there is still quite a bit of model rebuilding and cleaning.

6.1.1.2 Animation Games and Simulation

Animation and games mostly use rasterization to portray the concept and action scenes of a story. Occasionally, parts of a scene or frame will be ray-traced to convey the feeling of the scene. The casting of shadows, lighting, and colors are critical in getting the right mood conveyed, and artists and directors will spend days tweaking elements to get it just right.

Gaming has the potential (in terms of users) of being the biggest market for ray tracing.

Ray Tracing in Games

PC, console, and mobile games are available in several genres, and there is no single list of them; rather, it is more like a matrix. It is beyond the scope of this study to provide an exhaustive list, description, and taxonomy of all the gaming genre, but a few need to be discussed to understand the role of ray tracing in games.

Ray tracing today is hard to use and expensive—more expensive than the raster-based solutions we are used to. Tools and workflows exist to give a baked or dynamic lighting as well as somewhat convincing reflections. These have arisen in response to a demand for those effects, so they are wanted; it is just that they are expensive and time consuming to produce, so they are the first to be thrown out when gameplay (frame rate) is the priority.

If they were available at no performance or production cost, they would be universally used and as a consequence would become an integral part of gameplay (Fig. 6.5).

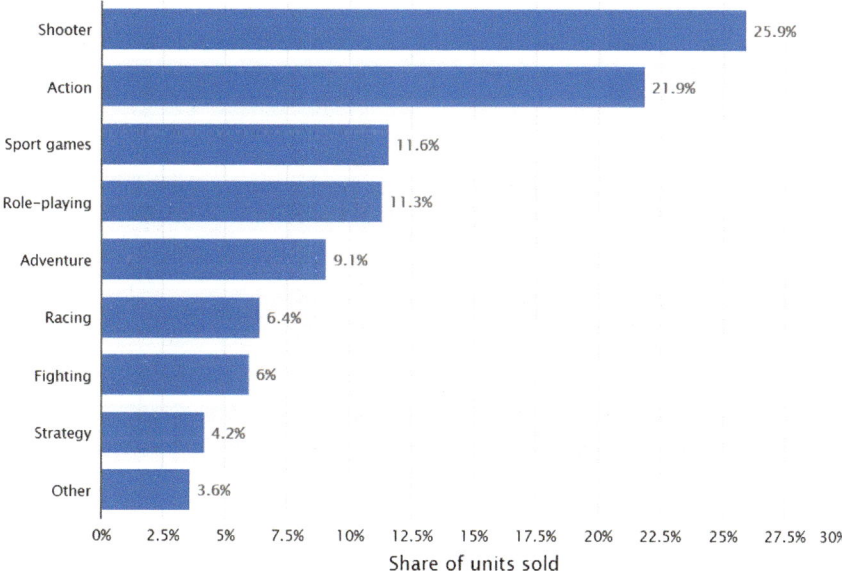

Fig. 6.5 The most popular video games sold in the USA in 2017. *Source* Statista

First-person shooter (FPS) is a video game genre centered around gun and other weapon-based combat in a first-person perspective; that is, the player experiences the action through the eyes of the protagonist. The genre shares common traits with other shooter games, which in turn makes it fall under the heading **action game** and is also referred to **action-adventure** (which gets confusing with adventure games). Since the genre's inception, advanced 3D and pseudo-3D graphics have challenged hardware development.

FPS games are very fact action with severe win/lose consequences more often described as kill or be killed. As such, the player has little to no time to carefully observe the environment and therefore ray tracing has little value in an FPS. Also, FPSs are the most demanding on the processors and any cannibalization of processing cycles for pretty effects is undesirable by the players.

Sport games don't seem to offer much opportunity for enhancement by ray tracing other than maybe shadows and sun flare/glare. Uniforms and fields will not benefit from ray tracing.

A **role-playing game** (RPG) also known as a computer role-playing game (CRPG) is a video game genre where the player controls the actions of a character (and/or several party members) immersed in some well-defined world. The world can be 2D or 2.5D.

An **adventure game** is a video game in which the player assumes the role of a protagonist in an interactive story driven by exploration and puzzle-solving. Included in the adventure game genre is a category known as **walking simulators**.

Walking simulators feature few or even no puzzles at all, and win/lose conditions may not exist. Such games allow players to roam around the game environment and discover objects like books, audio logs, or other clues that develop the story, because they are based on 3D models, they are an example of a game that could benefit from ray tracing.

Using ray tracing in games is controversial. Back in 1992, a few PC games used ray-casting algorithms. That was quite an accomplishment given the level of processor performance of that time.

Like ray casting, ray tracing "determines the visibility of surfaces by tracing imaginary rays of light from viewer's eye to the object in the scene" (Foley 701[1]). Ray casting, however, is faster than ray tracing (see Sect. 4.3.5).

Ray casting is faster because its world is limited by one or more geometric constraints (simple geometric shapes), a ray-tracing world can be almost any shape. Ray casting was developed in the early 1980s and was successfully exploited by John Carmack in his groundbreaking 3D shooter, *Wolfenstein 3D* (id Software) in 1992.[2] Ray casting is a technique that transforms a limited form of data (a very simplified map or floor plan) into a 3D projection by tracing rays from the viewpoint into the viewing volume.

Early PC games such as *Wolfenstein 3D* and the *Comanche* series[3] made use of ray-casting algorithms. In *Wolfenstein 3D*, the world was built using a square-based grid of walls which were of a uniform height. They were merged with solid colored floors and ceilings. While illuminating the world, a single ray was traced for every column of pixels on the screen. A vertical slice of the wall texture was then selected and scaled based on where it collided with the ray. This way the distance could be calculated, and the walls could be scaled accordingly. Since the ceiling and floors were uniformly colored, there was no need to worry about them. That also reduced the computational and memory overhead. The savings could then be utilized to render the bodies which were in motion in the open areas of the map (Fig. 6.6).

The *Comanche* series handled ray casting in a slightly different manner. Individual rays were traced for each column of screen pixels, and when the rays interacted with an object, it was plotted against a height map. It was then possible to determine which of the pixels were visible and which weren't and then use a texture map to pick the corresponding color for the pixel.

Ray Tracing in Contemporary Games

When *Quake*, a first-person shooter video game, developed by id Software and published by GT Interactive came out in 1996, it was a breakthrough,

---

[1]Foley, "Computer Graphics: Principles and Practice," p 701.

[2]https://en.wikipedia.org/wiki/Wolfenstein_3D.

[3]"Comanche," was a series of simulation games published by NovaLogic. The goal of each of these games is to fly military missions in a RAH-66 Comanche attack helicopter.

Fig. 6.6 Wolfenstein 3D made use of ray casting algorithms in 1992. *Source* Wikipedia

transformative, disruptive milestone in PC gaming and has been a legend and foundational example ever since.

Quake II release one year later had improved graphics and game mechanics and was an all-time hit—run, shoot, duck, die.

Battlefield V has fantastic graphics and is almost totally outside (no small rooms or long corridors like the original Quake), and yet the gameplay is almost exactly the same. Run, shoot, duck, die.

But Battlefield V could brag about something Quake couldn't—ray tracing. It *could*, but it can't anymore.

In 2017, Christoph Schied started adding ray tracing to Quake II as a spare-time project to validate the results of his computer graphics research in an actual game while at Karlsruher Institut für Technologie. The project was completed in 2018 and encompasses 12K lines of code, completely replacing the original Quake II graphics code. Take a look at the results in Fig. 6.7 and in this video (https://tinyurl.com/y7v5le3g). The explosions may seem disappointing, but that is due to the limited geometry in them, not the ray tracing.

However, Herr Schied was not the first to render a ray-traced version of Quake. Countryman Daniel Pohl was experimenting and demonstrating using ray tracing in real-time games, specifically Quake 3, in a cooperation of the Erlangen University and Saarland University in Germany in 2008. Pohl's work so impressed Intel, one of the patrons of Saarland, that they hired him after his master's thesis for the Larrabee project. In 2009, Herr Pohl faced the crowds at Intel's Research Day. But even that wasn't a first because as a student Herr Pohl was showing off his work at

Fig. 6.7 A scene from Schied's ray-traced version of Quake II. *Source* Christoph Schied (2018)

CeBit in 2007.[4] He actually started working on ray tracing in games in 2004 as part of his student research project under the guidance of graphics professor Philipp Slusallek. As part of his studies and diploma thesis, Pohl rewrote parts 3 and 4 of the first-person shooter Quake so that their graphics were calculated using the ray-tracing method. The source for Q3 and Q4 was not available. He actually never used the real Quake engine, and it was all rewritten from scratch to load the maps, models, textures, sounds, animations, even up to some simple AI to make it feel like a real game (Fig. 6.8).[5]

That was over 12 years before Nvidia showed their RTX-based Turing chip, and Pohl's results were not playable on a single PC. It took a high-end computer in the Munich Intel test laboratory, equipped with the latest quad-core processor to get barely 17 fps at 640×480—but the promise was there—Moore's law would prevail.

Pohl's work was visionary, and one might say ahead of his or the times. Schied's work is more accessible and testable. You can download his code (https://tinyurl.com/y7udr587), assemble it, and run the *Q2VKPT* game. If one has an RTX-equipped Nvidia add-in board (AIB), you can actually play the game—with real-time ray tracing turned on at greater than HD resolution.

Q2VKPT is implemented in the Vulkan API to be able to use the new hardware-accelerated ray-tracing features that were made available earlier this year. Thanks to those developments in 2017, the game could actually come close to

---

[4]Kremp (2007).
[5]Pohl (2008).

Fig. 6.8 Ray-traced Quake: the water reflects the environment and the player. *Source* Pohl (2006)

60 frames per second (fps) (2560×1440, RTX2080Ti), while being fully ray-traced and dynamically shaded with realistic global lighting models in real time.

Using Path Tracing for fully dynamic lighting, says Schied, allows for a lot more detail in the shading of game scenes, naturally producing complex interplay of hard and soft shadows, glossy material appearances, and perspectively correct reflections everywhere. Moreover, light can naturally flow anywhere, tying the scene together in the ways we would expect from the real world. Traditional approaches like precomputed lighting or coarse real-time raster approximations could never interactively reach this detail at a comparable resolution, since full storage of this lighting information would exceed any memory bounds.

The original *Quake II* engine uses precomputed light maps that contain soft shadows and diffuse indirect illumination. In contrast, Q2VKPT entirely replaces the static illumination using a fully dynamic simulation that unifies both the static and dynamic light sources.

Besides the use of hardware-accelerated ray tracing, Q2VKPT mainly gains its efficiency from an adaptive image filtering technique that intelligently tracks changes in the scene illumination to reuse as much information as possible from previous computations.

The first wave of PC games to employ some real-time ray tracing using DirectX 12 and Nvidia's RTX and running on a Nvidia RTX 2070/80/Ti AIB were all AAA first-person adventure shooters. As such with one notable exception, the ray tracing was actually wasted and not only didn't enhance the game but was distracting and silly.

The new *Shadow of the Tomb Raider* (SotTR) is an example of the issue and the exception. As mentioned above, in an action game where its kill-or-be-killed one doesn't have time to look around at the scenery, which in many senses is a shame because today's games have amazing and beautiful artwork and gigantic world models. The protagonist, the ever-suffering and indefatigable Lara Croft, quickly gets mud on her face and arms from jumping, crawling, failing, and fighting. But the mud is unrealistic, it looks like painted on makeup, and there is no depth or texture to it (Fig. 6.9).

However, once one stops gawking at the scenery and character and gets into the game, one no longer notices her mud (which comes and goes at odd times) or her hair. When one pauses and looks around at the scenery, one marvels at: A. the awesome size and complexity of the 3D models and map size and B. the textures and artwork. This is a delightful game world to be in. But does it need ray tracing? No. Would the game be any better with it? Not really. Except (read on).

I also looked at the demos of 4A's *Metro Exodus* and EA/DICE's *Battlefield V* (Fig. 6.10).

Metro is one of our all-time favorites. *Metro* and *Tomb Raider* have a story and really get one involved. As a take no prisoners, stressful game *Battlefield*, tests one's composure. There's no time for gawking—gawk and die. So why then do we need a ray-traced car that is in the middle of an intense sniper-filled house-to-house cleanup mission? No. One doesn't have time to look at it or appreciate it, and it could just as well be a big black box (Fig. 6.11).

And where is a war-torn place like Amsterdam is one going to find a perfectly clean, undamaged car with all its windows and no bullet holes?

Fig. 6.9 Lara's unrealistic dirty face and arms

Fig. 6.10 Artyom's perfectly clean mask and gun after a decade of fighting in tunnels and snow storms

Fig. 6.11 Car reflecting a nearby fire in Battlefield V

   The scene in *Battlefield V* is in Amsterdam after many years of war, in the early 1940s. In the 1940s, in Holland, there was no such thing as flat glass like we have today. It all had (and still does) ripples in it. Secondly, after many years of war deprivation, there weren't any clean windows. As fastidious as the Dutch are, during the war they were being starved to death by the Germans and didn't have

Fig. 6.12 Perfectly flat, perfectly clean Dutch windows in WWII Amsterdam

time or interest in washing their windows. Therefore, the depiction of perfectly reflecting windows like mirrors in the *Battlefield V* is superfluous and gimmicky (Fig. 6.12).

Rivers and pools of water, maybe, but you really don't need ray tracing for that, ray casting is fine, you're not going to be there long enough to appreciate it, and it's just burning cycles.

Now, if someone were to make a truly interactive, non-cartoonish fantasy game like *Myst*, that would invite you and let you wander around and discover things without fear of someone killing you, then ray tracing could, and would, be really great. But in action kill-or-be-killed games like *Tomb Raider*, *Metro*, or *Battlefield*, forget it. Give back those cycles, so they can be used for better physics, mechanics, and no latency, all with high frame rate and high resolution and FOV. Give better bump maps, so the mud on Lara is caked, and Artyom's stuff is dirty.

The Exception

There is one scene, the only scene, in SotTR where Lara is in a village, at night during a festival. She is not being chased and is safe. She is following some men. The village scene is very pretty with all the lights, their shadows, and reflections. In this situation, ray tracing does add something (Fig. 6.13).

Fig. 6.13 Market scene in Shadow of the Tomb Raider

So why, if ray tracing isn't really needed, plus it required a new and expensive AIB, and the first implementations were not very realistic, were the suppliers doing it? Because they could.

Computer graphics has always been about *because we can*. And, as has been pointed out many times, it is going to take years for the game developers to figure out what can (and what shouldn't) be done with ray tracing.

However, another point of view is that it is not eye candy that ray tracing will supply but visual cues to help gameplay. Reflections and shadows that alert gamers to a developing situation is the obvious one. So as with all media, the content needs to be more cleverly developed, and that just takes time as the developers figure out how to use it. Remember however, they never figured out how to use stereo 3D and as a result it died.

4A Games Metro Exodus

A4 has employed Nvidia's GeForce RTX for real-time ray-traced global illumination in PC-based games.

Game developer 4A Games has a video (https://youtu.be/Ms7d-3Dprio) of gameplay footage from its game, *Metro Exodus*. The story-driven first-person shooter (FPS) was one of the first titles to support real time ray tracing. The video is narrated by Benjamin Archard, a rendering programmer at 4A Games. In it, he explains some of the intricacies of real-time ray tracing and specifically global illumination (Fig. 6.14).

Nvidia's Turing-based add-in boards are designed to bring real-time ray tracing to consumers. The GeForce RTX 2080 Ti, 2080, and 2070 feature Nvidia's RT (ray tracing) and Tensor (AI) Cores and are used in conjunction with Microsoft's DirectX Raytracing (DXR) API. This combination makes realistic lighting effects attainable in gameplay.

Fig. 6.14 A ray-traced scene from A4's "Metro Exodus"

In the video referenced above, one can see several occasions where Nvidia's RTX ray-tracing operation is turned on and off to show what a difference real-time ray tracing makes.

Nvidia explained in a blog post (https://www.nvidia.com/en-us/geforce/news/metro-exodus-rtx-ray-traced-global-illumination-ambient-occlusion/), "By introducing real-time ray-traced global illumination (RTGI), 4A can have natural lighting from the sun and moon realistically illuminate a scene and have it genuinely affect the scene as the time of day changes. Before now, this was impossible —GPUs lacked the necessary hardware and performance to calculate real-time ray tracing, and no one had crafted technology and techniques to accelerate the process to such a degree that it could be used in graphically complex games."

Real-time ray-traced ambient occlusion (RTAO) can also be seen in the video. RTAO enables developers to calculate and display AO's contact shadowing based on the geometry of the scene. This is a different approach than traditional rasterization rendering, which uses rough approximations to generate shadows surrounding an object, rather than being based on an object's specific size, shape, and material construction.

The video also provides an indication of what kind of visuals GeForce RTX graphics add-in board owners will experience.

6.1.1.3 Architecture

Often lumped together as architectural, engineering, and construction (AEC), I make the distinction of not doing that because engineering and construction can be considered design and manufacturing respectively.

Fig. 6.15 Proposed mixed-use development. *Source* Tom Svilans, rendered with Indigo Renderer

Architectural conceptualization is what architects used to do with balsa wood and cardboard models, to give the prospect and idea of what his or her building or home would look like, or what a modification to a building, home, or garden would (could) look like. Ray tracing adds the ability to show the design concept in all hours of the day and all seasons, to show the secondary effects from the proposed building (such as reflections and/or shadows cast by it) (Fig. 6.15).

It is very common that architecture offices need to make renderings during the development of projects. For some stages and some types of projects, it makes sense to hire the services of a professional rendering company. But sometimes, it is too costly and the time consuming of the coordination doesn't fit in a tight schedule of a small project for example. However, even in these cases, one needs to be able to communicate to the client or other members involved in the development of a project how the space is going to look like.

Sun and Shadows

Because a ray-traced image is physically accurate and photorealistic, they are also used to show the shadow and reflections from a proposed building. Sometimes, such analysis is done after the fact. A classic case of doing the analysis afterward occurred in 2015 (Fig. 6.16).

London's 20 Fenchurch Street tower is known to Londoners as the "Walkie-Talkie," because if its concave shape. The glass-ensconced building has long been controversial among residents and architects alike. Built with sweeping curves, 20 Fenchurch inadvertently became the ideal platform for concentrating solar energy. As a result, the unfortunate owner of a new Jaguar found the interior of his car melted due to the concentration of sun rays from the building (Fig. 6.17).

Fig. 6.16 London's 20 Fenchurch Street tower. *Source* Nvidia

Fig. 6.17 Doing the analysis before would have revealed the risk. *Source* Nvidia

However, 20 Fenchurch wasn't the only building in the world to fall victim to its own designs. Los Angeles' Walt Disney Concert Hall has also been singled out for its solar harnessing properties and so there are such buildings in Las Vegas and other metropolises.

6.1.1.4   Film and TV

The film is similar to animations and games with regard to the use of ray tracing in the conceptualization stage. In the case of TV, ray tracing of products, especially products with shiny surfaces like ketchup bottles, clean floors, and even teeth, gives the sponsor the exact look and feel of the proposed commercial (Fig. 6.18).

Pitchvis can be used to create a pre-vis trailer to show investors and production companies that could help get one's project funded or greenlit. As the name suggests, Pitchvis is when one pre-visualizes some or all of a film, often for very complex scenes. That can include using storyboards and animatics (as well as asset building) to get a 3D visualization of the world of the story, therefore letting one try out every angle before filming.

Fig. 6.18   HBO logo ray-traced and animated as molten metal. *Source* © HBO

6.1.1.5   Medical and Scientific

Medical and scientific instruments have to be functional and at the same time pleasing and attractive to look at. Whether it is a dentist's chair, a full-body MRI scanner, a blood analyzer, or an electronic testing device, every supplier has competition and a differentiated and stylish look helps sell the product, makes the user and patient feel good about it, and helps the supplier get the maximum price. So, ray tracing contributes to the bottom line in several respects.

6.1.1.6   Vehicles

Automobiles, trucks, boats, airplanes, space ships, rovers, and satellites are all conceptualized using ray tracing. After the design has been accepted, it is then moved to final detailed engineering. During the presentation period, it is possible with many programs to make changes in the rendered image and have them be reflected back to the preliminary model. In the past, automobiles were conceptualized with a clay model and then measurements were made from it to create the manufacturing drawings. It was a very time-consuming and unreliable technique, but one that was critical to convey the slopes, angles, and surfaces. Ray tracing has all but eliminated the clay model practice (although it is still used in some cases). The same is true in the aerospace sector, and physical miniature scale models are still built for conceptualization. One person in the industry commented that people in these industries just like to build models, and others like to look at them; that is something ray tracing or any other computer simulation can never replace.

Autonomous vehicles however may pose a threat to the utilization of ray tracing for automotive design.

In the future, when self-driving cars represent the majority of vehicles on the road, car ownership and even driving licenses will be a thing of the past. If driverless vehicles become on-call transportation pods, taxis, or minibuses, the incentive to design beautifully looking vehicles will end. Consumers will no longer be subjected to advertisements for slick-looking cars, and the need for ray tracing and car designers will diminish (Fig. 6.19).

However, it will take decades for autodrive vehicles to replace the existing fleet of cars in service, unless there are insurance pressures or government mandates to accelerate the transition.

Fig. 6.19 Is this the future for automobiles?

And, while we may be seeing "peak cars" in our lifetime still, there are others who do not subscribe to the dystopian view that all pods the world over will look the same—on the contrary: services will likely distinguish themselves by offering rides in very different vehicles.

6.1.1.7 Products in General

Consumer products like an electric toothbrush, shaver, milk or whiskey bottles, lamps, and all sorts of other products used to be constructed with balsa wood, bits of plastic, and even tinfoil to try and convey the proposed design concepts. They were fragile and like the clay models of automobiles. They were time consuming to construct and not very easy to translate into a manufactured product. Watches were often built, a single copy, to show management and the sales department what could be developed. Today, it is all done with computer simulation. Also, most of the extraordinarily talented craftsman who handmade those models have died or retired and a new class of such people has not been trained to do it. So, ray tracing and computer simulation were essential in saving the watch design industry. Several other industries have a similar debt to ray tracing.

6.1.2 Design and Engineering—STAGE TWO

Once the concept has been accepted, it can move to the final, accurate, and detailed (including all subsystems) design. When a product, whether it's a robotic vacuum cleaner, a wing-tip fuel tank, or a 20 second TV commercial, manufacturing constraints, standards, and associated parts (including actors) will impact the design and shift it from the original concept into what's practical and possible. Now, the engineers and designers have to render it accurately and show it once again to the customer to get approval for the changes. If standards bodies are involved, the approval may involve certifications. To satisfy all those requirements, the ray tracer must be physically accurate and photorealistic.

Pre-visualization (also known as previs, pre-vis, pre-rendering, preview, or wireframe windows) is the visualizing of complex scenes in a movie before filming. It is also a concept in still photography. Pre-visualization is used to describe techniques such as storyboarding or the planning and conceptualization of movie scenes.

6.1.2.1 Photorealistic

Photorealism would seem like a basic characteristic in ray tracing, and it is the whole reason for ray tracing. However, many ray-tracing programs use the Monte Carlo stochastic technique and can, depending upon how many rays are cast and how long the ray tracer is allowed to run, give a slightly distorted representation known as biasing. Also, critically important is the material library used for the model. If the product is to be a certain type of leather, then the material model used has to be exactly that type of leather with exactly the correct tanning, dying, and surface texture. Anything less is not photorealistically accurate.

Physically Accurate

Automobile headlamps today employ complex illumination optics and are using projector-type headlamps which produce flexible and accurate illumination distribution. Such projector-type lenses for headlamp have tiny features on the exit surfaces to diverge a part of ray. Moreover, the headlamp light distribution is regulated by law in each country.

Physically accurate should not be confused with physically based rendering. Physically based refers to the fact that the algorithm in question is derived from physically based principles. It is not physically correct, and some approximations usually have to be made. In rendering, we always have to balance realism with computational cost, and physically based rendering is used when such compromises have to be made.

As mentioned above, a ray tracer can be biased. Nearly, every renderer is biased to some extent. Unbiased basically means that no shortcuts are taken when calculating a render. Every ray is treated equally, and there is no bias in terms of any importance whatsoever. If one's ray tracer is fast, it is more than likely biased. The degree to which it is biased depends on the developers of the ray tracer as well as the settings of the user.

6.1.2.2 Jewelry Design

Jewelers used to make elaborate multi-view drawings or revert to the actual construction of jewelry prior to selling it. Now, they use ray tracing to design the ring, necklace, brooch, or bracelet and make adjustments to suit the client before melting one drop of gold or silver. This gives the client exactly what he or she wants and eliminates very expensive waste (Fig. 6.20).

Ironically, Piñeiro Solsona worked so hard on the jewel and the diamonds and doesn't seem to have been interested in the band, which sadly detracts from the whole image.

6.1.2.3 Fashion Design

Using ray tracing in fashion design seems like an obvious application. But the dynamics of cloth and the many types of it is extremely challenging.

Design, development, and production in the fashion industry have largely relied on the same, often manual, methods despite all the technological advances happening in the world outside of fashion and apparel.

Fig. 6.20 Cut glass and jewelry design requires ray tracing to catch all the reflections of the piece and show it off best (Rendered in FluidRay RT, design by Manuel Angel Piñeiro Solsona)

Digital technologies in fashion are becoming more accessible, and now, any creative with a basic knowledge of fashion design and computing can create convincing still or animated 3D visualizations of styles, designs, and products. With this technology, the designer can present a lifelike design that shows how the fabrics will look and how the garment fits on the body. However, fashion designers must now learn about 3D software and the principles of working in three dimensions. They must learn about creating the mannequin avatar, garments, accessories, and textures and how to present and publish the finished article.[6]

Various programs are available now including Clo3D and Marvellous Designer for fashion-orientated design, and Maya, Mudbox, Rhino, and Photoshop for more general digital design, visual effects, and rendering.

Virtual Simulation in the Fashion Industry

Ten years ago, academic research investigated clothing companies' complaints on the lack of effective garment-oriented CAD packages to design directly in 3D and provide the model list with tools for shape modeling and cloth behavior simulation.[7] Although commonplace in other sectors, 3D virtual prototyping in the apparel industry had been slow and complex.

Digital prototyping in the textile and clothing industry enables the process of product development where various operators are involved in the different stages.

---

[6]Makryniotis (2015).

[7]Papachristou and Bilalis (2017).

Taking into account the recent trends in the industry and using new and various skills, and formalizing in a deterministic way the result of their activities, the product development cycle, and the use of new digital technologies can overcome the "typical cycle".[8]

Design, development, and production have largely relied on the same, often manual, methods despite all the technological advances happening in the world outside of fashion. Today with the demand from better-educated consumers, mass customization, e-commerce, and advances in virtual reality applications, the virtual garment development is seeking to optimize the apparel industry's design and development processes.[9] Although this is now commonplace in the aeronautical, automotive, furniture, and shoe sectors, development in the apparel industry has been slow and complex; mainly due to the dropping and stretching properties inherent in fabric, which are not only radically different between different fabric types and constructions, but also in the direction of weave or knit within the piece.

The 3D concept is an important development in the design process. It allows designers to create real-life visualization of designs that could previously only be imagined through 2D sketches. According to Dassault Systèmes though, many processes still do not live up to their full potential. Creative 3D materials have always been painful, whereas vendor software companies claim that with 3D virtualization is a fantastic way of starting the process of apparel product development.

The clothing industry has been transformed from a traditional labor-intensive industry into a highly automated and computer-aided one. However, the primary drawback for most of the existing commercial CAD systems in the past was that they relied on mere geometrical modeling and did not provide virtual simulation tools (with few exceptions). 3D technology started to get in that market but needed technological advancements to get there.[10]

Marvelous Designer offers the user the ability to create 3D virtual clothing with its design software. From basic shirts to intricately pleated dresses and rugged uniforms, one can, according to the company, virtually replicate fabric textures and physical properties to the last button, fold, and accessory (Fig. 6.21).

The program offers compatibility with other 3D software and interactive design interface so that one can instantaneously edit and drape garments onto 3D forms with high-fidelity simulation.

The company says their pattern-based approach has been adopted by game studios such as EA Konami and can be seen on the big screen in animation films including The Hobbit and The Adventures of Tintin, created by Weta Digital.

Clo3d offers 3D garment visualization technologies that the company claims to cultivate a more creative and sustainable landscape for the fashion and apparel

---

[8]Papachristou and Bilalis (2016).

[9]Fontana et al. (2005).

[10]Fontana et al. (2005).

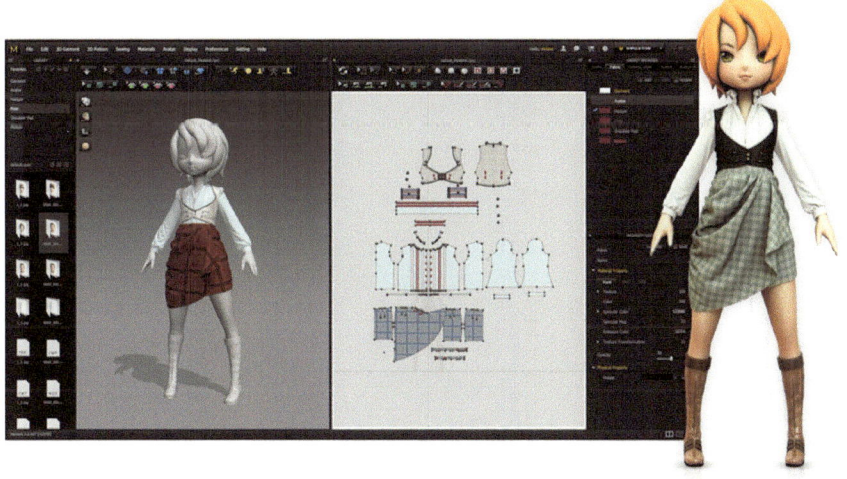

Fig. 6.21 Marvelous Designer's user interface and design tools. *Source* Marvelous Designer

industries. Boasting of over 15 years of extensive research and development, and multiple successful enterprise-wide adoptions, the company has a policy of maintaining a 1:1 ratio between expert engineers and fashion-industry veterans, which it says brings together the best of both worlds to build a user experience that focuses on the most essential element of one's process (Fig. 6.22).

The company uses Chaos Group's V-Ray ray-tracing engine for its final output.

6.1.2.4 Mechanical Engineering

3D simulation of ray-tracing model is developed for studying the radiation heat transfer, associated with laser-based additive manufacturing, in both thick and thin particulate beds by using the Monte Carlo method.

Another clever use of ray tracing was accomplished by Lunenburg Industrial Foundry & Engineering (LIFE), a company situated in the town of Lunenburg, Nova Scotia, that came up with a new geometry for solar concentrators to use solar energy to melt metal in their Foundry, reducing at the same time their use of fossil fuel.

Parabolic dish solar concentrator combined, and parabolic trough reflectors can achieve temperatures in the 350–400 °C range, while a solar tower can achieve temperature as high as 1000 °C but requires a large array of computer-controlled mirrors making it expensive. LIFE used ray tracing to design the parabolic mirrors and accomplish the concentration of solar radiation needed to melt metals (http://tcsme.org/Papers/Vol34/Vol34No2Paper6.pdf).

Fig. 6.22 Fashion design
with Clo3d. *Source* Clo3d

6.1.2.5   Molecular Modeling

Developed primarily for modeling and animation, ray tracing offers a high level of
flexibility with reference to photorealistic and surrealistic image rendering. Through
the use of existing software, the application of ray-tracing attributes to molecular
graphics is possible on a desktop computer. This application is especially pertinent
in view of rapid speed enhancements in PCs, which have enabled molecular
modeling and dynamics on such systems. In this regard, ray tracing provides
enhanced capabilities for molecular graphics rendering that are potentially equivalent to those achieved by workstations.

These effects require almost no additional effort to implement and are guaranteed
to be precise, unlike similar techniques in rasterization. The impact of the light
effects on depth perception is one can see that without the light attenuation and

shadows, any sense of depth is completely lost. The presence of shadows helps to clarify the relationship of the coils and molecule's surfaces, as well as the position of an ion or molecule attached to a metal atom by bonding (i.e., ligands) in binding pockets in proteins.

6.1.2.6 Packaging Design

To achieve photographic renders, packaging professionals and brand owners have relied on ray tracing, the current drawback being speed. This is especially noticeable when the scene contains materials such as glass and liquids.

Creative Edge Software was the first company to deliver full ray-tracing capabilities to all levels of packaging creatives with the launch of iC3D v4.0 in May 2016. By integrating ray-tracing technology into the iC3D all-in-one package, creatives and brand owners were able to achieve photorealistic design mock-ups at any stage without the need for specialist programs or third-party services (Fig. 6.23).

With the development of the iC3D Real-Time Ray Tracer, Creative Edge Software claims that they have succeeded in combining the speed benefits of OpenGL technology, but using ray tracing to enable simultaneous photographic

Fig. 6.23 Ray tracing used in packing design and marketing. *Source* iC3D

rendering of changes as they are made. This capability has the potential to replace previous methods for achieving high-speed ray-traced renders, such as via a render farm whereby the processing is shared between a group of top-specification computers.

6.1.2.7 Geophysical

Seismic tomography is a major research topic on geophysics and concerns the reconstruction of the Earth's interior. Accurate Source: Localization is a critical component of seismic monitoring. A seismic model accepts a description of the subsurface of the Earth as input and produces a synthetic seismic record as output. In raypath modeling, ray tracing is carried out for models of multilayered folded structures so as to generate ray diagrams and synthetic time sections. The purpose of seismic modeling is to provide the seismic interpreter with a tool to aid in the interpretation of difficult geological structures. Over the past few decades, the growing need for fast and accurate prediction of high-frequency wave properties (most commonly travel time) in complex subterranean structures has spawned a number of grid- and ray-based solvers. Traditionally, the method of choice has been ray tracing, in which the trajectory of paths corresponding to wave front normals is computed between two points. This approach is often highly accurate and efficient and naturally lends itself to the prediction of various seismic wave properties.

6.1.2.8 Optical Design

Optical designers use ray tracing to visualize rays in a CAD design to check optical properties, paths, and geometry. This improves optical performance and saves time by eliminating manual tests of design iterations. Ray tracers, especially those designed specifically for optical systems, provide analysis of multiple aspects of imaging systems, including stray light and polarization effects. Bulk properties including absorption, scattering, and fluorescence enable the design and analysis of devices for a wide variety of applications. They can be used to simulate and optimize light pipes, light guides, and non-imaging lenses and mirrors. Designers can simulate surface effects including absorption, specular reflection and trans-mission, and scattering.

6.1.2.9 Audio

Ray tracing has also been employed to visualize the acoustics of a space. Ray tracing is a way of following the sonic energy that is emitted through space. Rays are traced to generate an impulse response which represents the decay of sonic energy in time at the place of the listener. The impulse responses are generated for multiple frequency bands because material and air absorption parameters are different in respect to different wavelengths. Sound propagation, direct and indirect paths. Audio ray tracing takes into account occlusion for direct and indirect paths, directionality/head-related transfer function (HRTF), attenuation, approximate direct path diffraction, and material reflection, absorption, and transmission.

6.1.3 Manufacturing and Production—STAGE THREE

Virtual prototyping is not a new concept and dates back to the early 1990s.[11]

Virtual prototyping is a method in the process of product development. It involves using CAD, computer-automated design (CAutoD), and computer-aided engineering (CAE) software to validate a design before committing to making a physical prototype. This is done by creating 3D computer-generated geometrical shapes (parts) and either combining them into an assembly or testing different mechanical motions, fit and function. The assembly or individual parts could be opened in CAE software to simulate the behavior of the product in the real world.

In the movie industry, virtual prototyping is sometimes considered pre-visualization, but that is an incorrect designation. Pre-vis is the trial and design stage (see Sect. 6.1.2). Pre-vis often gets confused with virtual production.

The holy grail for filmmakers is to be able to work in real time, iterate in photorealistic environments, and do anything you want at the moment. As the technology of virtual production evolves and becomes more intuitive, the biggest benefactor may be the indie director.

One can't really discuss virtual production without discussing the stages that lead up to, or follow, it. Filmmakers don't often start production without a long period of pre-production, and so virtual production is often preceded by pre-vis, a world-building, planning aspect that is so closely linked to production that it is often inseparable.

The product design and development process used to rely primarily on engineers' experience and judgment in producing an initial concept design. A physical prototype was then constructed and tested in order to evaluate its performance. Without any way to evaluate its performance in advance, the initial prototype was highly unlikely to meet expectations. Engineers usually had to redesign the initial concept multiple times to address weaknesses that were revealed in physical testing. The world of virtual production is changing rapidly and getting faster.

Virtual Rapid Prototyping (VRP) is being opened up to all kinds of industries, and in filmmaking, it is getting the industry closer to that real-time iteration. VRP is a unique adaptation of the pre-vis process, accelerated with virtual production techniques. Utilizing only a small crew and an actor in motion capture suit, a

---

[11]"Virtual Prototyping: Concept to Production," Report of the DSMC 1992–93 Military Research Fellows, Defense Systems Management College, March 1994, https://apps.dtic.mil/dtic/tr/fulltext/u2/a279287.pdf.

director can stage, shoot, and edit sequences in real time, sketching the sequence quickly.

An entire film can be quickly and inexpensively pre-vised using VRP to test for marketability, providing a feature-length Pitchvis. An incredibly scalable solution, VRP can be executed with a compact team or full-scale production.

6.1.3.1 Fixture Design and Placement

Fixture design for interior spaces such as homes, lobbies, and conference rooms requires multiple forms of lighting to meet different needs. Linear fluorescent lamp fixtures commonly produce the general ambient light, and reflectorized halogen lamp fixtures produce the directional lighting, while light fixtures with LEDs to provide different beam distributions. Current lighting practice uses multiple light source technologies and fixtures to achieve the required illumination for various tasks. However, many light fixtures can create an unappealing architectural design, especially in a small space, and multiple light source technologies can cause maintenance difficulties.

Some companies such as Synopsys and DIAL specialized in the application of lighting design.

LightTools is a 3D optical engineering and design software program from Synopsys that supports virtual prototyping, simulation, optimization, and photo-realistic renderings of illumination applications (Fig. 6.24).

DIAL develops DIALux—the world's leading software for planning, calculation, and visualization of indoor and outdoor lighting (Fig. 6.25).

The company claims that their software makes professional lighting design easier and accessible to everyone as a platform and tool that connects planners and manufacturers.

6.1.3.2 Ray Tracing in Games' Manufacturing

Several game developers have used ray tracing in the generation of images in the game, then recorded those scenes or objects in the scene, and used them as texture maps. That is known as baking from baking in the image.

Japanese game designer Polyphony Digital, founded in 1998, is a subsidiary of Sony and the developer of the very popular racing game *Gran Turismo* for the PlayStation console. Polyphony Digital has developed their own ray-tracing software for in-house image generation and used it to create baked-in image that is applied in real time when the game is playing (Fig. 6.26).[12]

---

[12]http://cdn2.gran-turismo.com/data/www/pdi_publications/cedec2018_raytracing.pdf.

Fig. 6.24 LightTools'
illumination and lighting
design. *Source* LightTools

Fig. 6.25 DIAL's lighting
design software user's
interface. *Source* DIAL

The company and game are famous for beautiful exotic cars that the player can race on a track like Nuremberg or through the streets of Tokyo and other cities or places like the Circuit de Barcelona-Catalunya shown above.

Fig. 6.26 Gran Turismo the Circuit de Barcelona-Catalunya. *Source* Sony's Polyphony Digital

Polyphony used Nvidia Quadro RTX AIBs to render the scenes and objects they will place in the final game.

As mentioned in the hardware summary (Sect. 7.4.6), it doesn't take specialized hardware to do ray tracing. Polyphony did do ray tracing on the PS4, it is just a matter of how quickly it could render a scene, and it is doubtful it could be considered real time. However, a driving sim could do hybrid ray tracing in real time more easily than a first-person shooter because the scenery doesn't need to be ray-traced, just the automobiles.

6.1.4 Marketing—STAGE FOUR

As illustrated in the ray-tracing pipeline shown below, the marketing of a product using ray tracing can occur before the product is actually built. In the case of selling automobiles, for example, this is almost essential. Likewise, in the case of architectural design it is necessary to use the image of the proposed building to sell it, long before the building is built (Fig. 6.27).

In order to have customers lined up and hopefully prepaid, photorealistic images are used ahead of production. In the case of buildings, and product design, such rendering offers the opportunity of making changes before a design is committed to production and manufacturing. The line between virtual prototyping and marketing in some cases is very thin.

For most projects, marketing is done at the end, but for many projects, especially big ones (big being measured in either dollars, actual physical size, or number of units), marketing is done as soon as a design is finalized or almost finalized.

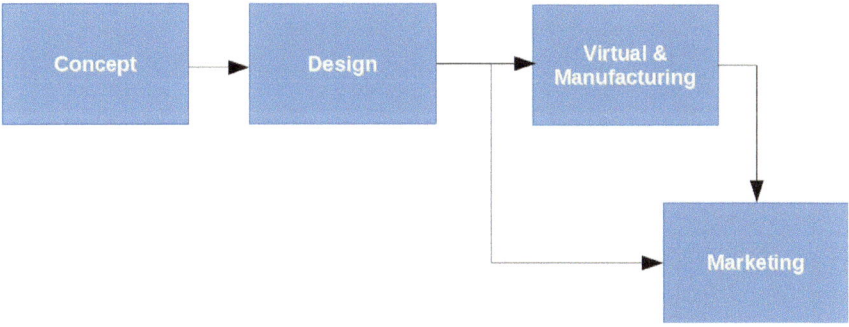

Fig. 6.27 Ray-tracing pipeline

Typically, the images used for marketing are the same as those used for manufacturing, why should they be any different. One of the advantages of a 3D model and ray tracing is the reality of the result. However, products may be put in situations or scenes that are not real, or difficult to obtain as some of the illustrations in the following paragraphs will reveal.

6.1.4.1 Advertising

In the case of product advertising, ray tracing is an advertiser's dream come true. It eliminates time-consuming product shoots which may be thwarted by weather, difficult lighting, actors, and product availability. It allows the advertiser to experiment and get just the image desired and at a fraction of the cost and time (Fig. 6.28).

Almost 95% of all vehicle advertisements for print and TV are done using ray-traced images of the vehicle which includes boats, buses, cars, forklifts, tanks, and trucks to name a few. All architectural advertisements are done using ray tracing which can be set at any time of day, with or without adjoining properties and geographic features (Fig. 6.29).

New consumer products from white goods to electric toothbrushes and frying pans are rendered for advertising using ray tracing. In several cases, the advertisers never get to see the actual product (Fig. 6.30).

Clever product placement programs such as MirriAd and Ryft can put ray-traced images in videos, movies, and games after the fact or in real time.

MirriAd is able to digitally place brand imagery into any video on demand and at scale using computer-vision-based technology for mobile and TV advertising. The software can replace a can of Coke with a can of Pepsi for instance or put a can of Coke in a scene that didn't have one (Fig. 6.31).

Ryff offers dynamic product placement in video streaming. Want to put a can of Diet Coke in the hand of the president while he is giving a press conference? Ryff can do that using AI-driven techniques; the company calls itself an "intelligent

Fig. 6.28 Ray-traced car with neutral background; any scene could be applied. *Source* Chevrolet

Fig. 6.29 Modern office buildings. *Source* Mike Mareen

image platform" company, which means the company does product placement in live or prerecorded video broadcast content. What makes it unique is that content can be placed dynamically, even changed. As a result, content can be tailored to the audience.

Advertising agencies and the studios who work for them have become one of the major customers of ray-tracing software and represent one of the growth segments for the technology.

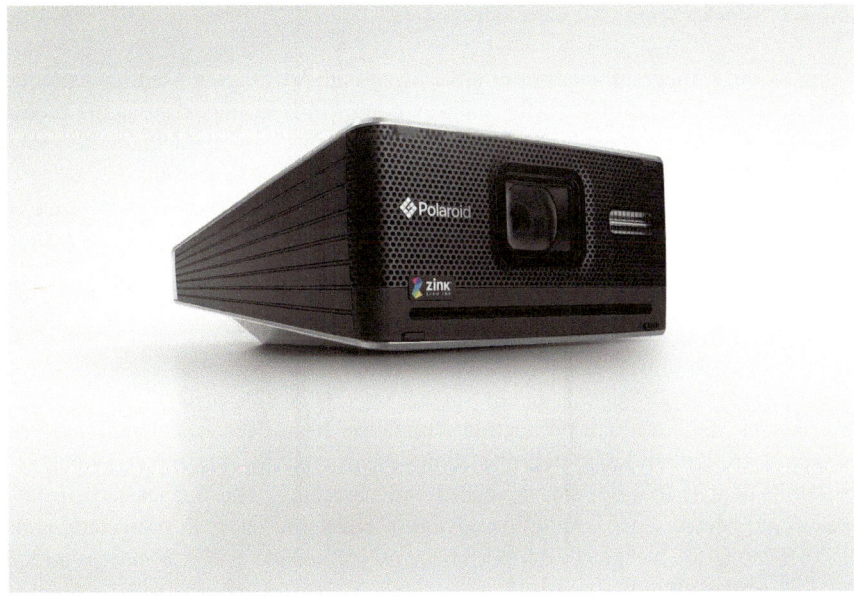

Fig. 6.30 Consumer product with neutral background. *Source* V-Ray

Fig. 6.31 Ryff lets advertisers place any virtual object into commercials and films. *Source* Ryff

6.1.4.2   Packaging

Akin to and sometimes a subset of advertising is the packaging used for a product. The box that a bottle of water or whiskey comes in is as important as the product itself in attracting a consumer's interest. Products that may not actually be shown, such as flower or salt, will be sold often based on its package (Fig. 6.32).

Curved and odd-shaped packages which reflect light in interesting ways much as an automobile's fender does are primary candidates for ray tracing in packing presentation.

6.1.4.3   Projection Mapping

Businesses and theatrical production companies have been using multi-projector systems to light buildings, storefronts, and stages creating amazing and sometimes startling images that delight audiences and passersby. The images have usually been prerendered videos. With the advent of HDR and lasers in projectors, a new quality capability presented itself for image projection and at 4K resolutions with up to 32K across multiple projectors.

One of the leading companies in that segment is Notch which has done major events at rock concerts, company presentation, museums, and events and offers ray-tracing capabilities in its visual creation tool for interactive motion graphics (Fig. 6.33).

Fig. 6.32 Packaging complex, nonlinear reflective surface containers. *Source* Creative Edge Software

Fig. 6.33 Notch makes clever uses of denoising filters to produce high-quality ray-traced videos in real time. *Source* Notch

Notch's content creation tool, Builder, allows creation from scratch as well as the ability to import elements from other industry tools. The company claims that a user can always see their final results in real time.

6.2 Summary

As the demand for photorealism continues to accelerate in all four stages, with no real end in sight, the demand for high-quality ray tracing will continue to grow with it. Anywhere that rendering is in use, ray tracing will be found. The users at all sizes of companies and in all stages will have multiple choices for how they obtain and employ ray tracing. And in many industries, the users in the pipeline, the four stages, will employ different ray-tracing programs from various suppliers. The goal and challenge for the supplier is to make the integrations with specific tools smooth and provide support for specific workflows—the suppliers must work to remove barriers to integration.

Speed Until recently, the primary barrier to wider ray-tracing adoption has been the hardware limitations of CPU and GPU architectures. With the advent of multi-core CPUs from Intel and AMD, as well as Nvidia's latest Turing architecture, those barriers are being eliminated, meaning that ray tracing will see even greater adoption as the rendering times are reduced.

Materials The ray-tracing suppliers are continuing to expand their material's libraries, as well as opening them up for sharing with other programs and making their own programs capable of accepting other libraries. Third-party material library suppliers are also expanding. Materials are the black hole of ray tracing, and there will never be enough. That suggests a meta-language, and taxonomy is needed to classify and make materials easier to select. That will require a consortium to balance open libraries from proprietary ambitions. Nonetheless, many suppliers will always maintain their own material libraries as will various users who want a differentiated look or have special paint, surface treatment, or characterization such as in animations.

Presentation The results of a ray-tracing rendering will be restricted in its portrayal of realism, or fantasy, by the presentation device. Local screens on workstations and mobile devices have reached densities of one billion colors, and 68 billion colors are available on some devices. Projectors follow that development, and printers do also. However, the presentation device will always be the limiting factor in how an image looks.

Future Looking forward, I expect suppliers to begin to incorporate more extensive techniques such as radiosity, light field, voxels, and other global illumination techniques in the quest for the ultimate realism in rendering.

References

Fontana M, Rizzi C, Cugini U (2005) 3D virtual apparel design for industrial applications. Comput Aided Des 37:609–622

Kremp M (2007) Cinematic-quality computer game graphics. Spiegel (online), Mar 2007. http://www.spiegel.de/netzwelt/tech/virtuelle-lichtstrahlen-computerspiel-grafik-in-kinoqualitaet-a-469418.html

Makryniotis T (2015) 3D fashion design: technique, design and visualization. Batsford, 17 Sept 2015

Papachristou E, Bilalis N (2016) Can 3D prototype conquer the apparel industry? J Fashion Technol Text Eng 4:2

Papachristou E, Bilalis N (2017) 3D virtual prototyping traces new avenues for fashion design and product development: a qualitative study. J Fashion Technol Text Eng 4

Pohl D (2008) Ray tracing and gaming—one year later. PC Perspective, 17 Jan 2008

Chapter 7
Ray-Tracing Hardware

Abstract Ray tracing and its associative techniques are mathematical functions and as such can be executed on any computational device. The question is how long is one willing to wait for the results? General-purpose processors, CPUs, with their large addressable memory space do an excellent job at ray tracing and are still the primary engine for ray tracing. Graphics processor units, GPUs, have been used, but the basic architecture of GPU isn't particularly well-suited for ray tracing, and GPUs have limited memory space. A new generation of specialized GPUs with specific ray-tracing features has been introduced and except for the memory space represents a real challenge to CPUs. Specialized, custom, application-specific integrated circuits (ASICs) have also been developed in an attempt to speed up the rendering time. None of them have had long-term success, and most have died still-born.

Hardware used for ray tracing is as important as the software requirements which are just as important as the need. Hardware is selected by the requirements of the software, and the software is selected by the requirements of the user's or the project's need. Most users won't update hardware until it reaches a pain point, i.e., too slow, not enough storage, etc.

How critical is hardware to ray tracing? It depends where the user is in the need to hardware spectrum.

7.1 Shortcuts and Semiconductors—The Need for Speed

Who cares about ray tracing and whether it is fast or slow?

Comparing the computational and hardware costs of ray tracing, some people have said that shininess for shininess purposes only makes no difference compared to some of the excellent quality that precomputed "baked-in" lighting techniques can produce.

© Springer Nature Switzerland AG 2019

J. Peddie, *Ray Tracing: A Tool for All*,

https://doi.org/10.1007/978-3-030-17490-3_7

However, baked-in lighting does not move, it is static, and it is only used for distance shading or games where the time of day does not change. It is also primarily used for finite worlds where the storage capacity is bounded. Large, dynamic worlds may require too much storage to hold precomputed lighting.

One can also use environment probes which renders the environment from a specific point in space. They are used to write the results to a texture map for an overlay of reflective surfaces, like water or windows, but again its static. If one has a line of trees next to a body of water, the fake reflections (of the trees and sky) only line up from a very specific angle if you move away from the scenery moves but the reflection doesn't.

The advantage is for the game artists and developers. Not having to create art with baked lighting and fake reflections, and workarounds for effects saves a lot of time that can be dedicated elsewhere, thus improving the graphics in other areas as well as giving us more accurate reflections and lighting.

Investigations to find clever ways to reduce the computational load by using intelligent algorithms to examine a scene and deterministically allocate what objects are visible and which surfaces need rendering will continue.

Hybrid techniques are being improved and evolved where only certain portions of a scene are ray-traced. Objects in the distance, for example, don't need to be ray-traced; flat, dull-colored objects don't need it (Fig. 7.1).

Semiconductors are being developed that specifically accelerate ray tracing. Imagination Technologies has a ray-tracing engine that when combined with the advanced techniques just described can render an HD scene with partial ray-traced elements several times a second. Also, Nvidia has introduced ways to make a standard GPU more ray tracing friendly and faster.

Fig. 7.1 Use of variance-based adaptive sampling on this model of Christmas cookies from Autodesk 3ds Max provided a better final image in record time. *Source* Chaos Group

All these ideas and developments will converge in the very near future, and real time, easy to use ray tracing will be realized.

Rendering is typically a stand-alone function because of the workload. However, like everything else, there are always exceptions due to resource limitations and project demands. With modern processors and modern software, users can model and render almost simultaneously, work in one domain, and see the results in the other.

There is no simple rule for rendering, each organization and user depending on the project, the available hardware and age of the software determine the workload protocol and procedure.

Ray tracing can be done with different processors and combinations of them:

- CPU only
- GPU only (regular GPU)
- CPU and GPU (Hybrid)
- GPU with ray-tracing hardware
- Dedicated ray-tracing processor (ASIC)
- CPU with ray-tracing acceleration using ASIC.

Obviously with so many options, there is no single best solution. In addition to the above choices for where the ray-tracing software is run, the location of the processor(s) is another variable as they can be:

- In a local workstation
- In a campus or departmental server
- In servers in the cloud.

And any combination of the above, ray tracing can be a distributed problem with different parts of the scene rendered on different processors or systems and then combined on a local system for viewing.

The industry has for some time been using third party suppliers in the cloud as it has come to be called for quite some time. Specifically, firms have engaged in independent rendering services from what are known as render farms.

Rendering is done on different platforms depending on where it is in the pipeline. In the concept stage, it is done on workstations and PCs because of the need for intimacy and if possible, interactivity. In the design stage, the demand for scene data and accuracy is required and the cloud is often used to off-load the local system. In the manufacturing stage, where more elements may be involved such as PLM and MIS aspects, more of the workload is sent to the clouds. And in the final marketing stage where the image has to absolutely and literally be picture-perfect, the work is sent to cloud (Fig. 7.2).

The transition between an on-premise local machine use for rendering and public cloud usage of visualization solutions over time is moving more to the cloud due to the savings in rendering time and cost, the cost of owning and maintaining software licenses, and the capital equipment costs of local machines and their maintenance.

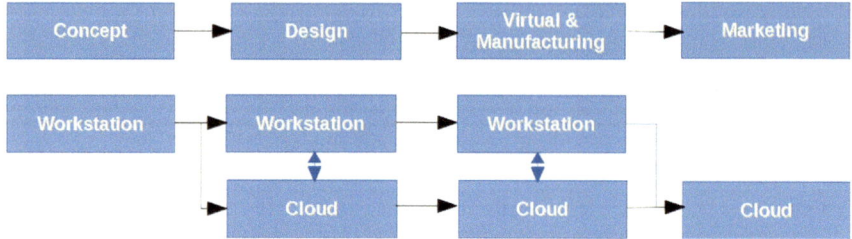

Fig. 7.2 Workload distribution through the pipeline

With improved bandwidth and virtual machine capability and ease of use, it is easy to visualize all rendering moving to the cloud other than localized activity in a trail-and-error development phase.

With the advent of real-time ray tracing on GPUs, the convenience of being able to experiment with a concept on a local machine will never go away. As ray-tracing programs improve the user interface and eliminate the clutter, and complexity of creating a ray-traced image, increased usage of local machines can be envisioned. It is a constant struggle for software developers to make the program so simple it is one button "Push to Render" capability, to one where every parameter of the scene and object can be tweaked. That is why there will never be a one-size-fits-all ray-tracing program and one reason why we have over 70 choices in ray-tracing programs.

7.2   Local

Local processing of ray-tracing workloads can be accomplished on PCs, workstations, and even tablets or smartphones in final or interactive situations. The processors these platforms can employ for the ray-tracing workload vary considerably from small (relatively speaking) ARM processors in SoCs such as a Qualcomm Snapdragon, to giant GPUs like Nvidia's Turing, or big CPUs like AMD's Epyic, Threadripper, and Intel's Xeon, or core I series. Once again, in the case of ray tracing, one size does not fit all.

7.2.1   CPU

Ray tracing only on the CPU one avoids bottlenecks and any intrinsic limitations of GPU rendering, which include the unsuitability of GPU architectures for full global illumination, limited memory, limited support for third-party plug-ins and maps, unpredictability, the need for specialist knowledge or hardware to add nodes, high cost, high heat and noise, and limited availability of render farms. Read our in-depth look at the advantages of CPU-based rendering. Of course, the GPU providers and devotees would argue with most of those points, and that is how it should be—there are no absolutes.

Up until recently almost all high-quality rendering for the film (at all the big studios, with all the major renderers) has been CPU only. There are several reasons why this is the case:

GPUs go fastest when everything is in memory. The biggest GPU add-in boards have 48 GB (and the size increases every year), and it has to hold everything. However, the studios routinely render scenes with 30 GB of geometry and 1 TB or more of textures maps. So, GPUs are unable to deal with the biggest (or even average) movie scenes. With CPU renderers, one can transfer pages from disk whenever needed and that can be even accelerated using smart high-speed solid-state memory (SSDs) that is tightly coupled to much larger (albeit slower) hard drives (HDDs) using technologies like Intel's Optane and Emotus FuzeDrive.

GPUs are great at highly coherent work (i.e., SIMD—doing the same process to lots of data at once). Ray tracing is very incoherent (each ray can go a different direction, intersect different objects, shade different materials, and access different textures), and so this access pattern used to be a criticism of a GPU's performance (because of the time needed to flush and load a new kernel or microprogram); however, newer GPU architectures have overcome that issue.

The Studio Point-of-View However, despite that recent GPU developments have enabled the GPU to match the best CPU-based ray-tracing code, and even though in some cases it has surpassed it, it is not by much, not enough to throw out all the old code and encourage new code specifically for GPUs. Nonetheless, in studio work the biggest, most expensive scenes are the ones where GPUs are only marginally faster. Being faster on the easy scenes is not that important to the studios (e.g., Blinn's law, see Conclusion under Sect. 7.2.2.7).

Studios with 50- or 100-man years of production-hardened CPU-based renderer code won't throw it out and start over in order to get a $2\times$ speedup. The cost of software engineering effort, stability, look and feel of the final product and fiefdoms are more important.

Similarly, if a studio has an investment in a datacenter holding 20,000 CPU cores, all in the smallest, most power and heat-efficient form factor you can, that is also a sunk cost investment and one doesn't just throw it away. Replacing them with new machines containing top of the line GPUs vastly increases the cost of one's render farm.

Amdahl's Law (1967)[1] was used as an argument against massively parallel processing. However, since 1988, Gustafson's Law has been used to justify massively parallel processing (MPP). But most people agree that you can only take multi-processing so far—how far has to do with the data structures being used and efficiency in threading (Fig. 7.3).

---

[1]Amdahl (1967).

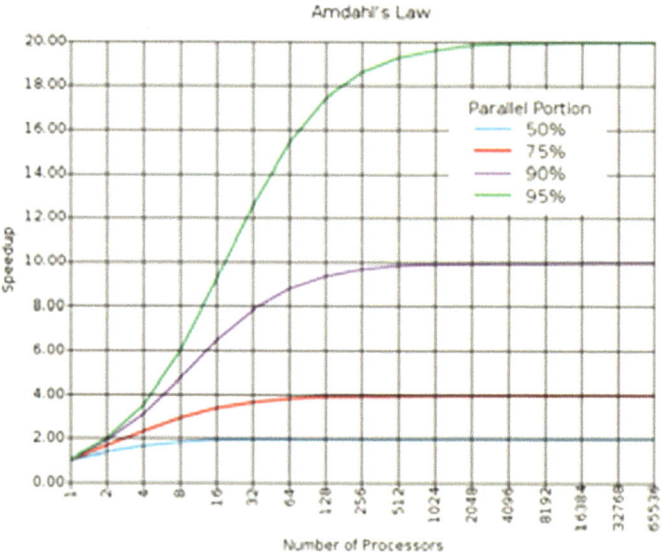

Fig. 7.3 Amdahl's Law. *Source* Wikipedia

In the case of a film, the actual rendering per se is only one stage in generating the scenes. But what is different about games? Why are GPUs good for games but not film?

When making a game it has to render in real time, no less than 30 frames per second (fps), or 33 ms per frame, and often the quality of the artwork, or the rendering features will be sacrificed to achieve that. In contrast, with film, the unbreakable constraint is making the director and VFX supervisor happy with the quality and look he or she wants, and how long it takes is (to a degree) secondary.

Also, with a game, you render frame after frame after frame, live in front of a user. But with film, you effectively are rendering once, and what is delivered to theaters is a movie file—so moviegoers never know or care if it took 10 h per frame, but they will notice if it doesn't look good. So again, there is less of a penalty placed on those renders taking a long time if the image looks fabulous.

With a game, you don't really know what frames you are going to render, since the player may wander all around the world, view from just about anywhere. You can't and shouldn't try to make it all perfect, and you just want it to be good enough all the time. But for a film, the shots are all hand-crafted. A tremendous amount of human time goes into composing, animating, lighting, coloring, and compositing every shot, and then it only needs to be rendered it once. Think about the economics —once 10 days of the calendar (and salary) has gone into lighting and compositing the shot just right, the advantage of rendering it in an hour (or even a minute) versus overnight, is small, and not worth any sacrifice of quality or achievable complexity of the image.

Most production renderers use CPUs. GPUs are incredibly powerful, and some benchmarks show 400% speed improvements over CPU-based renderers. The problem is though is that GPU-based renderers struggle with the scenes that are used in production. Typical production scenes contain over 250 GB of textures and over 10 s of GBs of geometry (pretessellation). This isn't going to fit in the memory of a GPU, and the GPU will spend most of the time loading assets from the hard drive (or network).

A lot of production renderers use the CPU as well most Dreamworks Animation and Pixar films are still mostly CPU-based rendered.

It is not that the studios are anti-GPU in any way, they just believe in using them for what they are good at. Soon, we will see the GPU used for rendering in films, just as we are seeing game engines being employed in pre-viz today. In-between we are seeing GPUs being used in areas where the architecture excels. This will be in functions like post-processing, e.g., Bloom & Glare, the generation of stochastic features like smoke, flames, waves, and clouds where the predictable, self-similar nature of each calculation can be shared between the processors in an efficient and effective way.

7.2.2 GPU

The GPU has been used to accelerate production ray tracing since 2009. However, the first application of ray tracing using a GPU was accomplished in 2002 by Carr, Hall, and Hart,[2] using an ATI Radeon 8500 AIB, and shortly after that Purcell, Buck, Mark, and Hanrahan[3] did a similar demonstration using an Nvidia GeForce 3.

These were primitive demonstration cases using only vertex and fragment shaders and simple instruction sets, integer-only (fixed-point) fragment shaders, a limited number of instructions per program, a limited number of inputs and outputs, and no loops, no conditional branching.

Dr. Professor, Alexander Keller, one of the developers of the Mental Image ray-tracing programs, and director of research at Nvidia commented, "Carr et al., used a regular grid as an acceleration data structure, which is very limited. Purcell et al. used a uniform grid (see Sect. 5: "In this research, we assumed a uniform grid. Uniform grids, however, may fail for scenes containing geometry and empty-space at many levels of detail. Since we view texture memory as random-access memory, hierarchical grids could be added to our system.")".

There is no difference between a "regular grid" and a "uniform grid?" Both Carr et al. and Purcell et al. used uniform grids, but Purcell admits that uniform grids

---

[2]Carr et al. (2002).

[3]Purcell et al. (2002).

"may fail for scenes containing geometry and empty spaces at many levels of detail."

Keller agrees and said, "This is also a big difference to Carr, as Carr is not using an acceleration data structure on the GPU."

"So, in fact, this architecture does not have a chance to compete." The end of Sect. 5.2 in Purcell (rtongfx.pdf) provides the fact: "Carr et al. [2002] have independently developed a method of using the GPU to accelerate ray tracing. In their system, the GPU is only used to accelerate ray–triangle intersection tests."

"[…] Our system differs from theirs in that we store all the scene triangles in a 3D grid on the GPU; theirs stores the acceleration structure on the CPU. We also run the entire ray tracer on the GPU. Our system is much more efficient than theirs since we eliminate the GPU-CPU communication bottleneck."

"Both teams," Dr. Keller continues, "were fair to each other, Carr at the end of Sect. 3 cites rtongfx, arguing about the issues of idle threads, which became a real issue with all GPU programming (divergence, etc.). Still, communicating with the GPU for intersection only, of course, the ray engine had no chance to compete."

Professor Dr. John Hart, at the University of Illinois, commented, "At the time, we were using AGP and PCI Express to communicate between the CPU and GPU, and we had really slow readback rates from the GPU to the CPU. Nowadays we have single-chip processors with both CPU and GPU elements and shared memory. Carr's approach was to use the CPU for what the CPU did best in handling the irregular program flow of ray management, and that approach may make better sense now given the faster CPU-GPU handoffs possible in modern system-on-a-chip architectures."

"So," said Keller, "I would conclude, they were independent at the same time - both important, although Carr at that time was a little bit more advanced, while the other predicted the coming problem. The one had all on the GPU, but no adaptive acceleration data structure, but kernels. The other one had recognized the issue of divergence, but lots of bandwidth limitations, which became more of a problem later on, when adaptive acceleration data structures were used."

"It depends a little bit on how far you want to take it, for example, in Szirmay-Kalos, Purgathofer's 1998 paper on global ray tracing,[4] used graphics hardware early to do ray tracing of ray bundles using parallel projection. That, of course, meant that all rays of a generation have to go in the same direction, which proved not to be practical, but it was ray tracing supported by the rasterizer. It had not been efficient, and won't be, as it touches all geometry all the time.

Attempts at using a GPU for real-time ray tracing date back 2009 or earlier. Limited resolution (256×256, or 512×512) and negotiated definitions of what constitutes real time: 24 fps as used by the cinema, 25 fps as used by European TV, or higher? As Margaret Wolfe Hungerford said, "… it's in the eye of the beholder."

---

[4]Szirmay-Kalos and Purgathofer (1998).

In 2018, Nvidia introduced a new GPU, the Turing, that the company claimed could deliver real-time ray tracing (RT-RT), and some examples were shown at SIGGRAPH 2018 to demonstrate it.

7.2.2.1 Real-Time Ray Tracing

Work on real-time ray tracing can be traced back to the REMRT/RT tools developed in 1986 by Mike Muuss for the BRL-CAD solid modeling system. Initially published in 1987 at USENIX, the BRL-CAD ray tracer is the first known implementation of a parallel network distributed ray-tracing system that achieved several frames per second in rendering performance.[5]

BRL-CAD's ray tracer, including REMRT/RT tools, continues to be available and developed today as open-source software. OpenRT, OptiX, OpenRL, and many other APIs have now risen to the challenge of enabling real-time ray tracing on GPUs.

Since then, there have been considerable efforts and research toward implementing ray tracing in real-time speeds for a variety of purposes on stand-alone. In 2001, Dr. Steven Parker while at the University of Utah used an SGI Origin 2000, considered a supercomputer at the time, to demonstrate almost real-time ray tracing at 15 fps (Fig. 7.4).

For real-time ray tracing, one would likely choose a GPU. However, as in all things there are compromises, and in its first instantiation, the AI-equipped, Nvidia Turing ray-tracing-accelerated GPU was limited to a lower scene complexity than typically used for the film. Nonetheless, it was and is extremely well-suited for ray-tracing prototyping, games, and pre-vis applications.

Ray tracing is a physics-based lighting system that does not require heavy custom implementation for each scene. GPUs with their massive compute density and low cost-per-GFLOP have been candidate for accelerating ray tracing, but the cellular construct of multiple SIMD (shaders) per cell and the nature of having to flush a kernel before a new one can be loaded has made using a GPU problematic. Recognizing that in 2014 AMD and Nvidia began adding special features to make the GPU more ray tracing friendly.

For a long time, hardware support for ray tracing has been held back by three main issues:

1. a large amount of floating-point computations needed
2. support for flexible control flow including recursion and
3. branching (necessary for traversal of hierarchical index structures and shading computations)

and finally the difficulty to handle the complex memory access patterns to an often very large scene database.

---

[5]3D Rendering, Editor: By Wikipedians https://tinyurl.com/y7jgy8jr.

Fig. 7.4 Portion of a 600 x 400-pixel image from Parker's system ran at 15 frames per second.
Source Steve Parker

The introduction of the highly parallelized SIMD architecture of the GPU, combined with the development of unified shader architecture led to a revolution in the computer industry. Since the task of tracing each ray is linear and repetitive, it is the exact same parallelized workload that benefits the most from the thousands of parallel cores (called shaders) in a GPU. However, ray tracing of a fixed scene is relatively straight forward, even easy. Ray tracing of a dynamic scene with moving objects is extremely challenging. The latter is much more intensive due to the changing nature of the scene. This requires more shaders (cores) and specialized algorithms that can compensate for the dynamic characteristics of the scene. Ray tracing, a dynamic scene, such as found in a game, simulator, or TV advertisement, has become a grand challenge known as real-time ray tracing—RT-RT. It has been a sort of holy-grail pursuit in the industry since the late 1980s.

Real-time ray-tracing performance was actually accomplished on single high-performance CPU by Ph.D. candidate (Saarland University) Ingo Wald in 2001[6]; however, higher resolutions, complex scenes, and advanced rendering effects still required a cluster of CPUs for real-time performance (Wald 2004). This large number of CPUs is also the main drawback of these software solutions. The large size and cost of these solutions are preventing more widespread adoption of real-time ray tracing.

7.2.2.2   Vulkan API Extension

The Khronos Vulkan API is available for GPU ray tracing to reduce the visual artifacts of CGI aliasing. Super-sampling consumes GPU processing cycles by requiring multiple passes through all or part of the 3D rasterization pipeline, with a different, shifted sample point per pass. Final pixel values are calculated through blending or accumulation of each pass. With recent improvements in GPU performance, mostly due to Moore's law, super-sampling has gained popularity in its usage.[7]

The AMD ray-tracing extension was introduced in September 2018 with the premiere Radeon graphics AIBs. With Vulkan 1.1.91, the extension is renamed to VK_AMD_memory_overallocation_behavior for ray tracing on the latest GPUs. It allows defining whether explicit overallocation beyond the device memory's heap sizes are allowed by the driver or not.

The Nvidia VK_NVX_ray tracing extension was introduced in September 2018 with the Nvidia GeForce RTX graphics AIBs. With Vulkan 1.1.91, the extension is renamed to VK_NV_ray_tracing for ray tracing on the latest GPUs.

DirectX and Vulkan

DirectX (DX) didn't copy so much from Vulkan. Both Vulkan and DX derive from AMD's Mantle API. However, both APIs took things in their own direction in significant ways. They are definitely not Mantle anymore—but you can tell they have a common ancestor.

Apple's Metal API is not derived from Vulkan—it is actually OpenCL with added graphics (even some section numbers were the same as OpenCL in the first versions of Metal). This is not so surprising when you realize OpenCL and Metal shared the same spec editor. It is why Metal has C++ shaders and more integrated compute. But is also not as full throttle "explicit" as Vulkan/DX12—which makes it a little easier and familiar at first—but Metal hides the lowest level of control over the GPU that game developers demanded to get the best performance from the hardware.

---

[6]Wald et al. (2001).

[7]https://www.khronos.org/registry/vulkan/specs/1.1-extensions/html/vkspec.html.

Things are definitely more fragmented than in the good "ol OpenGL days"—and definitely more fragmented when the industry had the truly universal (i.e., on every desktop and mobile phone) OpenGL ES 2.0 and 3.0, which also inspired WebGL 1.0 and 2.0 because of their ubiquity. However, things are not as bad as they first seem—the emerging theme of 2018 at Khronos is "Deployment Flexibility": running Vulkan over Metal, running Vulkan over DX12, running OpenGL over Vulkan, running DX12 over Vulkan, running OpenCL over Vulkan, etc. This is an emerging trend because all these APIs are becoming increasingly programmable—and so the layering is a trans-compilation exercise that can be efficient and not add any runtime overhead.

This will make Vulkan pretty much universally available. Vulkan over Metal is being used today to ship production applications at performance levels great than using the Apple OpenGL drivers. Vulkan over DX12 for Xbox app is a possibility.

So, although the platform vendors are trying to ringfence their walled gardens—Deployment Flexibility is fighting back.

7.2.2.3   AMD

At the Unite Berlin conference in the fall of 2018, AMD show ways developers could add real-time ray-tracing effects with Radeon ProRender and Radeon Rays software.

Radeon ProRender is a GPU and CPU renderer that handles ray casting and shading and is a physically based renderer that outputs rendered images (targeted at content creators and other developers.

Radeon ProRender supports hybrid rendering which combines ray tracing with rasterization. Rasterization will be used for primary visibility and lighting, whereas ray tracing will be used for secondary and complex effects.

In a hybrid mode, real-time ray tracing will be used for ambient occlusion, glossy reflections, refractions, diffuse global illumination, and area lighting. These effects will be handled by Radeon ProRender and can be turned on/off based on hardware capabilities according to AMD.

AMD did not add special features to make GPU more ray tracing friendly, but they did add general compute features that also help ray tracing.

In late 2017, ray tracing was still relatively new and isn't even yet supported on stable public versions Windows 10. At the time, AMD didn't think ray-traced games would become widespread until the technology was available on all tiers of GPUs, not just the most expensive, high-end options. 2020 and beyond likely bring more AIBs with ray tracing.

AMD has always looked to open standards, which always lags the proprietary (e.g., CUDA) which is why Nvidia tends to get the lead. That said, given DX is essentially an open standard (at least in respect to non-partisan adoption).

7.2.2.4 Nvidia

Nvidia made big announcements at SIGGRAPH 2018, Game Developers Conference and elsewhere about their new Turing GPU architecture with dedicated ray-tracing accelerator cores, plus specialized AI software for denoising.

Nvidia's RTX is showing a lot of promise in speeding up the **ray-casting** portion of rendering for scenes with simpler shading/textures, especially for renderers that are able to specifically utilize RT Cores (GPU/ray-tracing applications do not automatically support RTX—they need to be programmed to take advantage of it).

Turing followed a series of GPU developments by Nvidia, beginning with the Fermi in 2010. It was a loaded device with special functions and features which proved to not be the optimal fit, for graphics in particular. It hit solid performance levels for 3D graphics, but it fell short in expectations in price/performance and performance/watt metrics. Nvidia took note, and next-generation Kepler (2012) adopted a different strategy.

With Kepler, Nvidia for the first time delivered two distinct flavors: what I (not Nvidia) call "graphics-first" versions (starting with GK104) and heftier, "compute-first" versions (starting with the "Big Kepler" GK110 and culminating with the GK210). Compute-first chips weren't necessarily exclusively used in compute products (e.g., Tesla brand), and similarly, graphics-first chips weren't only built into graphics products (e.g., GeForce and Quadro brands). Still, with Kepler, there was a clear change in tack from the all-in-one Fermi approach to one pursuing two threads of products from the same GPU generation: one slanted toward compute and datacenters and the other slanted toward for bread-and-butter gaming and professional visual applications.

Next came Maxwell, which proved a bit of an anomaly in the context of both Fermi and Kepler, for good reason (at least at the time). Overriding the pursuit of the optimal graphics/compute balance came a different imperative: maximizing performance per watt. At the time, Nvidia was still hot on mobile opportunities, notably for automotive and mobile gaming applications (e.g., Shield) but also still likely toying with the prospects of tablets and possibly still phones. With Maxwell, Nvidia actually led with mobile GPU parts, later delivering higher performance parts for desktop applications. A "Big Maxwell" did appear in the form of the GM200 chip, but while it retained some of the lower-cost (or general-purpose) compute-oriented goodness, it didn't take on the big-cost compute-only features like fast FP64, instead of serving more as a maxed-out graphics chip. In fact, from a compute perspective, Maxwell stood out for its relatively paltry FP64 rates, compared to both Kepler before it and Pascal after.

With 2016s Pascal, Nvidia returned to a dual-pronged GPU strategy: one prong leaning toward compute and the other toward graphics, with both leveraging the same core architecture. Out first was "Big Pascal" GP100 bringing back fast FP64 and other features that gave it a very clear compute-first positioning. The

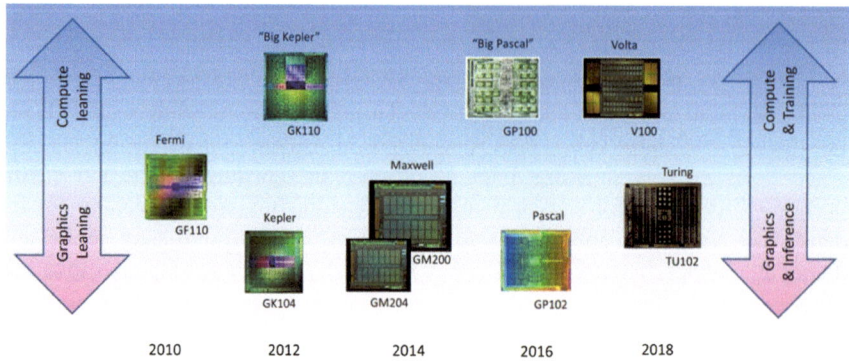

Fig. 7.5 Nvidia's last decade of GPUs, served more than just graphics applications

bifurcation of GPU products supporting compute versus graphics was pronounced, setting the stage—and speculation—for what the next generation, Volta, would bring (Fig. 7.5).

Things started to look different again with Volta, though we didn't recognize it at first. The Volta V100GPU was introduced in 2017 and seemed to fit Nvidia's established pattern: a big-time, no-holds-barred attack on compute-oriented applications. Nvidia gave "Big Volta" hefty FP64 support but took an even more aggressive path veering away (it appeared at the time) from graphics. Nvidia designed in features, cost and watts not only focusing on general compute-oriented applications but very deliberately focusing on one subspace emerging as the most interesting to the company (if not the computing industry as a whole): machine learning. Nvidia designed in dedicated Tensor Cores, useful in accelerating both training (the learning) and inference (the application of the learning for "judgment") applications.

Volta and Turing are shaped differently … but reflect a genuine, unifying inflection point in the future of GPU design

While the makeup of Big Volta made sense given Nvidia's aggressive push into machine learning, it led to the obvious speculation on what a graphics-focused Volta might end up looking like. What would Nvidia eliminate or trim from the flagship V100 chip? Would Tensor Cores, non-trivial in cost and power, remain or get the boot like high-performance FP64 has in past generations? We got a hint about what was coming next with the Quadro GV100 add-in card GPU Nvidia delivered in the spring of 2018. It leveraged the full-blown V100 chip, but packaged in a $9K product, the chip still didn't necessarily figure to be the eventual version of Volta that Nvidia would rely on to drive into more mainstream gaming and workstation-focused graphical markets.

Setting the stage for Turing was a new paradigm: RTX technology leveraging AI for traditional graphics markets

But what the Quadro GV100 did show off was RTX, software technology that harnessed Volta's AI goodness—especially Tensor Cores—to a new confluence of machine learning and graphics: AI-accelerated ray tracing. Nvidia's new darling market, machine learning, is finding compelling applications in virtually every corner of the computing landscape, including its core gaming and workstation applications. For the latter, consider machine intelligence used to generate the internal composition of objects to be 3D printed, taking into account the printing materials to create the optimal structure to balance weight, materials, and strength. Or digging deeper into CAD workflows, AI is and will be taking on some of the burdens in designing the form and function of the object itself. And the value of AI to more quickly and thoroughly analyze 2D, 3D, and even 4D (3D over time) imagery has obvious and compelling value in geoscience, surveillance, and medical applications.

But now—most significantly—we can add a 3D rendering application to that list of AI-assisted application. And we were not talking just any 3D rendering application, but the 3D rendering application: ray tracing, the holy-grail method of producing photorealistic images preferred by virtually every creator and consumer of synthetic 3D imagery, including game developers, film studios, architects, advertisers, and industrial designers alike. The Quadro GV100's claim to fame was not its economical price—far from it at $9000—it was the GPU's ability to ray-traced complex scenes with a credible level of detail at real-time speeds. Moreover, it was the AI in RTX technology that was just as instrumental in getting the GV100 to real-time status as any of the usual semiconductor-driven advancements like transistor density and switching frequencies.

Specifically, RTX software exploiting Volta's new Tensor Core hardware incorporated a deep learning neural network (DNN) in the ray tracer to accelerate image "convergence" by decreasing the computational load in the latter stages of rendering. Once the image congeals into something it can recognize, AI fills in remaining rays/pixels, denoising the image and wrapping up the time-consuming rendering process far faster than requiring the full per-ray processing. Specifically, think of this AI ray-traced acceleration as 2D image recognition implemented over time, polishing the image without any temporal artifacts (that might emerge if you individual processed each image independently without considering how the previous and following image pixels were filled in) (Fig. 7.6).

While the V100 chip was not the GPU Nvidia was optimizing for graphics/visual processing, it did mark what will likely prove a pivotal moment in Nvidia's ever-evolving strategy of GPU development. It demonstrated that, unlike some compute-specific features like FP64, those accelerating machine learning didn't have to be looked at as a cost-negative for a graphics product. On the contrary, it turned out to be a critical linchpin in finally closing the real-time performance gap for ray tracing. And that all leads up to the graphics-focused follow-on of 2018: Turing.

Fig. 7.6 RTX technology on Volta accelerates ray tracing through machine learning. *Source* Nvidia

Nvidia's Turing GPU: a Volta foundation optimized for visual processing

Proven by Volta, the applicability of machine learning on 3D visualization (ray tracing, specifically) turned the traditional trade-offs of compute-versus-graphics upside down. No longer did features that didn't enhance the conventional 3D graphics rasterization pipeline have to be considered a silicon tax to be eliminated for graphics-focused applications. That key premise set the stage for what a graphics-optimized Volta might look like, and while the premise held, the name did not. A graphics-optimized version did emerge, but it didn't come bearing the Volta name.

Instead, in late 2018 Nvidia introduced Turing, in which Nvidia dedicated a significant amount of effort and transistor budget to advancing the features GPUs need to advance: 3D graphics performance for gaming and professional visualization based on essentially the same rasterization pipeline the industry has always relied on. Turing had several significant enhancements in its fundamental 3D graphics programmable shader engine, the Streaming Multiprocessor (SM), especially in terms of chip registers and cache, and dialed up supporting infrastructure including external memory bandwidth. But all that represents are expected steps along the tried-and-true GPU evolution path, taking on cost and complexity for features and performance the company was pretty certain independent software vendors (ISVs) and end users alike would value in the near term, if not immediately.

More noteworthy than the more conventional 3D graphics features Turing added is what it didn't subtract. Nvidia leveraged in Turing much of what Volta brought forth, but without the assumed strip-down mandate for non-trivial AI acceleration features that past strategy might have suggested. With Turing, Nvidia architects not only didn't strip out Tensor Cores, but they also improved on them, most notably increasing performance for lower-precision 8- and 4-bit integer processing. Neither datatype is critical in graphics (not any longer, anyway), but can be often be used in place of 16-bit integer computation in AI inferencing. Adding lower-precision

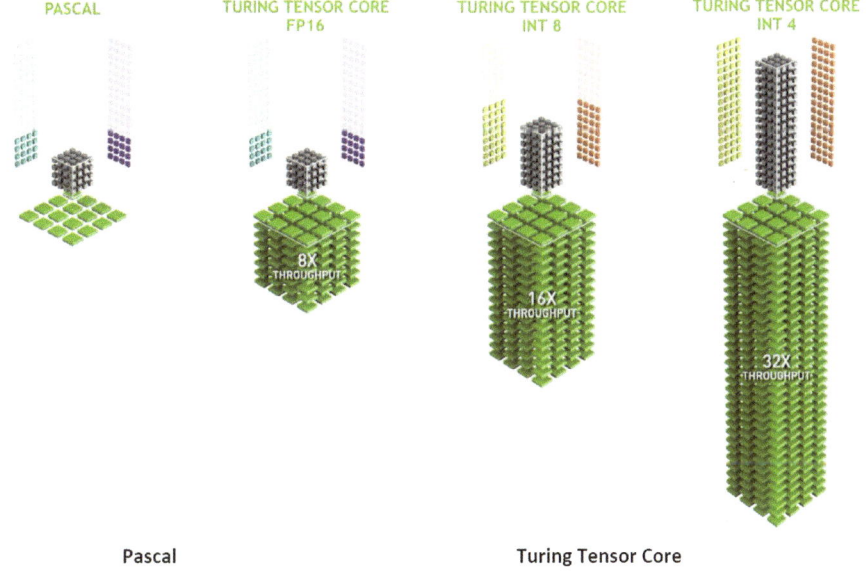

Fig. 7.7 Fast 8- and 4-bit integer processing improves inferencing performance and power efficiency. *Source* Nvidia

support is likely inexpensive to add and in place of 16-bit execution and would certainly improve inferencing performance and/or reduce power consumption (Fig. 7.7).

Nvidia didn't stop with simply keeping in Volta's Tensor Core, rather they took the further step of adding multiple (one per SM) instances of an entirely new core design: the RT Core. Short for ray tracing, the RT name signified a very deliberate design addition, one intended to parlay Volta's AI-spurred advancement for ray-traced acceleration into real-time processing for more economical, graphics-focused GeForce and Quadro GPU products.

The RT Core takes on critical ray-tracing computing tasks, which are inefficient and time-intensive on conventual GPUs. Determining whether a ray (shot from a viewport out into the scene) actually intersects an object (and which triangle on that object's surface) is one of those tasks that a traditional raster-based 3D shader wasn't designed for and therefore doesn't do particularly well. With Turing, that job was now assigned to the RT Cores, freeing up the SMs to spend cycles elsewhere, on shader processing they were more adept at executing (Fig. 7.8).

Nvidia as would be expected introduced a family of Turing GPUs (Table 7.1).

No doubt enthused by the successful synergy of machine learning and graphics with ray-tracing processing, Nvidia researchers searched for other ways to extract more visual processing goodness out of Turing's AI prowess. Extending on the DNNs employed in ray-tracing denoising, Nvidia formalized NGX, an enhanced set of DNN-driven image-enhancement features.

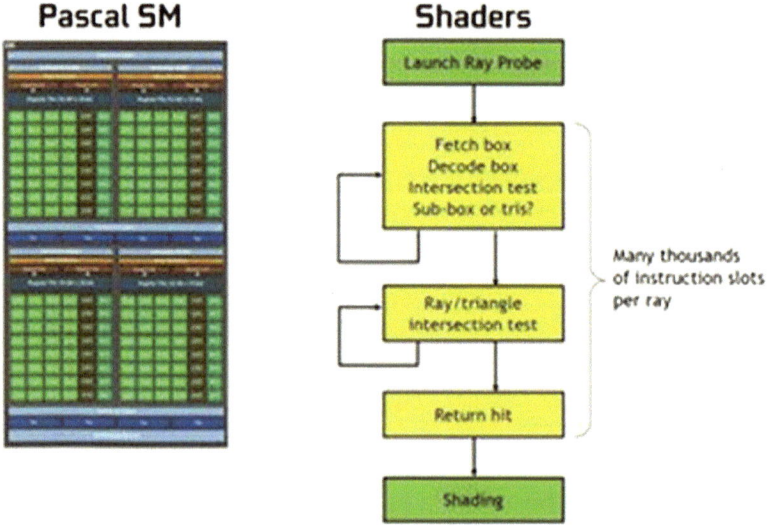

Figure 19.   Ray Tracing Pre Turing

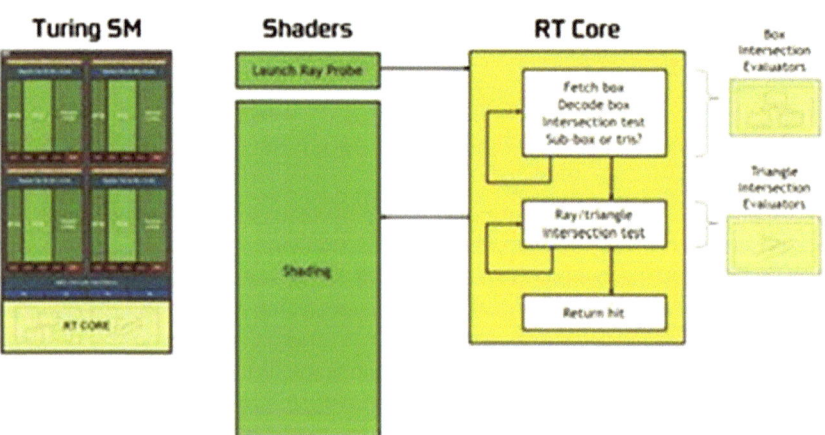

Figure 20.   Turing Ray Tracing with RT Cores

Fig. 7.8 Turing's RT Core focuses on determination of cumbersome ray/object intersection.
Source Nvidia

Table 7.1 Lower-cost Turing spins leverage same proportion of Tensor and RT Cores

Product	RTX 8000	RTX 6000	RTX 5000	RTX 4000
CUDA cores (% of RTX8000)	4608	4608 (100%)	3072 (75%)	2304 (50%)
SMs	72	72	48	36
Tensor Cores (per SM)	576 (8)	576 (8)	384 (8)	288 (8)
RT Cores (per SM)	72 (1)	72 (1)	48 (1)	36 (1)
Memory size/type	48 GB GDDR6	24 GB GDDR6	16 GB GDDR6	8 GB GDDR6
Memory bandwidth (GB/s)	672	672	448	416

Source Nvidia

- Deep Learning Super-Sampling (DLSS—see Sect. 7.2.2.6)
- AI InPainting
- AI Super Rez
- AI Slow-Mo.

I have no doubt Nvidia sees NGX today as anything but a fixed set of features, but rather an evolving and expanding toolbox of DNNs that can further harness machine learning for the benefit of Nvidia's traditional visual markets. For Turing's official launch, however, Nvidia's pitching four specific NGX features exposed to applications in the NGX API.

With the new Turing GPUs, the compute power and the ability to perform real-time ray tracing is present. However, the algorithms have also increased in complexity to account for greater realism. The number of rays that need to be cast per pixel has now gone up based on the scene as well as the objects that it must interact with. With the specialized ray tracing (RT) cores in the Turing GPU, along with denoising filtering techniques, the number of rays needed to be cast has been brought down to reasonable levels. Tracing every ray of light per pixel will provide the highest realism; however, there is the rule of diminishing returns—when is good, good enough. If the printed output or the display cannot reproduce the levels of realism possible it is inefficient to spend the processing cycles.

Nvidia's Turing GPUs accelerate ray tracing by using a combination of several techniques. Not all of the techniques are employed during the rendering stage.

- Reflections and refractions
- Shadows and ambient occlusion
- Global illumination
- Instant and off-line lightmap baking
- Beauty shots and high-quality previews
- Primary rays for foveated VR rendering
- Occlusion culling
- Physics, collision detection, particle simulations
- Audio simulation

- AI visibility queries
- In-engine Path Tracing.

The RT cores accelerate bounding volume hierarchy (BVH) traversal and ray/triangle intersection testing. These two processes need to be performed in an iteratively because the BVH traversal otherwise would need thousands of intersection testing to finally calculate the color of the pixels. Since RT cores are specialized to take on this load, this gives the shader cores in the streaming multiprocessor (a subsection of the GPU) capacity for other aspects of the scene (Fig. 7.9).

Nvidia says the Pascal GPU can generate 1.1 Giga Rays/s, while Turing can produce over 10 Giga Rays/s. That is accomplished because of the specialized RT cores are and the hybrid rendering pipeline in the Turing architecture.

In order to attain real-time frame rates, Nvidia advises developers to incorporate the hybrid rendering pipeline. Hybrid rendering is a multi-pass process that is composed of raster passes, ray-tracing passes, and compute passes. Ray-tracing passes can be used to add various lighting effects such as area light shadows, ambient occlusion, global illumination, reflections, refractions, and caustics. Compute is often used in denoising and compositing of lighting. For the ray-tracing passes, due to the volume of work, a scheduler orchestrates the tracing of rays in RT cores and shading work required to generate rays or use the results of ray-tracing operations.

The ray-tracing hardware is only part of the equation. For it to be useful and worth money to a consumer, there must be an infrastructure (APIs, operating systems support), and content. Content will be the biggest challenge (see Ray Tracing in Games under Sect. 6.1.1.2).

7.2.2.5 Denoising and Unbiased Ray Tracing

When a ray-tracing renderer uses machine learning (ML) or AI for denoising, it changes from unbiased to biased. Technically, unbiased means that the solution converges to the true answer in the limit. If one had a denoiser that made no

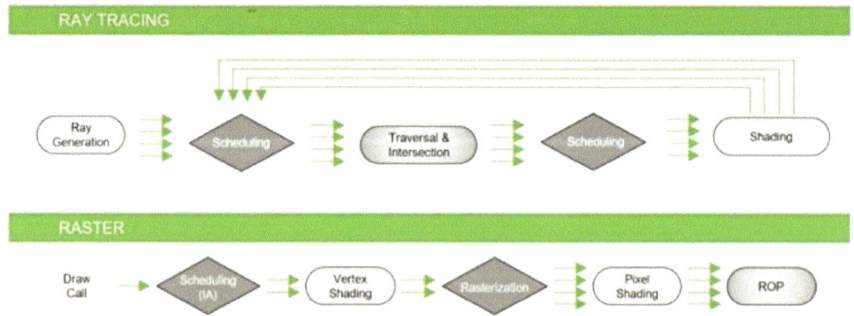

Fig. 7.9 Hybrid rendering pipeline

changes to perfect limit images, then the output would be unbiased because the input is unbiased. However, today's AI denoisers will still meddle with perfect images in some cases. Therefore, based on today's implementations it does become biased, but that is not a fundamental property of AI.

I explain it as being a biased first phase that gives one an 80–90% accurate impression of what the image will be like in 50% of the time, and then, one lets it resolve to the desired accuracy.

But the reality is, it is not that simple. The issue becomes biased versus unbiased versus consistent: What one wants is a consistent algorithm. Consistent means that it converges to the desired solution, i.e., the image that one wanted to compute. Consistency is a strong mathematical notion. No matter, how much developers have tried to educate the user that unbiased only converge on the average to the right image. So in principle, you can have an unbiased algorithm, but never get a correct image. Biased means that you may have a systematic error. But this error may decrease with the number of samples taken. The important point is consistency rules. Why? Because only convergence matters. For example, progressive photon mapping is consistent but not unbiased and still one of the most powerful algorithms.[8]

Convergence and ML The machine learning denoisers based on neural networks may work on the average, however, there is no guarantee other than that "it always worked so far." So, one cannot give any probability percentage. That does not exclude that hope that one day we may have a proof, but definitely not at this time. However, there are other denoisers based on classic methods, where one can argue in the sense of consistency as above. Therefore, there likely will not be any way around denoisers (or considering images instead of pixels) the faster one wants to create images. That is just because the convergence rate is limited, and denoising can buy you order (or maybe more) of convergence rate.

7.2.2.6 Deep Learning Super-Sampling

Deep Learning Super-Sampling (DLSS) is an Nvidia RTX technology that uses the power of AI to boost frame rates in games with graphically-intensive workloads. With DLSS, gamers can use higher resolutions and settings while still maintaining solid frame rates.

The DLSS team first extracts many aliased frames from a target game, and then for each one generates a matching perfect frame using either super-sampling or accumulation rendering. These paired frames are fed to Nvidia's supercomputer.

---

[8]Keller, Alexander, Quasi-Monte Carlo Image Synthesis in a Nutshell, https://web.maths.unsw. edu.au/∼josefdick/MCQMC_Proceedings/MCQMC_Proceedings_2012_Preprints/100_Keller_ tutorial.pdf.

The supercomputer trains the DLSS model to recognize aliased inputs and generate high-quality anti-aliased images that match the perfect frame as closely as possible. The company then repeat the process, but the next time they train the model to generate additional pixels rather than applying anti-aliasing. This has the effect of increasing the resolution of the input. Combining both techniques enables the GPU to render the full monitor resolution at higher frame rates.

The results of DLSS vary a bit because each game has different characteristics based on the game engine, the complexity of content, and the time spent on training. Nvidia's supercomputer never sleeps, and the company continues to train and improve its deep learning neural network even after game's launch. When the company has improvements to performance or image quality ready, it provides them to the user via Nvidia software updates.

7.2.2.7   GPUs for Rendering

Most users who must have high-quality rendering that purchases hardware exclusively or primarily for rendering have done so on the server side or in a render farm (via private datacenters, cloud outsourcing, or hybrid approaches). On the client side, very few buyers of client-side workstations and workstation GPUs are configuring for—and prepared to pay more—for either CPU or GPU-accelerated ray-tracing rendering. That does not mean those professional users are not rendering on their workstations as part of their workflow (regardless of time or volume of rendering). Rather, the vast majority that do render on their client are getting whatever performance they get, based on the machine they configured for more conventional CAD and DCC tasks (e.g., animations, simulations, 3D graphics).

Local

One can expect the advance of GPU-based rendering in both the client and the datacenter to boost rendering usage among both CAD, DCC, and other segments. The client-side buyers are unlikely to dramatically change their budgets and buying habits (average selling prices (ASPs) have been remarkably stable over the past several years); However, the advent of GPUs such as Nvidia's Turing that have an ability for ray-tracing rendering will present a key differentiation to buyers of workstations in the long term. In the short term, it will be uneven as ray-tracing adoption among ISVs and users alike embrace the potential speedup alleged by the new GPUs. By choosing the better raytracing performing GPU, users will be participating as consumers in the rendering market and getting what they can for free or close to free.

Dassault Systèmes and Autodesk, both big names in enterprise design, said they would use Nvidia's Turing-based GPU hardware for ray tracing. Autodesk's production ray tracer Arnold, previously CPU only, has been developed to make use of

Turing hardware for GPU ray tracing, with Arnold GPU capabilities. And Dassault Systèmes is using RTX GPUs in its 3Dexperience CATIA suite for design in electrical, mechanical, systems, and fluid engineering—particularly for accelerating VR rendering and design validation applications. Siemens NX is using Turing in its PLM software for applications such as AI-based denoising as well as MDL support.

Remote

Second, and arguably more dramatic, is the growing synergy of CPU and GPU rendering in the cloud and in the datacenter. The availability of more render-accelerating GPUs will encourage more users to adopt of GPU-accelerated rendering, which will in turn encourage more procurement of GPUs for rendering duty, in the client as well. Rendering is already one of the key components of the cloud computing landscape (e.g., Google Cloud/ZyncRender).

Most important when considering GPU-based rendering in the datacenter is the realization that cloud providers (and perhaps some private datacenters) do not need to justify GPU deployment strictly for rendering. The industry is at a point of synergy creating an environment for GPU adoption and deployment in cloud datacenters. Three trends are at a confluence:

1. GPU use for server-side general-purpose HPC (compute acceleration)
2. GPU use for machine learning and AI in both training and inference
3. GPU use for hosting remote graphics-intensive virtual machines (e.g., virtual workstations).

GPU use for rendering specifically is a fourth.

First is the steadily growing and accepted use of GPUs to accelerate complex, floating-point intensive applications that lend themselves to highly parallel processing. Maximum throughput FP64 is critical for some of these applications. All of the commercial cloud service providers (e.g., Amazon, Badu, Microsoft, etc.) are offering GPUs.

Second is the more recent trend to employ servers as datacenter-resident hosts for remote graphics desktops, including both physically and virtually hosted desktops for gaming and professional usage. The growing appeal of datacenter-based graphical desktops is being fueled by computing challenges that have begun to overwhelm traditional client-heavy computing infrastructures suffering (particularly) under the weight of exploding datasets and increasingly scattered workforces.

A third example is the rendering farms where large quantities of GPUs can be found and time on them can be rented for tenths of a penny per GFLOP second.

Now consider the procurement and investment decisions that both third party and enterprise datacenter providers contend with. Relevant to this context is one in particular: to what extent should an infrastructure build in GPU hardware? Should GPUs be deployed broadly, with a wide range of product performance and capability points, or should they be selected for sparing deployment, justified by specific demand and use cases? With the GPU's ability for inferencing, compute and hosting remote graphical desktops, those datacenters can justify the decision to go forward with more GPUs rather than fewer.

Conclusion

I see 3D rendering becoming more common as rendering times pick up and cloud resources become more accessible in terms of cost and ease of use. That is happening rapidly, and the synergy of cloud computing applications—for CPU-based rendering, yes, but perhaps especially for GPU-accelerated rendering—will expand the market in CAD and DCC.

But …

Blinn's Law and the paradox of efficiency

Blinn's Law asserts that rendering time tends to remain constant, even as computers get faster. Animators prefer to improve quality, rendering more complex scenes with more sophisticated algorithms, rather than using less time to do the same work as before (Fig. 7.10).

For the past three decades, the number of transistors per microprocessor chip has doubled about every two years, in step with Moore's law (top). Processor performance measured in GFLOPS has increased almost as quickly. Processors increased their clock speed until 2004 when speed increases hit an asymptote due to power consumptions and sequentially heat generation. The speed limit, which has been pushed up more slowly, has been offset my adding cores to obtain more processing performance.

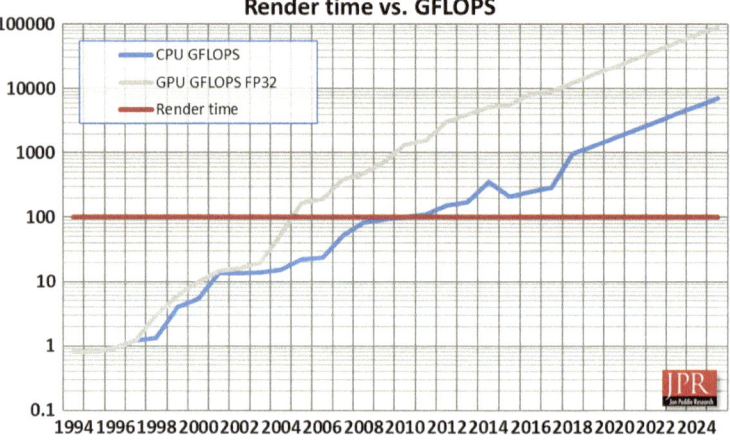

Fig. 7.10 Blinn's law of render time versus processor performance over time

Rendering performance and ray tracing in particular have had steady but slow (compared to Moore's law) improvements. Rendering time has remained the same because the artists make use of the increased performance in hardware and software to make better-looking images. Such enhancements are often referred to as nice to have but not critical. They become critical as artists and engineers get access to them.

Improved access and pricing declines will bring the larger nice to have market segments into more common usage. Therefore, rendering consumption will increase. However, most of that increase will be due to price elasticity drawing in those who will get as much as they can for free, or close to free.

Also, attitudes toward cloud use are changing among professionals. I see that happening faster for smaller companies. I also see hotspots where the cloud is used because the need is so critical, but users may be defying industry standards and practices. For instance, the Motion Picture Association of America (MPAA) has strong restrictions on the use of cloud-based tools, but contractors may sometimes turn to rendering in the cloud and the industry is rapidly moving toward certification for cloud-based workflows.

The CAD industry is moving more slowly on this, but I expect change to come rapidly as the obstacles start to fall and experiences and sophistication replace superstitious fears with facts.

With regard to GPU utilization for rendering, over 60% of the ray-tracing providers indicated they support a standard GPU (i.e., pre-Turing) for rendering. Of the companies surveyed a large majority of them said they were planning to adopt GPU supported rendering.

Consumer applications such as gaming have intermittently used ray tracing or Path Tracing, but it has not been a consistent trend. As mentioned previously (see Ray Tracing in Contemporary Games under Sect. 6.1.1.2), the type of game influences the benefit of ray tracing to the experience. It is reasonable to assume the game developers will embrace ray tracing in a hybrid fashion and use the benefits of improved realistic images as a differentiator. As they do, the consumers will embrace the hardware needed to realize it. Also, as future generations of GPUs include ray-tracing acceleration as a standard feature, the end-user engagement will approach 100%.

7.2.3 Dedicated

There have been a few attempts over the years to provide a dedicated ray-tracing processor. The pioneer and longest term producer of a dedicated ray-tracing chip was **Advanced Rendering Technology (ART)** in Cambridge UK, 1995.[9] They

---

[9]Peddie (1996).

ceased manufacturing in 2009 but continued as a company offering ray-tracing software and services and 3D rendering software for SketchUp.[10]

In 1996, Researchers at Princeton University proposed using DSPs to build a hardware unit for ray-tracing acceleration, named **TigerSHARK**,[11] a hardware accelerated ray-tracing engine.

Mitsubishi developed the **VolumePro** custom processor for volume rendering using ray-tracing algorithms in 1999.[12] Hanspeter Pfister[13] and researchers at Mitsubishi Electric Research Laboratories introduced the vg500/VolumePro ASIC-based system in 2002 with FPGAs by researchers at the University of Tubingen with VIZARD II. The chip's ray-casting pipeline construction consists of five basic stages:

- Data traversal for each pixel along a ray
- Resampling trilinear interpolation from eight surrounding pixels
- Classification assign RGBA to each sample
- Shading estimate gradients, per sample Phong illumination for depth cues
- Composition blend samples (along the ray) into pixel color.

The process is like ray tracing but does not have secondary or shadow rays.

In 2005, **Mercury Computer** Systems (founded in 1983), said it was entering the content creation market with a new product based on **IBM's Cell** processors. At SIGGRAPH, Mercury announced an alliance with the German company InTrace to create a ray-tracing product based on InTrace's **OpenRT**.[14] At the show, the companies revealed plans to develop ray-tracing applications by integrating OpenRT and SGI's Open Inventor to create a customizable approach for "thousands of existing applications" based on Open Inventor. Demonstrations at the show included a rendering application for Maxon.

One of the first implementations of a dedicated processor for real-time ray tracer was presented at the SIGGRAPH 2005 computer graphics conference. A custom processor designated "The ray-tracing processor unit" (RPU), developed by Sven Woop, Jorg Schmittler, and Philipp Slusallek from the Saarland University. It used a single **FPGA** running at 66 MHz and drove a 512×384 resolution screen (Fig. 7.11).[15]

Although running at only 66 MHz the prototype FPGA implementation, the authors claimed it could render images at up to 20 fps, which in many cases beat the performance of highly optimized software running on multi-GHz desktop CPUs.

---

[10]http://www.graphicshardware.org/previous/www_2001/presentations/Hot3D_Daniel_Hall.pdf.

[11]Humphreys, Greg, Ananian, Scott, C. (Independent Work), Department of Computer Science, Princeton University, May 14, 1996, cscott.net.

[12]Peddie (1998).

[13]Pfister et al. (1999).

[14]Peddie (2005).

[15]Woop et al. (2005).

Fig. 7.11 Real-time renderings on the RPU prototype using a single FPGA running at 66 MHz and 512 × 384 resolution: SPD Balls (1.2 fps, with shadows and refractions), a conference room (5.5 fps, without shadows), reflective and refractive spheres-RT in an office (4.5 fps), and UT2003 a scene from a current computer game (7.5 fps, precomputed illumination)

Imagination Technologies introduced an IP block for a dedicated ray-tracing processor, the PowerVR Wizard ray-tracing GPU based on technology from Caustics, a company Imagination acquired in 2011.[16] The company did not find any customers and has stopped investing in it. An implementation of the design has been shown at various conferences and provided some very impressive and real-time demonstrations. The IP is still for sale.

Two years ago, Imagination technologies showed a demo of a real-time hybrid ray-tracing demo (Fig. 7.12).

Imagination has been saying for a while that the PowerVR Wizard graphics IP processors can enable more immersive games and apps with real-life dynamic lighting models that produce advanced lighting effects, dynamic soft shadows, and life-like reflections and transparencies, previously unachievable in a mobile form factor.

As a by-product of the ray-tracing processor, Imagination Technologies' Caustic Professional division developed a ray-tracing API, OpenRL.

OpenRL is a flexible low-level interactive ray tracing API, available for download as an SDK for accelerating ray tracing in both graphics and non-graphics (e.g., physics) applications. A free perpetual license of OpenRL is available for integration, with either commercial or non-commercial applications.

In OpenRL, acceleration structures are built and maintained transparently, behind the scenes, and this eliminates the need for the client application to write any code to create or traverse them. This also allows for ray-tracing hardware acceleration of the acceleration structure assembly.

OpenRT, introduced in 2012, was an offshoot of OpenRL. The goal of the "OpenRT Real-time Ray Tracing Project" was to develop ray tracing to the point where it offers an alternative to the current rasterization-based approach for interactive 3D graphics. Therefore, the project consisted of several parts: a highly optimized ray-tracing core, the OpenRT-API, which is similar to OpenGL, and many applications ranging from dynamically animated massive models and global illumination, via high-quality prototype visualization to computer games.

---

[16]Peddie (2010).

Fig. 7.12 PowerVR ray tracing delivering real-time, photorealistic rendering

OpenRT was not open source; it was intended to be an open API like OpenGL. It was created and sponsored by Imagination Technologies.

In 2002, while at the Computer Graphics Group, Saarland University, Ingo Wald and Carsten Benthin demonstrated examples of interactively rendering complex and dynamic scenes with a ray-tracing-based renderer. The scenes show a prelighted theatre, robots moving through a city, large numbers of moving trees with sharp shadows, as well as the integration of volumes, light fields, and procedural shading in an office environment. Those examples ran interactively at a resolution of 640 × 480 using four to eight dual PCs.

The researcher presented a new rendering engine for interactive 3D graphics based on a fast, scalable, and distributed ray tracer. It offered an extended OpenGL-like API, supports interactive modifications of the scene, handles complex scenes with millions of polygons, and scales efficiently to many client machines.

Due to its superior scalability, usability, and efficiency, ray tracing was expected to play an increasingly important role in future interactive graphics applications. However, driving the technology with an API such as OpenGL would be complicated due to OpenGL's tight coupling to rasterization technology, which makes it less suitable for ray tracing. Therefore, the researchers proposed a new application programming interface called OpenRT.[17]

Siliconarts, founded in 2012, was a start-up in South Korea, developed a prototype of their RayCore in 2014.[18] However, the company couldn't find any

---

[17]Wald, Ingo; Benthin, Carsten, "A Flexible and Scalable Rendering Engine for Interactive 3D Graphics," Technical Report TR-2002-01, Computer Graphics Group, Saarland University.
[18]Peddie (2014).

customers or additional investors to sustain the development. They gave a paper at Hot-Chips and SIGGRAPH 2014 and showed demos. The company offered IP, not a chip.

FPGAs There are and have been experimental ray-tracing processors build as research prototypes using FPGAs. There are commercial dedicated hardware ray-tracing processors available on the market as of this writing. However, if Microsoft's DXR ray-tracing extension is enabling, and Nvidia is successful in convincing game developers to include ray tracing, that will create a user base that may stimulate companies with ideas for a dedicated processor, but lacking the scale needed to make one economically, to enter the market.

Nvidia introduced the concept of a dedicated ray-tracing appliance at Nvidia's GTC conference in 2014. The company called the rendering appliance the Iray Visual Computing Appliance. It was designed to eliminate the costly, lengthy process of building physical prototypes by rendering computer models with extremely high visual fidelity (VCA).

The VCA sold for $50,000 and included eight Kepler-based GPUs, 12 GB of memory per GPU, as well as two 1 GigE ports, two 10 GigE ports, and one InfiniBand connection.

It may be a stretch to think many budgets would support a VCA for a single designer's workstation. Justifying one or two shared among other workstations might make sense.

However, Nvidia had another thought on how to share a major investment in VCA and PBR technology: the updated Quadro Visual Computing Appliance (VCA). Announced at GTC 2015, the Quadro VCA houses twenty CPU cores, 256 GB of system memory, eight Quadro M6000s (for a grand total of 24,576 CUDA cores), the Quadro VCA will set back an IT budget the same $50,000. But with support for renderers Iray 2015, OptiX, V-Ray ray tracing (and thereby all the applications they support), it may be money well spent for a team of product designers and stylists looking to minimize iteration time and maximize product quality (Fig. 7.13).

The Iray VCA is sold through resellers CADnetwork, Fluidyna, IGI, and migenius. The cost includes an Iray license and the first year of maintenance and updates.

7.2.4 RT on Mobiles

Ray tracing has been one of the holy grails of computer graphics since the early 1980s. Always two years in the future, we have nonetheless seen it get faster, while screen resolutions have also increased. In the 1990s, if you could render a ray-traced 512×512 image in five to ten seconds you thought you really had something. We did just such a thing using 16 transputers, a 32-bit processor configured in a SIMD, cost a mere $10,000.

Fig. 7.13 Physically based rendering for the whole team: Nvidia's 56 TFLOPS (and $50,000) Quadro VCA. *Source* Nvidia

The movie studios use ray tracing extensively as special effect using CG becomes prevalent, so much so you no longer know when you are looking at a simulation and the real thing. Those images are rendered in 5K or 8K and scaled down to 4K for digital projectors in modern theaters—and one day your home. In addition to super-high resolution, the film industry operates in a minimum of 10-bits per color channel, and most of the time in 12-bit color (30 or 36-bit RGB or YCbCr) with a server that supports the DCI DCP. Rendering time at such a scale can take an hour and half per frame.

But what about more everyday issues? The next step down could be a PC game being displayed on a nice wide-screen 3440 × 1440 monitor, which currently is limited to 8-bit color. Many games, in particular racing games, are using hybrid ray tracing where just a portion (the shiny car bits) are ray-traced, and they manage to run at 30–45 fps, which is quite satisfying. But racing games are in very constrained worlds with limited FOV and scope.

Ray tracing can, however, be employed in real time in a more practical application, one that is near and dear to my heart—augmented reality. However, for AR, you can't use the brute-force techniques that are used in other applications.

For some AR applications, the visual quality and full integration of augmented content are critical for an immersive user's experience. The superimposed content over the real world must appear so realistic and integrative to be part of the real-world scene. Unfortunately, with the conventional graphics, the photorealistic AR visualization is still in its infancy. *"People are using today AR primitive tools because we're still early on the journey to creating better tools. Tomorrow, AR is going to help us mix the digital and physical in new ways"* Mark Zuckerberg, April 2017.

Adshir in Tel Aviv has developed a new approach to an AR/VR oriented ray tracing. If judiciously applied to an augmented object, it delivers real-time photorealistic ray tracing. It offers speedup of over 150× that of conventional approaches.

Similarly, to traditional ray tracers, it uses Path Tracing, which can provide physically accurate results.

The most basic operation in Path Tracing is the solving for visibility between each ray and millions of 3D scene polygons.

The cost of testing each ray against each polygon is prohibitive; therefore, accelerating structures are used to reduce the number of ray/polygon intersection tests. But still, traversals of billions of rays are the most expensive tasks in Path Tracing, making it one of the most complex applications.

The human way of solving visibility is different. A simple sight toward an object can tell whether it is visible or obstructed. The human sight can be simulated by the prevalent graphics pipeline. Adshir invented a unique technology to exploit the graphics pipeline in Path Tracing for visibility, replacing the expensive accelerating structures. It has been applied in their LocalRay technology.

Adshir has developed a technique they call Dynamically Aligned Structures and productized it into a toolkit they call LocalRay.

In LocalRay the costly traversals and reconstructions of acceleration structures are replaced by Dynamically Aligned Structures (DAS), a proprietary software mechanism based on graphics pipeline, for radical reduction of complexity (Fig. 7.14).

The DAS is a novel method for seeking ray/polygon intersections, specifically adjusted to augmented and virtual reality. It is based on a proprietary handling of hundreds of rays, enabling high utilization of the massive parallelism of the GPU graphics pipeline. Random samples assist in correctness of global illumination.

Key points of Adshir's AR/VR path-tracing technology are:

1. Path Tracing.
   Proprietary quasi-Monte Carlo ray-tracing technology, implementing global illumination, produces photorealistic integration of augmented objects in real life environment.
2. No traversals.
   The conventional traversals of accelerating structures are replaced by a novel, software based, ray hit mechanism (Dynamically Aligned Structures), gaining reduced computational complexity, high performance, and low power consumption.

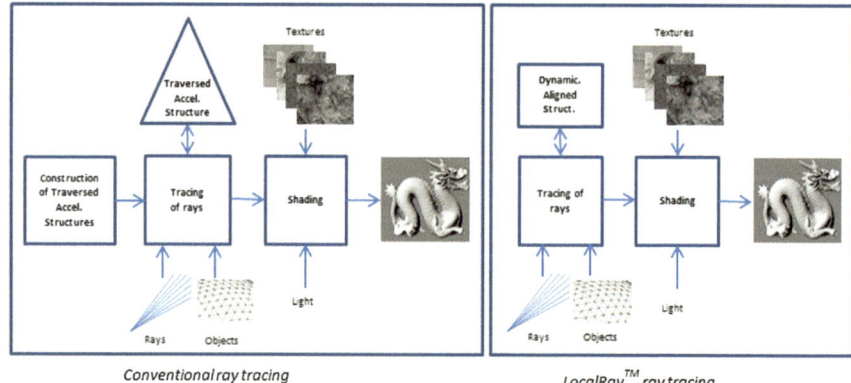

Fig. 7.14 Dynamically aligned structures versus conventional Path Tracing

3. Fast animation.
   There is no need to reconstruct acceleration structures for frequent scene changes.
4. Image convergence.
   Fast image convergence of milliseconds replaces the typical image convergence of seconds and minutes.
5. Data space parallelism.
   The ability to processing rays in data space, rather than in image space, highly utilizes the GPU parallelism.
6. Performance.
   The performance increases by two levels of magnitude over commercial ray tracers, on consumer class computing devices.
7. Power consumption.
   The energy consumption drops down, matching the power budget of consumer devices.

The product is a software development kit, that was available in Q3 2018 and function as a plug-into leading graphics platforms (Unity, Unreal, ARcore, ARKit, etc.), enabling the developers to create an immersive user's experience in VR/AR applications. It runs 100% on the GPU.

The other aspect is "to deal with overmodeled geometry, huge numbers of textures, sprawling shading networks, and massive datasets with large numbers of lights." The definition of "big data," Dr. Reuven Bakalash, Founder and CEO of Adshir Ltd and developer of LocalRay, believes that what is needed for rendering of big data (~ 1 B and up of polygons) is a radically different parallel rendering architecture, with minimized acceleration structures and maximized locality.

Recently, the company did a comparison between their ray-tracing algorithm, LocalRay running on a tablet and Nvidia's eight-GPU DX1 supercomputer running real-time ray tracing.

LocalRay algorithms make smart use of the screen-space raster pipeline in scene-space ray-tracing pipeline, achieving high coherence of secondary rays.

The lack of coherence in secondary rays has been always a problem in ray tracing, as compared to high coherence of primary and shadow rays. High coherency, along with massive parallelism of GPU, delivers outstanding performance (Fig. 7.15).

Adshir says their demo platform has 1.6% of the computational capability and operates at 2% of the power of Nvidia's DGX system.

Real-time ray tracing is and by itself an amazing thing to contemplate. Running on a smartphone seems almost like something out of StarTrek. Compromises will have to be made (the model for instance was reduced from 40K+ polys to 20K and the resolution has to be reduced, but those are parameters that are tied to Moore's law and will get better over time. And then there is the magic factor—Adshir could just surprise us again and come up with a tweak to the algorithm and increase everything. And lest we forget, this is a full-screen rendering, not a zonal rendering.

7.3 Remote

Remote ray tracing is that which is done in the cloud, either private or public, also known as cloud services.

Adshir's RT RT Performance
5 FPS in AR with 1M Polygons

Nvidia's RT RT Performance
24 FPS in Gaming with 1M Polygons (est.)

Adshir LocalRay Demo Platform
Microsoft Surface Pro tablet operating at 30W
Intel Iris GPU, 800 GFLOPS
1M polygons ray traced

Nvidia RTX GDC Demo Platform
Nvidia DGX computer system operating at 1500W
4x Tesla V100 GPUs, 49,152 GFLOPS
1M polygons ray traced (est.)

Fig. 7.15 Real-time ray-tracing performance comparison. *Source* Adshir

7.3.1 Cloud-Based Visualization

Several of the big CAD and Media & Entertainment software suppliers are offering their products and services as a cloud-based system. These are integrated end-to-end systems and include powerful visualization capabilities. Visualization systems typically employ large display systems in the form of wall-to-wall projectors, CAVES, or multi-monitor viewing walls. The visualization systems are used for engineering, proposals, advertising, and marketing.

Autodesk acquired Lagoa in 2014, maker of a cloud-based visualization and collaboration platform for product development. Lagoa has been rapidly building out an online rendering and real-time visualization platform and struck early partnership deals with SpaceClaim (since acquired by Ansys) and GrabCAD (since acquired by Stratasys). Earlier in 2014, it showed a technology preview of a new cloud-based MCAD tool based on the Parasolid 3D modeling kernel from Siemens PLM.

Autodesk offers their VRED suite of 3D visualization and virtual prototyping software as a local or cloud-based solution for automotive designers and digital marketers to create and present product renderings, design reviews, and virtual prototypes.

VRED came through the PiVR acquisition in 2013, primarily targeted at automotive visualization. Through VRED, in addition to the in-product integrated rendering, the company provides an on-premise interactive rendering cluster offering, but no cloud-based rendering (Fig. 7.16).

In addition to these new Autodesk options, a wide array of competitors continues to offer visualization solutions for both architecture and product design, including

Fig. 7.16 Cloud-based visualization car design concept. *Source* Autodesk

plug-in support for Autodesk's flagship products. As CPU cores become denser and faster, and as cloud and GPU support become more common, the next couple of years should be a time of rapid growth in the use of photorealistic rendering at all stages of the design process.

Bentley Systems' plans for becoming "the infrastructure digital twin company" don't end with those ambitions. The company acquired Stockholm-based Agency9, a provider of city-scale digital twin cloud services for city planning and related web-based 3D visualization.

Agency9 has already provided nearly half of Sweden's larger municipalities with city-scale digital twin cloud services for city planning and related web-based 3D visualization. Since 2012, Agency9 has used reality meshes created by Bentley's ContextCapture reality modeling software as the digital context for visualizing urban infrastructure assets represented in geographical information systems (GIS) data, terrain surveys, and BIM models.

7.3.1.1 Cloud Rendering

Redway3D offers their REDsdk 4.3 visualization toolkit with ray-tracing solutions, post-processing effects, as well as cloud-and-sky rendering.

REDsdk is a C++ graphics visualization toolkit that provides industrial designers, architects, and other CAD professionals with a single multifaceted rendering API. The REDsdk can be used for real-time 2D, 3D, and VR rendering and simulation.

One of the notable features in REDsdk 4.3 is cloud rendering (the fluffy white stuff, not the digital kind). This helps make any outdoor rendering look much more realistic, with REDsdk capable of automatically generating cloudy skies based on your prerequisites. This addition also affects indoor renderings, especially when many reflective objects and/or windows are present (Fig. 7.17).

REDsdk 4.3 ships with two different cloud-generating algorithms, one to simulate "true volumetric clouds" and another for simpler background clouds. Algorithm updates continue with new versions of three ray-tracing solutions: multiple importance sampling; probabilistic light sampling; and adaptive ray tracing. These serve to help increase the realism and efficiency of lighting simulations.

Designers will also be able to add a bit more shine to their work, with new post-processing features which include "sharpen," "glow," "blur," and "depth-of-field" tools, as well as updated color manipulation tools to tweak the brightness, contrast, and light saturation of images. Performance improvements are also hidden under the hood, with enhanced GPU light rendering, as well as a new error tracking feature included.

Fig. 7.17 Rendering created in REDsdk 4.3; note the cloudy skies in the background. *Source* intrimSIM

7.3.1.2   Block-Chain Render Farms

The concept of a distributed render farm is one based on block-chain. One example is **Render Token (RNDR)**, a distributed GPU rendering network and marketplace powered by Ethereum. The RNDR Network released a Beta Interest survey to get an idea of GPU supply and demand. The survey was quietly released to the RNDR community during a brief period toward the end of July and prior to major technology previews at SIGGRAPH 2018. The survey was focused on users that both provide and consume rendering power on the network—miner/users. The results were surprising and illustrated the ability of a decentralized GPU compute network to scale exponentially faster than centralized structures.

RNDR was able to accumulate over 14,000 unique GPUs with a total OctaneBench power of over 1.5 million. The quality of the GPUs was also very high, with over 40% of the GPUs as premium cards. RNDR allows miner/users to contribute their idle GPU power to the network to earn tokens, which they can then use when they are on a deadline or need to augment their local GPU capacity with cloud nodes for high resolution jobs.

However, this only works for very small rendering packages. Many jobs require thousands of small files and sometimes terabytes of data need to be transmitted to get a frame rendered. When that much data is sent, the internet is corrupted, and the rendering quite often fails.

CPUs in Visualization

CPU-based interactive and photorealistic rendering via SDV is (Software Defined Visualization) with the open-source Intel Rendering Framework is supplanting GPUs in many modern HPC supercomputing centers, asserted Intel in a guest post in Inside HPC, October 2018.

The ability to run and visualize anywhere with SDVis solutions, regardless of the scale of the visualization task and without requiring specialized hardware for interactive response, is the reason HPC centers no longer need to procure GPUs for visualization clusters.

Autodesk's VRED 3D visualization and virtual prototyping software utilize CPU-based ray-traced rendering with SDVis, while other software vendors such as Altair, Eastern Graphics, Kitware, and SURVICE Engineering Company are incorporating SDVis, claims Intel.[19]

"SDVis unlocks the full power of a compute node for visual analysis," said Dan Stanzione, Executive Director of the Texas Advanced Computing Center (TACC). "With it, even a single node becomes a powerful platform for analysis, as the full system memory is available to hold data."

In particular, the TACC Frontera supercomputer, which will be the fastest academic supercomputer in the USA when it becomes operational in 2019, will rely on CPUs for visualization. "CPU-based SDVis will be our primary visual analysis mode on Frontera, leveraging the Intel Rendering Framework stack," according to Paul Navrátil, Director of Visualization at TACC (Fig 7.18).

The Frontera design makes the switch from GPUs to CPUs for visualization concrete. Frontera includes a GPU subsystem, but one that is designed to primarily support compute codes that leverage single- and half-precision operations, particularly molecular dynamics (MD) codes and various machine learning stacks.

The "visualize anywhere" nature of SDVis means that visualizing locally or remotely is possible on devices that can display from memory with no GPU acceleration required. For researchers who want to enable visualization on supercomputers which are CPU-based, such a rendering framework would seem ideal.

"CPU-based SDVis will be our primary visual analysis mode on Frontera, leveraging the Intel Rendering Framework stack," said Paul Navrátil, Director of Visualization at the Texas Advanced Computing Center (TACC).

HPC users can view results on their laptops and switch to display walls or a cave. Professional visualization users literally see the same benefits regardless if they are rendering on an institutional cluster or in the cloud.

By switching rendering backends, visualization tools in the HPC community such as VisIt and ParaView allow users to switch between or even combine triangle-based OpenGL rendering with Intel OpenSWR and photorealistic ray-traced rendering with Intel OSPRay.

---

[19]https://itpeernetwork.intel.com/anyscale-visualization-intel-select-solutions/.

Fig. 7.18 OSPRay parallel rendering on TACC's 328 Megapixel Stallion Tiled Display. *Source* Intel

Jim Jeffers (Senior Director and Senior Principle Engineer, Intel Visualization Solutions) notes that the interactive performance delivered by the Intel Rendering Framework and SDVis "addresses the need and creates the want" for photorealistic rendering. Succinctly, interactive ray tracing with its inherent lighting capability lets scientists get more from their data. Again, this message has not been lost on the professional rendering community like movie studios and CAD/CAM software applications.

Navrátil notes, "We expect in situ workflows to become increasingly necessary on Frontera and across all large-scale simulation science." Pointing to the future he states, "In-transit analysis will also play an increasing role as simulations improve support for loosely coupled in situ frameworks. With an in-transit pathway, the simulation resources do not need to be shared for analysis tasks, which is favorable when the analysis is compute-intensive, or when the simulation requires all available resources itself."

"There is a real pull from submarkets like CAD and automotive. Photorealism is extremely important in improving 'virtual' vehicle design and manufacturing from commercial airplanes to military vehicles. Meanwhile, there is increasing pull from adjunct markets that include offline and interactive rendering for animation and photoreal visual effects." adds Jeffers.

Trillion triangle OpenGL hero runs performed by Kitware and the use of in situ and in-transit techniques to render both OpenGL and ray-traced images are examples of SDVis using visualization for peta- and exascale sized research efforts. In situ simulation means that the rendering occurs on the same nodes that perform the computation. This is the reason why Jim Jeffers states, "A picture is worth an exabyte," as no data movement is required! Of course, the in situ technique benefits commercial software vendors as well.

John Stone (Research Staff, The Beckman Institute) points out that improvements in the AVX-512 instruction set in the Intel Xeon Phi (and latest generation Intel Xeon processors) can deliver significant performance improvements for some time-consuming molecular visualization kernels over most existing Intel Xeon CPUs. Based on his recent results using the Intel Xeon Phi hardware exponential instruction Stone notes, "At present, I can say that the Intel Xeon Phi processor is the highest performance CPU result I've benchmarked for this molecular orbital algorithm to date." We discuss Stone's results in greater detail in this article.

Stone's results reflect a change in the visualization community where CPU-based visualization is now both accepted and viewed as fixing a community-wide problem. The 2016 University of Utah presentation, "Towards Direct Visualization on CPU and Xeon Phi,"[20] highlights this change in mindset by noting that "if computing is the third pillar of science then visualization is the fourth pillar" yet, "visualization currently can barely handle mid-gigascale data." This same presentation also notes that visualization "is two orders of magnitude and ten years behind simulation".

If computing is the third pillar of science, then visualization is the fourth pillar—John Stone

The reason is that traditional view to run with OpenGL GPU-based rasterization has been designed for millions of polygons while visualization needs to support billions to trillions of elements. The solution is large-scale CPU-based ray tracing using packages such as OSPRay running on big memory CPU nodes and the use of in situ visualization. Memory capacity is very important, hence the need to use big memory computational nodes. Thus, the mindset to "just use the same GPU graphics we use for games" is disappearing to be replaced with CPU-based Software Defined Visualization (SDVis).

Demonstrations at the Supercomputing 2017 and the Intel Developers Conference in Denver, Colorado, showed that even a device that simply displays an image in a framebuffer (e.g., that renders the image in memory and provides no hardware acceleration) can be used to interactively visualize even the most complex photorealistic images.

For OpenGL users, David DeMarle (visualization luminary and engineer at Kitware) observes that, "CPU-based OpenGL performance does not trail off even when rendering meshes containing one trillion (10^{12}) triangles on the Trinity leadership class supercomputer. Further, we might see a 10–20 trillion triangle per second result as our current benchmark used only 1/19th of the machine." The researcher believes the ability of the CPU to access large amounts of memory is key to realizing trillion triangle per second rendering capability.

---

[20]https://www.intel.com/content/dam/www/public/us/en/documents/presentation/sdvis-research-university.pdf.

However, this is an expensive operation and uses a lot of electricity to accomplish, so typically it is only the petroleum business or military that can afford it.

7.3.2 Public Cloud Rendering Services

Ray tracing is a compute-intensive process, prone to complexity.

With an increasing amount of digital content, the demand for 3D rendering from automotive and aerospace manufacturers, consumer product designers, film studios, graphic designers, animators, and special effects companies is growing rapidly, and as these creative industries adopt ever-higher resolutions (e.g., the transition to 4K video with 8K on the horizon), the compute-intensive nature of the rendering task increases still further. For example, a single frame in an animated movie might take several hours to render, for just one layer and 40 h for all the layers of a single frame one it is composited with an entire feature-length film potentially requiring millions of CPU hours to complete.

Some studios have made the decision to build on-premise render farms (a more mission-specific version of the corporate datacenter), comprising thousands of servers to handle this task—but that is not a cost-effective solution for all but the largest organization to construct and run firsthand. There are also third-party commercial services available that are running large infrastructure installations, but this solution has up to this point suffered from unpredictable performance and workload completion times, unclear total costs, and frequent occurrence of rendering errors.

A public cloud provider like Amazon, Baidu, or Microsoft Azure has servers with high-powered CPUs and GPUs, and most of the popular ray-tracing programs which can be rented for an average cost of a half US penny per GHz hour.

I believe where the ray-tracing software resides and is run will shift to off-premises. This will be due to ray tracing becomes more familiar and companies seek to shift from capital expenses to operational expenses.

The move to the cloud and block-chain render farms will not happen rapidly. There is still concern among many organizations about letting their intellectual property out of their control; old attitudes die slowly.

As users of ray-tracing software send their projects to the cloud and service bureaus, the suppliers of ray-tracing software will have to develop new pricing models and learn how to sell to a different type of client.

The cloud will have the greatest growth in revenue but not the greatest value. Render farms and cloud services providers seldom actually buy (license) a ray-tracing program. The software suppliers charge them a dollar value times the number of processors, per hour. The farms then charge by the clock speed of the processor times the number of cores (within a processor) per minute. Because the rendering farm market is so crowded and therefore competitive (with too many providers chasing too few customers, and a highly irregular demand), the difference (their margin) between what the farms pay the software suppliers and what the farms charge their customers is not very much.

After electricity, rent, internet (including Aspera) and the cost of servers, render farm operators margins can be marginalized. Massive server farms run by AWS/ Google/Microsoft/IBM use excess capacity from other operations to offer cut-rate server prices. Also, through their ability to negotiate preferential agreements with software suppliers smaller render farms need to rely on personal service or specialty rendering to compete. Companies like Scan in LA provide end-to-end VFX services for large difficult jobs that are too challenging even for the big production studios.

Aspera is a data transport and streaming technology company that provides high-speed data transfer solutions to send, share, stream, and sync large files and datasets. Aspera belongs to the hybrid cloud business unit of IBM.

As the cloud market matured, the principles of highly scalable, on-demand infrastructure capacity accessed on a pay-per-use basis became applicable to a wider range of business processes. In the software-as-a-service (SaaS) market, the infrastructure is already abstracted from the customer, who can potentially also make use of a PaaS layer for further application extension or composition.

Platform as a Service (PaaS) or Application Platform as a Service (aPaaS) or platform-based service is a category of cloud computing services that provides a platform allowing customers to develop, run, and manage applications without the complexity of building and maintaining the infrastructure typically associated with developing and launching an app.

At the Infrastructure-as-a-Service (IaaS) layer, despite improvements in management tools and automation, customers must still deal with the provisioning and management of the service. This has led to a rise in managed cloud services, particularly for business-facing applications, whereby customers can take advantage of the benefits of the cloud, without being concerned about the underlying intricacies.

The first question one must ask when it comes to using the cloud for a render farm is what cloud service provider to use?

There are many cloud providers to choose from, and typically each one provides the necessary tools and infrastructure to set up a cloud-hosted render farm. Examples can be found at Amazon EC2, Google Compute Engine, and Microsoft Azure. Google, Amazon, and Azure offer Linux and Windows instances. None of the providers offer Mac OS X instances.

Google has Preemptible Instances.[21] They only run for 24 h and can be terminated by Google prior to that.

Amazon has Spot Instances.[22] These instances work on a bidding system. Basically, when one starts an instance, they also set the maximum price they are willing to pay for it. If the going rate of that instance type is lower than one's bid, then they will get the instance. One then gets charged the going rate of that instance

---

[21]https://cloud.google.com/compute/docs/instances/preemptible.

[22]https://aws.amazon.com/ec2/spot/.

for an hour. At the start of the next instance hour, the bid price and going rate are compared again. If one's bid is lower than the going rate, then their instance will be terminated. This might happen if other people are willing to pay more for the instance type than the user. However, Spot Instances can be expensive during the Christmas season when the extra capacity that Amazon has is taken up for its primary purpose of Amazon sales.

If reliability is what one is looking for then bidding the On-Demand price should be done as, Spot Instances won't typically get that high. The user will get a discount and get the instances.

One of, if not the most important question one needs to ask is how do I want this to look? Will the cloud be used to supplement an existing render farm? Does one want a separate render farm in the cloud to run alongside their local render farm? Or does one not have a render farm and wants to create a farm in the cloud?

Don't think about the cloud as a strange new platform. Think of it as a remote office. Many of the concepts and considerations one would use when starting a remote office also apply to the cloud.

7.3.2.1   Assets

Getting one's assets to and from the cloud is an important step in the rendering process. Assets are any files your jobs need to render. Assets are also any output your jobs create. Getting your files up to the cloud and back down to your local network is a key part of cloud rendering.

One can create a Virtual Private Network (VPN) between their local network and the cloud network. The instances will be able to access one's assets the same way an on-premise node does.

Some companies do not allow for VPN use. In that case, one may have to move all required assets to a file server that is shared out to one's nodes. The files can be manually moved up and down, and one can use a Dropbox, OneDrive type service.

Another option is to use cloud storage. All of the providers offer cloud storage as a service, like Amazon S3 for example. They also charge for egress and ingress. Having Aspera is a requirement to make sure there are no faults for moving really big projects.

7.3.2.2   Render License

How does one license Deadline and all the software that is needed? Much like assets, one can set up a VPN between their on-premise network and their cloud network. With a VPN, one's instances will be able to connect to their current license server exactly like their on-premise machines do.

One can also put a license server in the cloud and have their instances get their licenses from there; however, instances can be terminated (due to outages, etc.). Restarting one's license server could become a problem as most licenses use the

MAC Address of the machine they are running on for authentication. A restarted license server won't have the same MAC Address as the old one, thus breaking one's licensing.

Another option is to use Deadline Usage Based Licensing. One only pays for the render time used, one can start as many nodes as they want (one doesn't need a floating license for each node), and one doesn't need a license server. One can use Usage Based Licensing to license Deadline itself along with several third-party rendering software. The Thinkbox Marketplace has pricing and availability.

Usage Based Licensing can also be used to supplement all of one's existing licenses. What's good about that is that all of one's on-premise render nodes can use the permanent licenses they already have, while the cloud render nodes only use what they need with Usage Based Licensing.

7.3.3 Private Rendering Services—Farms

A render farm is a high-performance computer system, e.g., a computer cluster, built to render computer-generated imagery (CGI), typically for film and television visual effects.

Render farm services are offered by private, third-party firms and individuals, and by hardware and software suppliers. For example, hardware companies like HP and Nvidia will sometimes make their render farms available to clients. Software vendors like Chaos Group have a render farm serve for V-Ray.

The term render farm was born during the production of the Autodesk 3D Studio animated short The Bored Room[23] in July 1990 when, to meet an unrealistic deadline, a room filled with Compaq 386 computers was configured to do the rendering. At the time, the system wasn't networked, so each computer had to be set up by hand to render a specific animation sequence. The rendered images would then be "harvested" via a rolling platform to a large-format optical storage drive, then loaded frame by frame to a Sony CRV disk.

The Autodesk technician assigned to manage this early render farm (Jamie Clay) had a regular habit of wearing farmer's overalls and the product manager for the software (Bob Bennett) joked that what Clay was doing was farming the frames and at that moment he named the collection of computers a render farm.

This is also where the term render wrangler came from. These are the people who keep the farm running and ensure that the frames are queued up with the correct priority. Described as "the keeper of the render," a render wrangler is the last person who sees the animation before its final output to film and video.[24]

A list of rendering farms by country, software, and hardware can be found at https://rentrender.com/all-render-farms-list/.

---

[23]https://www.youtube.com/watch?v=sCXqWO7FVzY.

[24]https://en.wikipedia.org/wiki/Render_farm.

7.3.4   Rendering Service Organizations

In addition to public and private rendering resources, organizations can employ a service bureau to do the rendering for them. Such service bureaus have trained experts in rendering in general and ray tracing specifically. They have most of the leading ray-tracing programs and probably all of the free programs.

One such firm is **VizSource** in San Diego, which has successfully completed thousands of projects and offers 3D renderings as low as $400 per rendering with a 5-day delivery of proof rendering.

Another rendering service organization is **Super-Cheap Architectural Renders**, a dedicated architectural visualization team (Fig. 7.19).

The company states its mission as providing premium quality photorealistic images at a fraction of the cost, with an exceptional level of customer service. The company offers to help architects in the property market get ahead by benefiting from the realism of images and taking advantage of the company's price point. It is a global company with offices in the USA, the UK, Dubai, Australia, and New Zealand.

Such bureaus offer architectural renderings, interior design renderings, product renderings, and more. Typically, one sends the bureau a CAD or hand drawing of what is desired to be rendered.

Fig. 7.19 Suplex development rendering. *Source* Super-Cheap Architectural Renders

7.4 Benchmarking Ray Tracing

Ray tracing, as everyone knows, is a simple algorithm that can totally consume a processor. But how much a given processor is consumed is an unanswerable question because it depends upon the scene and of course the processor itself. So, approximations have to be made, and parameters fixed to get a consistent comparison. Then it is left to the buyer to extrapolate the results to his or her situation.

Ray tracing is done on three platforms and soon four. Ray tracing is run on servers, workstations, and PCs, and has been demonstrated on tablets. Non-geometric-based ray tracing is also run on supercomputers in field simulations ranging from optical analysis to nuclear explosions and fusion reactions.

7.4.1 SPEC

At the workstation, server and supercomputing levels, the Standard Performance Evaluation Corporation—SPEC—has offered benchmarks based on professional applications since 1988.[25] SPEC is a nonprofit corporation whose membership is open to any company or organization that is willing to support the group's goals (and pay dues). Originally a bunch of people from hardware vendors devising CPU metrics, SPEC has evolved into an umbrella organization encompassing four diverse groups.

SPEC does not have a benchmark that focuses solely on ray tracing. That is because all SPEC benchmarks are based on applications, not specific functionality within applications. There are many tests within those application-based benchmarks (especially those from the SPEC Graphics and Workstation Performance Group—SPEC/GWPG) that test ray tracing functionality, but the performance measurement is related to how an application performs as a whole on the system being tested. These types of tests more accurately reflect what a user would experience in the real world when running a professional application.

SPEC/GWPG produces benchmarks that work on top of actual applications (SPECapc) and ones that are based primarily on traces of applications (SPECviewperf for graphics performance and SPECworkstation for comprehensive workstation performance). Members contributing to benchmark development include AMD, Dell, Fujitsu, HP, Intel, Lenovo, and Nvidia (Fig 7.20).

In 2018, SPEC released SPECworkstation 3, comprising more than 30 workloads containing nearly 140 tests to exercise CPU, graphics, I/O, and memory bandwidth. The workloads are divided by application categories that include media and entertainment (3D animation, rendering), product development (CAD/CAM/CAE), life sciences (medical, molecular), financial services, energy (oil and gas), general operations, and GPU compute (Fig. 7.21).

---

[25]https://www.spec.org/spec/.

Fig. 7.20 "Tribute to Myrna Loy" by Ive (2008). The figure is Vicky 4.1 from DAZ. The author, Ive, created it with Blender by using all images of her that he could find as reference. Rendered with POV-Ray beta 25 using 7 light sources (and the "area_illumination" feature)

Accurately representing GPU performance for a wide range of professional applications poses a unique set of challenges for benchmark developers such as SPEC/GWPG. Applications behave very differently, so producing a benchmark that

Fig. 7.21 Scene from the updated LuxRender workload

measures a variety of application behaviors and runs in a reasonable amount of time presents difficulties.

Even within a given application, different models and modes can produce very different GPU behavior, so ensuring sufficient test coverage is a key to producing a comprehensive performance picture.

Another major consideration is recognizing the differences between CPU and GPU performance measurement. Generally speaking, the CPU has architecture with many complexities that allow it to execute a wide variety of codes quickly. The GPU, on the other hand, is purpose-built to execute pretty much the same set of operations on many pieces of data, such as shading every pixel on the screen with the same set of operations.

The SPECworkstation 3 suite for measuring GPU compute performance includes three workloads. The ray-tracing test uses LuxMark, a benchmark based on the new LuxCore physically based renderer, to render a chrome sphere resting on a grid of numbers in a beach scene.

SPEC also offers viewsets within its SPECviewperf 13 and SPECworkstation 3 benchmarks that include ray-tracing functionality based on real-world application traces. For example, the maya-05 viewset was created from traces of the graphics workload generated by the Maya 2017 application from Autodesk.

The viewset includes numerous rendering modes supported by the application, including shaded mode, ambient occlusion, multi-sample anti-aliasing, and transparency. All tests are rendered using Viewport 2.0.

One thing to consider in benchmarking ray-tracing performance is that it doesn't happen in a void. Even in a SPEC test that is predominantly centered on ray tracing, there is a lot of other stuff happening that impacts performance, including application overhead, housekeeping, and implementation peculiarities. These need to be considered for any performance measurement to be representative of what happens in the real world.

In addition to benchmarks from consortiums such as SPEC, some ray-tracing software suppliers offer their own benchmark programs.

7.4.2   Underwriter Labs Futuremark

For PCs, the leading benchmark supplier is Underwriter Labs Futuremark team. Finland-based Futuremark has been making PC graphics benchmarks since 1997[26] and in 2018 announced their ray-tracing benchmark 3DMark Port Royal, the first dedicated real-time ray-tracing benchmark for gamers. One can use Port Royal to test and compare the real-time ray-tracing performance of any graphics AIB that supports Microsoft DirectX ray tracing (Fig. 7.22).

Port Royal uses DirectX ray tracing to enhance reflections, shadows, and other effects that are difficult to achieve with traditional rendering techniques.

As well as benchmarking performance, 3DMark Port Royal is a realistic and practical example of what to expect from ray tracing in upcoming games— ray-tracing effects running in real time at reasonable frame rates at 2560 × 1440 resolution.

3DMark Port Royal was developed with input from AMD, Intel, Nvidia, and other leading technology companies. UL worked especially closely with Microsoft to create an implementation of the DirectX ray tracing API.

Port Royal will run on any graphics AIB with drivers that support DirectX ray tracing. As with any new technology, there are limited options for early adopters, but more AIBs are expected to get DirectX ray-tracing support.

7.4.3   Blender's Open Data Benchmark

Blender Institute prepared six Blender files for testing its ray-tracing program Cycles. Rendering time with CPU and GPU, using various settings and design styles but based on actual production setups, is used for the testing.

---

[26]https://en.wikipedia.org/wiki/Futuremark.

Fig. 7.22 Real-time ray tracing promises to bring new levels of realism to in-game graphics. *Source* Underwriter Labs

The goal is to have an overview of systems that are used or tested by developers of Cycles. Blender plans to update the benchmark regularly, when new hardware comes in—and especially when render features improve in Cycles.

Most strikingly so-far is that the performance of CPUs is in a similar range as GPUs, especially when compared to the costs of hardware. When shots get more complex, CPUs win the performance battle.

"That confirms our own experience that fast GPU is great for previewing and lighting work," said Ton Roosendaal, Chairman of the Blender Organization. "A fast CPU is great for the production rendering. But … who knows what the future brings."

The six scenes shown in Fig. 7.23 have been selected by the Blender team and are based on production setups with various use cases; indoor, outdoor, characters with hair, hard surface.

The benchmark consists of two parts: a downloadable package which runs Blender and renders on several production files, and the Open Data portal on blender.org, where the results can be (optionally) uploaded. All results are open access and free to be shared.

The benchmark bundle is available for download on opendata.blender.org. Here, also thousands of test results can be reviewed and downloaded.

Fig. 7.23 Blender's Cycles six benchmark test scenes

7.4.4 Chaos Group

Chaos Group has a V-Ray benchmark. The V-Ray benchmark is a free stand-alone application to help users test how fast their hardware renders. The benchmark includes two test scenes, one for GPUs and another for CPUs, depending on the processor type you'd like to measure. V-Ray benchmark does not require a V-Ray license to run.

One launches the application and runs the tests. After the tests are complete, the user can share the results online and see how his or her hardware compares to others at benchmark.chaosgroup.com. The company recommends noting any special hardware modifications that have been made like water cooling or overclocking (Fig. 7.24).

Fig. 7.24 V-Ray benchmark tests. *Source* Chaos Group

Chaos Group says if one is looking to benchmark their render farm or cloud, they can try the command-line interface to test without a GUI. V-Ray benchmark runs on Windows, Mac OS, and Linux.

7.4.5 Redshift Benchmark

In 2017, the company introduced a benchmarking utility for its GPU-based production renderer. The benchmark, which is built into the current release works with the 3ds Max, Cinema 4D, and Houdini editions of the software, and with a little tweaking on Windows, Linux, and macOS.

7.4.6 Summary

Benchmarking will always be a challenge. There are two classes of benchmarking, synthetic or simulated, and application-based. SPEC uses application based, and UL uses synthetic. The workload or script of a benchmark is always subject for criticism, especially by suppliers whose products don't do well in the tests. The complaint is that the script (of actions in the application-based test) or the simulation (in the synthetic tests) doesn't reflect real-world workloads or usage. That is statistically correct to a degree. However, SPEC benchmarks either run on top of actual applications or are developed based on traces of applications performing the same work as in the real world. Also, the organizations developing these benchmarks have been doing this work, and only this work, for over two decades, longer than the life of some of their critics, and over that period and with that much-accumulated experience they can be considered experts.

Benchmarking is used to prove the performance of one processor over another. Ray tracing does not need specific hardware to support it explicitly. Any processor that can be programmed can execute a ray-tracing algorithm and produce a display file.

In Nvidia's case, they added RTX cores which are built in a way that makes them more suited for the calculations necessary for ray tracing and are explicitly supported it in their API. Including specialized processors just means one can do more of these calculations on less space, using less power and less time. It does not mean that hardware without these specialized processors can't do it, or even that it would be that much slower. In fact, GPUs are already pretty well-suited to this task as-is.

References

Amdahl GM (1967) Validity of the single processor approach to achieving large-scale computing capabilities. AFIPS conference proceedings 30:483–485. https://doi.org/10.1145/1465482. 1465560

Carr A, Hall JD, Hart JC (2002) The ray engine. In: Proceedings of graphics hardware 2002, Sept 2002, pp 37–46. Available from https://www.researchgate.net/publication/234783725_The_Ray_Engine. Accessed 26 Jan 2019.

Peddie J (1996) Advance rendering technology ray-tracing chip. The PC graphics report, 2 Jan 1996, vol IX, no 1, p 5

Peddie J (1998) Mitsubishi real-time volume renderer—vg500. The Peddie report, 19 Oct 1998, vol XI, no 41, p 1365

Peddie J (2005) Mercury takes off with new partners and cell processors. Jon Peddie's TechWatch, 15 Aug 2005, vol 5, no 16, p 27

Peddie J (2010) Imagination technologies to acquire caustic graphics developer of real-time ray-tracing graphics technology. Jon Peddie's TechWatch, 21 Dec 2010, p 9

Peddie J (2014) Siliconarts' RayCore ray-tracing processor. Jon Peddie's TechWatch, 26 Aug 2014, vol 14, no 17, p 19

Pfister H et al (1999) The VolumePro real-time ray-casting system. Mitsubishi Electric Research Laboratories, TR99, 19 Apr 1999. http://www.merl.com/publications/docs/TR99-19.pdf

Purcell TJ, Buck I, Mark WR, Hanrahan P (2002) Ray tracing on programmable graphics hardware. In: Proceedings of SIGGRAPH, July 2002. ACM Trans Graph 21(3):703–712

Szirmay-Kalos L, Purgathofer W (1998) Global ray-bundle tracing with hardware acceleration. In: Rendering techniques '98, proceedings of the Eurographics workshop in Vienna, Austria, 29 June–1 July 1998. Euro http://citeseerx.ist.psu.edu/viewdoc/download;jsessionid= 5828E586A04A651093455F4332F5FF8D?doi=10.1.1.79.1717&rep=rep1&type=pdf

Wald I, Slusallek P, Benthin C, Wagner M (2001) Interactive rendering with coherent ray tracing. Proceedings of EUROGRAPHICS. Comput Graph Forum 20(3):153–164

Woop S, Schmittler J, Slusallek P (2005) RPU: a programmable ray processing unit for real-time ray tracing. ACM Trans Graph 24(3):434–444

Chapter 8
Ray-Tracing Programs and Plug-ins

Abstract There are 70 or so ray-tracing programs available, plus ray-tracing capabilities in many major CAD, 3D modeling, and content creation programs. The idea of creating a photorealistic, physically accurate synthetic image is so compelling and exciting; literally, hundreds of people have tried to do over the past 60 years. It takes such specialized skill and such an extensive material library that no single program can satisfy all the needs of all applications or stages of a project. It is not uncommon for a film or design studio to employ two to five different ray-tracing programs on one project. That reveals how vast the requirements are and why there are so many programs. And many of the programs are free, so there is no economic barrier to using ray tracing.

I look at ray tracing as being used in a pipeline. I have approached it by visualizing a four-stage pipeline, starting with conceptualization, into the design, then manufacturing, and finally marketing. I see the use of ray tracing in the stages of development of a product in the four stages of the pipeline from idea to consumer. Moreover, please note, by a product I mean, and include anything from a washing machine to a movie, from a medical training scenario to an analysis of a body scan, from an airplane or car design to the simulation of the airplane flying or the car crashing. Physically accurate modeling, virtual prototyping, and data analysis are essential for product satisfaction, safety, reproducibility, and reliability.

- Stand-alone
- Integrated
- Plug-in
- Middleware
- Other

The market for ray tracing is entering a new phase. This is partially due to improved and readily available low-cost processors (thank you Moore's law), but more importantly because of the demand and need for accurate virtual prototyping and improved workflows (Fig. 8.1).

© Springer Nature Switzerland AG 2019   181
J. Peddie, *Ray Tracing: A Tool for All*,
https://doi.org/10.1007/978-3-030-17490-3_8

Fig. 8.1 Rendering in the cloud using GPUs. *Source* OneRender

With any market, there is a 20/80 rule, where 20% of the suppliers represent 80% of the market. The ray-tracing market may be even more unbalanced. There would appear to be too many suppliers in the market despite failures and merger and acquisition activities. At the same time, many competing suppliers have been able to successfully coexist by offering features customized for their most important customers.

This section includes all the popular stand-alone ray-tracing programs. The caveat "well-known" is used to excuse me if I missed a program that the reader thought should be included. As mentioned earlier, this book is about geometry-based ray tracing and does not embrace field, optical, audio, or other non-3D (virtual or real) ray-tracing applications or software.

The programs are listed followed by the company name.

I have segmented the market into four categories: integrated (e.g., Autodesk's Raytracer), stand-alone (e.g., V-Ray), plug-in (almost everyone), and middleware (e.g., OptiX). I have identified 71 ray-tracing programs from integrated to stand-alone and plug-ins. Of that population, I have found 21 that are free.

In some cases, there is a version of a stand-alone program that is a plug-in. In a few cases, some plug-ins are all that are offered by a supplier (Fig. 8.2).

In a few cases a supplier may offer a stand-alone, and integrated, and plug-in versions, or a supplier that offers a stand-alone and plug-ins, may have their program integrated into a modeling program. So just about every combination that can be imagined found.

Many stand-alone ray-tracing programs are also available as a plug-in for other applications. Therefore, they are listed twice, albeit briefly in the plug-in section.

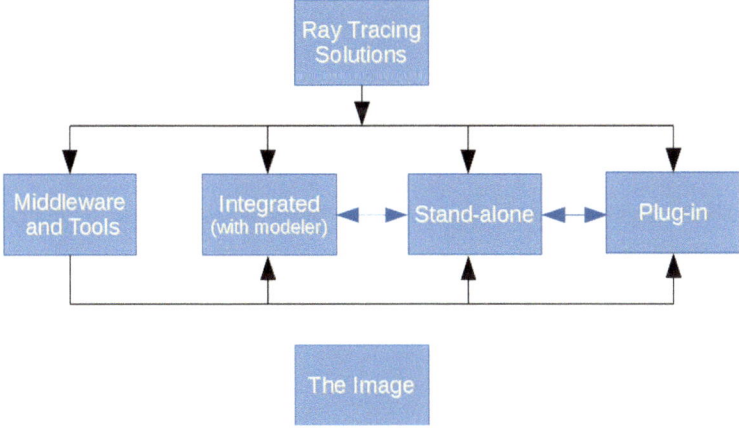

Fig. 8.2 Ray-tracing taxonomy

On average, three ray-tracing companies a year have been started since 1968 amounting to 93 organizations totally. I plotted the start dates of the surviving 61 companies (Fig. 8.3).

The following sections list some of the more popular programs.

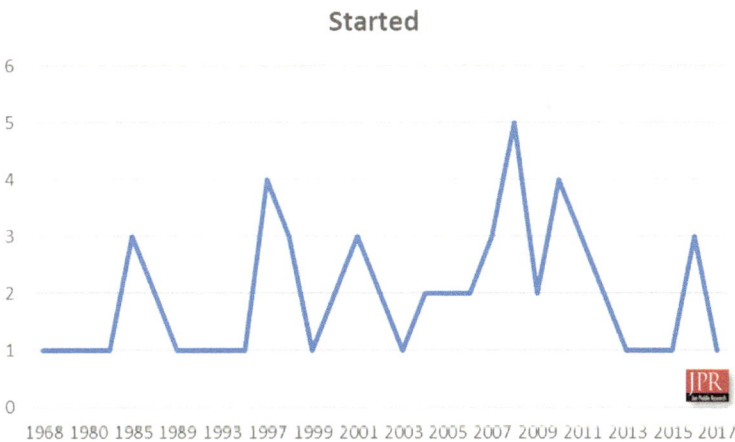

Fig. 8.3 Start-up of ray-tracing companies over time

8.1 Stand-Alone Ray-Tracing Programs

Stand-alone software is any software application that does not come bundled with, or require, another software package in order to run. Essentially, it is software that can stand on its own without help from the Internet or another computer process.

The programs listed in this section are such stand-alone programs that create ray-traced images from data files from other programs and put out an image file for display and printing.

Many of the companies offering a stand-alone program also offer a plug-in version.

8.1.1 3Delight—Illumination Research

It is founded by Pierre Lachapelle and Aghiles Kheffache in 1999. In 1985, when computer-generated character animation was in its infancy, Lachapelle won international acclaim and a host of awards with his animated short, *Tony de Peltrie*, which gave the world a look into the future of computer-generated characters. That was a year before Pixar was spun out from Lucas as a private corporation.

Since then, Lachapelle has been actively building an elaborate 3D animation studio in Montreal, further advancing state-of-the-art character animation. Some of his accomplishments include many firsts: computer-animated crowd, hair, clothing, and 3D paint.

3Delight runs on Microsoft Windows, OS X, and Linux. DNA Research developed it and for a while was a subsidiary of Taarna Studios. In 2003, the company renamed itself Illumination Research and left Taarna who had been an early investor and customer. The administration/head office is in Singapore. A core R&D team is in Montreal. Additional development contributors spread all over the world.

The renderer became first publicly available in 2000 and was the first RenderMan-compliant renderer combining the REYES algorithm with on-demand ray tracing. The only other RenderMan-compliant renderer capable of ray tracing at the time was BMRT. BMRT was not a REYES renderer though.

3Delight was meant to be a commercial product from the beginning. However, DNA decided to make it available free of charge from August 2000 to March 2005 to build a user base.

Illumination Research specializes in rendering solutions for the VFX and animation production pipeline. 3Delight was their first program and introduced in 2002, and the company takes pride in the software was used in countless feature films and commercials.

With 3Delight, one has the option to choose between two rendering engines: Path Tracing (default) and REYES. The choice is made through the simple Render Mode menu option in the render engine group of attributes of the render settings.

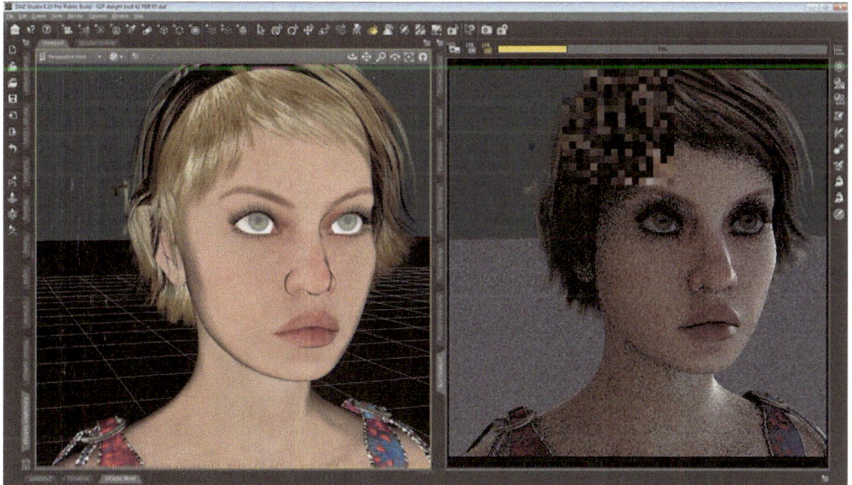

Fig. 8.4 An example of 3Delight capabilities. *Source* Illumination Research

Using REYES does not preclude one from using ray tracing, which can still run on top of REYES for any secondary rays (Fig. 8.4).

Their current product line includes 3Delight, 3Delight for Daz Studio, Maya, and 3Delight for Katana. They also made public their upcoming rendering service in the form of 3Delight Cloud which is still in testing.

3Delight Core technologies

3Delight is a unidirectional forward path tracer, said to be able to withstand the needs of modern production rendering. The company mentions the software as being able to render large scenes with an optimal memory footprint and efficient processing scalability. To accommodate efficiency and versatility, 3Delight interfaces through the below technologies:

- **Nodal Scene Interface**—It enables 3Delight to be light and flexible in live rendering. Additional functionality can be added easily to the open standard API, making it usable for many programs and production needs.
- **Open Shading Language**—3Delight has the OSL technology at its core which enables efficient coupling of shading and ray tracing.

Key features

Raytrace Motion Blur—Enables or disables motion blur for traced rays. For example, a moving object as seen in a mirror shows motion blur only if this option is enabled.

Raytrace Displacements—Enables or disables ray tracing of accurate geometric displacements. The default is to ray-trace displacements as bump maps (a displaced surface appears bump-mapped in a mirror reflection). Enabling this feature makes ray tracing slower and forces 3Delight to use more memory so one should use this option with care.

Raytrace Bias—It specifies a bias for rays starting point to avoid potentially erroneous intersections with the emitting surface.

Unified sampling

3Delight has been equipped with a rapidly converging light sampling algorithm which allows rendering large amounts of light sources. A multiple importance sampling algorithm can combine samples from lights, materials, and environments to produce anti-aliased images along with the earlier mentioned algorithm. Volumes, such as atmospheres and OpenVDB (see Glossary), leverage from the same technology. This results in a single point of control on shading quality. The artist is thus happy not to be involved in sample count adjustments on both materials and lights.

Cloud rendering

3Delight has cloud rendering integrated at the core which allows the user to decide if the rendering is to occur through the CPU or remotely. 3Delight takes care of data management where a registered user account is utilized with rendering credits with the 3Delight Cloud rendering service.

Multi-light technology

3Delight can pass each light or group of lights through its own AOV/layer which allows the correct light manipulation during compositing. These kinds of light layers can also be the output to 3Delight Display for real-time interactive adjustments in HD resolution.

Incandescence lights

3Delight has an option of incandescence lights which is used to the incandescence of scene objects that are not originally illuminated. This functionality is also utilized to light grouped objects using a single incandescence light and control their light emission together.

Multi-camera rendering

3Delight can render a scene or image from multiple views simultaneously using shared scene geometry which allows for efficient stereo rendering. Each of the several cameras can have their own quality and color settings.

Precise geometric surfaces

3Delight renders curved surfaces free of faceting artifacts, while displaced geometry is rendered to subpixel level. The absence of pretessellation geometry leads to faster start-up times.

Network caching

3Delight optimizes network traffic by caching of server-side textures and NSI geometries into local storage without user intervention.

3Delight Cloud is a technology that allows artists to render interactively from their workstation using thousands of cores, and 3DelightNSI is a fast and simple-to-use path tracer built on top of the nimble Nodal Scene Interface (NSI) and Open Shading Language (OSL).

3Delight Cloud and 3DelightNSI are available through artist-friendly integration with Foundry's Katana and Autodesk Maya.

3Delight Cloud features ease of use. It is as simple as selecting 3Delight Cloud and pressing "Render." No manual data upload or download is required. Also, images render interactively with thousands of cores. An image that takes hours to render on a powerful workstation renders in mere minutes using 3Delight Cloud. It also features simple and affordable per-minute billing at a rate of two-cents per minute per slice of 24 cores. There are no storage fees and no data transfer fees.

8.1.1.1 Summary

Being in the industry for a decent period and with the connections the company has built over the years coupled with the technical superiorities, 3Delight has been a successful product in the market. Users have been praising its operational speed and rendering quality of complex objects like hairs, furs, etc. However, some people feel that they should have more options particularly with the functions available to the users particularly when compared to V-Ray and Indigo Renderer. As the company brings out new versions, they will surely improve upon this function as well.

Used mainly in Europe by people who liked the RenderMan style interface, it is not supported by any render farms except maybe Rayvision in China, and Rayvisiosn was just a small operation in 2019.

8.1.2 Appleseed

Appleseed was founded in May 2009 by François Beaune, a former rendering engineer from the core R&D team at Mental Images.

In October 2011, the development of Appleseed benefited from a technology sharing agreement with Jupiter Jazz Limited and received funding for one year. Since October 2012, Appleseed relies on the continued effort of talented volunteers. Appleseed is an open-source, physically based global illumination rendering engine primarily designed for animation and visual effects.

Appleseed implements a modern workflow based on Path Tracing that enables artifact-free, single-pass rendering with minimal technical tuning. It is

Fig. 8.5 Country Kitchen by Blend Swap user Jay-Artist

simultaneously capable of strictly unbiased rendering when total accuracy matters, and biased rendering when artistic freedom and shorter rendering time are paramount (Fig. 8.5).

Appleseed supports fully programmable shading via Sony Pictures Imageworks Open Shading Language (OSL), RGB, and spectral rendering, fast and robust transformation and deformation motion blur, ray-traced subsurface scattering, exhaustive Python and C++ APIs, and many other production-oriented features.

The program has support for all kinds of motion blur on par with all kinds of commercial renderers like V-Ray or mental ray. Appleseed supports transformation motion blur with as many steps as one wants and also curved, plus deformation motion blur with as many segments as desired, and it is fast.

Appleseed is a CPU renderer. The reason why it is CPU only is that it supports programmable shading through OSL which is only available (currently) for the CPU. It also supports other forms of programmability, for example, Disney SeExpr, which allow it to combine layers with formulas. It does not run on the GPU, and if it did run on the GPU, it is questionable whether it would be very efficient. The organization doesn't have plans for GPU support yet. The team is also interested in rendering large scenes with lots of geometry and textures. Right now, one cannot do that on the GPU unless one has expensive GPU with like 24 GB of RAM and there are not so many on the market. Appleseed wants to support large scenes and lots of flexibility by programmable shading which is not feasible on the GPU.

Regarding the market, it is true that GPU rendering is attractive for smaller studios because it cuts rendering times by an order of magnitude. However, the company believes there is a market for a more flexible renderer that can do things you may not be able to do with a GPU renderer. You also have to keep in mind that Appleseed is still kind of a hobby project which the developers do in their free time, and they don't want to fight with GPU incompatibilities, driver problems, and things like the split between OpenCL and CUDA. That is another reason why they are not engaging with the GPU right now.

Along with the core renderer, the team is actively developing high-quality integrations for common digital content creation applications:

- Appleseed for Maya
- Appleseed for 3ds Max
- Appleseed for Blender

Appleseed is also the default rendering engine of Image Engine's Gaffer.

Appleseed is actively developed by a small, international team of volunteers from the animation and VFX industry. Its core mission is to provide individuals and small studios with a complete, reliable, fully open rendering package.

Over the years, Appleseed has been used on several projects including TV documentaries, ads, promotional videos, and animation short.

Volume rendering is a major feature the team is developing. Just like for the rest of Appleseed they want robust support for volumes in the sense that are fully path-traced volumes, so the only bias they will get will be noise. Together with subsurface scattering, volume and subsurface scattering are interconnected fields. Subsurface scattering is a form of volume. A considerable research about fast path-traced volumes has been published, some of it by Solid Angle, the makers of Arnold.

8.1.2.1 Summary

Founder Beaune lives in Annecy; the town of the Annecy animation festival is a large festival for animation with worldwide reach.

Somewhat similar to LuxRender, Appleseed is an open-source volunteer group of CG enthusiasts who are contributing their time and passion to the development of a powerful ray-tracing rendering tool. As mentioned elsewhere, "I have identified 21 organizations offering free ray-tracing software. However, although there are a lot of open-source renderers on the market none of them," says Beaune, "really targets animation."

In 2019, Autodesk added the toon shader to Arnold as part of a non-photorealistic rendering (NPR) solution that is provided in combination with the contour filter.

8.1.3   Arnold—Autodesk (Solid Angle)

One evening in 1999, Marcos after working with Station X Studios in Los Angeles, he and two friends went to see an Arnold Schwarzenegger film, "End of Days." His friends imitated the Arnold accent from the rear of the theater, cracking up the audience. Marcos had never realized what a distinctive voice Schwarzenegger had since he had only seen Arnold films in Spain, where US films are dubbed. Andy Lesniak, one of the friends at the theater, suggested "Arnold" as a joke, and Marcos liked it. Marcos then started showing images from Arnold on the Web. The code name was picked up by people, so the name became permanent. He is thought of choosing something more professional, but "Arnold" now has a reputation, so he hasn't changed it (yet).

Marcos Fajardo is the chief architect of Arnold. The beginnings of what is now Arnold emerged in 1997 when Fajardo, 24 at the time, decided to write his own renderer. That year, he attended SIGGRAPH, where his interest in stochastic ray tracing (a foundational part of Arnold's rendering technology) was piqued in discussions with friends attending the conference.

Arnold is an unbiased, physically based, ray-tracing 3D rendering application created by the company Solid Angle. Solid Angle, and the Arnold Renderer were acquired by Autodesk in 2016. As part of the ongoing integration process, Arnold transitioned to the Autodesk Licensing Framework on July 25, 2017.

Arnold is an advanced unidirectional stochastic Monte Carlo ray-tracing renderer targeted at animation and visual effect studios. Unlike RenderMan, Arnold uses ray tracing for direct and indirect lighting. Arnold has about 200,000 lines of highly optimized C++ code, and it is considered a very direct implementation without a lot of software hacks or tricks.

Arnold has supported plug-ins available for Maya, Houdini, Cinema 4D, 3ds Max, and Katana. The Arnold plug-in for Softimage is now available under an Apache2.0 open-source license.

The program has evolved and had features added to it over the years including hair and fur, a memory-efficient ray-traced curve primitive to help create complex fur and hair renders, 3D motion blur that interacts with shadows, volumes, indirect lighting, reflection, or refraction, and volumetric rendering for effects such as smoke, clouds, fog, pyroclastic flow, and fire.

In the latest version, some of the highlights are:

- new path-traced, random walk SSS engine that provides more accurate results in concavities and thin geometry
- frustum-based tessellation
- new car paint shader
- revamped and optimized triplanar
- flakes and shadow matte shaders
- improved UDIM accuracy
- AOV/alpha transmission, improved volume sampling of low-spread area lights
- big memory savings in procedural namespaces
- A new maketx binary (to convert images to tiled, MIP-mapped textures) with optimizations and improved color space support.

Random walk subsurface scattering

In 2017, Arnold introduced random walk subsurface scattering, a new, more accurate way of calculating SSS. Unlike the empirical BSSRDF method (see Glossary) based on diffusion theory, this method traces below the surface with a random walk and makes no assumptions about the geometry being locally flat. This means it can take into account anisotropic scattering like brute-force volume rendering and produces better results around concavities and small details. It can also be substantially faster for large scattering radius (i.e., large mean free path) compared to the other methods (Fig. 8.6).

On the other hand, the new method can be slower in dense media and it does not support blending two surfaces together, may require redialing materials to achieve a similar look, and is more sensitive to non-closed meshes, "mouth bags," eyeballs, and internal geometry potentially casting shadows. The default is to use the old empirical diffusion method in order not to break the look of the existing scenes.

Subdivision frustum culling

Arnold allows subdivision patches outside the view or dicing camera frustum to not be subdivided. This is useful for any extended surface that is only partially visible as only the directly visible part will be subdivided, potentially saving memory and subdivision time in complex scenes. Similarly, no subdivision work will happen if a mesh is not directly visible. This can be turned on globally and can be turned off for specific meshes. The global option adds a world space padding to the frustum that can be increased as needed to minimize artifacts from objects that straddle the frustum boundaries.

Materials

The company currently provides a limited library of sample materials in its documentation, with many third-party vendors providing additional material libraries

Fig. 8.6 Diffusion versus random subsurface scattering. *Source* Autodesk

(i.e., Greyscalegorilla). With material interoperability, Autodesk has been a strong supporter of the MaterialX open-source material standard, contributing directly as well as creating the ShaderX library to help facilitate MaterialX interop with other 3D DCC applications.

Car paint shader

A dedicated car paint shader has been added to the latest version of Arnold, which can be thought of as the combination of a simplified version of shaders. This shader can create a range of car paint looks without having to connect several nodes. For example, a pearlescent effect can be added to both the specular and flakes layers by tweaking a few parameters.

An arbitrary number of layers of flakes can be used. The flakes at a deep layer are covered by the ones closest to the surface and more tinted by pigments.

GPU acceleration

Arnold GPU has run beta tests and is now getting it in the hands of users. Arnold GPU makes full use of Nvidia's RTX technology and says the company has been developed in jointly with Nvidia.

Arnold GPU is built using Nvidia's OptiX library and currently runs exclusively on Nvidia hardware.

Typically, 30–50% is spent tracing rays; the rest is mostly shading. With RTX, tracing time is cut in half and render time is now mostly shading.

Cached Playback

Autodesk offers a feature in Maya for fast viewport viewing called Cached Playback. It isn't really about real-time ray tracing, but it is about caching data in a scene in advance, so it can be played back much faster than if Maya had to calculate each frame in real time when the user clicks the play button.

Caching the individual frames would be more like what a Playblast does in Maya —it renders a viewport camera video playback for each frame that is animated, so it can be watched in real time. That means the one camera angle plays back and it is not interactive, so changes cannot be made as you watch it.

Since Cached Playback is caching the data from a scene, it means the playback can be watched within the actual viewport of Maya. The extension of this is that it is possible to tumble or zoom the viewport camera, while the animation is playing back to see it from different angles. It also means that the animator can interact with the animated content (i.e., make changes) right away.

It is precaching the frames. Within Maya, the artist can see the progress of Cached Playback as the little blue bar that progresses along the timeline. Blue (or the set color) means that frame is cached. When a file is opened, it takes a moment for Maya to cache the data. Then, when a change is made in the scene, the frame will change from color to grayed out, and then back to color when it is recached.

Sheen

Shader enhancements include a new Cell Noise shader and new Sheen function in the Standard Surface shader to render cloth-like microfiber materials or the peach fuzz on a face. Sheen layer can be used to approximate microfiber, cloth-like surfaces such as velvet, and satin of varying roughness. Sheen is layered onto the diffuse component, and its weight is determined with this attribute. Sheen can be thought of as the density or the combination of the density and length of the fibers. Sheen is an approximation in the sense that it does not model the fabric structure itself but is nevertheless a good model for a large variety of cloth-like materials.

8.1.3.1 Summary

Autodesk recognized the importance of rendering and ray tracing specifically and felt Arnold represented the right mix of proven technology with a great product road map, as well as many happy users. It is also worth mentioning that the Arnold team, from Marcos Fajardo to Fred Servant and everyone else on the team, are all passionate about the art and science of rendering.

Ray-tracing technology has many applications. Arnold has been focused on the M&E space, specifically VFX and animation, but with its integration with 3ds Max, and Autodesk is seeing many new users in design (i.e., architectural visualization and design visualization) who are adopting it. Pipelines vary across industries, but Arnold's architecture and API are very flexible, so expect Autodesk to integrate it in other areas where it makes the most sense.

Some of the target markets are arch viz, industrial viz, motion graphics, and FX. Before the acquisition by Autodesk, if one worked at a small studio and only does furniture rendering for example, then Arnold may have been too expensive. However, Arnold interactive rendering is now available for free in Maya and Max makes it interesting for small studios, and more and more students are now trained in Arnold because it is shipping with those DCCs by default. However, granted, furniture rendering is not the company's traditional market and is new for them.

If one does only FX, well then Arnold may be the right choice as is evidenced by its use in *Game of Thornes* and *X Men Apocalypse*.

Ray tracers are often created to answer specific creative demands, and in the case of Autodesk Arnold, to handle the demands of feature film-quality photorealistic visual effects and animation. Any renderer, whether a ray tracer or otherwise, will have to make design compromises according to the users that it is trying to serve. With Arnold, Autodesk felt that its performance capabilities with very large datasets gave it an excellent foundation on which to build for a broader range of industries.

However, it has been criticized as very difficult to use without a really good crew of VFX people. It also has a host of other assets that need to be taken into consideration. Significant training is required to make it work.

Originally co-developed with Sony Pictures Imageworks (and it is now their main renderer), the company claims Arnold is used at over 300 studios worldwide including ILM, Framestore, MPC, The Mill, and Digic Pictures. Arnold was the primary renderer on dozens of films from Monster House and Cloudy with a Chance of Meatballs to Pacific Rim and Gravity. It is available as a stand-alone renderer on Linux, Windows, and Mac OS X, with supported plug-ins for Maya, 3ds Max, Houdini, Cinema 4D, and Katana. It is the built-in interactive renderer for Maya and 3ds Max.

8.1.4   Cero—PTC

PTC is a computer software and services company founded in 1985 and head-quartered outside of Boston, Massachusetts. The company developed parametric, associative feature-based, robust computer-aided design modeling software

Luxion's KeyShot powers the Creo Render Studio Extension. With it, one can produce photorealistic renderings with sophisticated handling of light, scenes, and model appearances. It is fully integrated with Creo Parametric, so the user can move between rendering and modeling modes without the need to exit the rendering application. Moreover, with real-time ray tracing, one can leverage existing scenes and appearances for their designs. The image is constantly rendering itself, so there is no waiting (Fig. 8.7).

Creo Render Studio is fully integrated with Creo Parametric, so you can switch between the rendering and modeling modes without the need to exit the rendering application. See Luxion's KeyShot description in the following section.

Fig. 8.7 Creo Render Studio uses Luxion's KeyShot (PTC)

8.1.4.1 Summary

PTC began developing Creo in 2009 and announced it using the code name Project Lightning at Planet PTC Live, in Las Vegas, in June 2010. In October 2010, the company unveiled the product name for Project Lightning to be Creo and released it in June 2011.

Creo is part of a broader product development system developed by PTC. It connects to PTC's other solutions that aid product development, including Windchill for Product Lifecycle Management (PLM), Mathcad for engineering calculations, and Arbortext for enterprise publishing software.

8.1.5 Indigo Renderer—Glare Technologies

Nicholas Chapman, Managing Director of Glare Technologies, makes Indigo, started in the late 2000s, based on code and research that he was doing on Monte Carlo path tracers. "I was fascinated by the way such realistic images could be generated with such relatively simple algorithms," said Chapman.

Nicholas Chapman and Ralph Chapman started Glare Technologies Limited in 2008 in Wellington, New Zealand. It is the parent company of the Indigo Renderer and Chaotica. The company is based in Wellington, New Zealand. Indigo Renderer works as an unbiased, photorealistic GPU and CPU renderer which the company claims to provide ultimate image quality.

Indigo Renderer is an unbiased, photorealistic GPU and CPU renderer aimed at ultimate image quality, by accurately simulating the physics of light. State-of-the-art rendering performance, materials, and cameras models—it is all made simple through an interactive, photographic approach with few abstract settings, says the company.

"In 2011, with Indigo 3.0, we added support for offloading ray tracing to the GPU via CUDA and OpenCL," added Chapman. It became clear to them that a full GPU rendering solution (materials, ray tracing, lighting, etc., all running on the GPU) was needed to exploit the performance available with GPUs. They started to work on that, and now it is available with the release of Indigo 4.0. "This development," added Chapman, "has been worth it as Indigo now renders approximately ten times faster on the GPU and that speedup increases when more GPUs are added."

The latest version in Indigo Rendering is Indigo 4 which was launched in early 2018 and has many benefits over the previous versions (Fig. 8.8):

Multi-GPU rendering

Indigo RT utilizes the new open CL-based GPU engine which provides their performance for Nvidia and AMD graphics cards on all major operating systems. The recent GPU boasts of a 10x faster speed compared to the CPU code of Indigo 3.8.

Fig. 8.8 A demonstration of Indigo Renderer. *Source* Glare Technologies/Indigo

More cards can be added to the computer and get the power to render 4K images and animated movies.

Fast, flexible region rendering

Indigo Renderer 4 enables the user to render multiple regions at once by shift and enable a transparent background with a single checkbox (Fig. 8.9).

Fig. 8.9 A demonstration of fast flexible region rendering. *Source* Glare Technologies/Indigo

Aperture controls

The tool allows the user to better render the image by controlling the aperture shape with Indigo's generated aperture. It even allows the addition of aperture maps as per the requirement, and the camera lens needs to be covered by the maps to create image flare.

RGB color curves

RGB color response curves are a great way to tweak the raw image to get photographic effects. Indigo's native RGB curves are recommended for this as it means it is done in high precision and doesn't need to be repeatedly added in post-process for multiple renders (Fig. 8.10).

Material preview window

Indigo 4 has a customizable material preview window for modifying the scene materials in a neutral lighting environment. There are multiple sample objects available, and the user can change resolution and render quality of the preview.

Sequence overrides

It is a new tool which is used for rendering batches of images and animations with the render queue overriding to change render settings for all the frames in the queue, on the fly (Fig. 8.11).

Product comparison

See Table 8.1.

Fig. 8.10 RGB color curves. *Source* Glare Technologies/Indigo

Fig. 8.11 An example of sequence overrides which can render multiple regions at once. *Source* Glare Technologies/Indigo

Table 8.1 Product comparison of RT 4 and Renderer 4 (*Source* Glare Technologies/Indigo)

	Indigo RT	Indigo Renderer
Price	€ 145	€ 595
Ultimate Image Quality	●	●
Multi-GPU Rendering with OpenCL	●	●
Realtime Updates While Editing	●	●
Physically Accurate Sun and Sky	●	●
HDR Lighting	●	●
Subdivision and Displacement	●	●
Realistic Camera and Lights	●	●
Lab-measured Metal Materials	●	●
Subsurface Scattering	●	●
Object Instancing	●	●
Fully Accurate Motion Blur	●	●
Production-ready Commandline Build	●	●
Section Planes	●	●
Orthographic Camera	●	●
Spherical Camera	●	●
Invisible-to-camera Objects	●	●
Shadow-catcher Material	●	●
Light Layers	●	●
IES Lighting	●	●
Network Rendering	●	●

Materials

Indigo Renderer has a moderate collection of materials compared to some of its competitors. They consist of:

Ceramic—22

Gemstones—26

Glass—44

Leather—12

Lights—16

Liquids—33

Metals—68

Plastics—30

Skin—5

Special paints—30

Stone—71

Textile—33

Vegetation—19

Wood—90

Chaotica is a fractal art application that is designed for both new and experienced artists. Professional users are supposed to prefer the fast rendering engine from the company which publicizes the high-quality animations and complex images for print that are easily produced, with real-time imaging controls. Indigo is now available commercially. After 5 years of development, Glare Technologies is releasing a commercial version of Indigo and has made an intuitive user interface, and stability improvements.

8.1.5.1 Summary

The product has been able to gather good support because of its better quality of output and metal finish materials which are broad in variety compared to its competitors. However, there are a few areas which drew criticism such as it is a little expensive compared to its competitors of similar age and is not too easy to learn. However, as more versions come, the company is expected to clear up these expectations from its clients and will likely create a problematic arena for its competitors to sustain.

8.1.6 Cinema 4D—Maxon Computer

First released commercially in 1993 on the Amiga platform, Cinema 4D debuted on Mac OS and Windows OS in 1996. In 2000, BodyPaint 3D followed, an innovative 3D painting application available as an integrated part of Cinema 4D or as a stand-alone product for use with other 3D applications. In early 2000, Maxon was partially acquired by the Nemetschek Group.

Maxon introduced Cinema 4D release 20 at SIGGRAPH 2018. Cinema 4D's largest user base is 3D modeling and animation with a strong presence in the VFX industry and for motion graphics artists mainly in European VFX houses. Rebus farm is the main commercial supplier although when Maxon raised their price from $5/node to $100/node, there were significant service interruptions. They now have a GPU-based renderer which has been praised; however, it needs a plug-in for each render node to make it work properly especially when doing tile rendering with multiple nodes.

The company has added on to its capabilities with an expansion of its motion graphics toolset, MoGraph, as well as new volume-based modeling tools, simplified CAD files importing and a node-based material system.

Volume-based modeling—The OpenVBD-based Volume Builder and Mesher in Cinema 4D R20 offers an entirely new procedural modeling workflow. Any primitive or polygon object (including the new Fields objects) can be combined to create complex objects using Boolean operations. Volumes created in R20 can be exported sequentially in OpenVBD format and can be used in any application or render engine that supports OpenVBD. Also, OpenVBD, is an open-source C++ library, part of the growing portfolio of open-source tools that the VFX community is building for itself.

Dreamworks maintains OpenVBD, and many major software companies support it. Houdini, Pixar's RenderMan, Arnold Solid Angle, Next Limit RealFlow, Clarisse, Guerilla Render, Maxwell Render, Foundry Modo V-Ray, OctaneRender, and 3Delight are listed on the OpenVBD site.

Houdini requires a 10 GbE network or Mellanox to make this run in a render farm and also needs an expensive storage server. It is designed for big studios and has an expensive license.

File compatibility

Cinema 4D plays well with others: Third-party applications can read and write native .c4d files. And formats such as .fbx, .dae (Collada), .dfx, and .dwf can be used for seamless file exchange with Cinema 4D. File exchange is particularly easy with CAD applications from the Nemetschek family of products, to which Maxon also belongs. For example, a Cinema 4D visualization can be easily modified and updated from within Allplan, ArchiCAD, or Vectorworks.

Node-based material system

More than 150 different node-based shaders offer customers a new and streamlined workflow to quickly and conveniently create shading effects from simple reference materials to highly complex shaders. The existing standard material system's interface can be used to get started with the new node-based workflow. Node-based materials can be made available as parametric assets with a reduced interface. Each node performs specific functions from color correction to camera distance, generating noises, gradients, patterns, flakes, or scratches.

ProRender improvements

The GPU-based ProRender in Cinema 4D is a GPU-powered ray-tracing renderer that can create physically accurate renders. In R20, key features such as subsurface scattering, motion blur, and multi-passes are now available. Other enhancements in ProRender include updated code, support for Apple's Metal 2 graphics technology, and the use of out-of-core textures (Fig. 8.12).

Out-of-Core Textures. The company claims that ProRender eliminates the memory limits on the GPU and allows streaming of high-resolution textures to the AIB on demand. It is also possible to optimize render speed and quality with individual control over the diffuse, glossy, refraction, and shadow depths.

Global Illumination

Global illumination, which simulates diffused, reflected light, is essential for creating great-looking, realistic renderings. Cinema 4D offers a much greater diffuse depth than CineRender, which gives interior spaces as well as exteriors a much

Fig. 8.12 Maxwell's ProRender comes with an extensive material library (Maxwell)

more natural illumination and makes them look even more realistic —giving them that extra edge for any visualization.

ArchiCAD

With the release of ArchiCAD 18, Graphisoft introduced Maxon's CineRender for its integrated visualizations. CineRender is Cinema 4D's high-end render engine and lets ArchiCAD users quickly and easily create compelling renderings.

Vectorworks

Vectorworks has licensed Maxon's Cinema 4D rendering engine and integrated it into their Renderworks visualization program (Fig. 8.13).

The company offers it to produce renderings and presentations. Renderworks is fully integrated into the Vectorworks software interface, so it lets one seamlessly visualize their work throughout the design process. The company also offers connectivity with Maxon's Cinema 4D Visualize.

Cinema 4D Visualize

Cinema 4D Visualize adds to the range of functions of the Prime version to help you create perfect images for architecture or design visualizations and much more. Cinema 4D Visualize offers huge libraries that provide you with high-end objects and materials. Using the Physical Camera, one can simulate many of the optical properties of an SLR or a film camera, including realistic lighting. This adds even more realism to your images and animations.

8.1.6.1   Summary

Maxon's parent company Nemetschek has always been an interesting company, more a group of independent companies with a layer of infrastructure on top to provide some management and bookkeeping. The structure has served the company well since its founding.

Maxon is in Nemetschek's Media and Entertainment group. In July 2018, Nemetschek increased its share of Maxon from 70 to 100% of Maxon. At that time,

Fig. 8.13 Cinema 4D rendering in Vectorworks' Renderworks visualization program. *Source* Vectorworks

David McGavran, an industry veteran who most recently worked at Adobe, was appointed CEO and the company plans to increase its share in the AEC, AR, and VR markets.

8.1.7 Corona Renderer—Render Legion

Corona Renderer is a new high-performance unbiased photorealistic renderer, available for Autodesk 3ds Max and as a stand-alone CLI application, and in development for Maxon Cinema 4D.

The company is described in the plug-in section on Sect. 8.3.3 because it is best known as a plug-in for 3ds Max and Cinema 4D.

8.1.8 Iray—Nvidia

Who thought the study of theoretical physics was the way to make it in Hollywood? Maybe Rolf Herken who once labored through a Ph.D. on quantum gravity did, and that was why he started Mental Images to produce the mental ray tracing program.

"Artists like [Albrecht] Dürer and Leonardo da Vinci knew all about the concepts of ray tracing—they just didn't have computers," said Herken, the former CEO of Mental Images, which he founded in 1986.

"The idea behind ray tracing is that it should be entirely programmable and not introduce any filter or artistic interpretation in the result," says Herken, "Just like you may tell the photographer from his pictures but not the camera he used."

The company name is a reflection of Herken's main interests. At that time, he had been working as an artist for 17 years besides doing theoretical physics, mathematics, and computer science with emphasis on complexity theory and artificial intelligence.

The first five years the company was self-funded by means of its professional computer animation department with talent imported from the USA such as Stefen Fangmeier, John Nelson, and John Berton.

The first major commercial software development and license agreement was with Wavefront Technologies in 1991 to develop the universal .obj object file format and a modeling library that could generate the free-form surfaces needed for advanced industrial modeling and rendering, e.g., in automotive design. The format is still widely used, and the modeling library became the mental matter product. It is still contained in 3ds Max, for example.

Academy Award

In 2003, after being honored by the Academy of Motion Picture Arts and Sciences with a Technical Achievement Award for its "mental ray" technology, the Wall

Street Journal referred to the company as "The German Eggheads Who Stormed Hollywood," pitting the European upstarts against US-based Pixar Animation Studios. At the time, mental ray had been used in 120 movies—including *Star Wars* and *Harry Potter* films and thousands of television commercials, such as a Levi Strauss & Co. advertisement featuring 600 stampeding bison. Executives at The Mill, a London graphics firm that created the bison images, praise mental ray's ability to create lifelike hair on the beasts.

The former CEO of Mental Images and now CEO of MINE, a novel form of incubator for the creation of new technologies and technology companies, whose interest was born from his academic work on computer simulations the physical world, says the [mental ray] software's first incarnation took programmers working in a 300 m^2 Berlin flat three years to develop. Herken credits mental ray 0.1 as being written by Robert Hoedicke, "an extremely talented mathematician with a broad range of interests in computer science, in particular in novel approaches to programming."

"We bought the first Silicon Graphics workstations in Europe," Herken recalls. "That meant we had burned our entire first round of venture capital before we even started working."

Once that money was gone, funding came from computer-generated trailers and television advertisements produced by special effects pioneers that Herken had lured to Germany who doubled as test pilots for the program.

By the end of the last century, Herken predicted then that 90% of all visual effects would use ray tracing under one guise or another. He recalled at the time of the Academy Award that "we could produce any visual effect you might think of. We had reached the point where, if it is unconvincing, it was due to financial rather than technological constraints." Thus, the best effects often go unnoticed. Special effects generated in a computer allow camera movements that would not have been possible to perform on a physical set. He cited one scene in The Matrix which shows Keanu Reeves riding a bike on a busy motorway slaloming precariously between cars that do not exist except as lines of code.

Mental images' Ray was one of, if not, the first to patent and launch what we now call cloud-based rendering. The goal was to allow users around the world to have access to and manipulate three-dimensional scenes drawn from centrally stored data, for instance, a maintenance manual for a nuclear submarine or the mathematical description of a car prototype without having to download it on to their computers. That would not only allow large numbers of people to use data without the need for powerful local computers but would also enable companies to control its dissemination preventing intellectual property theft or accidental security leaks.

Herken knew at the time there that were obstacles, but he had made technological bets before such as his gamble that computers would be able to simulate physical phenomena by the mid-1990s. So, he was confident that the demand would be there, from online gaming to industrial design and sophisticated terrain-mapping map-sharing for the military.

Despite the many question marks hanging over the project at the time, one thing was certain to Herken: By the early 2000s, he saw enough growth potential in it to have ruled out selling his company for the foreseeable future, and instead new several investors supported the company.

Four years later, Nvidia acquired Mental Images for $100 million—and a decade later, cloud-based, multi-user ray-tracing applications have entered the mainstream. (Rolf Herken stayed with the company until 2011 and then went on to found MINE, a novel form of incubator for the creation of new technologies and technology companies that he now heads as CEO.)

After Nvidia had acquired Mental Images, the company introduced Iray, an unbiased ray-tracing program, and claimed it was the first fully GPU-accelerated, commercially supported, turnkey rendering solution for a wide range of 3D graphics application developers. Iray technology leveraged Nvidia's GPUs and promised to deliver fast photorealism to designers, engineers, visual artists, and consumers (Fig. 8.14).

Watching Iray at work, the viewer sees a grainy image of the rendering almost immediately. As time passes, the granularity resolves itself into a true-to-life image. This process contrasts with earlier versions of Mental Images mental ray software that rendered portions of an image in square tiles as it worked. The advantage of the Iray approach is that users may be able to quickly see if colors or other settings are not right, stop the rendering process, and change them.

In 2009, Dassault Systèmes, the global French leader of professional CAD and PLM software that had used mental ray as the ray-tracing engine of its CATIA product, licensed Iray (which is CATIA's ray-tracing engine to this day).

In 2010, Bunkspeed, an independent U.S.K. developer of product visualization applications (since 2013 owned by Dassault Systèmes' SolidWorks unit) ray-tracing rendering technology adapted its Shot program to be the first end-user application to use Mental Images in Iray. In Shot, users can turn off ray tracing to move the model around, set the scene and other functions, and then turn ray tracing back on to begin the render. This kind of interaction is harder almost impossible to

Fig. 8.14 A living room rendered using Iray. *Source* Nvidia

do if the rendering software displays the image in tiles, thus bringing ray tracing into interactive workflows.

In 2013, Lightwork Design, an independent UK developer of ray-tracing rendering technology company for CAD and 3D software developers (whose main customer is Siemens' Industrial Software/PLM unit who acquired Lightwork Design in 2018; see Sect. 8.1.26), announced that it had formed a partnership with Nvidia to bring its "Iray+" implementation to the market as a GPU-based ray-tracing rendering SDK with enhanced shader handling workflows.

In Nov 2017, Nvidia transferred sales and support of the Iray plug-in products for 3ds Max, Iray for Maya, Iray for Rhino, and Iray Server—to the Iray integration partners (AKA Iray Plugins), Lightwork Design/Siemens PLM, migenius, in Hawthorn, Australia, and [0x1] Software in Hamburg, Germany. In October 2018 migenius and Siemens PLM licensed the Iray SDK bought, and then Siemens bought Lightworks, making them a partner, and the latter is also the depository and store for Iray plug-ins, as well as Lightworks' Iray+ customers via irayplugins.com.

At SIGGRAPH 2018, Nvidia introduced their new RTX GPU architecture with a specific ray-tracing hardware accelerator called RT Core. The RT Core was accessed by Nvidia's RTX API and was exposed by Microsoft DirectX driver in early October 2018, followed by Vulkan and a newer version of OptiX.

Nvidia says Iray runs on all current-generation (and Pascal) boards and supported RT Core later in 2019.

Iray has many features available in the latest version:

Iray with artificial intelligence: AI denoising

Iray with AI is bringing the power of deep learning to the frame and interactive photorealistic rendering. This capability of Iray called "AI Denoising" enables the completion of final output much faster and can be used to make interactive rendering much smoother for complex images (Fig. 8.15).

Iray and virtual reality

Iray supports virtual reality (VR) presentations in head-mounted displays (HMD) in both prerendered VR walkthroughs from panoramic snapshots and dynamic presentations based on light-field technology (Fig. 8.16).

Physically based lighting

Iray implements rendering technology that generates imagery by simulating the physical behavior of light interaction with surfaces and volumes. Images are progressively refined to provide full global illumination including caustics, sun studies, and luminance distributions (Fig. 8.17).

Physically based materials and MDL

Nvidia Material Definition Language (MDL) defines the properties of materials for Iray and other rendering products that support this open language. These range from the color of surfaces to their reflection or refraction properties, light emission of

Fig. 8.15 Iray with artificial intelligence on and off. *Source* Nvidia

Fig. 8.16 Iray with virtual reality. *Source* Nvidia

surfaces, scattering, absorption properties of volumes and geometric shapes and cutouts (Fig. 8.18).

Materials

The Iray+ Material from Lightworks is a monolithic shader that is used to create a majority of the other Iray materials. These materials, numbering nearly 100, are under the groups of base components, decal components, coating components, and surface components. There are also couples of groups of special materials named ocean and metal categories.

Fig. 8.17 Physically based lighting. *Source* Nvidia

Fig. 8.18 Physically based material. *Source* Nvidia

Iray+ Ocean is a material designed for creating bodies of water that includes particles and volumetric effects.

Volume: This function controls the color of the material (Figs. 8.19 and 8.20).

Distance: This scale maintains the overall strength of the subsurface absorption and scattering effects.

Particle Density: This feature controls how much of the volume is taken up by particles which controls the transparency of water (Figs. 8.21 and 8.22).

Refraction: The index of refraction controls the margin by which the material refracts (or distorts) the transmitted light.

Fig. 8.19 Changing impact of color control through a material. *Source* Nvidia

Fig. 8.20 Changing impact of distance control through material. *Source* Nvidia

Fig. 8.21 Changing impact of particle density. *Source* Nvidia

IOR: **1.0**   IOR: **1.34**   IOR: **20**

Fig. 8.22 Changing impact of change of index of refraction. *Source* Nvidia

Fig. 8.23 Comparison between photorealistic and interactive processes. *Source* Nvidia

Interactive 3D rendering

Iray provides interactive visual feedback throughout the entire design process. The Iray interactive rendering mode uses approximation algorithms to mimic realism while minimizing unwanted noise. This improves performance during interaction (Fig. 8.23).

Light path expressions

Iray offers compositing elements that isolate lighting components, using a technique called light path expressions (LPEs) rendered in parallel and saved to output buffers. These LPEs are calculated on a per object and light basis, which allows for complete control in post-processing (Fig. 8.24).

Fig. 8.24 Light path expressions. *Source* Nvidia

In 2015, Nvidia adopted Iray to plug-ins for tighter communications with 3D modeling and design programs, beginning with 3ds Max, and today, there are over a half dozen versions such as Max, Maya, Rhino, SketchUp in addition to CATIA, SolidWorks Visualize, and Siemens NX.

Nvidia stopped developing the mental ray program in 2117 in favor of Iray, primarily because the structure of the program did not offer any advantage via GPU acceleration, and Iray did. Nonetheless, there are still tens of thousands of users of mental ray around the world including many in North America. The program is now royalty-free (albeit without any support), and the company has given free, unending licenses to everybody who asked (including all preexisting users). Incidentally, mental ray is still a favorite among Japanese Manga artists because of their specially developed toon shaders.

8.1.8.1 Practicing What They Preach

In 2013, Nvidia began planning a new building. It was to be as eco-friendly as possible and use as much natural light as possible. As might be expected, the design was rendered in Iray to get physically correct lighting simulations (Fig. 8.25).

The building is triangular in shape, reflecting the basic GC element. Nvidia people and the architecture firm Gensler accomplished the whole design process with Iray. They used measured materials for the interior and verified physical correctness by modeling existing premises and comparing their simulations of them with real measurements. The company named the building Endeavor, after the space shuttle. The story about how Iray was used for the design can be seen here: https://tinyurl.com/ybfeda3v.

Fig. 8.25 Nvidia's ray-traced visualization of its proposed building Endeavor. *Source* Nvidia

However, the Iray plug-in program didn't do that well for Nvidia, and so the company decided in 2018 to transition it to other firms, such as Siemens's Lightworks team.

8.1.8.2   Summary

The mental ray program has been admired and is in daily use by tens of thousands of professionals. Integrated with leading CAD products like CATIA, Siemens NX, and SolidWorks Visualize and offering plug-in tools for Maya, 3ds Max, and Rhino, Iray is a well-known and used program. People like the performance, quality of rendering, and the image quality, particularly with photorealism. However, the issue with GPU consumption during rendering is what people expect the company to address. People somewhat absorb this issue but expect the company to develop a more efficient product with future versions.

However, when Autodesk bought Arnold in 2016 and dropped Iray/mental ray from being an integrated free resource, many others dropped it too, which lead to Nvidia transferring sales and support of the Iray plug-ins to migenius, and [0x1] Software in 2017. There are still several users in India who are using the old version of mental ray in old versions of Maya/3ds Max to get it for free.

The name mental images reflect on the fact that there are no digital images, only mental images. The tagline of the company was "Rendering Imagination Visible." The goal was to render anything that one can imagine as realistic or surrealistic as desired with nature recorded with the highest-quality camera being the benchmark for fidelity.

Founded with the intent of developing fundamental technologies such as image synthesis as well as for image understanding, mental images intended to go into robotics and artificial intelligence. For that reason, its first computers were PCs with Inmos Transputer networks. They were focusing on massively parallel computer architectures for both purposes, looking at the human brain as guidance. Unfortunately, those ideas were so far ahead of the times (and the computer hardware development) that they had to abandon that part of the business for lack of funding. (The original business plan could still be submitted unchanged today and would most likely get funded given the attention and funding that is being directed in that area of research now.)

Herken is proud of the name, and when he met Danny Hillis, founder of the famous Thinking Machines, and gave Hillis his business card, Hillis said, "mental images—that is also a good name for a company."

8.1.9   KeyShot—Luxion

Henrik Wann Jensen is a Danish computer graphics researcher and is best known for developing the photon mapping technique as the subject of his Ph.D. thesis, but has also done significant research in simulating subsurface scattering and the sky. He was awarded an **Academy Award for Technical Achievement** in 2004 together with Stephen R. Marschner and Pat Hanrahan for pioneering research in simulating subsurface scattering of light in translucent materials as presented in their paper. A few years later, he helped form Luxion.

Luxion has been an erstwhile player in the usage of computer-based lighting simulations for creating art. They take pride in being one of the leading developers of 3D rendering animation and lighting technology including areas related to daylighting (atmospheric scattering), light scattering by materials (BRDF, see Glossary, and BSSRDF models), light transport algorithms such as photon mapping, and real-time rendering technology. The company is also into creating proprietary applications and libraries for customers in need of software capable of precisely calculating the scattering of light in complex 3D environments.

KeyShot

KeyShot is an application program from Luxion that makes the creation of 3D renderings and animations fast and easy, with support for a wide number of 3D file formats on both Mac and Windows. It is real-time rendering with every change from material, lighting, cameras, or animation being seen simultaneously in a viewport as work continues. The product has some of the key parameters such as very good physical lighting and color combinations, patterns and image styles, and good control and connectivity features. The animation features of the KeyShot are also a thing to be looked at, and the company claims to have much better features compared to its competitors (Fig. 8.26).

Fig. 8.26 Abilities of the KeyShot program. The initial picture is the input with the final picture being the last drawn image from the tool. *Source* Luxion

The company recently launched the KeyShot 8 on October 8, 2018, with better features over its previous versions.

Image styles

KeyShot 8 has introduced the image styles which allow the user to make photographic adjustments to the KeyShot scene in real time prior to or after rendering. The tool also allows the creation of multiple image styles and is added to a list for a range of different styles that can then be used in KeyShot Studios with adjustments for tone mapping, curve control, color adjustments, and background color override added to the image.

Cutaway

Cutaway is an innovative approach that allows the user to use parts and 3D primitives to slice the image by geometry. The cutaway material also allows adding and defining the cutaway Caps as a shaded color, the same material as the object to be cut or as a custom material, including the elimination of all of them.

Scattering media

KeyShot 8 supports the creation of scattering media to simulate particle scattering and volumetrics such as smoke and fog with physical lights for visualizing rays of light. This comes with the additional option to add a density texture to any material.

Geometry nodes

The company claims to have added a new approach to apply geometry in KeyShot. Using the options in the Material Graph, the user can have three new types of geometry nodes to modify an object: displacement, bubbles, or flakes.

The latest version comes with other new features like:

- Faster movement through the process to make it easier for the user.
- Better visuals and enhanced color and light experience.
- Better style and control of image creation.

- Providing the user with the capabilities to fine-tune, controlling, or adjusting shadows, mid-tones, and highlights separately.
- Removing the hassles of cutting and pruning the images before importing to the tool.
- The company claims to create one of the best-finished images with various looks like juicy, liquid shots, creation materials, or sparkle.
- Creation of amazing rays to create the magic of foggy morning or a forest cover.

GPU rendering

KeyShot was the first such real-time ray-tracing and global illumination program that uses a physically correct rendering engine to be certified by the CIE (International Commission on Illumination), employing the GPU.

Direct import

KeyShot directly imports over 40 different 3D file formats from 20+ 3D modeling applications with no plug-in required. From the File menu, one selects Open or Import to bring up unique options for the 3D data one needs to import. Direct import of all major 3D modeling applications as well as generic 3D file formats is included in KeyShot HD, Pro, and Enterprise.

KeyShot 8 was released with advanced rendering capabilities such as displacement mapping, bubbles, and flakes, a unique approach to creating cutaways, volumetric materials including volume caustics, and interactive image color and intensity curve adjustments (Fig. 8.27).

Fig. 8.27 KeyShot has increased stability and improved workflow options. *Source* Specialized Levo by TB&O

KeyShot 8.1 introduced in-app problem reporting, 16-bit PSD (Photoshop document) output, in-view indicators for geometry shader, full-resolution HDRI update, and invert selection capabilities, along with many other improvements and bug fixes.

8.1.9.1   Summary

KeyShot faces a fair amount of competition from the products like Maxwell Renders, OctaneRender, V-Ray, and others in the market. The product commands a little higher pricing from its competitors like Maxwell Renders; however, the users are of the opinion that the program offers speed of operations. It can render difficult images and shaders in real time without any noise, and the latest version KeyShot 8 has helped strengthen the reputation which the company has garnered from through old versions. However, the product seems to be behind its competition with similar price in terms of quality. The company has taken steps in that direction and demonstrated a robust performance improvement in view of market competition.

KeyShot is one of the few programs that is integrated (into PTC Creo), is stand-alone, and is also available as a plug-in; see Sect. 8.3.7.

8.1.10   Lumion 8 and Pro—Act-3D B.V

After years of experience creating 3D simulations, training tools, 3D movie technology, and architecture, Marcellis has steered the company specifically toward architectural visualization and proudly boasts that 65% of the top 100 architectural firms are using Lumion for their renderings.

"Software is not something architects necessarily love to work with," says Marcellis. "So, our goal from day one was to offer a design tool that doesn't fight you. Rather, it works with you as an architect to bring your ideas to life quickly and easily with uncompromising style and precision."

Act-3D was among the pioneers when the first 3D acceleration hardware became commonplace. Lumion is a stand-alone ray-tracing program that is compatible with all 3D design software programs, such as Revit, SketchUp, and ArchiCAD. It is also available as a plug-in.

Act-3D was one among the pioneers of 3D acceleration and image rendering when being developed. After years of experience in training, architecture, and simulation, the company decided to focus on architectural visualization. Act-3D developed multiple software solutions which are being used all over the world, and Lumion is the most popular visualization solution among them. Lumion 9 was launched in November 2018 and was available as a free update for Lumion licenses (Fig. 8.28).

Fig. 8.28 Introductory image for Lumion 9. *Source* Act-3D B.V.

According to the company, they have built the fastest 3D rendering software for architects with Lumion. Within a concise amount of time, just a few seconds, the user can visualize the CAD models in a video or image with true-life environments or artistic designs. The company says not requiring training is one of their significant achievements. Act-3D claims that the ease of their rendering tool allows users to create images, videos, and 360 panoramas very quickly (seconds for images and minutes for videos). It is beneficial, says the company, for architects to collaborate using different CAD software and bring landscapes, roads, buildings, or urban constructions together into a Lumion render including real-time environments using LiveSync.

Lumion and the later versions have several changes and improvements:

New Hand-drawn feature—Lumion 8 helps the user to demonstrate architectural designs using the new "hand-drawn" feature (Fig. 8.29).

LiveSync for Lumion 8.3—Using the new LiveSync, Lumion allows the user to set up a live visualization of the SketchUp or Revit model.

Sky Light—Sky Light is a daylight simulator used for softening and dispersing the scene's surrounding lights. The feature can be used in combination with soft shadows and fine detail shadows.

Soft and fine shadows—Versions above the Lumion 8 allow the user to inject realism into the render by turning on the soft shadows and fine detail shadows as part of the shadow effect. Immediately, the shadows become softer with a growth in their penumbras (Fig. 8.30).

Hyperlight for videos—Hyperlight increases the power for better lighting quality and accuracy. With Lumion 8 and above, the user can apply the Hyperlight effect when rendering videos or images.

Fig. 8.29 Image showing the ability to use a hand-drawn outline. *Source* Act-3D B.V.

Fig. 8.30 Image showing the soft and fine shadows feature. *Source* Act-3D B.V.

<u>**New grouping function**</u>—Lumion 8 and above enables the user to bunch multiple objects together and control them all at once, be it trees, cars, people, or any other objects (Fig. 8.31).

<u>**Mass placement for curved shapes**</u>—This is a functionality preferred by landscapers where they can use the mass placement feature to place multiple objects in different shapes, including curves.

Fig. 8.31 Image showing the new grouping function of Lumion. *Source* Act-3D B.V.

New tools for OpenStreetMap—OpenStreetMap is a tool for directly placing the designs in a real-life environment. In Lumion 8, it becomes possible to put the model in the center of a big city without any other buildings getting in view.

Softening of hard edges (Pro only)—The new edge slider in Lumion 8 allows the user to make the surfaces appear a little rounded or worn to give it a more natural and weathered feel (Fig. 8.32).

Fig. 8.32 Image showing the softening of hard images. *Source* Act-3D B.V.

New realistic materials—Lumion 8 has 168 new materials, including 100 HD materials from Poliigon. The tool allows the user to add city sidewalks and streets with realism and texture or structures with new materials.

168 new materials included in Lumion 8 Pro. Their key features are:

- 20 new water presets with specific color and style
- 17 new soil types which include gravel and pebbles
- 51 new metal materials
- 15 new concrete and 23 new stone materials
- 12 city street sidewalks
- 10 new wallpapers
- 1 wet glass (Pro only)

With the new additions, the total number of materials in Lumion 8 Pro is 1,019.

New objects in the content library (Pro only)

The features of the newly added content library include:

- 74 new tree species from across the globe.
- 595 indoor objects.
- 26 outdoor objects.
- 14 new vehicle models, including HD cars.

8.1.10.1   Summary

The tool is appreciated by architects for its photorealistic visualizations from a rendering engine. It improved the quality of some images subtly, while for others, it was dramatic. Speed and clarity were two of the most liked properties of the tool and neutralized the higher price which the software makers charged from their users. Another factor which attracted people is its ability to make it possible to use rendering as a design option tool and not show directly as the final product. The company's strong customer support team is also applauded by its users. However, there are a few shortcomings which the company has to work on like the menu options where most of the drawing software appears hidden from the users and viewports not being available for providing plan and positioning of objects. However, the users appreciate the new features, and this goes in favor of the company in their trade war against the Revit or 3ds Max/V-Ray.

8.1.11   Maxwell Render—Next Limit

Victor Gonzalez of Madrid, not be confused with the Mexican television director/ actor with the same name, founded Next Limit with his partner Ignacio Vargas in

1998. In 2008, he was one of the co-awardees of the "Technical Achievement Award" by the Academy of Motion Picture Arts and Sciences. The firm has developed technologies in the field of digital simulation and visualization and created RealFlow—a dynamics and fluid simulator for film production. RealFlow which was used in the production of The Lord of the Rings: The Return of the King.

The company also developed a division and computational fluid dynamics program called XFlow and in December 2016 sold it to Dassault Systèmes.

However, the company is best known for the Maxwell Render—a physically correct light simulator and render engine it introduced in 2004. It was the first unbiased spectral physically based render engine available, inspiring others to follow that vision. Maxwell Render was nominated twice to the Academy's Technical Achievement Awards.

The software was used to render the Waterfall for the Salesforce headquarters lobby in San Francisco as well as the new MGM Cotai in Macau. Since it is a progressive renderer, people use it to get amazingly precise renders trading off time for beauty.

In 2018, Victor Gonzalez, who describes himself as a tech entrepreneur, fascinated by computers and simulation from a very early age, became the sole owner of the group, expanding the company portfolio toward new markets and industries.

Maxwell Render is a stand-alone unbiased 3D render engine, developed by Next Limit Technologies in Madrid, Spain. This stand-alone software is used in the film, animation, and VFX industry, as well as architectural and product design visualization. It offers various plug-ins for 3D/CAD and postproduction applications.

Maxwell Render was released to the public as an early alpha in December 2004 (after 2 years of internal development) utilizing a global illumination (GI) algorithm based on a Metropolis light transport variation. Next Limit Technologies released Maxwell Render V3.2 in October 2015.

"The main aim of Maxwell is to make the most beautiful images ever," says Juan Cañada, the Head of Maxwell Render Technology. "That's the main idea we had in mind when we started the project. Apart from that, we wanted to create a very easy to use the tool and make it very compatible, so everybody can use it no matter what platform you wanted to use."

Next Limit has been a pioneer in high-fidelity simulation and visualization technologies with an aim to develop high-fidelity rendering, making artificial intelligence more robust and safer, upgrading the data visualization and physical simulation techniques. The company takes pride in its strong research and development division which is a key to the company's success and is in collaborative touch with many public and private organizations. They have developed several tools and products ranging from Maxwell Render for rendering, and RealFlow, RealFlow 4D, and CaronteFX for the other operations and have generated a good response from the market.

Maxwell Render

Maxwell is a 3D rendering tool and a stand-alone, unbiased 3D render engine, which finds the maximum applicability among the architects and designers. The renderer is known for its quality, realism, and decent speed of operations. The latest version 4.2 was launched in 2018 and has multiple improvement features over its previous edition 4.1. Properties like having a powerful denoiser, optical memory handling, and Maxwell multi-light are some of the updated features the latest version possesses.

The algorithms of Maxwell use an advanced bidirectional Path Tracing with a hybrid Metropolis implementation that is unique in the industry. Interestingly, in the last few years, the whole industry has been moving more toward Maxwell's "physically based lighting and shading approach," while the Next Limit engineers have been making Maxwell Render faster and better using key technologies such as MIS and multi-core threading to optimize the speed in real-world production environments.

The software can fully capture all light interactions between the elements in a scene, and all lighting calculations are performed using spectral information and high dynamic range data; an excellent example of this is the sharp caustics which can be rendered using the Maxwell bidirectional ray tracer with some Metropolis light transport (MLT) approaches as well.

One of the most challenging things for an unbiased renderer is subsurface scattering. As stated above, many solutions are point-based. In Maxwell, Act-3D will not apply biased techniques, as it is important that Maxwell is used not only in effects to create good images but also in a scientific way, producing predictable results to help you with and guide the user in making real-world design decisions.

Maxwell Studio

Maxwell Studio is an independent scene editor with a full 3D environment that offers an alternative workflow for those Maxwell Render users that work with 3D or CAD applications for which the company does not currently offer a plug-in.

It is also useful as an MXS editing tool—an MXS file generated by any plug-in currently offered by Next Limit can be imported into Maxwell Studio. For example, if one's scene is not rendering as intended, usually the most efficient way of seeing what is wrong is opening the MXS in Maxwell Studio and checking that the scene has been exported by the plug-in (cameras, materials, geometry, and others) (Fig. 8.33).

The company claims that rendering in Maxwell is available for any 3D platform through Studio. One can export one's models in any of the compatible formats, import them in Studio, and there adjust the cameras, assign and edit materials, set up the environment and lighting, and launch the render. This product is also known as Maxwell Render V4 and Maxwell Render Studio.

Fig. 8.33   Maxwell Studio has been used in several architectural presentations

Materials

The Maxwell materials gallery is an online library with thousands of free Maxwell materials available for download.

The Material Editor is one of the most critical components of Maxwell Render. It provides a robust set of parameters for advanced editing of a Maxwell material. This panel in Studio is precisely the same as the stand-alone Material Editor application (also named MXED, stands for Material Editor) that is also included with the Maxwell installation.

Denoiser

Maxwell 4.2 can integrate a powerful denoiser from Innobright's Altus technology, to preserve the texture and geometric details to save time. It claims to be able to save time to the tune of two to six times, depending on the complexity of the image. The most significant advantage of this feature is to be able to keep the sampling level low and allow the denoiser to accomplish the remainder of the job (Fig. 8.34).

Fig. 8.34   Before and after example of the denoising program. *Source* Next Limit

Denoiser integration to Maxwell is offered as a free solution for all customers without any need for an extra license.

GPU—optimized handling memory

The company's R&D team has done a few optimizations to the GPU which is now a lot better in handling memory which means the device can render bigger and complex images with much lesser utilization of GPU memory. The new device uses a CUDA-capable Nvidia graphics card which uses all the power generated by the GPU for the rendering process. The company claims to reduce GPU usage without any effect on the rendering of the image. Using a GPU significantly speeds up ray tracing by leveraging CUDA using proprietary acceleration techniques while providing physically correct fidelity (that is also why Dassault and Siemens picked it for their CAD systems).

Maxwell multilight

Maxwell Multilight allows the user to avoid rerendering and save time and energy in the process while getting the same quality output image as done through the process of multiple rendering. It allows the user to play with the intensities of light and scene emitters after the completion of the rendering process. However, the best part is the avoidance of Maxwell tool for using the Maxwell Multilight; however, it needs a stand-alone app and an MXI file. It has several benefits as follows:

- Tone mapping and camera response features which help fine-tune the look of the images
- Indefinite lighting changes and setups in real time
- Quick and smart operations by editing lights before and after the render function
- Creation of a lighting catalog for the user's client
- With various lighting positions and geometry, the catalog is updated directly.

Multilight is not a ray tracer but offers tone mapping and camera response features, so you can fine-tune the look of your images. This, says the company, offers limitless lighting setups in real time. One can create a lighting catalog for one's client and can automatically update one's catalog with different lighting positions or geometry.

The company advertises it as one render, multiple lights, no Maxwell needed (Fig. 8.35).

One can tweak the lighting setup over and over, saving as many images of the same scene as you like. Moreover, one does not need Maxwell. Multilight is a free stand-alone program.

Fig. 8.35 Multilight offers the flexibility to change lights even without a Maxwell license. *Source* Net Limit

8.1.11.1 Summary

Next Limit's Maxwell renderer has been around for over 15 years and is one of the most respected in the industry. It is affordable and compatible with over a dozen other programs and is an unbiased stand-alone renderer. It competes favorably with Arnold, V-Ray, and Iray.

However, some users are abandoning it for other options like Redshift, Octane, Corona, and V-Ray. Next Limit's move to a GPU version diluted their offering, especially in being able to maintain feature parity between their CPU and GPU offering. See chart here: http://www.nextlimit.com/maxwell/cpu_gpu_chart/.

8.1.12 Mitsuba

Mitsuba is the name of Japanese wild parsley and a large Japanese automotive motor control company. Neither of them has anything to do with the Mitsuba ray tracer.

Mitsuba is a research-oriented rendering system in the style of PBRT, from which it derives much inspiration. It is written in portable C++, implements unbiased and biased techniques, and contains heavy optimizations targeted toward current CPU architectures.

Mitsuba is a personal project of Dr. Wenzel Jakob of Lausanne, Switzerland, and consists of over 150K lines of code. It has been used in research projects at Cornell, MIT, University of Virginia, Columbia University, UC Berkeley, NYU, Berlin, TU

Dresden, Nvidia Research, Disney Research, Volvo Car Corporation, Square Enix, and Weta Digital. Interestingly, Jakob worked at Weta Digital as an intern and has screen credits in R&D in the first two Hobbit films, but he started writing Mitsuba in 2007 and today does research. He is an assistant professor leading the Realistic Graphics Lab at EPFL's School of Computer and Communication Sciences.[1]

Mitsuba is extremely modular: It consists of a small set of core libraries and over 100 different plug-ins that implement functionality ranging from materials and light sources to complete rendering algorithms.

In comparison with other open-source renderers, Mitsuba places a strong emphasis on experimental rendering techniques, such as path-based formulations of Metropolis light transport and volumetric modeling approaches. Thus, it may be of genuine interest to those who would like to experiment with such techniques that haven't yet found their way into mainstream renderers, and it also provides a solid foundation for research in this domain.

The renderer currently runs on Linux, macOS X, and Microsoft Windows and makes use of SSE2 optimizations on x86 and x86_64 platforms. So far, its primary use has been as a test bed for algorithm development in computer graphics, but there are many other exciting applications.

Mitsuba comes with a command-line interface as well as a graphical frontend to interactively explore scenes. While navigating, a rough preview is shown that becomes increasingly accurate as soon as all movements are stopped. Once a viewpoint has been chosen, a wide range of rendering techniques can be used to generate images, and their parameters can be tuned from within the program.

Mitsuba instances can be merged into large clusters, which transparently distribute and jointly execute tasks assigned to them using only node-to-node communication. It has successfully scaled to large-scale renderings that involved more than 1000 cores working on a single image. Most algorithms in Mitsuba are written using a generic parallelization layer, which can tap into this cluster-wide parallelism. The principle is that if any component of the renderer produces work that takes longer than a second or so, it at least ought to use all of the processing power it can get.

The renderer also tries to be very conservative in its use of memory, which allows it to handle large scenes (>30 million triangles) and multi-gigabyte heterogeneous volumes on consumer hardware.

Mitsuba supports the most commonly used scattering models: Lambertian surfaces, ideal dielectrics, and mirrors as well as the Phong and anisotropic Ward BRDFs.[2] A range of microfacet models are also available, including rough glass, plastic, and metal. Subsurface scattering can either be simulated using a BSSRDF approach (see Glossary) or more rigorously using volumetric light transport.

For volumes, the supported scattering models are isotropic, Henyey–Greenstein, Kajiya–Kay fiber scattering, and microflakes (Fig. 8.36).

---

[1] http://www.mitsuba-renderer.org/ ∼ wenzel/.
[2] Ward (1992).

Fig. 8.36 Voxelized scarf model rendered using full multiple scattering and an anisotropic scattering model (microflakes). *Dataset courtesy* Jon Kaldoe and Manuel Vargas

Mitsuba can compute global illumination solutions in scenes containing large isotropic or anisotropic participating media. The underlying volumes can be represented as sparse voxel octrees or as hierarchical grids, where grid cells are directly mapped from files into memory.

Mitsuba internally uses a $O(n \log n)$ SAH kd-tree compiler with support for primitive clipping (aka. perfect splits). The ray-tracing core is built on Havran's fast traversal algorithm. On Intel platforms, it is possible to trace coherent rays' packets using SSE2. Mitsuba supports analytic shapes such as cylinders and spheres and makes use of additional SSE2 accelerations when working with triangle meshes, which allows it to intersect up to four triangles at a time.

8.1.12.1 Summary

In comparison with other open-source renderers, Mitsuba places a strong emphasis on experimental rendering techniques, such as path-based formulations of Metropolis light transport and volumetric modeling approaches.

Mitsuba is a research renderer, rather than a production renderer, and uses the CPU, not the GPU. Mitsuba lacks features that are necessary for production: There is no proper support for hair (Mitsuba has a simple Kajiya–Kay shader and no specialized acceleration structure for ray intersections), there is no support for subdivision surfaces, there is no support for displacement mapping, and there are some other features necessary for production.

Mitsuba is excellent for research though. It has support for a lot of experimental rendering algorithms (such as Metropolis light transport), which are not supported in production renderers. Due to Mitsuba's modular structure, it is also incredibly easy to implement new algorithms, which makes Mitsuba an excellent framework for comparing rendering algorithms. A lot of papers use Mitsuba to compare their new algorithm to other algorithms.

8.1.13 Nebula Render

In the process of preparing this ray tracing and rendering book, I have searched for all the ray-tracing programs and suppliers I could find.

One of the newest entries into this category is Nebula in Montreal, and the developer Yann Clotioloman Yéo released the first version on GitHub in February this year. Before working on Nebula, he was studying software engineering at Laval University in Quebec and is currently working in the video game industry (Fig. 8.37).

It is a physically based, unbiased stand-alone renderer with real-time DirectX 12 preview written in C++. It runs on Windows 10 (64-bit) and requires SSE4 to run. However, it is a ground-up design and does not use Intel's Embree middleware. Nebula will automatically choose at runtime between SSE4 and AVX2 depending on the device. The program uses Intel's TBB—task scheduling framework (Fig. 8.38).

General features:

- Intuitive user interface with multiple settings (materials, lights, and more)
- Create scenes from model files and save it in xml files
- Material import/export
- Free play camera
- Render photorealistic images.

The program supports refractive materials, depth of field, area lights, soft shadows, ambient occlusion, subsurface scattering, homogeneous participating medium, post-process denoising, standard image filtering (brightness, hue, bloom, etc.) and allows to save renders to a file. Currently, there is no material library supported. The Nvidia MDL is being considered (Fig. 8.39).

As an **off-line renderer**, it offers multi-threaded Path Tracing with two modes:

- Pure CPU intersection kernels. It is the default mode.
- Hybrid. Use the CPU for secondary rays and the GPU with AMD's Radeon-Rays for primaries.

Fig. 8.37 Golden dragon rendered with a model downloaded on Archive 3D

Fig. 8.38 Urban exterior modeled by Hai le. Sun and the sky are the light sources. Cube map is courtesy of Spiney

Fig. 8.39 A BMW i8 downloaded model with an aluminum material. Lightning is mainly from an environment map made by Emil Persson

Nebula comes with a fully featured editor. The application viewport uses the DirectX 12 API. The software also supports real-time (progressive) ray tracing, allowing users to interactively edit scenes and see a preview of the final result, and finally launch a production render (with support for post-process denoising with OpenCV).

The off-line and real-time renderer supports physically based rendering, directional and omnilights, cube maps, transparent materials, and normal mapping. Also, it doesn't do AI denoising since Nebula is an unbiased renderer.

The future

Yéo has a road map too and is planning the following additions:

For the general features, he wants to add an animation timeline and skeletal animation. In the off-line renderer, he is looking at including The Open Shading Language, heterogeneous participating medium, as well as other integrators: bidirectional Path Tracing and photon mapping.

Moreover, for the real-time renderer, he plans to replace DirectX 12 by Vulkan (for macOS) and add shadow mapping.

Nebula Render is free software, for both personal and commercial use.

8.1.13.1   Summary

Nebula is currently a free and partially open-source project. For the future the company is planning on making it a fully open-source project are options that are being considered. Yéo originally developed Nebula to learn new technologies. In the past, he only knew graphics programming using OpenGL. Then DirectX 12 and Vulkan came out. Working on Nebula gave him the opportunity to learn DirectX, a modern graphics API, and also CPU rendering.

So, just as many ray-tracing programs have found their origins as a graduate project, or what is called a science project, Nebula is in a similar class. However, such projects have yielded great successes like V-Ray and Arnold so who's to say Nebula couldn't be the next big thing. At the very least, it could be a technology pickup for a larger company and wouldn't be the first time we have seen such a thing happen.

8.1.14   OctaneRender—Otoy

OctaneRender is a real-time 3D unbiased GPU-based ray tracer that was started in 2010 by the New Zealand-based company Refractive Software Ltd. Otoy took over the company in March 2012. The first non-beta stable version, v1.0, was released on November 28, 2012, and later versions of OctaneRender continue to be deployed as a Web release software.

Otoy claims that it is the first commercially available unbiased renderer to work exclusively on the GPU and thus, due to the parallel processing power of the GPU, can work in real time, or at least render faster than most CPU-based path tracers. Using GPUs allows users to modify materials, lighting, and render settings "on the fly" because the rendering viewport updates immediately whenever a change is made. OctaneRender ran exclusively on Nvidia's CUDA technology (which restricted it to running on AIBs from Nvidia). In 2016, the company released Octane 3.1 with cross-compilers for other AIBs.

Figure 8.40 is not a photograph. It is a ray-traced image created by artist Enrico Cerica using OctaneRender software. Ray tracing allows for details such as distortion in the glass, light diffusion in the windows and floor, and realistic light reflections of various objects. Now, imagine images and environments like this being rendered in real time (Image source: Nvidia/Enrico Cerica).

Although the company says they already have an AMD-compatible alternative to CUDA in the shape of OpenCL, the company felt the open standard has never entirely made the headway within the DCC market that its supporters initially hoped. While major apps do support OpenCLAdobe uses it for GPU acceleration in Photoshop and Premiere Pro, and Autodesk uses it for Bullet physics in Maya—its use in GPU-based renderers is spotty.

Otoy believes CUDA is superior to OpenCL and that it enables richer graphics software, so it chose to develop a CUDA cross-compiler for non-Nvidia hardware.

Fig. 8.40 OctaneRender image of a living room. *Source* Otoy

Each frame of video accurately simulates every ray of light in a given scene or environment and every interaction that each light ray has with the surfaces and materials therein. Every reflection, refraction, and absorption of that field of light is modeled as it would be in the real world. Otoy's GPU-based rendering and cloud graphics platform further enables live post-processing, motion graphics, and foveated compositing inside VR and light-field video content. The experience works both off-line and for live-streaming holographic videos.

The company says it has a steady stream of R&D and is planning the following features for Octane 4:

- **Brigade Engine Integration** Otoy's real-time game engine has been integrated into Octane, shrinking scene load times and expanding what you can do today. You will enjoy a new game engine-like scene graph, and the ability to move large meshes nearly instantly.
- **Out-of-Core Geometry** Support and Scene AI Octane 4 fully supports out-of-core geometry and scene data, in addition to textures. All meshes and textures can, if desired, be stored in CPU memory while rendering. Scene AI models' visibility of surfaces gets the maximum speed for out-of-core geometry.
- **Spectral AI Denoiser and AI Light Denoise** Both are used to create scenes on-the-fly very quickly. Octane's AI Denoiser operates on internal perceptual models of material, spectral irradiance, and scene data deep in the engine. Domain-specific denoisers help with glass, refraction, SSS, and other features. AI Light complements the AI Denoiser; it is unbiased and tracks emissive points live, in real time. It can be used in conjunction to reduce the number of samples to work in photoreal precision.

The company claims that OctaneRender can predetermine the necessary lighting information for a given **light field** and retrieve it in real time on consumer VR devices powered by mobile GPUs. Given the viewer's position and orientation, ORBX holographic video can turn a typical display screen into a virtual window, projecting the proper light path from a curved or VR display directly into the viewer's eyes.

8.1.14.1 Summary

Otoy has been an adventurism company experimenting with and pushing the boundaries of several technologies, intending to produce movies and games faster and more efficiently. In addition to its rendering technology, Otoy has LightStage, a facial scanning technology.

The company was the first company to demonstrate real time light-field capture for virtual reality. Its light-field sampler system rotates two cameras in a circle to capture the light-field data of the entire spherical area around it. The data is processed and rendered with Otoy's technology to create a virtual environment that can be explored by a user wearing a head-tracking HMD.

Otoy's Octane is a cloud rendering platform that works directly within Autodesk products such as Autodesk 3ds Maya and Autodesk 3ds Max. And the company says it will make it much more comfortable and less expensive to create animated films. Autodesk has invested an undisclosed amount in Otoy.

At the time, Otoy acquired Refractive Software, Otoy was also working on Brigade. Brigade is a real-time fast GPU path tracer rendering engine for video games. It provides global illumination and accurate reflections/refractions. Brigade is now available in the first experimental release of Octane 4 and will be rolled into all Octane 4 integrations.

8.1.15   OSPRay—Intel

OSPRay is an open-source, scalable, and portable ray-tracing engine for high-performance, high-fidelity visualization on Intel Architecture (IA) CPUs. OSPRay is released under the permissive Apache 2.0 license. Intel says it provides high-performance kernels for CPU ray-tracing operations and specifically provides high RT perf on Intel Xeon and Xeon Phi processors.

OSPRay is a library, with a low-level, C-style API. It primarily targets visualization-style rendering. Its developers emphasize that it is not trying to compete with GPUs in games or with global illumination renderers in production rendering.

High fidelity is an option, but not required (one can always do GL-style shading). OSPRay was developed to focus on visualization-like capabilities (volumes, large data, etc.), not pretty pictures. It is for visualization-style rendering.

The developers say it aims at being a "workhorse" for visualization tools like the Visualization Toolkit (VTK) and a scalable application built on VTK called ParaView. ParaView runs on some of the largest supercomputers in the world. The goal is to provide a free, open-source, high-fidelity alternative to GL.[3]

OSPRay provides the rendering layer on top of Embree (i.e., frame buffers, geometry types, volume types, shading modes, Message Passing Interface (MPI), and conflict of interest modes (COI modes) where required. All bounding volume hierarchy (BVH) traversals and construction are done through Embree's tree structure on a set of geometric objects (see BVH, Glossary). All SIMD-relevant code is written in Intel's single program, multiple data (SPMD) program compiler (ISPC). ISPC compiles a C-based SPMD programming language to run on the SIMD units of CPUs and the Intel Xeon Phi architecture. All instruction set architectures (ISA)-specifics are hidden by Embree and ISPC.

Interactive CPU rendering

OSPRay features interactive CPU rendering capabilities geared toward scientific visualization applications. Advanced shading effects such as ambient occlusion, shadows, and transparency can be rendered interactively, enabling new insights into data exploration.

Global illumination

OSPRay includes a path tracer capable of interactively rendering photorealistic global illumination.

Volume rendering

OSPRay supports high-fidelity interactive direct volume rendering with a number of state-of-the-art features.

MPI distributed

OSPRay can run on large-scale distributed memory systems with a high-performance MPI backend.

Visualization

OSPRay supports several visualization programs and is integrated into Kitware's ParaView implementation for VisIt, an open-source, interactive, scalable, visualization, animation, and analysis tool that runs on Unix, Windows, and Mac.

Open source

OSPRay is open-sourced under the Apache 2.0 license.

The purpose of OSPRay is to provide an open, easy-to-use rendering library that allows one to quickly build applications that use ray-tracing-based rendering for interactive applications (including both surface- and volume-based visualizations).

---

[3]Wald et al. (2017).

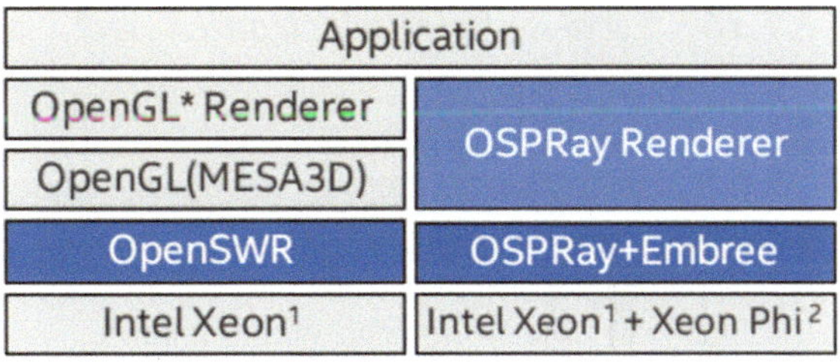

Fig. 8.41 OSPRay's
software stack (Intel)

Application	
OpenGL* Renderer	OSPRay Renderer
OpenGL(MESA3D)	
OpenSWR	OSPRay+Embree
Intel Xeon[1]	Intel Xeon[1] + Xeon Phi[2]

OSPRay is CPU-based and runs on anything from laptops, to workstations, to compute nodes in high-performance computing systems (HPC).

OSPRay internally builds on top of Embree and Intel's SPMD Program Compiler and utilizes instruction sets like Intel SSE4, AVX, AVX2, and AVX-512 to for rendering performance; thus, a CPU with support for at least SSE4.1 is required to run OSPRay (Fig. 8.41).

OSPRay is under continuing development, and the company does its best to guarantee stable release versions a certain number of bugs, as-yet-missing features, inconsistencies, or any other issues are still possible. Should one find any such issues, they are reported to OSPRay's GitHub Issue Tracker (https://github.com/ospray/OSPRay/issues).

8.1.15.1 Summary

Intel launched its Larabee project in 2009, and ray tracing was chosen as one of the showcase applications. The company hired experts in ray tracing and was engaged with universities in developing the Embree kernels and sequentially the OSPRay application to exhibit and exploit the benefits of a CPU for running ray-tracing software. Due to the branching characteristics of ray tracing, the CPU with its large memory area has been the processor of choice for most applications. Specialized hardware features have been added to GPUs to minimize the CPU's advantage which has only served Intel to increase their developments. The net result is ray tracing, in general, and has significantly benefited from this competition.

The Intel Rendering Framework includes high-performance, parallel software, rendering libraries such as Intel OpenSWR, Intel Embree, Intel OSPRay, and Intel OpenImage Denoise. These libraries have been created using a methodology and open-source community initiative known as Software Defined Visualization (SDVis) from Intel and industry collaborators. The goal of SDVis to improve the visual fidelity, performance, and efficiency of prominent visualization solutions—with a particular emphasis on supporting the rapidly growing big data usage on workstations, 3D motion picture animation, and visual effect infrastructures, and HPC supercomputing clusters without the memory limitations and cost of GPU-based solutions. For example, many primary visualization tools such as ParaView, VisIt (binary packages), and VMD have adopted the Intel Rendering Framework as well as professional, photorealistic rendering solutions like Dreamworks MoonRay renderer, and Chaos Group V-Ray and Corona rendering solutions.

8.1.16 Pica—SEED/Electronics Arts

At the start of 2018, Electronic Arts' Dice division (acquired in 2006) was the Swedish gaming sectors' biggest employer, with over 700 employees in Sweden. SEED is an internal incubator, focusing on high-technical innovation. The team is based in Los Angeles and Stockholm and works on advanced subjects such as deep learning, neural networks, and virtual humans.

SEED's research into new technologies and development techniques support EA's other studios, with AI being just one of many areas which are being looked into to enhance future games.

The Pica project was a real-time ray-tracing research effort done at SEED, a cross-disciplinary team working on graphics technologies and creative experiences at Electronic Arts. The Pica project also featured a mini-game for self-learning AI agents in a procedurally assembled world. SEED used their "Halcyon" research engine for the Pico ray-tracing demo.

Microsoft announced their DirectX Raytracing (DXR) extension; however, EA SEED had already been working on software, looking into how it could be applied in future games. The studio had already integrated ray tracing into their Halcyon research engine, revealing how it can impact future games with enhanced shadows, reflections, light refraction, and more, simulating light in a way that can't be replicated using traditional methods. DXR is only the start of ray tracing in gaming

Pica features a hybrid rendering pipeline where rasterization, computation, and ray tracing work together and enable real-time visuals with almost path-traced quality. PICA is a mini-game that SEED built for AI agents rather than humans. Using reinforcement learning, the agents learn to navigate and interact with the environment. They run around and fix the various machines, so that conveyor belts keep running efficiently.

SEED's demo illustrates what can be expected in future games which will exploit AI, ray tracing, and other technologies (Fig. 8.42).

SEED built the mini-game from the ground up using their Halcyon R&D framework. The team had the opportunity to be involved with DirectX Raytracing, with Nvidia and Microsoft, to explore some of the possibilities with the technology. SEED decided to create something a bit different and unusual. For the demo, they wanted cute visuals that would be clean and stylized yet grounded in physically based rendering. The team wanted to showcase the strengths of ray tracing, while also taking into account their small art department of two people. SEED used procedural level generation with an algorithm that drove layout and asset placement.

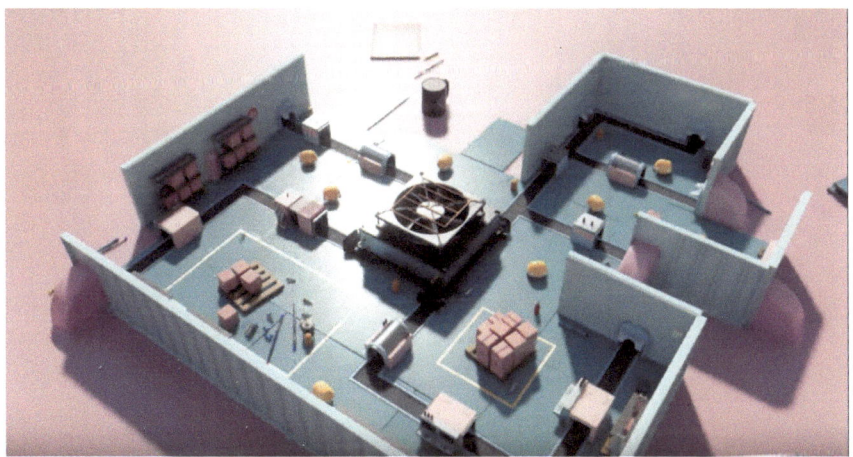

Fig. 8.42 Electronic Art's SEEd Pico AI simulator using ray tracing. *Source* EA

8.1.17 ProRender—AMD

AMD introduced its Radeon FireRender in early 2016 as a physically based rendering engine that can produce photorealistic images. In July 2016, at SIGGRAPH, the company renamed it ProRender.

Built on the company's Radeon-Rays middleware technology, Radeon ProRender's complete, scalable ray-tracing engine uses open industry standards to harness GPU and CPU performance for swift, impressive results. AMD uses Embree for the CPU implementation of ProRender.

Radeon-Rays is a GPU intersection acceleration library with support for heterogeneous systems. It exposes a C++ API for scene construction and asynchronous ray intersection queries. The current implementation is based on Metal for Mac platforms, and for Windows and Linux platforms with OpenCL, and supports execution on all platforms conforming to the OpenCL 1.2 standard. The company says it is not limited to AMD hardware or a specific operating system (see Sect. 8.4.3) (Fig. 8.43).

Radeon ProRender is a GPU-based ray-tracing renderer that offers features such as ray casting and shading. It is a physically based renderer that outputs rendered images and is targeted at M&E content creators and is also available for developers.

Materials

ProRender has an Uber shader which is adaptable to behave like Nvidia's MDL, Substance PBR maps, and other material standards such as MaterialX. The company's goal is to have a system which can be a drop-in replacement for others. Also, AMD is looking to add OSL support (for texture nodes) to the GPU renderer (Fig. 8.44).

Fig. 8.43 AMD's out-of-core render (AMD)

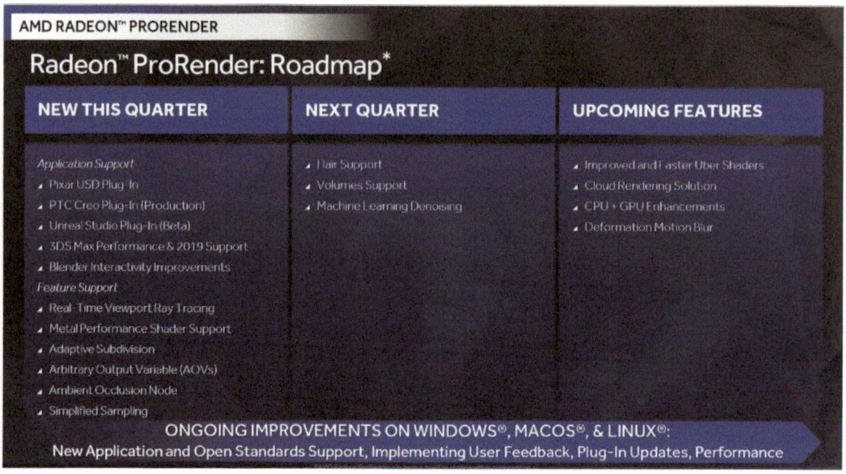

Fig. 8.44 AMD's ProRender road map

In the second half of 2018, AMD updated ProRender with several new features including an enhanced Uber shader and an ambient occlusion node for enhanced procedural texture workflows, such as making textures look dirty. Camera Motion Blur was added to recreate accurately a moving camera when rendering animations. Adaptive Subdivision, previously only available in the plug-in for Blender, has been added to the 3ds Max and Maya 1 plug-ins, allowing artists to render complex shapes from simple meshes.

Optimizations for plug-ins to accelerate multi-app workflows when working with large and complex scenes, and the plug-in for 3ds Max was updated to support 3ds Max 2019.

Along with the plug-ins and add-ins currently available for many popular 3D content creation applications, Radeon ProRender now offers open-source availability for developers.

The first content creation application to integrate ProRender natively was Maxon Cinema 4D R19, released in 2017. Maxon recently announced that R20 has new ProRender features such as subsurface scattering (SSS) for rendering realistic-looking skin, motion blur for animations and deformations, and multi-pass rendering for compositing.

The Foundry has also integrated ProRender natively into its Modo modeling program.

In 2018, Pixar made an open-source Universal Scene Description (USD) available for content creation pipelines with software that provides interchange and augments arbitrary 3D scenes that may be composed of many elemental assets.

Part of the USD toolset is the USDView interactive viewport to preview complex scenes. The Foundry has integrated this viewport into their Katana 3.0 application.

The PTC Creo plug-in supports exporting to Unreal Engine for VR visualization when used with ProRender Game. The SolidWorks plug-in importer has the same including decal support.

AMD released the code for open-source ProRender USD Hydra render delegate plug-in on GitHub that adds path-traced rendering for accurate previews when compared to the default OpenGL renderer. ProRender is open source via MIT license https://github.com/GPUOpen-LibrariesAndSDKs/RadeonRays_SDK.

8.1.17.1 Summary

AMD developed ProRender because the company believes strongly that ray tracing is the future and wants to bring it to as many users as possible in a way that is open. The company doesn't see themselves as a competitive product to traditional solutions in the ray-tracing market. They believe everyone should be rendering and hope to drive the adoption of rendering by as many users as possible so that they can make decisions in real time; this is especially true in the product design space.

Their goal is to get people using higher-quality rendering that can run on any hardware, but of course, preferably AMD's hardware. They are working with ISVs such as Maxon Cinema 4D to build that into Maxon's software. AMD says they would instead enable software providers such as Maxon or even other renderers to work on all hardware. However, if that is not possible, AMD has Radeon ProRender plug-ins that run just as well.

8.1.18 POV-Ray

As the story goes, it was in the 1980s that David Kirk Buck downloaded the source code for a Unix ray tracer and ran it on his Amiga. It intrigued him, and he decided to write his own ray tracer, calling it DKBTrace, his initials. In 1987, Aaron A.

Collins downloaded DKBTrace and produced an x86-based port of it. He and Buck then collaborated by adding more features. They posted results on the "You Can Call Me Ray" bulletin board system in Chicago. The program proved to be more popular than they expected, and they couldn't keep up with the demand for more features.

In July 1991, David turned the project over to a team of programmers working in the GraphDev forum on CompuServe and renamed it the "Persistence of Vision Raytracer", or "POV-Ray." Features of the application and a summary of its history are discussed in an interview in February 2008 with David Kirk Buck and Chris Cason on episode 24 of the free and open-source software (FLOSS) Weekly.

POV-Ray is a ray-tracing program that can generate images from a text-based scene description and is available for several platforms. POV-Ray is free and open-source software with the source code available under the AGPLv3.

In 2002, POV-Ray became the first ray tracer to render an image in orbit, rendered by Mark Shuttleworth inside the International Space Station (Fig. 8.45).

POV-Ray has evolved and matured considerably since its beginning. The most recent version contains a robust set of features including the following:

- Atmospheric effects such as fog and media (smoke, clouds)
- Image format support for textures and rendered output, including TGA, PNG, JPEG, among others

Fig. 8.45 A ray-traced image of glasses rendered in POV-Ray showing the perfect reflections and refractions, as well as shadows. *Source* Gilles Tran

- Library of ready-made scenes, textures, and objects
- Radiosity
- Reflections, refractions, and light caustics using photon mapping
- Support for a number of geometric primitives and constructive solid geometry
- Surface patterns such as wrinkles, bumps, and ripples, for use in procedural textures and bump mapping
- Turing—complete scene description language (SDL) that supports macros and loops
- Various light sources.

Like Blender, one of the main benefits of POV-Ray's is the ecosystem and third-party support such as tools, textures, models, scenes, and tutorials.

The current official version of POV-Ray is 3.7. This version includes:

- 16- and 32-bit integer data to density file
- 64-bit compatibility
- Bounding using BSP trees
- High dynamic range imaging (HDRI), including the OpenEXR and radiance file formats
- Symmetric multiprocessing (SMP), to allow the renderer to take advantage of multiple processors
- UV mapping to more primitives
- Official POV-Ray versions currently do not support shader plug-ins.

In addition to standard geometric shapes like tori, spheres, and heightfields, POV-Ray supports mathematically defined primitives. The primatives include isosurface (a finite approximation of an arbitrary function), the polynomial primitive (an infinite object defined by a 15th order or lower polynomial), the Julia fractal (a three-dimensional slice of a four-dimensional fractal), the super-quadratic ellipsoid (intermediate between a sphere and a cube), and the parametric primitive (using equations that represent its surface, rather than its interior).

8.1.18.1   Summary

Official modifications to the POV-Ray source tree are done and approved by the POV-Team. Most patch submission and bug reporting are done in the POV-Ray newsgroups on the news.povray.org news server (with a Web interface also available). Since POV-Ray's source is available, there are unofficial forks and patched versions of POV-Ray available from third parties; however, these are not officially supported by the POV-Team.

POV-Ray can be ported to any platform which has a compatible C++ compiler.

8.1.19 Redshift Renderer

Founded in 2012, Newport Beach-based Redshift claims that it has the world's first fully GPU-accelerated, biased renderer. The company offers a suite of features integrated with industry standard CG applications. The company also offers plug-ins for 3ds, Cinema 4D, Houdini, Katana, Maya, and Softimage.

Redshift Rendering Technologies was created with the ambition of developing a production-level, GPU-accelerated renderer with ample support for biased global illumination techniques that only ran on the CPU. With its latest version, the company claims to have created the world's first GPU-accelerated renderer which can meet the specific needs of contemporary high-end rendering. Redshift offers a lot of new features in the latest versions and helps to support the specific demands of the rendering, including the complicated ones.

Instead of approaching the problem of GPU rendering from a production CPU renderer perspective, the founders of Redshift come from a background in games and the real-time GPU rendering requirements they have.

Robert Slater, one of the co-founders of Redshift, says that it is not just another GPU renderer. The company's goal was to create a final-frame production-ready renderer that "brings the flexibility of biased CPU rendering to the power of the GPU." They have a flexible material system, multiple biased global illumination modes for diffuse bounces and caustics and have full sampling controls for cleanup of noise. However, the real magic is their memory management scheme.

One of the criticisms of using a GPU for ray tracing is the limited (relative to a CPU) memory space. A CPU can be equipped with up to 256 GB of RAM, whereas the largest GDDR memory available on an AIB is 32 GB. Redshift, says Panos Zompolas, CTO and co-founder, can support a virtually unlimited number and size of bitmap textures, which means an artist can render scenes containing a terabyte of textures without running out of memory or crashing. They do this by using out-of-core paging technology, meaning that all assets don't need to be in GDDR at once. They also have built-in UDIM (see Glossary) and UVTILE texture tile support, which allows artists to efficiently texture tiles without having to rely on complex shader node graphs.

GPU and biasing

The company says Redshift has the quality and features of a CPU renderer, but at speeds which are identical to a GPU renderer. However, unlike the conventional GPU renderer, Redshift is a biased renderer which enables the user to fine-tune the settings of individual techniques to get the best possible performance to quality ratio for their product. It uses approximation and interpolation techniques to achieve noise-free results with relatively few samples, making it much faster than unbiased rendering.

Redshift supports several biased global illumination techniques including:

- Brute-force GI
- Photon mapping (with caustics)

- Irradiance cache (similar to irradiance map and final gather)
- Irradiance point cloud (similar to Importons and Light Cache).

Users choose the techniques that work best for their particular scene.

Benchmark—In 2017, the company introduced a benchmarking utility for its GPU-based production renderer. The benchmark which is built into the current release works with the 3ds Max, Cinema 4D, and Houdini editions of the software, and with a little tweaking on Windows, Linux, and macOS.

Out-of-core geometry and textures

The memory management system allows rendering of scenes which contains hundreds of millions of polygons and terabytes of texture information. Redshift uses an out-of-core architecture for geometry and textures, allowing you to render large scenes that would otherwise never fit in video memory (Fig. 8.46).

A common problem with GPU renderers is that they are limited by the available memory (GDDR) on the AIB and can only render scenes where the geometry and textures fit entirely in video memory. This poses a problem for rendering large scenes with many millions of polygons and gigabytes of textures.

Burtnyk says with Redshift, one can render scenes with tens of millions of polygons and a virtually unlimited number of textures with off-the-shelf hardware.

Global illumination

In real life, light photons originate from light sources, bounce off several surfaces, have their colors modified by these surfaces, and eventually reach our eyes.

Fig. 8.46 Out-of-core geometry and textures. *Source* Redshift

Fig. 8.47 Without (left) and with (right) GI—notice the color bleeding. *Source* Redshift

In computer graphics, global illumination (GI) attempts to simulate those photon bouncing interactions. This simulation adds realism to lighting and helps achieve more lifelike images. Burtnyk says Redshift Renderer can achieve fast indirect lighting by utilizing biased point-based GI techniques, as well as brute-force GI (Fig. 8.47).

GI can have a profound effect even on straightforward scenes, as shown above. The light that reaches object surfaces without any bounces is referred to as direct lighting. Once the light has bounced off one or more surfaces, it is referred to as indirect lighting. So what GI essentially computes is indirect lighting.

Proxies

Redshift allows the user to export objects and lights to Redshift Proxy files, and then other scenes can easily reference them. Proxies allow for powerful shader, matte, and visibility flag overrides as often required in production. However, getting the proxies to run in a render farm can be challenging, but possible.

Additional features that can be found in Redshift include the following:

Transformation and deformation blur—Redshift also supports multi-step transformation blur and two-step deformation blur.

Volumetric rendering—Redshift supports OpenVDB (see Glossary) rendering in each of the 3D apps and native volume rendering in Houdini. Redshift lights can cast volumetric lighting around the images.

Hair rendering with "Min Pixel Width"—There is a possibility that thin hair can generate noisy renders. Hence, Redshift supports "MPW" rendering which smoothens the look of thin and hard-to-sample hairs.

Tessellation and displacement—Redshift's tessellation supports edge and vertex creasing with separate UV smoothing control.

Per-object flexibility—Objects have advanced matte features and tracing options such as self-shadowing and primary/secondary ray visibility.

Shading and Texturing—Redshift supports advanced shading networks and texturing capabilities as needed for production-quality rendering. There can be different types of shading employed:

- Physically based materials
- Ray switches
- Hair shader
- Dedicated skin shaders
- Round corners
- Displacement mapping with "autobump"
- No texturing limitations
- Powerful shading attributes
- Sprite node
- A large variety of nodes.

Materials

There are 135 premade complex materials:

- Ten ceramic materials
- Eight concrete–asphalt materials
- Three emissive materials
- Seven fabric materials
- Four ground materials
- Four leather materials
- Twenty-one metal materials
- Two organic materials
- Four paint materials
- Ten paper materials
- Three plastic materials
- Eleven plastic–rubber materials
- Thirteen stone materials
- Two terracotta materials
- Eleven translucent materials
- Twenty wood material.

8.1.19.1 Summary

Though launched in 2012, the product has created a fan-following for itself with the users up for praises for the speed and quality of the product. With the upcoming versions, improvements like having more materials seem a norm. However, it can be a little taxing for the GPU which the company needs to take care in the future versions. So, while playing against the likes of V-Ray and Maxwell, Redshift has made its presence felt among the users and will surely be a steady company of the future.

Redshift has been used for several Hollywood projects including one by Nickelodeon. Redshift is fast and is helped by using the biggest GPU's one can get —up to eight times faster than a CPU doing the same work.

8.1.20 RenderMan—Pixar

The "group now known as Pixar" came together in about 1975 on Long Island and had the original vision then to make a completely digital movie. They changed their name several times but held the vision. Pixar began in 1979 as the Graphics Group, part of the Lucasfilm computer division, before it was spin out as a private corporation in 1986, with funding by Apple's co-founder Steve Jobs, who became the majority shareholder. Twenty years later in 2006, Disney purchased Pixar for $7.4 billion.

Pixar's RenderMan (formerly PhotoRealistic RenderMan) is proprietary photorealistic 3D rendering software program produced by Pixar Animation Studios. Pixar uses RenderMan to render their in-house 3D animated movie productions, and it is also available as a commercial product and licensed to third parties.

On May 30, 2014, Pixar announced that it would offer a free non-commercial version of RenderMan that would be available to download in August 2014. The product's release was postponed to early 2015. As of March 23, 2015, RenderMan was available for free for non-commercial use. However, some users have complained that it was difficult to use without a Pixar-sized team to do the shading, lighting, and other functions.

Historically, RenderMan used the REYES algorithm to render images with added support for advanced effects such as ray tracing and global illumination. Support for REYES rendering and the RenderMan Shading Language were removed from RenderMan in 2016. RenderMan currently uses Monte Carlo Path Tracing to generate images. An excellent history of RenderMan can be found at Fxguide.[4] https://tinyurl.com/y7fuqh9p.

REYES (Renders Everything You Ever Saw) was the brainchild of Rob Cook, Loren Carpenter, and Ed Catmull, and it is not actually 'RenderMan'. It is a part of the RenderMan-compliant renderer that Pixar has used and sold and predates what might be thought of as RenderMan. It was in May 1988 when the original RenderMan interface 3.0 was launched, but it was more than 25 years for the REYES renderer which was released in 1984 and different from PRMan which was released in 1989.

It was at SIGGRAPH 1987, Anaheim, that Cook, Carpenter, and Catmull delivered the original paper the REYES image rendering architecture. The paper

---

[4]https://www.fxguide.com/featured/pixars-RenderMan-turns-25/.

Fig. 8.48 A scene out of Incredibles 2. *Source* Pixar/Disney

was given at a time when a full ray-traced system just wasn't viable. REYES provided a way to render complex scenes, but it is just a component of what makes RenderMan the powerhouse it is and has been for two and a half decades.

RenderMan has been developed using Pixar's core rendering technology starting 32 years ago and is designed to meet the increasing challenges of 3D animation and visual effects. The tool is utilized for all the rendering work from Pixar production, including feature films, shorts video content, video materials for theme parks, and marketing. The tool has been liked and appreciated by people across the world, and this is visible from the success of various films which have used RenderMan. The tool has been used in almost every Visual Effects Academy Award Winner and Nominee for over 15 years (Fig. 8.48).

The latest release of RenderMan is version 22 which the company claims to have a redesigned core for interactive rendering of shaders, lights, and geometry, as well as new studio tools which provide cutting-edge pipeline groundwork. It has several new features compared to the previous versions as follows:

Live rendering

The company says it rewrote each bridge product to provide an optimal user experience for always-on live rendering.

Pixar unified

With this functionality, one can use the same advanced light integrator developed at Pixar, which includes unique ways to employ indirect light. This integrator combines different types of light transport in a single production-focused tool. Pixar Unified offers unidirectional and bidirectional Path Tracing which can be controlled on a per-light basis that allows usage of both. The tool also offers techniques based on computer learning from Disney Research where indirect light is guided with light paths. The Pixar Unified Integrator has been used on movies like *Finding Dory*, *Cars 3*, *Coco*, and *Incredibles 2*.

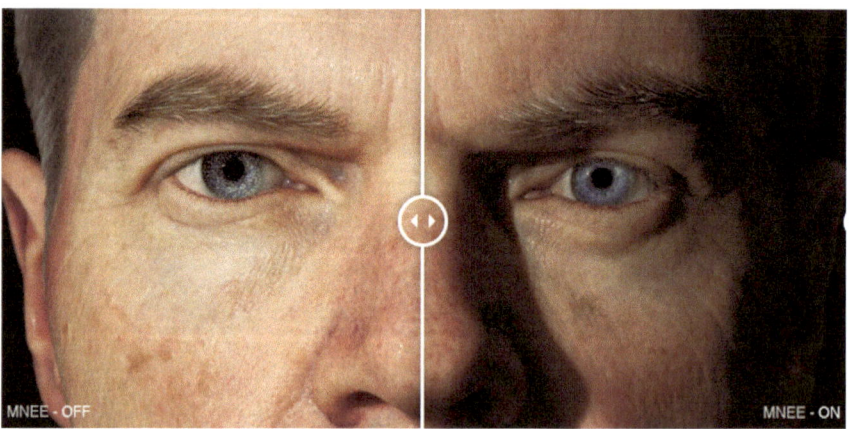

Fig. 8.49 Impact of MNEE on the image. *Source* Pixar/Disney

Photorealism

Effects, such as caustics, are taken care of by Pixar Unified. The Pixar Unified Integrator contains functionality for quickly resolving caustic paths, a technique called Manifold Next Event Estimation (MNEE), allowing caustic paths to resolve in a short time. This option allows for creating realistic eyes, which is required for achieving realistic digital humans, as illustrated in the next image (Fig. 8.49).

Performance improvements

The company has worked on the performance and speed in their latest version. Pixar claims that speed has gone up by almost 2X across the board and almost 6X in curves and the company has thanked their architecture designs and new curved description for this enhancement.

Performance breakdown

The performance is compared between RenderMan 21.5 versus 22.0:

- Faster overall—10% to 2x
- Memory reduction—10–30%
- Time to first pixel—from 20% to 10X
- New ray-tracing core—pure tracing 3X
- Light discovery—large numbers of lights render 25% faster
- Curve rewrite—from 2x to 6x faster and less memory
- Particle improvements—2X faster and 30% less memory
- Better sampling—convergence looks better, earlier.

Preset browser upgrade and materials

Pixar says RenderMan has an improved Preset Browser which now supports new features in all three bridges, which makes sharing assets (lights, shaders, and textures) between DCCs simple.

Rendering at Pixar

Pixar continues to elevate and enhance RenderMan and has introduced the RenderMan XPU project. XPU is addressing the challenge of rendering Pixar-scale production assets on systems with a mix of CPU and GPU capabilities. From a single set of assets, XPU produces film-quality renderings by seamlessly using all available compute cores concurrently. XPU is a single renderer that can operate on a variety of systems, from render farm machines with mid-range CPUs only all the way up to workstations or servers having many-core CPUs and multiple extreme GPUs.

Scene complexity and artist dexterity

Demands on artists and tools continue to evolve, and scene complexity grows. Film, television, and other formats call for more realism as well as more fantastic fictional realms. With tighter production schedules, maximizing artist productivity is essential. Artists require both greater interactivity and finer-grained control when dealing with tremendous, high-quality assets. Artists are also more productive when rendered previews accurately reflect the look of the final frames coming off the farm.

The mission of XPU is to leverage available CPU automatically and GPU compute power to provide artists with optimum performance and flexibility on production scenes, all from within the art tools that they are already using. XPU is in active development at Pixar and was available after the commercial release of RenderMan 22.

At Pixar, each of their productions is more complex than the last, with unique technical innovations required to allow their artists to create the richness and detail that define each of the studio's films. Artists demand speed and flexibility—requiring the ability to tweak lighting and shading at the very last moment to enhance an image in service of the story and the director's vision. Many studios are familiar with these demanding trends.

Today, it is common in VFX and animation to have to deal with overmodeled geometry, vast numbers of textures, sprawling shading networks, and massive datasets with large numbers of lights. Every part of the scene must be editable, so artists can enhance a shot at any time up to final render, all in service of enhancing the story (Fig. 8.50).

The average shot in Coco took 27 GB of memory with outliers requiring 70 GB or more. There were shots with millions of point lights. RenderMan has always been inspired by these technical challenges and is focused on providing high-quality results, at any scale, with the most adaptable versatility, while responding to the constantly evolving artistic landscape.

Fig. 8.50 Rendered by XPU, a massive scene from Coco (without shaders and lights)

Over the past several years, and predating the RenderMan XPU project, Pixar's internal tools team developed a GPU-based ray tracer, built on Nvidia's CUDA and OptiX. An application called Flow was built around that renderer to deliver a real-time shading system to Pixar's artists. To date, Flow has helped artists shade hundreds of assets across several feature films like *Coco* and *The Incredibles 2*.

The Flow system was engineered so that the GPU renderer shares as much core shading logic as possible with the final renders coming from RenderMan, making it far easier for Pixar to keep the two renderers in sync. However, exact matching is difficult since RenderMan has features and resources beyond what Flow was currently able to deliver on the GPU only.

This is interesting, though not new

One aspect is to enable running on CPU or GPU, or a mix of both. Renderers like V-Ray or AMD FireRay (and others) do the same. However, maybe the XPU delivers higher flexibility by rendering quickly on the artist desktop and rendering quickly on farms. That render farm may be on a set of desktops running at night, a rented rack with specialty GPUs, a dedicated on-premises CPU-based datacenter, or in the cloud on a set of economically provisioned instances. In the latter two cases, a GPU with the capacity to handle the complexity of production assets may not be available.

8.1.20.1 Summary

The ray tracer, being from a company which has been around for 32 years and used in so many movies, has built a strong confidence among the users of the program. Its speed and efficiency are also appreciated; however, some users feel the lack of user-friendliness and options as a point which the company can improve in, particularly when so many companies like Maxwell and Redshift have entered the market in the last ten years.

The company acknowledges that mental ray was an early commercial ray-tracing renderer although not certain if it was the first commercial ray tracer offered. And they agree that RenderMan has never been a classic ray tracer. It started with

REYES instead, added an interesting hybrid tracer, and evolved into the sophisticated path tracer available today.

One of the rationales for developing the REYES algorithm was to avoid the slowness of ray tracing, while also having something that could scale to the requirements of feature film animation—but still providing nearly photoreal lighting and shading effects. Dynamic, programmable proceduralism for shading and geometry creation was another part, that is distinct from the rendering algorithm itself, but trickier to do well in a pure ray tracer. Therefore, the people at Pixar bristle a little at RenderMan being described as "never capable of useful ray tracing." REYES was plenty useful and delivered hundreds of commercially successful customer films, and classic ray tracing per se was never the end goal—that is the all-important context.

8.1.21 Rigid Gems—FerioWorks.LLC

Yoshihiro Fukurono living in Ebisu, Tokyo, had been developing 3D graphics program since he was 17 years old. Skipping college to pursue his dream, he made a demonstration program to get a job; he thought it would be important to demonstrate his skills. So, in 2008 he began developing a ray-tracing program to present and presumably sell jewelry. Part of his inspiration came from Stéphane Guy, and Cyril Soler's paper in SIGGRAPH about presenting gems,[5] and Arvo and Kirk's 1987 paper on ray tracing.[6]

Fukurono-san used assets from 3D Lapidary and TurboSquid to create his collection. All of the software was written by Fukurono; he didn't even use any kernels such as Embree, OptiX, or Radeon-Rays, or any open-source ray-tracing software (Fig. 8.51).

Because expensive equipment is was necessary to make it an off-line renderer. The demo is able to run at 60 frames per second (fps) with the latest GPU. It is a hybrid ray-tracing technique, and the non-critical part of the scene does not use ray tracing. Fukurono-san started developing the hybrid software in 2010. Today, hybrid is part of the latest API DirectX Raytracing. To keep the frame rate up, he chose a fixed number of bounces, with some exceptions in highly faceted regions. DirectX Raytracing technology is also in use.

FerioWorks offers a demo presentation program of their software http://www.rigidgems.sakura.ne.jp/files/RigidGems2_2.zip which generates a small (855 kB) program and a 35 mB data file. It contains about 12 examples of stone presentation with reflections and caustics.

The company's software has been used by other firms for displaying their products.

---

[5]Stéphane and Cyril (2004).
[6]Arvo and Kirk (1987).

Fig. 8.51 Sparkly ray-traced gems. *Source* FerioWorks

8.1.22   Tachyon

When John Stone was at the University of Illinois, he developed a parallel ray-tracing library in 1998 named *Tachyon*, for use on distributed memory parallel computers, shared memory computers, and clusters of workstations. Stone is now on the research staff at the Beckman Institute, but Tachyon lives on. Tachyon supports Message Passing Interface (MPI) for distributed memory parallel computers and threads for shared memory machines and can support both simultaneously for clusters of shared memory machines. Tachyon has been selected for inclusion in the SPEC MPI2007 benchmark suite. Tachyon supports the typical ray tracer features, most of the standard geometric primitives, shading and texturing modes. It also supports fewer common features such as HDR image output, ambient occlusion lighting, and support for various triangle mesh and volumetric texture formats beneficial for molecular visualization (e.g., rendering VMD scenes) (Fig. 8.52).

Tachyon is heavily used as a built-in ray-tracing engine within VMD, where it is frequently used to render scenes containing hundreds of millions of objects, often with ambient occlusion lighting, depth cueing, angle-modulated transparency, and other features that are well suited for molecular visualization. Tachyon has been used to render Volume Management Device (VMD) movies in parallel on the NCSA Blue Waters supercomputer, on over 15,000 CPU cores. I'm currently evaluating the use of GPU acceleration techniques for Tachyon, using Nvidia OptiX as a backend, and possibly with the use of some custom CUDA/OpenCL kernels.

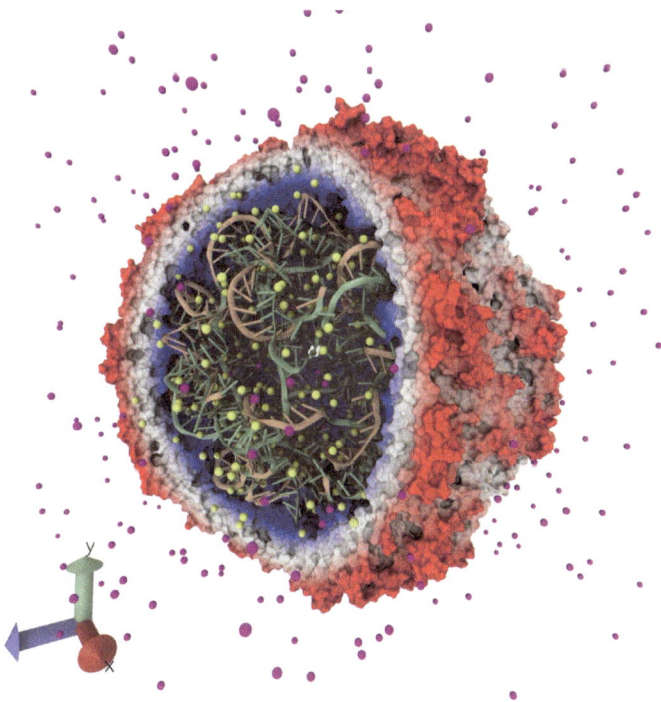

Fig. 8.52 Satellite tobacco mosaic virus molecular graphics produced in VMD and rendered using Tachyon (John Stone)

8.1.23 V-Ray—Chaos Group

The Chaos Group began in 1997 as a 3D design and animation studio in Sofia, Bulgaria. One of their early projects required them to render atmospheric effects, but a proper plug-in wasn't available, so they had to develop their own, and a few years later Phoenix FD (originally called Atmos Blender) was born.

Later, needing a way to cast realistic shadows with Phoenix FD, they started writing their own ray-tracing solution. Impressed by its speed, Peter and Vlado realized it could be a tool other artists and designers might be interested in, and the development of V-Ray officially began. In late 2001, Peter and Vlado release the first public beta of V-Ray.

Chaos Group is a pioneer in the computer graphics industry and has a history of helping artists and designers create photorealistic images and animation used for design, television, and movies. The company takes pride in the diversity of their markets, as it has grown to be a standard in leading design studios, architectural firms, advertising agencies, and visual effect companies around the globe.

In March 2002, the Chaos Group released their first official version of V-Ray for 3ds Max and today provides ray-tracing software for thousands of customers across

Fig. 8.53 Architectural image rendered in V-Ray. *Source* Chaos

a wide variety of content creation applications. While best known for its Academy Award-winning V-Ray renderer, the company also produces Corona Renderer, Phoenix FD for fluid dynamics, and VRscans, which is a patented material scanning technology. In 2019, Chaos Group had over 300 employees worldwide and claims to be the largest company solely dedicated to rendering research and development.

The company's research and development division has been aggressive in developing new designs and products in cloud rendering, material scanning, and real time and is collaborating with various artists, industry leaders, and academic researchers to advance ray tracing.

Chaos Group's first rendering product, V-Ray for 3ds Max, has been one of the most popular plug-ins of any kind developed for Autodesk's 3ds Max. And the company claims it is the renderer of choice for most 3ds Max-based visual effect work and the leading renderer in architectural visualization (Fig. 8.53).[7]

The success of V-Ray for 3ds Max led to the development of V-Ray for additional digital content creation applications such as Maya, SketchUp, Rhino, Revit, Modo, Nuke, Katana, Blender, Unreal Engine, and Houdini. Each version is custom integrated to match the application's native workflow as closely as possible. Also, each version includes the ability to run V-Ray on a network, either as a host application or as a command-line stand-alone version.

Chaos Group provides the V-Ray AppSDK for control of the rendering pipeline, as well as for integrating V-Ray within custom applications. As examples, both Adobe Dimension and formZ use a licensed version of V-Ray AppSDK for their rendering.

---

[7]Mottle (2018).

Fig. 8.54   Ray-traced image rendered in V-Ray for 3ds Max. *Source* © Toni Bratincevic

Academy Award

In 2017, The Academy of Motion Picture Arts and Sciences presented Chaos Group co-founder Vlado Koylazov with a Scientific and Engineering Award for the "original concept, design and implementation of V-Ray."[8] The academy noted, "V-Ray's efficient production-ready approach to ray tracing and global illumination, its support for a wide variety of workflows, and its broad industry acceptance were instrumental in the widespread adoption of fully ray-traced rendering for motion pictures" (Fig. 8.54).

Since 2002, V-Ray has been used on over 200 feature films including *Avengers: Infinity War*, *Black Panther*, and *Ready Player One*. V-Ray use is also widespread on television and streaming productions, helping to increase ray-traced realism on series like *Game of Thrones*, *The Walking Dead,* and *Westworld*.

V-Ray's, ray-tracing technology

Over the years, the company has continuously updated and upgraded its program to embrace the latest hardware and software developments.

Modular ray-tracing architecture

V-Ray was one of the first renderers to have a modular ray-tracing architecture. While most renderers had relied on special hard-coded shaders, Chaos abstracted its ray-tracing algorithms, separating them from the scene materials, objects, and light sources. That provided a means to implement different ray-tracing methods such as brute force, irradiance mapping, photon mapping, and the company's proprietary Light Cache technique. Also, to achieve cleaner, noise-free images, this modular

---

[8]"18 Scientific and Technical Achievements To Be Honored With Academy Awards," January 4, 2017,   https://www.oscars.org/news/18-scientific-and-technical-achievements-be-honored-academy-awards-0.

approach also allowed for the implementation of new and adaptive image samplers, with V-Ray adopting variance-based image sampling with the release of V-Ray 3.3.

Adaptive ray tracing

Adaptive ray-tracing techniques such as variance-based adaptive sampling allow V-Ray to optimize its calculations automatically, without custom input from the user. Additional adaptive features had to be developed to make V-Ray more automated. That put more of the analytic workload onto V-Ray and removing the need for artists to control local values for lighting and materials. As part of this trajectory, Chaos Group released Adaptive Lights in 2017, which dramatically reduced the number of calculations required to render scenes with many lights.

Scene intelligence

Capping three years of R&D, Chaos Group introduced V-Ray Scene Intelligence, an automatic scene analysis feature built on machine learning techniques. Inspired by information gathered from V-Ray's Light Cache global illumination algorithm, scene intelligence automatically analyzes 3D scenes to produce faster, cleaner renders. The technology debuted in V-Ray Next for 3ds Max and provides the backbone for smart features like adaptive dome light, automatic exposure, and automatic white balance.

Maximizing hardware

Chaos claim several hardware acceleration advancements with their program including GPU, GPU and CPU, as well as distributed rendering.

GPU rendering

V-Ray has one of the longest histories with GPU ray tracing, showing its first GPU-based renderer (V-Ray RT) at SIGGRAPH 2009 (Fig. 8.55).[9]

While V-Ray RT started as an interactive ray-tracing engine initially used for *look* development, it has grown with successive editions into V-Ray GPU, a fully featured production render, now included with every new version of V-Ray. V-Ray GPU is optimized for Nvidia CUDA and was the first commercial renderer to support Nvidia's NVLink.

GPU + CPU hybrid rendering

In 2017, Chaos Group introduced GPU + CPU hybrid rendering, adding CPU support to its Nvidia CUDA-powered GPU renderer. Using this method, artists could utilize all available hardware by rendering scenes using GPUs, CPUs, or a combination of both. For artists that have a GPU-powered workstation and a CPU-based render farm, hybrid rendering has opened up more flexibility on production workflows.

---

[9]Suarez (2009).

Fig. 8.55 Image rendered in V-Ray GPU. *Source* © Double Aye

Distributed rendering

In addition to standard network rendering, where a single computer renders one image, V-Ray was one of the first to implement a distributed rendering system. In a distributed rendering system, a single image is calculated across multiple computers. By leveraging more compute capabilities, professional artists and production teams have been able to be more responsive to requests for higher-resolution imagery at a much faster pace.

Cloud rendering

Chaos Group entered the cloud rendering market through partnerships with Chaos' service and Chaos Cloud. Chaos Group's early partnerships with companies like AWS Thinkbox Deadline and Google Cloud's Zync made V-Ray accessible to production artists on all major services and render farms. In 2012, Atomic Fiction used a combination of Zync and V-Ray to render the first fully cloud-rendered film in *Flight*. They followed this up with the second cloud-rendered film, *The Walk*, in 2015.

However, Rebus Farms and many other small render farms did this before AWS bought Thinkbox; even then, it took several years for AWS to figure out how to do V-Ray. Ralph Alvarez' SquidNet distributed computing software was doing V-Ray well before then on a least 10 independent commercial render farms including RenderStorm.

Chaos is stating that these are two important cloud rendering partnerships, rather than the first relationships of its kind.

Introduced in 2017 and at SIGGRAPH 2018 Chaos Group partnered with Google Cloud Platform (GCP) on Chaos Cloud and offered a free public version. The GCP-built service is notable for simplifying the cloud rendering experience to a single click. The goal is to open up a fast form of cloud rendering to professional artists without the complexity of having to track assets, manage licenses, or set up virtual machines. Chaos Cloud launched in Q1 of 2019.

Ray tracing meets real time

The launch of V-Ray for Unreal in 2018 was the first direct connection from an off-line renderer to the popular game engine, effectively consolidating two work-flows for artists and designers (Fig. 8.56).

For markets exploring immersive experiences, especially in the architectural and design sectors, the requirement to learn how to navigate a game engine has proven difficult. V-Ray for Unreal operates as a bridge, letting artists bring V-Ray scenes into Unreal that feature fully baked lighting and global illumination. The bridge also works in reverse, letting users render content from their experiences with full ray tracing.

Real-time ray tracing and Project Lavina

Filmmaker Kevin Margo create a short film with real-time ray tracing was on the CONSTRUCT project in 2014,[10] which saw independent filmmaker Kevin Margo create a short with the help of cutting-edge virtual production techniques. Chaos Group designed a special prototype of V-Ray for Autodesk's MotionBuilder, enabling Margo to apply live motion capture to predesigned virtual characters in real time.

In 2018, Chaos Group announced the world's first real-time ray tracer. Accelerated with Nvidia's RTX ray-tracing-enabled GPUs, the Project Lavina demo represented one of the first major applications for the technology and a course change for real-time ray tracing, which until this announcement was assumed to require a game engine. Game engines have shortcuts to accomplish real-time ren-ders, which can affect the final look. Project Lavina, on the other hand, promises direct compatibility and translation of V-Ray assets, so artists can see an immediate representation of their vision with physically accurate lighting, reflections, and global illumination (Fig. 8.57).

---

[10]Starr (2014).

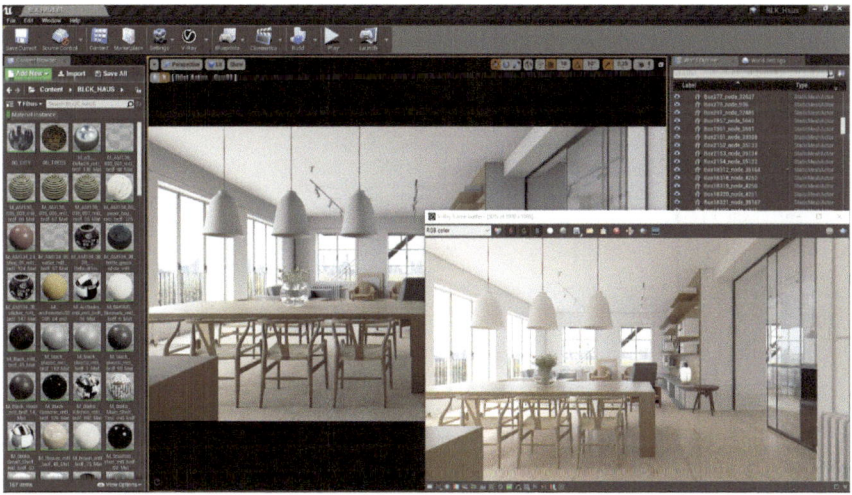

Fig. 8.56 Screenshot of V-Ray for Unreal. Image courtesy of Chaos Group

Fig. 8.57 Screenshot of Project Lavina ray tracing 300 billion triangles in real time. Image courtesy of Chaos Group

The Project Lavina demo depicted a massive forest scene with 300 billion triangles and 80,000 instances running at 24–30 fps. Unlike game engine rendering, there were no rasterized graphics or reduced level of detail.

The opportunity for Chaos Group is that they are taking over a significant piece of the gaming engine value proposition and enabling different types of applications to access real-time rendering. The company mentions applications such as virtual

Fig. 8.58 Image rendered in V-Ray using VRscans scanned materials. *Source* © Visual State

productions and VR, 3D configurators and CAD walk-throughs, product demos, etc., also fall into this category.

Material scanning, industry standards support, and research

Materials are critical to the success of a ray-traced image, and all of the ray-tracing suppliers have spent great sums of time and money in developing their material libraries and classification techniques.

VRscans

In 2016, Chaos Group announced VRscans, a patented material scanning technology that can produce an exact digital replica of a physical material with sub-mm precision. VRscans is a combination of a hardware-based scanning service and a software-based rendering plug-in that work together to create material properties for realistic renderings, without the usual workflow of texture maps and shader settings (Fig. 8.58).

The process begins with a scan of an existing real-world object surface. VRscans uses bidirectional texture functions (BTFs) instead of typical BRDF approximations (such as Phong, Blinn, and Ward) to capture a material's true surface appearance, texture data, and its unique response to light.

Stored in a proprietary VRscans material format, the scanned material is then read into the CG scene using the VRscans plug-in and is ready for rendering through V-Ray without much (if any) additional tweaking required to match the original scanned material's surface.

The company also introduced the VRscans library which included over 650 photorealistic materials for automotive, industrial design, and architectural projects.

Fig. 8.59 Procedural Stochastic Flakes material rendered in V-Ray. Image courtesy of Chaos Group

Industry standards

While V-Ray comes with a library of materials, Chaos Group has shown a commitment to supporting standard initiatives that seek to bring consistency to physically based rendering (PBR), visual effects, and design-based workflows (Fig. 8.59).

That includes participation in TurboSquid's StemCell Advisory Board[11]; support for Nvidia's Material Definition Language (MDL) format; support for Open Shading Language (OSL); and compatibility with X-Rite's AxF format and Allegorithmic's (Adobe) PBR-based substances. In 2018, Chaos Group added direct PBR compatibility by adding a metalness[12] reflection option to their standard V-Ray material shader, further connecting real-time and ray-traced workflows.

Stochastic Flakes research

Research and development into the simulation of car paints, snow, and other glittery materials led to a breakthrough in 2017 with the debut of the Stochastic Flakes material in V-Ray 3.6.[13] The material works by procedurally simulating the aggregated effect of a large number of flakes scattered over the surface of an object at render time.

---

[11]https://www.turbosquid.com/3d-modeling/stemcell/stemcell-advisory-board/.

[12]Nichols (2018).

[13]Seymour (2016).

Fig. 8.60 Comparison of original versus denoised render using the V-Ray Denoiser. Image courtesy of Chaos Group

Denoising

V-Ray comes with two denoisers that help artists address different parts of the rendering/denoising equation (Fig. 8.60).

The V-Ray Denoiser is the production option that allows users to render an image up to a certain threshold or time limit and then lets V-Ray denoise the image based on all available information coming in from the various render elements that will make up the final composite.[14]

The AI Denoiser, based on Nvidia AI-accelerated denoising technology, is designed specifically for non-final interactive rendering.[15] Its speed and clarity make it well suited for lighting and general scene composition. The AI component was trained using thousands of 3D scenes and images and can dramatically reduce the time it takes to render a noiseless image.

Acquisitions and investments

In August 2017, the Chaos Group acquired Prague-based **Render Legion**, creator of the Corona Renderer (Fig. 8.61).

With this new product and Chaos's V-Ray, the company was able to offer even more rendering solutions for the architectural visualization industry. The Render Legion acquisition was Chaos Group's largest investment to date. It was the third investment by the visualization company in the previous two years, including interactive presentation platform **CL3VER** and virtual reality pioneer **Nurulize**.

---

[14]Nichols (2018).

[15]Nichols (2017).

Fig. 8.61 Image rendered in Corona. © Gustavo Coutinho Alves

8.1.23.1 Summary

Chaos' V-Ray has found its way into dozens of specialized applications from movie production to toothbrush ads, from clothing design and fitting to architectural renderings.

Marianna Yakimova from an art studio "Pompidou" has recently presented a stunning work with a girl in a pink dress. The artist and her team created the model for a perfume ad with an idea of a dress looking like a blooming flower bud (Fig. 8.62).

The artists used ZBrush for sculpting, Marvelous Designer for the dress, Ornatrix for her hair, and V-Ray for the final render.

Looking at the future, Chaos' approach to AI is not strictly machine learning and doesn't give the data to multiple machines to learn but does give the V-Ray Light Cache capabilities to learn as much as possible from a scene. The first example of this was in the version when Chaos added adaptive lights and the system could learn where all the lights were in the scene. Another example was the introduction of variance-based adaptive sampling. Chaos eliminated the need to set individual subdivisions on materials and lights, or even camera effects like depth of field.

Fig. 8.62 Fashion design firms use ray tracing and CAD mesh to design perfectly fitting clothes. © 3D art-studio Pompidou

8.1.24   VRED—Autodesk

VRED is the predecessor of Autodesk's Showcase 3D visualization and 3D presentation software which the company stopped offering after March 2017. Showcase was used in several industry categories from manufacturing to M&E and automotive design, and Autodesk has now segmented applications for visualization in those categories. However, VRED Design cannot open or import Showcase files. Autodesk's cloud-based rendering system is called A360.

VRED is a sophisticated real-time rendering engine Autodesk acquired from Germany-based PI-VR in 2013 and is a high-end tool, intended for photorealistic design visualization in product development. VRED supports pixel fidelity surface display of native CAD data through unique support for interactive NURBS rendering (Fig. 8.63).

PI-VR specialized in real-time visualization technology for product development, primarily automotive. Software acquired included the VRED line of highly realistic 3D visualization tools. Autodesk uses the acquired technology to enhance its software for automotive design. Alias Studio is Autodesk's flagship product in automotive, but the new technology is also used in products including 3ds Max, Maya, and Showcase.

In 2011, Autodesk acquired Numenus for its ray-tracing technology, at the time also designated for automotive users first and foremost. And in April 2016, the company acquired leading ray-tracing supplier Solid Angle, producer of the popular Arnold ray tracer.

Autodesk's goal with Arnold GPU is to have a single renderer, feature/pixel/API compatible with the CPU. So, the GPU renderer will have no more bias than the CPU one. Windows and Linux are supported now. Autodesk says they will support Mac as soon as there is support for Nvidia eGPUs.

Autodesk doesn't have any plans to implement bidirectional Path Tracing in Arnold, at least not immediately. The company is looking at alternate light transport techniques to tackle interior renders and caustics.

Renders can be completed locally or sent to a cloud service. The technology uses CPUs, not GPUs, making it cheaper to run as a cloud option where time on GPU

Fig. 8.63 Autodesk's VRED supports ambient occlusions and baked shadows. *Source* Autodesk

clusters is more expensive. Autodesk places a heavy emphasis on VRED's support for the design tools in Autodesk Alias industrial design software, and its suitability for quick turnaround of visual prototypes.

Autodesk's history of ray tracing

2005—Autodesk acquired its first family of ray tracers with the acquisition of Alias. Autodesk acquired Alias from Silicon Graphics in 2005. The Maya software from the original Alias became a separate program within Autodesk and the Wavefront software formed a new software group that Autodesk called Showcase. Showcase was like Wavefront in that it was targeted at the automotive industry.

1984—Wavefront was founded, the company began focusing on photoreal-istic images of automobiles. It had a patented paint library combined with a state-of-the-art ray tracer that put it in a unique position and made it a leader in the field.

1995—Wavefront and Alias were acquired by Silicon Graphics and com-bined into the division Silicon Graphics called Alias/Wavefront.

1983—Alias was founded and had been best known for its media enter-tainment graphics program called Maya. SGI later combined the two com-panies named just Alias.

1998—Opticore started in Sweden and known for its visualization software

2007—Opticore was acquired by Autodesk.

2009—A small German startup called Numenus was founded.

2011—Acquired and incorporated into Showcase.

2012—Lagoa was started and specialized in cloud-based visualization and collaboration.

2014—Autodesk acquired Logoa and incorporated its technology into Showcase.

2017—Autodesk ended the Showcase product line and initiated a new pro-duct line called VRED, again targeted at the automotive industry as well as others.

1997 in Madrid Spain Solid Angle was started and created the Arnold ray tracing program. Arnold was a very successful ray tracing program used by several companies and tens of thousands of users.

2016—Autodesk acquired Solid Angle and incorporated the Arnold ray tracer into various other Autodesk products as well as continuing to offer the pro-gram separately as a standalone and plug-in for other applications.

VRED has two modes of user interaction. In simple mode, it is a matter of letting the software use default settings. For those ready to dig in deeper, the complex mode offers camera control, surface analysis, comprehensive material libraries, real-time ray tracing, animation, and stereo display; the Professional version even supports the Oculus Rift virtual reality headset.

VRED is sophisticated enough to allow selective resolution, where certain parts of the model are rendered at a higher resolution as a special effect. This variable resolution is handy for creating advertisements that draw the viewer's eye to a particular part of the image. Unlike most renderers, which work with the materials data supplied from the CAD program (if available), VRED requires that the user adds material designations, in addition to setting the lighting and scene conditions.

8.1.24.1 Summary

The addition of the VRED team brought new energy and high-end technology to Autodesk's visualization offerings and has contributed to the development of Autodesk Raytracer, which is now packaged with its flagship products. As with every technology, however, there are trade-offs. The addition of Raytracer makes rendering part of the design workflow, but in a limited fashion; it lacks the bells and whistles of a dedicated product. In contrast, VRED is a dedicated, full-featured visualization engine, but it is not integrated into the design workflow. If something changes in the product model, one has to start again with the VRED visualization.

8.1.25 Other

Radiosity, light-field, photon, etc., and historical.

8.1.26 Lightworks Design

Lightworks is one of the oldest ray-tracing companies in the industry, and has undergone several transformations, partnerships, and sometimes ironic interconnections. I've included it here in the integrated section, but it could have been in the stand-alone or plug-in section a few months, or years ago.

Lightwork Design was founded in 1989 in Sheffield England. In 1994, it was sold to Tektronix, who were not successful at developing the company's products. In 1999, it was sold on to the newly formed Lightworks Inc., then owned by Fairlight Japan, and then purchased by Gee Broadcast in May 2004. In August 2009, the UK- and US-based company EditShare acquired Gee Broadcast and the Lightworks editing platform.

The company developed a proprietary ray-tracing program for CAD software companies including Autodesk, PTC, Siemens, and Dassault at one time or another. The company did not sell its products directly to the end users.

Lightwork Design supplied rendering technology to Siemens for over twenty years. In 2013, the company stopped developing new ray-tracing software and switched to Nvidia's GPU-powered Iray ray-tracing program and created specialized visualization tools for its customers in the CAD industry. It also said it would bring Iray+ to the market as a GPU-based ray-tracing rendering SDK.

In November 2017, Nvidia transferred sales and support of the Iray plug-in products for 3ds Max, Iray for Maya, Iray for Rhino, and Iray Server—to the Iray integration partners (AKA Iray Plugins), Lightworks. Then, in October 2018, Siemens PLM bought Lightworks, making them a partner and depository for Iray plug-ins, as well as Lightworks' Iray+ customers. Iray+ is the full Iray toolkit from Nvidia that Lightworks have wrapped in their own easy-to-integrate-and-support API. See, Iray—Nvidia, Sect. 8.1.8 for additional background on Iray.

As an example of the type of work Lightworks Design has been doing with Siemens, Lightworks introduced Slipstream in 2017. It is a tool that enables customers to create a workflow for exporting complex models into game engines. The same kind of procedural methods are required to enable models to be visualized, analyzed, simulated, and mechanized. All the sort of things, Siemens and their customers will need to realize the digital twin strategy.

Slipstream which Lightworks announced at SIGGRAPH 2017 isn't so much a product as a service bundle to address the same sorts of problems being addressed by Epic's Datasmith. Lightworks has a long history of providing integrated rendering to PLM tools.

As a longtime provider of rendering backends, its own, and now Iray, the company has integrated rendering in multiple PLM products. It did some of its early development work for Slipstream with Siemens, which uses Lightworks Iray in its CAD programs. Lightstream is familiar with CAD pipelines and understands the complexities of the model.

As a result, Lightworks approached the creation of Slipstream as a service plus technology depending on the end-user requirements and the types of models. At the end of the process, customers then have an easy-to-use recipe for getting models out of CAD and into a game engine. "The beauty of Slipstream," says Lightworks CTO David Hutchinson, "is that companies can work with their intellectual property, without having to send it off to an agency to create a visualization or application and they retain the ability to change up the work, redo, and repeat."

Siemens acquires Lightworks

As mentioned above, In September 2018, Siemens announced the acquisition of Lightwork Design. Lightworks began life as an OEM provider of rendering software to many CAD companies including Autodesk, PTC, Siemens, and Dassault at one time or another. The company did not make products that sold directly to customers.

In a letter announcing the acquisition, Tony Hemmelgarn, president and CEO of Siemens PLM Software, a business unit of the Siemens Digital Factory Division, said that Siemens customers are increasingly making photorealistic rendering and visualizations. Also, the company sees opportunity in augmented reality, virtual reality, model-based engineering, digital mock-ups, and mobile visualizations.

Lightworks Design will be combined with Siemens PLM Components business. The company says more than 240 companies integrate Siemens PLM Software technology into 350 commercial applications for six million end users.

The plan for Siemens is to continue to supply Iray+ to all the existing licensees of the product and to include it within the Siemens PLM Components division alongside programs like Parasolid. In addition, the plan is to include it in other products across the Siemens PLM portfolio, but I cannot give more details of that.

Iray is used in Siemens NX, Dassault Catia, and SolidWorks—as such it dominates the market in rendering for top end CAD.

8.1.26.1   Summary

Given the nature of its business, Lightworks Design is a company that stays in the background, but throughout much of its history, CAD companies have chosen it as their rendering engine. At one time, the company could claim more customers for its rendering technology than any other product on the market because of the high installed base of CAD users. That doesn't mean everyone was using the tools, but Lightworks' rendering technology was accessible to the highest number of customers. Lightworks footprints can be found in many companies and products from CAD systems to game engines.

Rendering has become much more critical in the workflows of CAD customers. The Lightworks team is battle-hardened, responsive, and adaptive. They should be an asset within Siemens, and while Siemens is an enormous organism, it tends to preserve the companies it assimilates.

8.1.27   Manuka—Weta

Weta of New Zealand is one of the most respected and admired special effects companies in the world. The list of movies they have worked on is amazing.

In order to accomplish some of the astounding effects they create, the company has developed an elaborate, and much envied, set of software tools, including a world-class ray tracer. Mike Seymour of FX Guide wrote extensively in his 2014 article.[16]

Weta's ray tracer Manuka is a physically based production renderer. Manuka was a great development in that it produced accurate and beautiful scenes and

---

[16]https://www.fxguide.com/featured/manuka-weta-digitals-new-renderer/.

Fig. 8.64 A frame from the War for the Planet of the Apes movie, rendered in Manuka. Image courtesy of Weta Digital, ©2017 Twentieth Century Fox Film Corporation. All rights reserved

managed the complex render requirements of the huge worlds and scenes in the big movies (Fig. 8.64).[17]

The third Hobbit film was Weta Digital's first major motion picture with Manuka as the primary renderer. The renderer was put to the test in *War for the Planet of the Apes*, with subtle things like snow in the fur of the apes.

Eric Veach's Monte Carlo path-tracing work and Manuka were the most complete implementation of this approach for physically based production rendering to date. Manuka was started as a technical validation of the approach.

Manuka is focused on production, concerning both the controlling of a real-world feature film production pipeline and allowing a much larger model complexity to be rendered. One of the benefits from Weta's work in real time was the development of hardware GPU-based rendering that gave artists an accurate preview of the final image.

A path-tracing ray tracer using Monte Carlo produces a noisy image at first and then progressively improves it. That feature allows Manuka to be used as a progressive refinement Render Preview tool, leveraging an artist's ability to work with partially rendered images.

---

[17]Fascione et al. (2018).

Manuka is both a unidirectional and bidirectional path tracer and encompasses multiple importance sampling (MIS). Interestingly, and importantly for production character skin work, it was the first production renderer to incorporate spectral MIS in the form of the hero spectral sampling technique.[18]

The term hero spectral samples comes from the film industry jargon of the hero shot. Skin, for example, is handled very differently for different wavelengths. One can deal with this in R, G, and B or in a proper light spectrum. The wavelength is not a trivial distinction, not only for the accuracy of the results (less noise for the similar effort) but to work one needs the pipeline spectral—including materials/BSSRDF (see Glossary). A hero wavelength is the basis then for an MIS-style directed spectrum.

The spectral work also helps match computer-generated objects to real ones, more closely matching colors and responses—making CG objects ever more difficult to pick from reality.

Lighting is based on area lights and IBL/environment lighting. An arbitrary shape can be a light source so that a fire simulation can be a light source. Any volume or shape can be a full-area light emitter. The renderer was always designed to handle a ridiculous amount of lights, more than say a million. Also, that allows you to do all sorts of things, suddenly volumes, multi-colored lights, and textured lights; it all just becomes a non-issue—and that is cool.

Weta Digital does not support Open Shading Language (OSL) as Manuka was designed to work with the studio's current shader pipeline. The studio needed to make it a streamlined transition process. Essentially, both RenderMan and Manuka can run on the same shaders with a minimal amount of additional Manuka specific code.

A critical part of adding production value and scene complexity is volumetrics, and there has been much research in this area. There are many solutions on offer, namely photon-mapped volumes and beam solutions in addition to more brute-force approaches. Various approaches have proven to provide other exciting speed/quality trade-offs. Manuka can do full volumetric scattering simulations, which has proven enormously useful in verifying and validating our other models and approximations.

Regarding the pipeline, everything rendered at Weta was already completely interwoven with their deep data pipeline. Manuka very much was written with deep data in mind. Concerning camera models, Manuka offers orthographic and projection mapping. Manuka has a highly advanced depth of field and motion blur.

Manuka has instancing support, but it is different from most other production renderers. Weta believes their implementation is extremely efficient but with certain limitations and they are still investigating.

---

[18]Wilkie et al. (2014).

8.1.27.1   Summary

To make Manuka, the Weta team worked for years on hardcore rendering research with contributors and interns from around the world. They made some unexpected and novel algorithmic choices, all with particular production biases in mind. At Weta, the farm runs every night producing shots for dallies the next morning. The challenge is one has to make sure the shots can render and be there in the morning no matter how complex.

8.2   Integrated (Programs with Native Ray Tracers)

Some modeling and design programs have dedicated, built-in ray-tracing programs. These ray-tracing programs are not sold separately and don't offer plug-ins to other design programs. However, the baseline modeling or design program may accept plug-in renderers from other suppliers.

8.2.1   Cycles—Blender

The Blender Foundation is a nonprofit organization responsible for the development of Blender, an open-source 3D content creation program (Fig. 8.65).

In 1988, Ton Roosendaal co-founded the Dutch animation studio NeoGeo which became the largest 3D animation house in the Netherlands. In 1995, it was decided that the current in-house 3D toolset needed to be rewritten from scratch. It was and became Blender. In 1998, Roosendaal founded Not a Number (NaN) to market and developed Blender. In early 2002, the NaN investors decided to shut down all operations including the development of Blender.

Fig. 8.65 Astro, Pratik Solanki

Enthusiastic support from the user community and customers couldn't justify leaving Blender to disappear into oblivion. Since restarting a company with a sufficiently large team of developers wasn't feasible, in May 2002 Roosendaal started the nonprofit Blender Foundation.

In 2011, the foundation introduced Cycles a new rendering engine built into Blender. The developers claimed that it was flexible and fast and, above all else, produced more realistic results (Fig. 8.66).

Although Blender and Cycles are tightly integrated, Cycles is also available as a stand-alone library, which has been adopted by Rhino and Poser, and available as a plug-in for Cinema 4D.

When Blender speaks about their render engine, they call it "Cycles." For mentioning it outside of Blender context, the name "Blender Cycles" is the preferred reference.

Cycles is an unbiased, physically based, path-tracing render engine that is designed to be interactive and easy to use, while still supporting many production features. It comes installed as an add-on that is available by default and can be activated in the top header. It produces an image by tracing the paths of "rays" through the scene. Specifically, Cycles is a "backward" path tracer, which means that it traces light rays by sending them from the camera instead of sending them from the light source(s). This is typical. Almost all path tracers do this.

GPU rendering

Cycles supports GPU rendering which is used to help speed up rendering times. There are two GPU rendering modes: CUDA, which is the preferred method for Nvidia graphics cards, and OpenCL, which supports rendering on AMD graphics cards. Multiple GPUs are also supported, which can be used to create a render farm —although having multiple GPUs doesn't increase the available memory because each GPU can only access its own memory (Table 8.2).

Fig. 8.66 Cycles is used as a production rendering engine for animation movies. Frame from "Agent 327, Operation Barbershop"—by Blender's animation studio

Table 8.2 Cycle's features by processor type

Supported features			
Feature	CPU	CUDA	OpenCL
Basic shading	Yes	Yes	Yes
Transparent shadows	Yes	Yes	Yes
Motion blur (https://en.wikipedia.org/wiki/Motion_blur)	Yes	Yes	Yes
Hair	Yes	Yes	Yes
Volume	Yes	Yes	Yes
Smoke/fire	Yes	Yes	Yes
Subsurface scattering	Yes	Yes	Yes
Open shading language (https://en.wikipedia.org/wiki/Open_Shading_Language)	Yes	**No**	**No**
Correlated multi-jittered sampling	Yes	Yes	Yes
Branched path integrator	Yes	Yes	Yes
Displacement/subdivision (https://en.wikipedia.org/wiki/Open_Shading_Language)	Experimental	Experimental	Experimental

Integrator

The integrator is the rendering algorithm used for lighting computations. Cycles currently supports a path-tracing integrator with direct light sampling. It works well for various lighting setups but is not as suitable for caustics and some other complex lighting situations. Rays are traced from the camera into the scene, bouncing around until they find a light source such as a lamp, an object emitting light, or the world background. To find lamps and surfaces emitting light, both indirect light sampling (letting the ray follow the surface BSDF) and direct light sampling (picking a light source and tracing a ray toward it) are used. Cycles defines its materials in a BSDF.

There are two types of integrators:

Progressive Integrator. The default path-tracing integrator is a true path tracer. At each hit, it bounces light in one direction and picks one light from which to receive lighting. That makes each sample faster to compute but typically requires more samples to clean up the noise.

Branched Path Integrator. The alternative is a branched path-tracing integrator which at the first hit splits the path for different surface components and takes all lights into account for shading instead of just one. That makes each sample slower, but reduces noise, especially in scenes dominated by direct or one-bounce lighting.

Blender Internal

BI is a biased rasterization engine, which means that it works by calculating which objects are visible to the camera and not by simulating the behavior of light. Blender Internal has been removed per version 2.80 (November 2018). It has been replaced with an OpenGL-based PBR render engine that runs in the 3D viewport and tools environment in real time.

Open shading language

Blender users can create their own nodes using the Open Shading Language although it is important to note that there is no support for it on GPUs yet.

Portal lamps

Portal lamps are a new feature in Blender 2.75 that help Blender understand your scene and thus speed up rendering significantly. To create a portal, one adds an area lamp and checks the "Portal" box in the lamp settings in UI. That tells Blender not to emit any light from the area lamp, but instead use it to guide rays toward the environment light. That usually means less noise in ones render, and thus, it can use fewer samples and finish rendering sooner.

8.2.1.1 Summary

Blender has proven to be a popular, durable, and robust program and development ecosystem. It has grown into a worldwide community and found its way into many films and TV studios, most design and engineering offices, and game developers. It is also popular with animators and amateurs.

One of the unique features of Blender is the massive community of users. Although not too many VFX professionals are using Blender for their final work, there are hundreds of thousands of amateurs and artists who use Blender as their free tool of choice for VFX design and rendering.

It is an easy-to-use and very flexible tool that uses a CPU or GPU to render and is easy to set up for distributed rendering. While its appeal is its popularity, Blender also attracts a set of artists who are trying to either make their first mark as a VFX Pro or students trying to complete a college course in animation or a hobbyist trying to create a masterpiece.

The downside of this is the enormous amount of rendering that is required to complete some of these projects which on a modest or even a single high-powered computer would take a very long time for even a minute of the reel which requires 1800 frames (much more for a VR film).

That leads them to find alternative methods such as using commercial render farms to accomplish their rendering quickly, but, since the farms are too expensive for most students and first-time animation artists, they run out of funds well before the project is complete. What follows then us the students try to use free render credits whereever they are offered, and they leave behind a trail of their frames across any render farm that offers Blender and a small number of trial credits. That also takes up render farm storage, Internet bandwidth, and time cleaning it out which render farms cannot afford to support.

The major VFX studios hardly use Blender, but small/mid-size ones do already. A good example is Barnstorm VFX in LA; they used it for The Man in the High Castle and Silicon Valley.

Fig. 8.67 Blender was used for concept art in Jurassic World. *Source* Jama Jurabaev

The famous artist Jama Jurabaev, Senior concept artist at Lucasfilm, used Blender for pre-viz and story art on Solo and Jurassic world (Fig. 8.67).

Blender is used by every studio now. But it is rising for sure.

Render time is also more of a secondary thing for studios (to decide to use Blender). The costs of render time are high, but it is also well possible to manage, especially if one knows the renderer well. The decision for Bender or Cycles is mostly beneficial in the production pipeline.

Google Cloud and Azure support Cycles render well on their infrastructure. It doesn't have to be free, and it can be managed efficiently, for example, using preemptive rendering, which means one gets all the spare time on servers. For that to be effective and efficient, the render should be able to stop (and save work) within a 30 s notice. Cycles can do that.

8.2.2 Carrara—Daz 3D

Daz Productions, Inc., commonly known as Daz 3D, is a 3D content and software company specializing in providing rigged 3D human models, associated accessory content, and software to the hobbyist as well as the prosumer market.

The history of Carrara started in 1989 when a group of individuals founded Ray Dream with the idea of creating graphics software for the new Mac computers with color displays. Two years later, the first version of their new 3D graphics program which they named Ray Dream Studio was released.

In 1996, Ray Dream, Inc. was sold to Fractal Design (then the developer of Corel Painter and Poser). Fractal Design Corporation was in turn acquired by MetaTools (developer of Bryce, KPT) shortly after that. The combination of the two companies was given the new name MetaCreations. Around the same time, another 3D graphics program named Infini-D was acquired from Specular International. Now owning two 3D graphics programs, MetaCreations decided to merge Ray Dream and Infini-D into one application giving it the new name Carrara.

In 2000, when MetaCreations was divesting itself of most of its products, it sold Carrara to a new company named Eovia founded by former employee Antoine Clappier. Eovia developed Carrara for several versions culminating with version 5 in 2005. That same year, Eovia shipped a new 3D modeling application, Hexagon.

In 2006, Daz 3D (developers of Daz Studio and a line of articulated 3D figures) acquired Eovia along with Carrara and Hexagon. Daz 3D was started in 2000 by Dan Farr.

In May 2010, the company launched Carrara 8.0. Carrara is a full-featured 3D computer graphics application featuring figure posing and editing, as well as nature modeling, in addition to traditional modeling, animation, texturing, and rendering (Fig. 8.68).

Notable new features for Carrara users that are now integrated into Carrara: GPU rendering, unbiased rendering, HDR/EXR with multi-pass rendering.

The program even supports network rendering, dynamic hair rendering, IES photometric lighting (excellent for architecture), and displacement vertex modeling. Rendering wise, it supports OpenGL of course and ray tracing, global illumination, ambient occlusion, caustics and irradiance maps, and more.

Carrara's rendering process can create photorealistic images because it considers all of the objects in a scene simultaneously and calculates not just forms, color, and texture, but the interaction of lights and surfaces within the scene. Carrara rendering options include soft shadows, blurred reflections, blurred transmission, correct ambient lighting, caustics, global illumination, ambient occlusion, HDRI, motion blur, subsurface scattering, shadow catch, transparency with absorption, depth of field, and more. Using the program's multi-pass rendering, one can retouch or edit images without having to rerender.

MatCreator is a large material multi-pack library of material/shader presets for Carrara.

Fig. 8.68 Daz 3D's Genesis 8 figure platforms produces photorealistic 3D composition results. *Source* Daz 3D

Grid for Carrara

The Grid site license enables one to build a render farm of up to 50 nodes with up to 100 CPU's, $199.

Daz Studio

Daz Studio is a software application developed and offered for free by Daz 3D. Daz Studio is a 3D scene creation and rendering application used to produce images as well as video and is offered for free by Daz 3D.

Using Daz Studio, one can:

- Use 3D morphing, posing, animation, and rendering
- Get GPU-accelerated real-time rendering, photorealistic results.

Daz 3D offers the following comparison of their program to others (Table 8.3).

One of the main differences between Daz Studio and other software applications such as Poser is that Daz 3D has also included support for its various generations of the Genesis technology which is used as the basis for its human figures (Fig. 8.69).

The Genesis 8's figure platforms are more than just a figure or a character. It is a real character engine that allows one to choose the desired characters, modify and

Table 8.3 Software comparison

Software	Modeling	Texturing	Scene building	Rigging	Morphing	Animation	Rendering	Physically based rendering	Cost
Daz Studio			Yes	Yes	Yes	Yes	Yes	Yes	$0.00
Poser			Yes	Yes	Yes	Yes	Yes	Yes	$450.00
LightWave 3D	Yes	Yes	Yes	Yes	Yes	Yes	Yes	Yes	$1000.00
3ds Max	Yes	Yes	Yes	Yes	Yes	Yes	Yes	Yes	$3600.00
Maya	Yes	Yes	Yes	Yes	Yes	Yes	Yes	Yes	$3600.00

Source Daz 3D

Fig. 8.69 Daz 3D's renderer is well known for its realistic human and non-human figures. *Source* Daz 3D

enhance them to meet one's needs, or even mix and blend them with other characters to create a unique vision. All of this while providing an extensive library of content will adjust to fit characters and a global network of artists.

Daz 3D's business model is to offer free SW and be paid for models and shaders. The company also offers a rendering service.

LuxCoreRender

The LuxCoreRender engine is a Carrara plug-in and supports GPU-accelerated rendering and interactive photorealistic rendering (IPR) inside Carrara. It works on both AMD and Nvidia AIBs using the OpenCL language which requires updated graphics drivers. It also runs on CPU which supports more functions than GPU only.

Iray

Daz 3D has a license to embed Iray into any of their products. When Nvidia did the agreement, they included Daz Studio.

The Iray Uber shader adds an extra layer in the Base > Diffuse > Overlay group. This layer is useful for adding details like makeup or tattoos in the diffuse section of the Iray Uber Material.

8.2.2.1 Summary

Daz Studio is a 3D scene creation and rendering application used to produce images as well as video. Renders can be done by leveraging either in the 3Delight render engine or the Iray render engine, both of which ship for free along with Daz Studio, or with a variety of purchasable add-on render engine plug-ins for Daz Studio from various vendors and companies.

Daz 3D follows the "Razor and blades business model"—Daz Studio is the "razor" free-of-charge core program with the required features for the creation of imagery and animations while relegating other features to the "blades" add-on "plug-ins," usually commercial, which the user may add. Initially, it was possible to create new content in another DAZ program, Carrara easily. Beginning in 2017, Daz 3D began offering another of their programs, Hexagon, and distributing that as a package with Daz Studio.

8.2.3 Dimension CC—Adobe

Adobe Dimension is a 3D, photo-based mock-up editor, developed and published by Adobe Systems for macOS and Windows. It started as Project Felix on March 2017 and became Dimension on October 2017. Unlike other modeling programs, models are not created in Dimension. Users can import 3D models created in other software, assign materials, textures, and HDRI lighting via a simple drag-and-drop workflow, and render images as layered PSD files for post-processing in Photoshop.

Dimension CC is a design tool which provides access to high-quality 3D built from the ground up for graphic designers. It cannot create custom shapes, only either preloaded shapes or from the Adobe Stock library. However, one can import custom shapes with.obj files created with another 3D software.

In January 2017, Adobe announced the public beta of Project Felix—a 3D application for graphic designers with photoreal rendering powered by V-Ray.

Project Felix is a new type of 3D application, simple for anyone to use, and targeted at 2D designers familiar with Photoshop. It sits alongside the photograph editing software in Adobe's Creative Cloud.

With Project Felix, users can place, scale and rotate 3D objects, select and customize their materials, and alter the lighting. A real-time Render Preview shows exactly how the final image will come together (Fig. 8.70).

In October 2017, Adobe added a native rendering engine to Dimension— Adobe's own, in-house developed, ray-tracing engine. According to the company, the new engine offers "faster interaction and Render Preview times."

Adobe says V-Ray remains in the product as an option, but that that new native renderer can be used for final-quality output as well as preview work.

Nvidia has published a blog post announcing support for its RTX ray-tracing technology within Dimension, promising over $10\times$ faster performance on the firm's RTX graphics cards.

Dimension uses three types of rendering:

- **Canvas**. The canvas in design mode is fast, but it is not accurate. It is designed for one to interact with the content to make selections, move objects, and assign

Fig. 8.70 Dimension enables people with absolutely no 3D skills to create a composite shot of a 3D model within a 2D environment. *Source* Adobe

materials. Some effects like translucent glass, soft shadows, and reflections are not displayed on the canvas.
- **Render Preview**. The Render Preview window gives one a real-time update of how one's final render looks, every time one edits the scene. The Render Preview gives one a sense of the final lighting, shadows, reflections, and translucency. However, it is limited on quality to preview the render faster.
- **Render Mode**. Render Mode allows one to configure one's final render and uses a production renderer to give one the best results. One can receive the full-quality image after the rendering is complete (Fig. 8.71).

Rendering is a complex process, and the time for rendering to finish has many contributing factors.

- **Hardware**. The most significant contributing factor to rendering time is the hardware of the machine. Rendering requires many calculations that powerful GPU and CPU components speed significantly. Review the system requirements for minimum and recommended hardware setups.
- **Resolution**. The size of the render significantly impacts the time of renders. It is recommended that one preview renders at a lower pixel size to get a sense of the lighting before committing to a final resolution render. One can change the size of the render in design mode.
- **Materials**. The combination of materials used in the scene has a high impact on render times. Plastics, metals, and matte materials render quickly, while translucent materials like glass, water, or gels render slower.

Adobe is offering a wealth of **materials** with their new standard format Adobe Standard Material. The format is built on Nvidia's free MDL material format which is being widely used in the industry. Adobe Dimension supports the OBJ model format, which is also a broad industry standard for content creation software. The company is also offering models and materials through Adobe Stock. New materials can be developed with Allegorithmic's Substance Painter and captured using Adobe Capture.

Fig. 8.71 (Left) Interactive view of the design mode canvas. (Middle) The Render Preview window. (Right) A final render produced from Render Mode. *Source* Adobe

8.2.3.1 Summary

Rendering is the process of turning 3D information into a 2D image. To create images that appear photorealistic, Dimension simulates how light behaves in the real world. When one renders an image in Dimension, the computer starts running a simulation which follows the paths of light rays from their sources (the sun, the sky, lights in the scene).

Adobe's Dimension CC technology enables artists to combine 3D content with photographs or 2D content in a realistic way. True to Adobe's roots in commercial art, it is ideal for product placements and advertising pieces, but it is also fun and an excellent entry for people who want to experiment with 3D work. Adobe has been refining its 3D tools in Photoshop and Premiere, but Dimension is a function-built tool that addresses this one challenge—compositing 3D and 2D content. It is an app.

The interface is simple with just a few controls. The process is that users bring in their desired image. What's really beautiful about it though is that it enables the non-artist and especially those who aren't good at 3D content creation.

8.2.4 Mantra—SideFX

Beginning from Omnibus company, two animation experts Kim Davidson and Greg undertook the production and wrote their software, creating visual effects for film and broadcast, finally coming up with 3D graphics software in 1987. They developed SideFx Software and released PRISMS which laid the groundwork for Houdini. The Academy of Motion Pictures Arts and Sciences has recognized SideFX's Houdini four times in four years for its breakthrough procedural based technology and awarded the firm the prestigious Award of Merit. The company has also been recognized as being used by several movies in the Academy awards for their visual effects.

Mantra is an advanced renderer included with Houdini. It is a multi-paradigm renderer with scanline, ray tracing, and physically based rendering. Mantra has deep integration with Houdini, such as an efficient rendering of packed primitives and volumes. Mantra has got several features embedded in the latest version. They are:

Preview rendering

The Render view shows a rendered image that updates as the user moves lights and objects, and other parameters (Fig. 8.72).

Mini render

The Render region tool lets the user outline a rectangle in the 3D viewer that acts as a Mini Render view or viewport. It renders that part of the view and updates the rendered rectangle as the changes are done (Fig. 8.73).

Fig. 8.72 A demonstration of preview rendering. *Source* SideFx

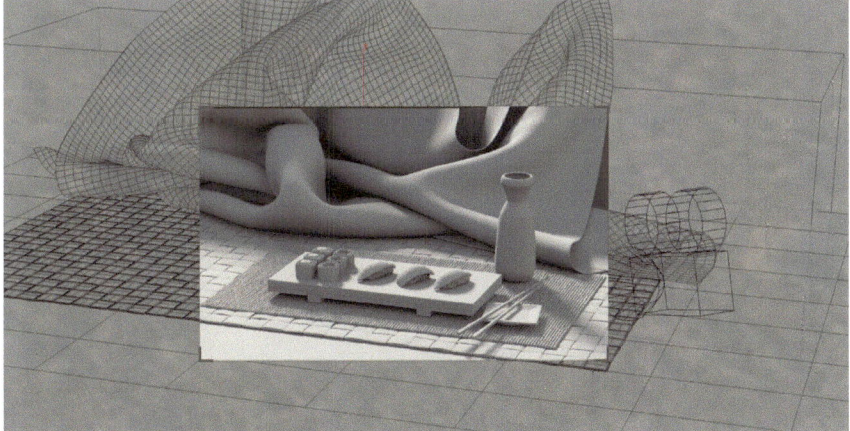

Fig. 8.73 A demonstration of Mini Render. *Source* SideFx

Sampling and noise

When generating an image, Mantra determines a color value for each pixel by examining the scene behind the image plane by sending out some rays from the camera's position until they hit an object in the scene and it returns some piece of information, specifically the color of the object (Fig. 8.74).

Direct and indirect rays

When the need to send more direct rays in the renders arises, it can sometimes be challenging to separate one source of noise from another. Adding the image plane allows the user a view of the direct contribution of each component separately. When attempting to optimize the number of direct rays in the scene, the "Direct Samples" image plane can be added. This plane will show the number of direct rays used throughout the image displayed as the intensity.

Indirect rays can be described as rays which deal with objects and their surface properties. That means that rays travel from some position in the scene in directions determined by the shader attached to the object. Similar challenges can be faced as

Fig. 8.74 A demonstration of sampling. *Source* SideFx

with the direct rays when evaluating the effect of sending more indirect rays in the renders. When attempting to optimize the number of indirect rays in the image, the "Indirect Samples" image plane can be added. This plane will show the number of indirect rays used throughout the image.

Volumes

Even operating at low sampling rates, it can be costly to render clean images of volumetric data due to the shading being made to run for every step through the volume. However, Mantra has a variety of ways to optimize volume rendering which can decrease render times without sacrificing detail (Fig. 8.75).

One optimization, called as stochastic transparency, decouples the accumulation of density values from the shading samples.

Houdini

In late 2018, Toronto-based SideFX released the latest Banshee version of its leading-edge Houdini procedural animation software, which handles the many elements of physics in CGI entertainment. From scores of smaller digital effects workshops, in movies to big studios like Disney/Pixar and Weta Digital as well as video games from Bethesda, Sega, Gameloft, Xbox, and others, SideFX's Houdini effects engine is behind an extraordinary amount of the entertainment content.

Houdini focuses on the procedurally generated parts of the action, more than the artists' creations themselves, and Houdini touches many more parts of an animated scene than is obvious. It is the engine behind hair and fur and feathers that react to wind and rain, as well as to a character's movements. It is the engine that lets one drape muscle, skin, and clothes onto a model and have them each react to motion captured animation in realistic ways, with finely tuned material properties that have their inertia, bounce, stretchiness, and tendency to tear (Fig. 8.76).

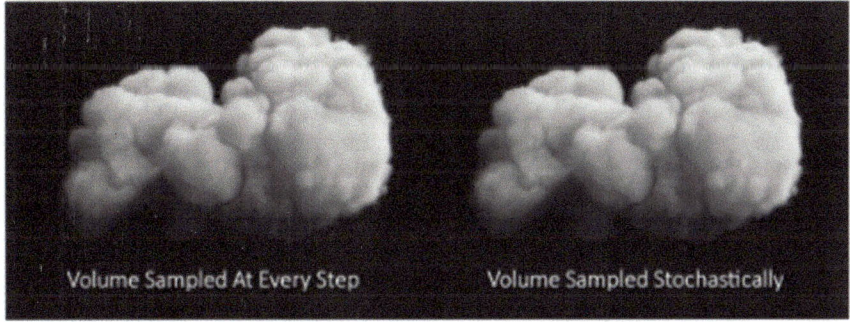

Fig. 8.75 A demonstration of volume modification. *Source* SideFx

Fig. 8.76 Houdini's white-water simulator renders video-realistic waves that interact with rocks, sand, and one another. *Credit* Igor Zanic

It handles particle animations to depict what would happen if one emptied a bag of marbles or wet sand. It handles flames, smoke, mist, lighting, and magical elements that don't follow traditional physics.

It is also responsible for procedurally generated environments, literally simulating the processes of hydro and thermal erosion to turn a wrinkled surface into a set of mountains, valleys, and rolling hills that look and feel like they've been there for millions of years. Procedurally generated terrain allows one to build a set of lumps and then simulate the processes.

Houdini also handles water effects, from ripples and splashes to a newly developed module that generates unbelievably realistic surf, complete with foam, spray, and backwash patterns.

The program has been behind many of the most memorable and spectacular CG visuals audiences seen.

8.2.4.1 Summary

With the company being around for 31 years and the integration of the software with Houdini, there is decent support for Mantra. Its ability to render complex images in acceptable time has been the significant advantages, so is the ability to manage workloads by its adherence to Houdini. It has been compared to Arnold which is a winner in the speed of operations; however, Mantra comes as the better product when quality is of importance. Moreover, with more versions to come in the future, improved and better products are expected from the company.

8.2.5 ART (Autodesk Ray Tracer)

For years, a network of third-party solutions (including V-Ray from Chaos Group, AccuRender from Robert McNeel & Associates, and many others) has been providing alternatives to and augmenting the existing rendering and visualization technology inside Autodesk applications such as AutoCAD, Inventor, and Revit. Even Autodesk's two best-known animation and visualization products, 3ds Max and Maya, work with a variety of third-party rendering products.

ART, also known as RapidRT, is based on technology from the Autodesk's acquisition of Opticore in 2007. Since then, the renderer has been integrated into Autodesk design products such as Showcase (2009), Inventor (2011), Revit (2011), Fusion 360 (2013), Navisworks (2013), AutoCAD (2015), 3ds Max (2015), as well as the Autodesk Cloud Rendering service (since 2017). The cloud rendering service is integrated into, and accessible out-of-the-box from, AutoCAD, Revit, Fusion, Navisworks, and 3ds Max.

At the time the rendering engine in Revit was Nvidia's mental Ray and Autodesk had to pay to use the program. Also, they were not able to change or enhance it. Autodesk owns the ART engine and can be modified and enhanced as needed to parallel other changes in Autodesk's offerings. This new technology is also available in AutoCAD, Navisworks, and Showcase.

As of April 2017, Autodesk ended the sale of mental ray Standalone to new customers of all Autodesk products. That change did not affect existing licenses of mental ray Standalone. However, new licenses of mental ray Standalone would have to be obtained directly from Nvidia. On November 20 2017, Nvidia discontinued mental ray.

Autodesk ART is the in-product rendering engine, allowing one to create high-quality rendered images and animations. It is a physically based and unbiased rendering engine. The rendering process simulates the flow of light according to physical equations and realistic shading/lighting models to accurately represent real-world materials. As an unbiased renderer, ART calculates the path of light as accurately as statistically possible.

Rendered scenes are based on physically accurate lights, materials, and reflected light. Two essential terms of lighting, reflection, and diffusion describe the most basic separation of surface/light interactions.

Reflection: When light hits a surface boundary, some of the light will reflect or bounce off of the surface at an opposing angle.

Diffusion: Not all light reflects from a surface. In most cases, some light penetrates the illuminated object. This light is either absorbed by the material or scattered internally. The scattered light that makes its way back out of the surface becomes visible once more to the eye and to cameras. This light is referred to as diffusion or diffuse light.

Using physically based rendering, different types of surfaces (such as metal, brick, plastic, and glass) should look "natural" because of the calculated way light reflects off of the material, and the accuracy with which shadows are created.

8.2.5.1 Summary

Autodesk has two integrated ray tracers, VRED and Raytracer. It also has a stand-alone ray tracer, Arnold. Also, there are several plug-in ray tracers like Nvidia's Iray, Chaos V-Ray, and others available to Autodesk users.

8.2.6 Unreal Studio—Epic Games

The latest version of Unreal Studio has several new features such as photorealistic rendering. BY incorporating it, the company says one can eliminate the wait for renderings and thereby achieve stunning photorealistic visuals in real time.

Features such as physically based rendering, area lights, advanced dynamic shadow options, screen space reflections, and lighting channels are now available.

Datasmith for Revit

Through Unreal Studio Datasmith, Epic has supported high-fidelity autoconversion of data import workflows for Autodesk, 3ds Max, SketchUp Pro, and a host of CAD formats. The company has extended Unreal Studio Datasmith with a new exporter for Autodesk Revit; new importers for DWG and Alias Wire formats; improved VRED/Deltagen import. Plug-ins are supplied for the source applications that write out data in a format directly understood by the source program. Datasmith offers final conformation and translation of many popular CAD formats. One can convert entire scenes into Unreal Engine, automating many of the time-intensive processes involved with data prep.

Epic Unreal announced its acquisition of Datasmith at SIGGRAPH 2017. The tool was originally introduced at SIGGRAPH 2016 as Motiva Unreal Scene (MUS). Datasmith enables structured transfers of necessary data from CAD models to game engines where the data can be used in content creation. It supports 20 CAD and digital content creation sources as well as modeling and animation tools such as Autodesk 3ds and Max. As an interesting side note, the Datasmith effort is being led by former Autodesk director Ken Pimentel who has long experience in professional visualization and animation.

Epic announced plans to offer the Datasmith toolbox through a private beta program. Epic has been saying that the ability to work in real time with rendering is the game changer for game engines, but without good ways to get and manage content, the game never really gets started. At Autodesk University, where the Unreal team pitched their engine for use with CAD data in manufacturing, AEC, and content creation, Epic's Mark Petit told the audience that Unreal customers want real time in every aspect of content creation. "They don't want V-Ray in real time, they want everything: the physics, the materials, everything." Moreover, that means dealing with lots of data, but only the necessary data. Petit said they have also found that customers don't want to pay for services to get the data into for Unreal Engine. "That's why we bought Datasmith."

Unreal has also been able to incorporate Alembic into its pipeline to deal with assets from 3D animation.

Datasmith helps users to import models with all the necessary components including assembly components, surfaces, materials, physics, animations, into Unreal Engine with assets organized in a way the application understands and users can also see and understand.

Enhanced 3ds Max material translation

The company claims that it has improved BRDF (see Glossary) matching from V-Ray materials (especially for metal and glass) and added support for most commonly used 3ds Max map (Fig. 8.77).

Also, the company has added the ability to translate 3ds Max material graphs to Unreal graphs on export, making the materials more straightforward with which to work and understand.

Fig. 8.77 Unreal Studio has expanded its material library's support. *Source* Epic

Epic has also improved its Nvidia MDL and X-Rite AxF import capability and improved the shading fidelity.

Jacketing and defeaturing

Traditionally, it can take a bit of work and time to prepare and optimize a complex CAD model for real-time performance (Fig. 8.78).

With Unreal Studio, Epic has added features such as jacketing, which automatically hides or removes unseen elements, and defeaturing, which lets one remove unnecessary details—like through-holes, blind holes, and protrusions.

Sun position calculator

One can now set the azimuth and altitude of the Sun in Unreal Engine based on the latitude and longitude of ones intended location, and for a specific time and date. That enables the user to accurately visualize the lighting and shadowing effects the Sun will have on their design and the surrounding environment.

8.2.6.1 Summary

Unreal Studio is a new real-time visualization product based on Unreal Engine and its Datasmith toolkit. The toolset is primarily intended to provide architects and designers with a more user-friendly way to produce photorealistic content. Unreal Studio is the architectural workspace where one imports all the files and adds the materials, and Unreal Engine is the renderer. However, one can also import

Fig. 8.78 Jacketing and defeaturing in Unreal Studio. *Source* Epic

materials and lights from 3ds Max too. Datasmith streamlines the process of importing 3ds Max scenes and CAD data into Unreal Engine, so Unreal is a lot more than a renderer.

8.2.7   Visualize—Dassault Systèmes/SolidWorks

Founded: 2002 by Philip Lunn (Bunkspeed)
CEO (now): Gian Paolo Bassi (SolidWorks)
Status: Public
Headquarters: Waltham MA
Number of employees: 1.790
2018 Revenue: $348.4M (est)
Price: $2995*

   SolidWorks Visualize is a rendering tool offered by Dassault Systèmes that is derived from Bunkspeed. Dassault has three ray-tracing renderers: 3Dexcit, PhotoView 360, and Visualize; all three can be obtained in the company's main program 3Dexperience. SolidWorks Visualize is a stand-alone product * SolidWorks Visualize Standard is available at no cost for SolidWorks Professional and Premium customers on subscription and doesn't tie up one's SolidWorks CAD license.

Dassault Systèmes acquired SolidWorks (founded in 1993) in 1997. SolidWorks annualized revenues in 1997 were approximately $25 million.

Bunkspeed (founded in 2002 by Philip Lunn) was an independent privately held ray-tracing company in Carlsbad, California, that offered a ray-tracing program the company developed. The company's customers in late 2013 included Audi, Cartier, Dell, Ford Motor Company, Gensler, Gulfstream, Harley-Davidson, Honda, Jaguar, Kohler, Land Rover, Newell-Rubbermaid, Nike, Nissan, Pininfarina, Procter & Gamble, Siemens, similar to many of SolidWorks and Dassault's. Bunkspeed SHOT sold for $995, about the same as the competitive KeyShot ray tracer. Before the acquisition, the company had 12 employees and did $650k in sales.

In July 2010, Bunkspeed released a revamped version of Shot, an application for making realistic renderings quickly. It was the first end-user application of mental images Iray interactive realistic rendering technology. Iray was able to employ Nvidia GPUs to run ray-tracing algorithms. At the time, the company asserted ray tracing provided the only physically correct rendering. Mental Images became a subsidiary of graphics-chip maker Nvidia in December 2007.

In October 2013, Real-time Technologies (RTT) acquired Bunkspeed. RTT AG was founded 1999 in Munich and was listed on the Frankfurt Stock Exchange.

Then, in December 2013, Dassault Systèmes acquired RTT. RTT also had a similar customer base and some that used Siemen's software. RTT's customers at the time consisted of Adidas, Audi, BMW, Daimler, EADS, Electrolux, Ferrari, General Motors, Harley-Davidson, Porsche, The North Face, and Volkswagen. The RTT Group employed over 750 staff at 15 locations in 2013.

Visualize

Dassault Systèmes added Bunkspeed rendering software to SoildWorks in 2015. The company renamed the product Visualize as a stand-alone suite of rendering tools included with SolidWorks 2016 Professional and Premium versions. SolidWorks Visualize will be included in subscriptions. Based on Bunkspeed, Visualize is designed for people who want "to take a picture" of their work (Fig. 8.79).

Visualize already comes with an appearance library that is community-driven, and new appearances are being added frequently. At the time of this writing, visualize only recognizes the native ".svap" appearance file format. That means that third-party appearances cannot be imported for use in Visualize.

However, there is a workaround process by which the Luxology Modo appearances available in PhotoView 360 can be "imported" and saved to the SolidWorks Visualize appearance library.

The latest release of the tool is its 2018 version which has a decent number of additional features over their previous release like new area lights. Now, the user can create light sources which can be simulated as rectangles, disks, spheres, cylinders, and many more. With extreme efficiency of lighting the exact position the user wants, these new area light sources are also available in "Fast mode" and can replace the manual techniques available in the earlier versions. The latest versions

Fig. 8.79 Ray tracing a model in Visualize. *Source* Dassault Systèmes

also boast of "on-the-fly" light creation which is synced with the camera's position, direction, or wherever the user wants the light to shine.

The latest version has several additions over the previous versions. They are:

Refreshed user interface

The first feature which catches the attention of every new user is the look and feel of the interface in Visualize 2018. The buttons of the tool are mostly in the same position though refreshed to give a new modern look and give the benefit of touch-enabled devices to the customers. SolidWorks Visualize has the goal of being sleek in the options provided to the user which the company claims makes its use very comfortable. Several of the workflow issues brought out by their customers of old versions have been resolved. Subtabs in the Palette keep settings and features organized, which means less scrolling. There is a new View Presets button in the Main Toolbar, with a lock and zoom to fit icons. The tool can also be themed either Light or Dark.

Better integration with SolidWorks files

The SolidWorks files were not entirely integrated with the older SolidWorks visualize tool, hence causing difficulty in importing cameras, lights and other custom saved views. The 2018 version comes equipped with this feature and allows the user to get the final image much faster than before. This new feature is handy for the PhotoView 360 users as well. SolidWorks completely revamped the Decal System allowing the user to import any decal types from their SolidWorks files. Several other enhancements were also added, including better initial decal placement, several masking options, reordering layered decals, and increased stability.

Create virtual reality content

Creating graphics content involves the final review process and finalizing it. With the older version, having an issue with the review process, which involved the annoying process in going through the entire visual tenure, the 2018 version comes equipped with the ability to preview the image or graphics before rendering. A proper stereo (left eye, right eye) can be created as well; however, it is not a must for 360 VR content. An updated feature in the new tool is the ability to create animations for VR with this new 360 camera.

Area lights with ease of placement

Visualize 2018 has introduced a new way of lighting places of the user's choice. This new functionality is known as the new "Area" lights which can be in multiple shapes (sphere, plane, tube, disk) and can be used to recreate any real-world lighting environment. These new area lights are said to cast shadows extremely well which look much closer to the actual world than its older versions (Fig. 8.80).

These new area lights can work in "Fast" mode which can conduct 20 times faster renders. That is a great parameter for many of the users.

Fast raytracing mode switch

SolidWorks Visualize includes an option on Fast Render Mode: Speed or Quality. You can access this switch from the Main Toolbar.

Fast Render Mode includes photorealistic features found in Accurate mode, but with the faster ray-tracing speeds of Fast mode. Fast Render Mode allows for greater usage of Fast ray-tracing mode throughout more and more projects. Accurate ray-tracing mode is only needed for interior scenes.

Fig. 8.80 Lighting makes all the difference in a rendering of a shiny product with no flat surfaces

- Speed: Recommended for fastest interactivity in the Viewport. Speed removes self-shadowing and time-consuming reflections. Speed is ideal for projects without glass, clear plastics, or transparent objects.
- Quality: Recommended for final renders.

Ray tracing is a technique for rendering 3D scenes. Ray tracing traces the path of every ray of light from its source until it either leaves the scene or becomes too weak to have an effect. The term also applies to the reverse method: tracing the path of every ray of light from the camera back to the light source.

PowerBoost (available in SolidWorks' Visualize Professional) provides a Render Mode that streams ray tracing directly to your Visualize Viewport. An Internet connection is required, and a multi-GPU machine for a Visualize Boost computer or a Nvidia Quadro VCA is recommended for the best performance.

Plug-in capability with Iray support

Dassault Systèmes SolidWorks new photorealistic rendering software can also work with Nvidia's Iray technology, progressively refining its image through constant feedback.

Visualize started as a third-party application; therefore, it can import more than 20 file types for other design tools including:

- 3ds Max
- Alias, Rhino Autodesk
- FBX
- Maya (binary)
- Pro/Engineer
- SketchUp

Several other CAD formats are also being added. Nvidia is happy with the move because Bunkspeed is built on Nvidia's Iray technology and optimized for Nvidia's GPUs. SolidWorks is also promoting rendering as part of the design process, a tool that can validate design ideas before they are committed to prototype. Also, rendered models of production designs can be delivered to marketing earlier, speeding up the concept-to-design-to-market pipeline.

8.2.7.1 Summary

Although Dassault Systèmes offers three ray-tracing renderers (3Dexcit, PhotoView 360, and Visualize), it did not create any of them, and all are the result of acquisitions or partnerships. However, all three can be obtained in the company's main program 3Dexperience (Fig. 8.81).

Dassault is a giant company (3.3 Billion Euro 2017), and its 3Dexperience platform presents all the company's brand applications, serving 12 industries, and provides a portfolio of industry solution experiences. 3Dexperience is not a thing, other than maybe a UI, and if you search for it, you won't find a technical

Fig. 8.81 Dassault's 3Dexperience UI logo

description of it. The platform is available on premise and on public or private cloud. Enabled with our 3Dexperience platform, the platform is about eliminating silos within companies, moving from a static, file-based world to a digitally connected world, where live data drives innovation, processes, and business decisions.

8.2.8   *PhotoView 360—Dassault Systèmes/SolidWorks*

Visualize is not the only rendering tool in the SolidWorks arsenal, and PhotoView 360 has been around since the 2009 release. PhotoView 360 is a visualization and rendering solution included with SolidWorks Professional and SolidWorks Premium. Providing a highly interactive environment for viewing designs as well as for creating photorealistic renderings can be used to showcase your designs.

Based on SolidWorks Intelligent Feature Technology (SWIFT), the software helps CAD users of any level achieve expert results. Its simple-to-use progressive rendering tools let users' photorealistically render a scene while allowing the user to continue working on the same scene, unlike software that forces users to wait until scenes are complete.

PhotoView 360

PhotoView 360 tool for SolidWorks is built on Modo technology from The Foundry. The news that Visualize was going to be widely available was met with some apprehension by fans for PhotoView 360, which is lauded for its ease of use. So far, though, SolidWorks is just adding on Visualize as another rendering option.

SolidWorks Visualize is a rebranded Bunkspeed, which Dassault Systèmes got in late 2013 when it acquired RTT, whom earlier that year acquired Bunkspeed (see Visualize—Dassault Systèmes/SolidWorks) (Fig. 8.82).

The Modo for SolidWorks kit is for design and engineering visualization professionals wanting to import SolidWorks parts, bodies, and assemblies into Modo.

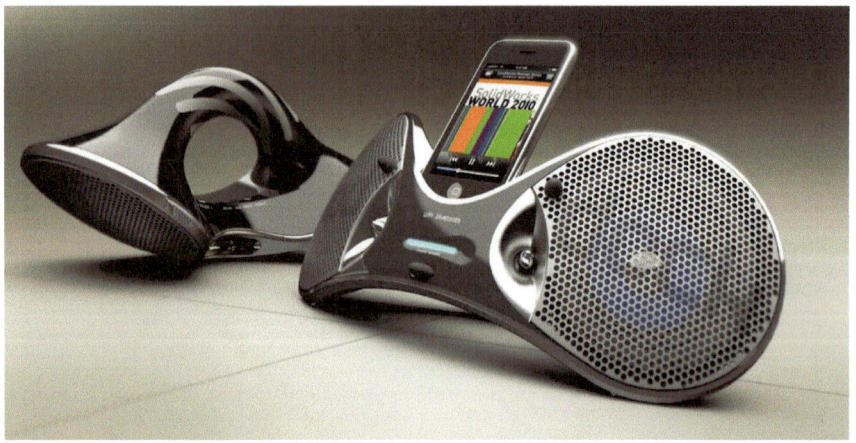

Fig. 8.82 PhotoView 360 example rendering. *Source* SolidWorks

The kit can be used to convert bodies and part to meshes or static meshes for further editing, animation, or even dynamic simulation within Modo.

Proof sheets

Proof sheets have been added to PhotoView 360 within the options. Proof sheets offer turnkey settings that optimize lighting options to ensure a quality rendering. That is the type of thing that is easy to play with but hard to get exactly right, and these proof sheets offer a compelling shortcut to making things look polished.

Dassault has three ray-tracing renderers: 3DEXCITE, PhotoView 360, and Visualize; all three can be obtained in the company's main program 3Dexperience.

3DEXCITE—Dassault Systèmes

In 2014, Dassault Systèmes created a new brand, 3DEXCITE, from the acquisition of RTT providing professional high-end 3D visualization software, marketing solutions, and computer-generated imagery services to extend the company's offerings to marketing professionals (Fig. 8.83).

Dassault acquired Munich-based Real-time Technologies (RTT) through a stock buyout in 2013. At the time, Dassault said it planned to build a new brand to extend its business into marketing, a long-held ambition of Dassault's management. The deal was reported to be valued at €179 million about 2.4x RTT's revenues for 2012, and RTT was founded in 1999 and had seen steady growth. It reported €73.7 million in revenue for 2012, a 34% growth over 2011. With the acquisition, Dassault got a complete product visualization business division with desktop rendering from Bunkspeed and rendering and visualization tools and services from RTT.

RTT's technology included Deltagen and PictureBook, software used to create visualizations for sales and marketing tools and also for product prototyping.

Fig. 8.83 Realistic ray-traced Corvette rendered using 3DEXCITE Deltagen. *Source* Dassault Systèmes

In 2014, 75% of the company's business was in marketing, and 80% of their business came from the automotive industry. Only about 25% of the company's business comes from software sales.

3DEXCITE Deltagen ray-tracing software has been positioned for realistic display of 3D visualizations with real-time interaction. Dassault says it supports the full value chain from design and engineering to marketing and sales. The company claims that rapid virtual prototyping and validation provide earlier product maturity using Deltagen.

With the launch of 2018X, 3DEXCITE debuts software tools for content creation and experience staging. The company says they have developed a simple, intuitive interface that will be appreciated by its existing customers and in particular the new users. Being hardware agnostic like other tools from 3ds/3Dexperience, it allows the user to be logged on to any system without any special hardware requirements.

Naturally, there was some overlap in the customer lists of Dassault and RTT in automotive including Audi, BMW, Ferrari, Toyota, the Volkswagen Group, and GM. Also GM is interesting because it is also a customer of Siemens. Siemens had been working with RTT to integrate visualization tools into Siemens' products. Siemens held an equity position in RTT since August 2010, and in 2012, Ralf Schnell of Siemens' venture capital group took a seat on the RTT board.

The deal also tightened some relationships already in place. Nvidia had been involved with RTT because RTT takes advantage of Nvidia's technology on every level, from CUDA to Grid. Also, Bunkspeed uses Nvidia's Iray technology. Dassault and Nvidia have demonstrated productivity gains with Nvidia's Maximus technology in rendering, design, and simulation. Bunkspeed's business model wasn't working—they wanted more money for rendering than most people wanted to pay—but as a tool for push-button rendering for consumers who might want to try out different "looks" or for designers who want to demonstrate the superiority of their design, it is an asset.

8.3 Plug-in Programs

Included in this section are the most popular (but not exhaustively all) ray-tracing programs that are plug-ins for other programs such as 3D modeling, medical, AEC, CAD, and visualization. The following table summarizes the plug-ins and the programs they are available for. This list changes monthly, and so this table should be viewed as a snapshot and general view of the market and not a comparative or shopping guide (Table 8.4).

Table 8.4 is a partial listing of the most popular programs.

8.3.1 3Delight—Illumination Technologies

Their current product line includes 3Delight, 3Delight for Daz Studio, Maya and 3Delight for Katana. They also made public their upcoming rendering service in the form of 3Delight Cloud which is still in testing.

8.3.2 Arnold—Autodesk

Arnold has supported plug-ins available for Maya, Houdini, Cinema 4D, 3ds Max, and Katana. The Arnold plug-in for Softimage is now available under an Apache2.0 open-source license.

The company points out that there are several players in the space, including RenderMan, V-Ray, Redshift, Octane, and others. Autodesk DCC tools like Maya and 3ds Max are built to make third-party rendering easy to implement, and the company believes that the open ecosystem is essential, which is also why Arnold licenses include a range of third-party plug-in integrations such as 3ds Max, Maya, Cinema 4D, Houdini, and Katana.

The company points out that there are several players in the space, including RenderMan, V-Ray, Redshift, Octane, and others. Autodesk DCC tools like Maya and 3ds Max are built to make third-party rendering easy to implement and the company believes that the open ecosystem is important, which is also why Arnold licenses include a range of third-party plug-in integrations such as Cinema 4D, Houdini, and Katana.

8.3.3 Corona Renderer—Chaos Group (Legion Team)

Corona Renderer is a photorealistic renderer which has the capacity of working in biased and unbiased capacities. The tool is available for Autodesk 3ds Max, as a stand-alone CLI application and Maxon Cinema 4D.

Table 8.4 A table of programs [y] with plug-ins [x]

	3Delight	Cycles	ProRender	Arnold	Corona	Iray	KeyShot	Lumion	LuxCoreRender	Maxwell	Redshift	V-Ray
ArchiCAD								Y				
Autodesk 3ds Max			Y	Y		Y	Y		Y		Y	Y
Autodesk Katana	Y			Y							Y	Y
Autodesk Maya	Y		Y	Y		Y	Y		Y		Y	Y
Autodesk Revit								Y				Y
Bentley MicroStation								Y				
Blender		Y	Y						Y			Y
Dassault SolidWorks			Y				Y					
Dassault Catia						Y						
Daz Studio	Y								Y			
Epic												y
formZ												Y
Houdini				Y		Y					Y	Y
Lumiscaphe												
Maxon Cinema 4D		Y	Y	Y		Y	Y		Y		Y	Y
Modo			Y						Y			Y
Nuke												Y
Pixar's USD Hydra viewport			Y									
PTC Creo			Y									
Rhino		Y	Y			Y	Y	Y		Y		Y
Siemens NX						Y	Y					
SketchUp							Y	Y	Y			Y
Vectorworks							Y	Y				

The development of Corona Renderer started in 2009 as a solo student project of Ondřej Karlík at Czech Technical University in Prague. Corona has since evolved to a full-time commercial project after Ondřej established a company together with the former CG artist Adam Hotový and Jaroslav Křivánek, Associate Professor and Researcher at Charles University in Prague. In August 2017, the company became part of Chaos Group, allowing for further expansion and growth.

Chaos Group positions its renderer as being "Proudly CPU Based." The company states that the Corona Renderer does not need any special hardware to run. It uses the CPU, and one can run it on any processor from Intel or AMD released in the past decade.

Corona is intended mainly for use by power users and third-party plug-in developers with particular exporters. It does not come in a "studio" version with graphics interface. All from the host application properties are exported into Corona Renderer, so developers of exporters have access to all features.

One cannot create a scene in a 3D application that does not have a Corona Render plug-in and render that scene using Corona Standalone. The only option available for now is to import the model to other supported application (3ds Max, Cinema 4D, etc.), or to create an exporter script that saves the model, lights, and materials as an OBJ file.

Corona Renderer 2.0 for 3ds Max came out in June 2018, while the previous version 1.7 came in October 2017. The company claims to have focused on the following points in the latest version:

- Heterogeneous media (FumeFX, OpenVDB, Phoenix FD)
- Initial steps in V-Ray compatibility
- About 110 new materials introduced in the material library
- The introduction of Corona toolbar
- An overall reduction in memory requirements by 5–10% in almost every scene
- Improved denoiser for bump mapping
- Updated material override functionality option to preserve predefined materials.

Corona Renderer does not need any special hardware to run. It uses the CPU and can run on any processor from Intel or AMD released in the past decade. Corona Renderer uses Intel's Embree ray-tracing kernels.

Adding feature to heterogeneous media shading

A support feature was introduced for various volumes which include Phoenix FD, FumeFX, OpenVDB (see Glossary), and 3ds Max texture maps.

Phoenix FD is a V-Ray feature that is characterized by the same technology which lets Corona Renderer generate 3D volumes utilizing the corona volume material. However, there are a few limitations that only Phoenix FD 3.10.00 or newer support such as foam rendering and isosurface rendering modes which are currently not supported by Corona.

FumeFX is similar to Phoenix FD. However, there are a few shortcomings as well such as only FumeFX 5.0 or newer is being supported and options like Motion blur, space warps, illumination maps, and the channel data shader are not covered by Corona 2 (Fig. 8.84).

Open VDB (see Glossary) support (Corona Volume Grid)—Open VDB files allow the user to store voxels in a 3D grid, along with optional additional data such as density, velocity, and temperature. These files can be created using a wide range of software like SideFX Houdini and Phoenix FD and can be loaded and rendered using the Corona Volume Grid Object, which then allows the properties of absorption, scattering, and emission to be set and can be driven by the parameters of density, velocity, temperature, etc.

3D volume materials

There are two nodes in the corona volume material—the old "on-surface" mode and the new "inside volume" mode. The new mode permits the corona volume material to render exact volumes inside the objects, in place of simple calculation of the surface of the object. The tool can work with old versions of 3ds Max noise maps which calculate noise in 3D space. The company claims that the uses of this tool are tremendous which would allow one to create low-lying mist, clouds, ice, and other atmospherics and used them either on its own or with other tools like Corona distance map (Fig. 8.85).

Additional support for core V-Ray features

Corona Renderer can support V-Ray Light (plane, disk, mesh, and sphere) and V-Ray MTL. However, there are a few limitations as well such as the renderer supports only images created in V-Ray 3.60 or later and all the exclusion or inclusion list of V-Ray light requires the installation of V-Ray.

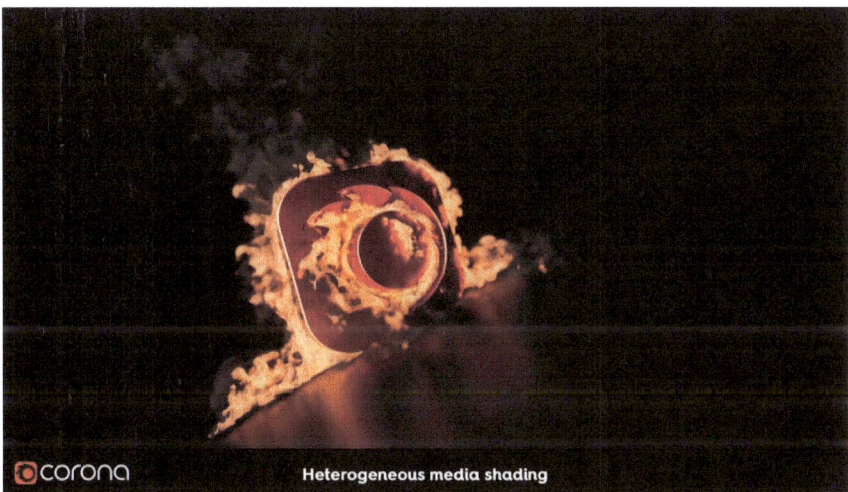

Fig. 8.84 Heterogeneous media shading. *Source* Corona Renderer

Fig. 8.85 Old "on surface" versus new "inside volume". *Source* Corona Renderer

Corona Camera, new bokeh controls

The corona camera has been added with advanced bokeh controls for center bias, vignetting, and anisotropy. Positive values of center bias expand the bokeh, while it contracts with the negative scores. Similarly, positive values of vignetting presents a harder outside edge to the bokeh, while negative values do the same toward the center of the image (Fig. 8.86).

Corona Renderer has received many useful ideas and comments from its users. Most of them prefer this tool because of its speed where it has earned much applause. There are others who prefer it because of reduced dependency of GPU as Corona is a CPU-based rendering tool (Fig. 8.87).

Users also like the quality of the output, and that is one reason for its growth in the past years. However, there are a few areas of improvement suggested by the users. Memory becomes an issue particularly in case of big/complex scenes with frames over 4K which need lots of RAM, even 32 GB of RAM may not be enough.

8.3.3.1 Summary

Being a new player in the group, Corona Renderer has built a good market and reputation for itself with its ability to handle operations with good speed and other benefits. There is fierce competition with V-Ray, Arnold, and others, and even

Fig. 8.86 Material Library Update. *Source* Corona Renderer

Fig. 8.87 Motion blur example. *Source* Corona Renderer

though companies like Chaos Group/V-Ray have been in the market for more than 20 years, Corona Renderer can produce a decent level playing field for itself and its products.

8.3.4   Cycles—Blender

The ray tracer found in Blender is also available as a plug-in for other programs. Cycles is natively integrated into Blender, Poser, and Rhino. The Cycles 4D plug-in for Cinema 4D and a plug-in for 3ds Max is available as well.

8.3.5   finalRender—Cebas

Cebas partners mainly with Autodesk and develops on Autodesk industry standard 3D software: 3ds Max. Autodesk has been incorporating cebas technologies into their offerings for many years. finalRender is a ray-tracing program developed as a plug-in renderer for 3ds Max.

Cebas says finalRender is the new breed of light simulation software offering unique algorithms and approaches to light simulation not found in any other renderer for 3ds Max. finalRender was the first renderer to practically apply exact global illumination rendering to the large-scale vfx movie production with the film *2012*.

finalRender uses spectral wavelengths in real-world physics, and Monte Carlo sampling simulates light energy transport within a 3D scene that recreates optical effects on materials which are impossible for older generation ray-tracing systems. Cebas claims that spectral-based rendering, the way it is used in finalRender, is able to simulate effects such as diffraction, dispersion, absorption, iridescence, and interference (Fig. 8.88).

Cebas says finalRender serves to debunk the myth that unbiased rendering needs unlimited random rays like natural light, resulting in speed lost and noise. Cebas claims to have developed a solution that resolves the speed and the noise issue while providing photorealistic accuracy. They call the technology Drop 1, and it uses adaptive sampling and an AI Denoiser to interpret and recalculate pixels in a complex feedback loop while staying faithful to unbiased rendering and physics accuracy. Texture baking (render to texture) is now incorporated as well.

The company also claims that finalRender is the first renderer of its kind for 3ds Max to offer a rendering engine that supports GPU rendering or pure CPU, as well as both technologies at the same time. Cebas calls this feature trueHybrid technology and says it allows the user to experience all the power within one application, no need for a separate GPU only product.

finalRender supports all of the standard lights in 3ds Max and comes with its own optimized and fully multi-threaded IES light. This native area light is

Fig. 8.88 A soap bubble rendered with spectral wavelength rendering. *Source* Cebas

configurable and is meant to replace all light types one might need. Setting up lights and especially changing light setups becomes as simple as clicking a button on the mouse.

finalRender offers the benefit of multiple global illumination engines for artists to choose from. The newest GI rendering method offers an unbiased, physically accurate path-tracing method, with fast GPU-based global illumination.

Other options or methods include:

- Irradiance caching
- Unbiased rendering
- Light Cache rendering

Core render qualities (real time and non-real time):

- Newly developed: content-aware sampling (CAS)
- Physically based wavelength/spectral light transport
- Biased and unbiased rendering including direct lighting/ambient occlusion support
- Full physically based IES light support
- Physically based material shading model
- Highly optimized geometry instancing for GPU and CPU.

One of the issues in GPU renders is noise or grain. Cebas developed a new sampling method that smoothens out such renders and produces more even and smoother results.

The program comes with dedicated materials and supports the thousands of preset Autodesk materials in addition to the mental ray materials. However, to deliver the best possible result with the utmost control, finalRender offers a dedicated car paint material. It features metallic flakes, special coating, and a reflection layer.

8.3.5.1   Summary

Cebas has proven that a company can specialize on a platform (3ds Max) and offer an esoteric very technical product and do quite well. Many of its competitors offer plug-ins for several programs and as such may be spread thin regarding support and feature development. Furthermore, 3ds Max is a somewhat specialized program appealing to a specific segment of the market, mainly media and entertainment (M&E).

8.3.6   Iray—Nvidia

As mentioned above (see Sect. 8.1.8.2), in December 2015, Nvidia announced it would enter the plug-in market with versions of Iray for popular design and modeling programs.

Nvidia's software integration partners have created state-of-the-art workflows that give one access to Iray within popular 3D content creation applications such as Autodesk Maya, Autodesk 3ds Max, and McNeel Rhinoceros.

8.3.7   KeyShot—Luxion

A KeyShot plug-in links the 3D modeling software and KeyShot together, rather than putting KeyShot inside the modeling application. Plug-ins add a menu button to one's 3D software that transfers 3D data and other model information into KeyShot.

Luxion has one of the most extensive lists of plug-ins for KeyShot of all the companies in the industry.

3D systems	3ds max	Alibre	AutoCAD 360	Cinema 4D
Creo	Deadline	Delcam	ESKO	Geomagic Design
IronCAD	JewelCAD	Maya	NX	Probeer
Rhinoceros	SketchUp	Solid Edge	SolidThinking	SolidWorks
SpaceClaim	ZBrush	ZW3D		

Plug-ins are developed by Luxion or by its partners who distribute and support them.

8.3.8   *Lumion*

Lumion is both a plug-in and a stand-alone ray-tracing program and is discussed in the stand-alone section above (Sect. 8.1.10). It is compatible with SketchUp, Revit, ArchiCAD, MicroStation, Allplan, Vectorworks, Rhinoceros, and 3ds.

8.3.9   *LuxCoreRender*

LuxCoreRender is an open-source physically based renderer that began in 2007. The program is an undertaking of hundreds of people sharing their knowledge in computer graphics papers, books, Web sites, and university courses. Among all these people, LuxCoreRender started particularly thanks to all involved in the development of LuxRender v1.x, to Matt Pharr and Greg Humphreys and their excellent book and project. LuxRender is based on PBRT, the unbiased ray tracer developed by Matt Pharr and Greg Humphreys for academic use. Pharr and Humphreys were kind enough to provide the source code of their program under the terms of the GPL, thus making the program free software.

In 2007, a small group of programmers led by Terrence Vergauwen took on the challenge to modify the program and make it suitable for artistic use. Late 2007, the initial version of LuxRender was released. With the release of LuxRender 0.5 in June 2008, the program was considered to be usable enough for general use. Since then, the rendering speed and the number of features and available exporters have been growing steadily.

During the 2017 winter, LuxCoreRender v2.0, the company defined it as the LuxCore API render package, dropping all old code related to LuxRender v1.x. A new Web site, forum, wiki, and Blender exporter were developed in order to mark a new fresh project restart.

Lux(Core)Render is one of the oldest open-source projects (Fig. 8.89).

LuxCoreRender is a physically correct, unbiased rendering engine. There are LuxCoreRender plug-ins for 3Ds Max, Blender, Maya, Modo, Cinema 4D, Daz Studio, Poser, SketchUp. All the code included in LuxCore repository was released under a new license: Apache License v2.0.

8.3.9.1   Summary

LuxRender was a free and open-source software rendering system for physically correct image synthesis. The program runs on Linux, Mac OS X, and Microsoft

Fig. 8.89 Lux and Love by Charles Nandeya Ehouman (Sharlybg) using BBBB and LuxCoreRender

Windows. The project changed the name in the last part of 2017 and restarted with the name of LuxCoreRender.

LuxRender features a 3D renderer; it relies on other programs (3D modeling programs) to create the scenes to render, including the models, materials, lights, and cameras. This content is then exported from the application it was created in for rendering using LuxRender. Fully functional exporters are available for Blender, Daz Studio; partially functional ones for Cinema 4D, Maya, SketchUp, and XSI. LuxRender is also fully supported as production renderer in 3ds Max.

LuxRender was very popular with Blender users. However, since Blender developed its ray tracer, Cycles, Blender users have gravitated toward it. Luxrender has a different approach than Cycles, so it always was two separate independent projects; however, LuxRender is still available for Blender. https://www.blender.org/download/external-renderers/.

8.3.10 Maxwell

Maxwell has a fully integrated workflow so that one can set up render scenes from the comfort of your usual 3d/CAD platform. There is a wide range of Maxwell plug-ins from Next Limit.

3ds Max	ArchiCAD	Softimage	Bonzai3d	Cinema 4D
formZ	Houdini	Lightwave	Maya	Modo
Revit	Rhinoceros	SketchUp	SolidWorks	Nuke
Photoshop	After Effects			

Maxwell SketchUp

The latest version of the Maxwell Sketchup was launched in early 2018. It allows the user to work at ease within the SketchUp Make and Pro. This product has been introduced for rendering in SketchUp with a simple but extensive Maxwell toolbar. It brings on the table all the advanced features the new version of Maxwell in a simple yet detailed manner (Fig. 8.90).

The Maxwell 4.2 has worked on several of the challenges their users faced earlier. They became much faster than the older version, and they gave the option of either CPU or GPU for rendering. That helps in the cost/speed ratio for the system.

Moreover, their introductions of multi-light stand-alone, new searchable library and multiple host support are beneficial for the user. However, they lack regarding GPU rendering support for MAC users. Maxwell always had a reputation for delivering high quality, but their speed of operation had been an issue for them which they have worked upon in Maxwell Renders 4.2. However, their usage

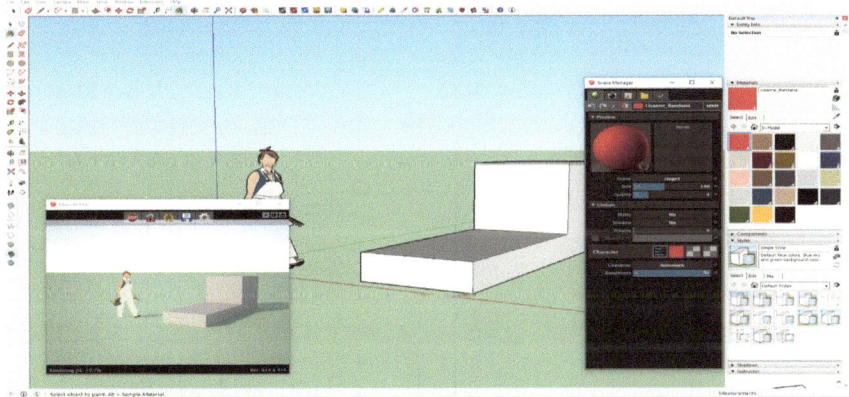

Fig. 8.90 Using Maxwell renderer in SketchUp. *Source* Next Limit

remains simple but exhaustive and is supposed to be their biggest strength in the years to come.

Maxwell targets their 3D rendering software at architects and designers.

8.3.11   ProRender

ProRender is both a plug-in and a stand-alone ray-tracing program and is discussed in the stand-alone section above (Sect. 8.1.10). It is available as a plug-in for

Autodesk 3ds Max	Autodesk Maya	Blender	Maxon Cinema 4D	Modo by Foundry
Pixar's USD Hydra viewport	PTC Creo			

8.3.12   Redshift

Redshift is both a plug-in and a stand-alone ray-tracing program and is discussed in the stand-alone section above (Sect. 8.1.17). The company has plug-in for 3ds Max, Cinema 4D, Houdini, Katana, Maya, and Softimage.

8.3.13   V-Ray, Chaos Group

V-Ray is both a plug-in and a stand-alone ray-tracing program and is discussed in the stand-alone section (Sect. 8.1.23).

V-Ray is available as a plug-in for several popular programs:

V-Ray for 3ds Max	V-Ray for Adobe CC (Felix)	V-Ray for Maya	V-Ray Render Node
V-Ray for Cinema 4D	V-Ray for Modo	V-Ray for Nuke	V-Ray for Katana
V-Ray for formZ	V-Ray for SketchUp	V-Ray for Rhino	V-Ray for Revit
V-Ray for Unreal	V-Ray for Blender	V-Ray for Houdini	

V-Ray Next Scene Intelligence

V-Ray Next Scene Intelligence delivers faster ray tracing, cleaner sampling, and more accurate rendering compared to its previous version. There are multiple benefits to this version which are:

- Better lighting, shading, and rendering tools
- Can handle biggest projects without toughest scenes
- Less time consuming and allows more time being creative
- New versatile features
- Seamless Integration

Good acceptance among the top design firms.

New features in the support modules for various software

V-Ray 3.6 for 3ds Max (Fig. 8.91)

• Scene intelligence	• Adaptive dome light
• Point-and-shoot camera	• 2 times faster GPU rendering
• GPU volume rendering	• Nvidia AI Denoiser
• Lighting analysis	• Physical hair material
• Switch materials	• Denoised render materials
• Layered Alembic workflows	• Cloud-ready
• Metalness	

Fig. 8.91 Sample picture for V-Ray tool integration for 3ds Max. *Source* Chaos Group

V-Ray 3.6 for Modo

• GPU hybrid rendering	• GPU device select without restarting
• Realistic grass and fur	• Over 650 extremely realistic scanned materials
• Full light select render element	• Cryptomatte render element

V-Ray 3.6 for SketchUp

• Viewport rendering	• Powerful GPU rendering
• Hybrid GPU–CPU Rendering	• Adaptive lights
• Smart UI	• V-Ray color picker
• V-Ray scene import	• Sunlight studies
• Implementing fog scenes	• New texture maps
• 2D displacement	• Animated proxy objects and proxy reviews
• Better viewport materials	• Better denoising

Similar new features can be seen for the other software as well (Fig. 8.92).

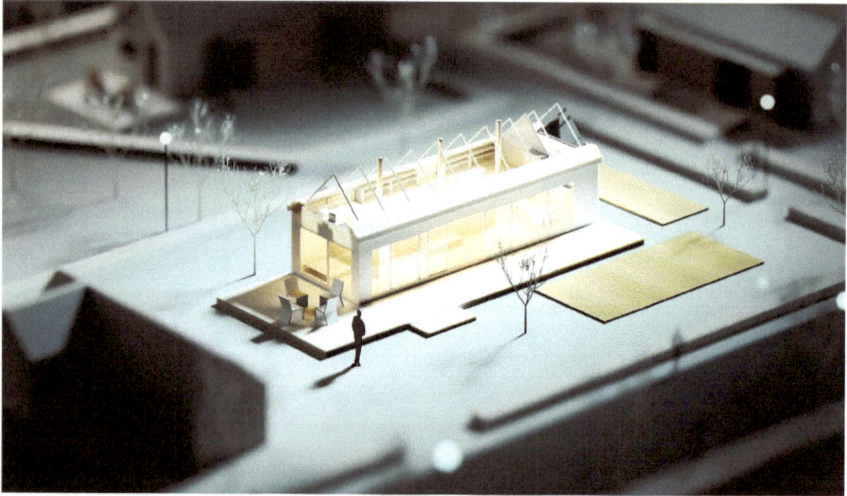

Fig. 8.92 Sample picture for V-Ray tool integration for SketchUp. *Source* Chaos Group

Applicability

The version 3.6 is applicable for multiple industries as follows:

• Architecture	• Automotive
• Television VFX	• Interior design
• Advertising	• Film VFX
• Product design	• Games
• Software development	

8.3.13.1   Summary

The V-Ray software is used by many of its users for its fitment with various programs, and this is a reason for its wide adaptability as well. However, there are a few points which displease the users as well. Parameters such as the speed of operations and the number of materials included in the latest version are not up to the mark compared to the other competitive tools available in the market. So, while V-Ray enjoys a good presence in the market, they need to work on these points to counter the progress made by the new entrants like Corona and Redshift.

8.4   Middleware

Middleware is computer software that provides services to software applications beyond those available from the operating system. It is e described as "software glue."

Middleware makes it easier for software developers to implement communication and input/output so that they can focus on the specific purpose of their application. It gained popularity in the 1980s as a solution to the problem of how to link newer applications to older legacy systems, although the term had been in use since 1968. The term is used for software that enables communication and management of data in distributed applications.

8.4.1   Embree

Introduced in 2011, Embree is a collection of ray-tracing kernels, developed at Intel.

Embree is an open-source ray-tracing framework for x86 CPUs. Embree is explicitly designed to achieve high performance in professional rendering environments in which complex geometry and incoherent ray distributions are common. Embree consists of a set of low-level kernels that maximize utilization of modern CPU architectures and an API which enables usage of these kernels in existing renderers with minimal programmer effort. The developers state that in secondary rays, in particular, the performance of Embree is competitive with (and often higher than) existing state-of-the-art methods on CPUs and GPUs.

The target users of Embree are graphics application engineers who want improved performance of their photorealistic rendering application by using performance-optimized ray-tracing kernels. Intel optimizes the kernels for the latest Intel processors with support for SSE, AVX, AVX2, and AVX-512 instructions. Embree supports runtime code selection to choose the traversal and build algorithms that best matches the instruction set of one's CPU. Intel recommends using Embree through its API to realize the highest benefit from future improvements. Embree is open-sourced under the Apache 2.0 license.

Intel Embree supports applications written with the Intel SPMD Program Compiler (ISPC, https://ispc.github.io/) by also providing an ISPC interface to the core ray-tracing algorithms. That makes it possible to write a renderer in ISPC that automatically vectorizes and leverages SSE, AVX, AVX2, and AVX-512 instructions. ISPC also supports runtime code selection; thus, ISPC selects the best code path for your application.

Embree contains algorithms optimized for incoherent workloads (e.g., Monte Carlo ray-tracing algorithms) and coherent workloads (e.g., primary visibility and hard shadow rays).

Embree provides a Monte Carlo ray tracer as an example. This renderer demonstrates how an efficient rendering system is designed and implemented using Embree's key technologies. The renderer is also an excellent framework for evaluating and comparing different ray-tracing kernels in a realistic application scenario.

In Fig. 8.93, a single machine with four Intel Xeon processors computes preview images of this 3D model at interactive frame rates (left). The image converges to a better solution within a few seconds (middle). A perfect image (right) only takes about a minute to compute.

The single-ray traversal kernels of Embree provide high performance for incoherent workloads and are very easy to integrate into existing rendering applications. Using the stream kernels, even higher performance for incoherent rays is possible, but integration might require significant code changes to the application to use the stream paradigm. In general, for coherent workloads, the stream mode with coherent flag set gives the best performance.

Fig. 8.93 Progressive rendering of the imperial crown of Austria. Model courtesy of Martin Lubich, http://www.loramel.net

Intel Embree also supports dynamic scenes by implementing high-performance two-level spatial index structure construction algorithms.

Embree is not targeting the end users of rendering technology directly. Instead, the kernels are for integration into existing and future rendering applications. By using the open-source Embree ray-tracing kernels, researchers and developers can achieve the highest level of performance on Intel CPUs.

8.4.1.1 Summary

Embree provides highly optimized ray-tracing kernels that speed photorealistic rendering on Intel CPUs by up to 2x. Intel has released these kernels as open source under the Apache 2.0 license.

Please visit the Embree project page http://Embree.github.io for more information. Read the article: Embree: Photo-Realistic Ray Tracing Kernels (https://software.intel.com/en-us/articles/embree-highly-optimized-visibility-algorithms-for-monte-carlo-ray-tracing).

8.4.2 OptiX—Nvidia

Nvidia's OptiX (OptiX Application Acceleration Engine) is a general-purpose ray-tracing API for rendering, baking, collision detection, and AI queries.

OptiX is not a renderer but can implement many types of renderers; it implements a modern shader-centric, stateless, and bindless design. The computations are offloaded to the GPUs through either the low-level or the high-level API introduced with CUDA. CUDA is only available for Nvidia's graphics products.

Nvidia OptiX is part of Nvidia DesignWorks. OptiX is a high-level or "to-the-algorithm" API, meaning that it is designed to encapsulate the entire algorithm of which ray tracing is a part, not just the ray tracing itself. That is meant to allow the OptiX engine to execute the larger algorithm with great flexibility without application-side changes.

Fig. 8.94 A Julia set drawn with Nvidia OptiX—this is a sample of the SDK

OptiX is not a renderer, but renderer-enabling middleware. It provides a simple framework for accessing the GPU's massive ray-tracing power using state-of-the-art GPU algorithms. Loosely inspired by the Manta interactive ray tracer developed at University of Utah in 2006 by Steven Parker[19,20] the program has evolved extensively since then (Fig. 8.94).

OptiX works by using user-supplied instructions (in the form of CUDA kernels) regarding what a ray should do in particular circumstances to simulate a complete tracing process.

When a light ray or some other kinds of ray might have different behaviors when hitting a particular surface rather than another one, OptiX allows one to customize the hit conditions with user-provided programs. The programs are written in CUDA C or directly in PTX code and are linked together when used by the OptiX engine.

To use OptiX, a CUDA-capable GPU must be available on the system, and the CUDA toolkit installed (Fig. 8.95).

The ray generation shader is the first thing invoked in a ray-tracing dispatch. This function casts a single ray into the scene to search for intersections, triggering other shaders in the process. Intersection and any hit shaders get invoked for potential intersections between the ray and the scene. The intersection shader determines whether the ray intersects an individual geometric primitive. The most common type is, of course, triangles, for which the API offers special support through a built-in, highly tuned intersection shader. Once an intersection is found, the any hit shader may be used to process it further or potentially discard it. Any hit shaders commonly implements alpha testing. Finally, either the closest hit or a missed shader is invoked, depending on the outcome of the search. The closest hit shader is typically where most shading operations take place: material evaluation, texture lookups, and so on. The miss shader can be used to implement environment lookups, for example. Both closest hit and miss shaders can recursively trace rays by calling the ray generation program themselves.

---

[19]Bigler et al. (2006).

[20]Stephens et al. (2006).

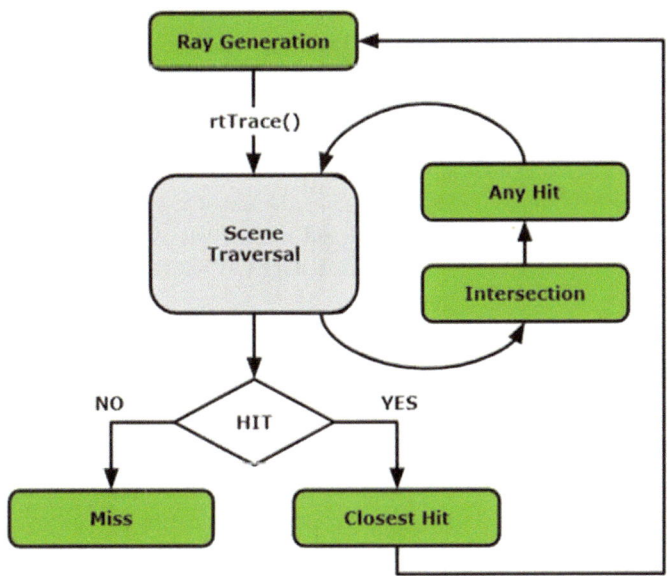

Fig. 8.95 Nvidia's OptiX block diagram

Several examples for these programs are available with the program's SDK License: proprietary software, free-of-cost for non-commercial use.

8.4.2.1   Summary

According to Nvidia, OptiX is designed to be flexible enough for "procedural definitions and hybrid rendering approaches." Aside from computer graphics rendering, OptiX also helps in optical and acoustical design, radiation and electromagnetic research, artificial intelligence queries, and collision analysis.

Nvidia OptiX is a ray-tracing API. The computations are offloaded to the GPUs through either the low-level or the high-level API introduced with CUDA. CUDA is only available for Nvidia's graphics products. OptiX also utilizes RT Cores introduced in the Turing architecture for ray-tracing acceleration.

8.4.3   Radeon-Rays—AMD

Radeon-Rays was released by AMD in 2015 and is a GPU intersection acceleration library with necessary support for heterogeneous systems. AMD developed Radeon-Rays to aid developers to exploit AMD GPUs and CPU or APUs and eliminate the need to maintaining hardware-dependent code. Originally called FireRays, AMD first demonstrated the ray-tracing kernels in a prototype form at SIGGRAPH 2014.

Radeon-Rays is middleware for enabling renderers to run on GPUs and is cross-platform based on standard programming APIs (OpenCL today, moving to Vulkan next). FireRays 2.0 brings support for Windows, OSX, Linux, AMD, NV, Intel GPUs and CPUs with many backends.

Radeon-Rays exposes a C++ API for scene construction and performing asynchronous ray intersection queries. The current implementation is based on OpenCL 1.2 standard. It is not limited to AMD hardware or a specific operating system. Radeon-Rays can be easily distributed and through its API helps assure compatibility and best performance across a wide range of hardware platforms.

Radeon-Rays 2.0 key features are

- Performance improvements on FATBVH for fast BVH
- Support for geometry and ray masks
- Ray filtering support
- Calc abstraction computation layer for low-level API support

Radeon-Rays is an open-source developer's tool that conforms to the OpenCL 1.2 standard, so it can be deployed with non-AMD hardware and in multiple OS environments. AMD's Radeon-Rays (and the latest release of ProRender) can support real-time GPU acceleration of ray-tracing techniques, mixed with traditional rasterization-based rendering on the Vulkan 1.1 API, which is fully supported by GNC-based AMD GPUs loaded with the latest version of Radeon and RadeonPro Software.

Radeon-Rays has a smaller feature set than AMD's full ray tracing program, Radeon Render Pro, and is only a ray intersection library. It is also cross-platform.

Game developers can use Radeon-Rays for real-time ray tracing in a hybrid rendering method mixing ray tracing with rasterization. Rasterization is used for primary visibility, lighting, and backgrounds, and ray tracing is used for secondary and complex effects of specific objects.

In this hybrid mode, real-time ray tracing with Radeon-Rays is used for ambient occlusion, glossy reflections, diffuse global illumination, and area lighting. These effects are turned on/off based on hardware capabilities.

Radeon-Rays comes with an open-source stand-alone renderer and is available for download on GPUOpen. Future versions will support the Vulkan API. The Radeon-Rays SDK has the following requirements:

- A PC with 64-bit Windows 7, 8, 10, Linux, or Mac OS X installed.
- Any OpenCL 1.2-capable device
- Microsoft Visual Studio 2013 installed to compile the sample renderer.
- The Visual Studio 2013 redistributable is required to run precompiled SDK sample binaries.

OpenCL, Vulkan, and C++ backends can be used as an important building block of a renderer supporting global illumination on rendering, sound rendering (through TrueAudio Next), and AI (Fig. 8.96).

Fig. 8.96 Previous lightmapping solutions would take hours to compute even moderate-sized scenes. Expansive outdoor environments could take days. *Source* AMD

Unity announced GPU Progressive Lightmapper with AMD Radeon-Rays integration claiming to revolutionize render times and workflows for realistic light effects was one of the dominant themes at GDC 2018. The announcement of AMD's Radeon-Rays integration in Unity's GPU Progressive Lightmapper should be exciting to game developers looking to boost the visual fidelity of their games assisted by an interactive baking workflow.

Powering the GPU Progressive Lightmapper is the integration with AMD's Radeon-Rays—an open-source GPU-accelerated ray-tracing engine for low low-level engine developers and supporting OpenCL, Vulkan, and C++ backends. Radeon-Rays can be used as an important building block of a renderer supporting global illumination rendering, sound rendering (through TrueAudio Next), and AI.

Radeon-Rays can be used for lightmap baking and light probe calculation using ray tracing and is being integrated by developers to improve the lighting effects in their games.[21]

8.4.3.1 Rendering Times: CPU Versus GPU

Unity's previous light mapping solutions were entirely CPU-based and could require several hours to compute for a moderately sized scene. Expansive outdoor environments could take days to lightmap. Unity said that by using Radeon-Rays GPU acceleration sped up the process of tuning lights and baking up to 10× the speed of CPU-based baking, giving instant feedback to the artist. The new Lightmapper also adds an interactive baking mode which allows lighting artists to

---

[21]Harada (2017).

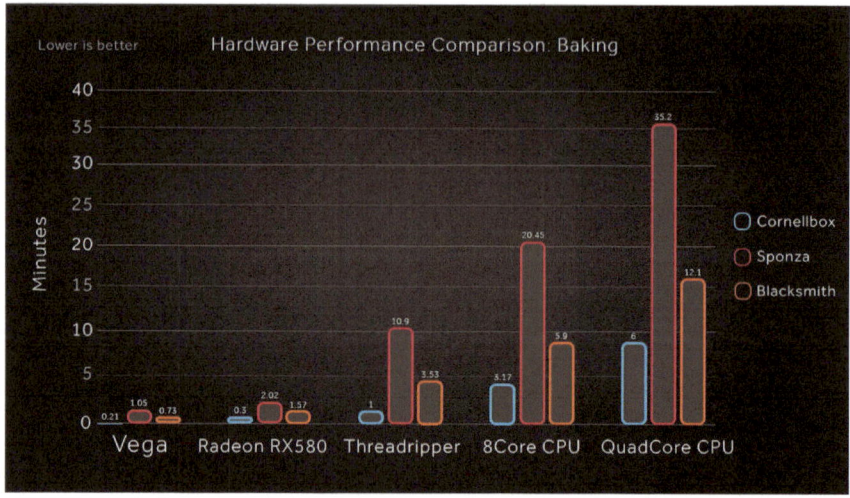

Fig. 8.97 Baking hardware performance comparison. *Source* AMD

navigate the scene to see the baking process in real time. It also allows them to change lighting and material and immediately see how it affects their bakes.

Just how much does GPU hardware accelerate the lightmapping process compared to previous CPU-based methods? In benchmark tests run by AMD comparing lightmapping hardware performance across models commonly used for benchmark (the simple Cornell box, moderate sponza) and a production model (the complex blacksmith), the difference was substantial. GPU-based lightmapping generated close to 200 million rays/s, around $10\times$ more than the level of CPU-based approaches (Fig. 8.97).

With the new GPU-based Progressive Lightmapper, Unity says users can achieve faster bakes on a Radeon Vega in their system. The tool enables a faster workflow for artists to design while they bake. That means that when designers make any changes to lighting, materials, and textures, they can immediately see how that affects their baked global illumination quality. Because of the simple, elegant API of Radeon-Rays, developers can focus on the actual algorithm of the Lightmapper instead of spending time on the integration. That means more efficient use of system resources, faster workflows, and overall better experience for Unity users as they create better quality assets (Fig. 8.98).

The real-time ray tracing with GPU Progressive Lightmapper was released in 2018.[22]

---

[22]https://gpuopen.com/.

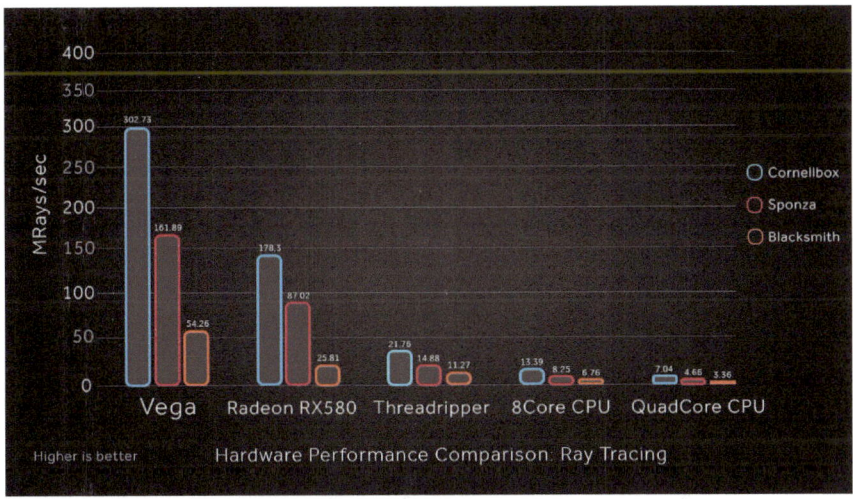

Fig. 8.98 Ray-tracing hardware performance comparison. *Source* AMD

8.4.3.2 Summary

AMD developed Radeon-Rays to help developers get the most out of AMD GPUs and CPU or APUs, as well as save them from maintaining hardware-dependent code. Radeon-Rays exposes a well-defined C++ API for scene construction and performing asynchronous ray intersection queries. The current implementation is based on OpenCL, which means Radeon-Rays supports execution on all platforms conforming to the OpenCL 1.2 standard. It is not limited to AMD hardware or a specific operating system. Radeon-Rays can be easily distributed and through its API helps assure compatibility and best performance across a wide range of hardware platforms.

8.5 Cloud-Based

Cloud-based rendering engines that create photorealistic images from one's 3D models became available in 2006, but so far are limited to two suppliers, OneRender and RealityServer.

Cloud-based is different than using cloud services. For example, Chaos V-Ray cloud which is integrated in V-Ray can render to the cloud. Chaos had designed fit or fast and simple setup, with just a few settings for resolution and image format. There is no hardware to configure or virtual machines to set up. The distinction here is cloud only vs. cloud capable. OneRender is cloud only, whereas V-Ray (and several others) is cloud capable.

8.5.1   CL3VER—Cloud Rendering

Barcelona-based CL3VER introduced a proprietary cloud solution based on Nvidia's RTX to visualize real-time 3D content directly in a Web browser (Fig. 8.99).

This technology is based on CL3VER's 3D ray-tracing engine that renders 3D scenes, regardless of its complexity says the company, in the cloud, live-streaming the visualization to the browser using standard H L5 technology compatible with any recent device (desktop or mobile) without the need of any plug-in.

The company claims that the technology offers photorealistic results, immersive 3D navigation, fast loading times, and immediate changes, making it a choice for Web-based 3D applications such as real estate and product configurators, training and educational modules, interactive storytelling, and so on.

With this solution, CL3VER targets all types of companies that want to improve engagement with their users, offering them a new way of interacting with their products with improved visual quality.

"Our new solution is going to make a big impact in the market and lead the next generation of 3D user experiences in the browser, helping companies to engage their customer in ways they couldn't even imagine before," CL3VER's CEO, Daniel Iborra, said. "Seamless 3D navigation in the browser has been in the radar of industrials, advertising agencies, video game companies and so on for many years and now CL3VER finally delivers it to the user."

CL3VER's cloud solution is available through a variety of business models, including a SaaS platform.

Fig. 8.99 CL3VER real-time cloud rendering

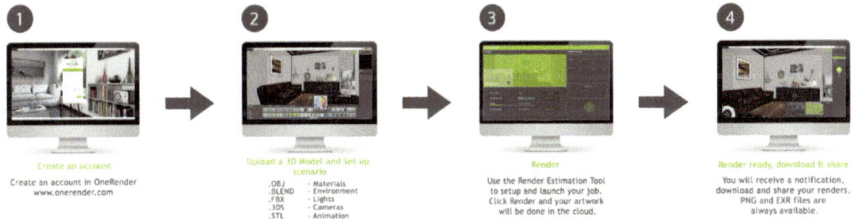

Fig. 8.100 How OneRender works. *Source* OneRender

CL3VER is also working on integrating this new technology into CL3VER Presenter, its presentation authoring tool, which will allow 3ds Max and Revit users to create photorealistic real-time 3D presentations from their 3D scenes and share them, in a few clicks, without rendering times or any additional production time, thanks to its compatibility with V-Ray content.

Founded in 2011 in Barcelona, CL3VER is a real-time rendering technology company focused on bringing photorealism to mobile and Web-based applications.

8.5.2   OneRender—Prefixa

OneRender is a cloud-based render engine that creates photorealistic images from your 3D models (Fig. 8.100).

The 3D CAD program Onshape, which can use Luxon's KeyShot. Onshape is only available from the cloud, but KeyShot is available in several forms (see Sect. 8.1.8.2).

8.5.3   RealityServer—Migenius

In 2012, migenius of Melbourne began offering RealityServer, a software development platform for integrating cloud-based photorealistic 3D rendering in applications. It provides Web services and API frameworks that developers can utilize to easily integrate 3D rendering in any Web-based or desktop application.

RealityServer runs as a server, much like a standard Web server like Apache or Microsoft IIS, it accepts requests and responds with streams of 3D rendered imagery. RealityServer is provided for developers to install either on their servers or on those of popular cloud providers. Continue reading to learn more about what makes RealityServer different from conventional client-side rendering approaches.

RealityServer is built directly on Nvidia Iray, the very same rendering technology chosen by firms such as Dassault Systèmes, Siemens, and Allegorithmic to power photorealistic rendering in their applications. Using the power of the GPU, Iray provides multiple rendering modes to address a range of use cases.

Fig. 8.101 Before and after: a typical SketchUp architectural model before (above) and after (below) using Bloom Unit. *Source* Migenius

The Bloom Unit is a plug-in for SketchUp, offering interactive photorealistic model rendering in real time using cloud computing. The rendering can be shared with any device on the Internet through a browser; a copy of SketchUp on the viewing end is not required (Fig. 8.101).

Iray delivers a uniform user experience while supporting the demands of both interactive editing and final-frame, photorealistic rendering. Physically correct, Iray can produce accurate simulations of the actual behavior of light in any scene and does so with push-button simplicity.

8.5.3.1   Summary

The cloud-first nature of RealityServer makes it perfect for direct integration in Onshape, the cloud-based CADA system.

migenius RealityServer enables the development and deployment of interactive and photorealistic applications and Web services, allowing product designers, architects, and consumers to visualize 3D scenes with remarkable realism. The RealityServer platform is a powerful combination of Nvidia GPUs and 3D Web services software that delivers interactive, photorealistic applications over the Web. Migenius says

RealityServer is the first Web services platform that enables anyone to interact remotely with complex, 3D models and environments, from any perspective and under customizable lighting conditions. Netbooks, and smartphones can use used thus enabling 3D Web applications to scale based on utilization requirements dynamically.

8.6   Other

Specialized ray tracers used for optical design and other applications are reviewed in this section.

In addition to all the commercial and free professional ray-tracing programs, one can experiment with some interesting ray-tracing tools and code.

8.6.1   *The Ray Tracer Challenge*

Can one build a photorealistic 3D renderer from scratch? It is easier than you think says Jamis Buck the author of the book, *The Ray Tracer Challenge: A Test-Driven Guide to Your First 3D Renderer.*[23]

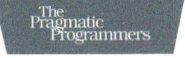

---

[23]Buck (2019).

In just a couple of weeks, according to Buck, one can build a ray tracer that renders beautiful scenes with shadows, reflections, brilliant refraction effects, and subjects composed of various graphics primitives: spheres, cubes, cylinders, triangles, and more. With each chapter, implement another piece of the puzzle and move the renderer that much further forward. Do all of this in whichever language and environment you prefer, and do it entirely test-first, so you know it is correct. Recharge yourself with this project's immense potential for personal exploration, experimentation, and discovery.

Each chapter presents a bite-sized piece of the puzzle, building on earlier chapters and setting the stage for later ones. Requirements are given in plain English, which you translate into tests and code. When the project is complete, one can look back and realize they have built an entire system test-first.

There is no research necessary—all the necessary formulas and algorithms are presented and illustrated right there. Dive into interesting topics from fundamental concepts such as vectors and matrices; to the algorithms that simulate the intersection of light rays with spheres, planes, cubes, cylinders, and triangles; to geometric patterns such as checkers and rings. Lighting and shading effects, such as shadows and reflections, make your scenes come to life, and constructive solid geometry (CSG) enables you to combine your graphics primitives in simple ways to produce complex shapes.

Aside from a computer, operating system, and programming environment, one will need a way to display PPM image files. On Windows, programs like Photoshop will work, or free programs like IrfanView. On Mac, no special software is needed, as Preview can open PPM files.

Another interesting resource is Pete Shirley's *Ray Tracing in One Weekend*.[24]

8.6.2 Tiny Ray Tracer Fits in 64 Bytes

People often try to make the biggest, or the fastest, or the smallest. The Hellmood ray caster is in the latter category and proves it with a 64-byte interactive 3D application for MS-DOS.

Since 2013, says the author, he tried several approaches in little intros for MS-DOS, except for 3D ray casting. As a computer scientist with a specialization in computer graphics, he just was not interested enough in manually asm-coding a brute-force ray caster, about already existing, excellent examples like "Spongy" (128b, TBC, 2009) and "Wolf128" (128b, Baudsurfer, 2014). However, he coded several "2,5D" effects like "Lucy" (64b, 2014) and recently "Projektbeschreibung" (32b, DESIRE, 2018). So naturally, at some point, he asked himself, what is the smallest 3D ray caster which is perceived as one, being centered, having decent textures and colors, and runs on all common systems (MS-DOS, FreeDos, WinXP

---

[24]Shirley (2018).

Fig. 8.102 Video of 64-byte ray caster. *Source* Hellmood

Dos, Dosbox) while being smooth at least on real hardware? The (his) answer is: It is a.COM file format is lean, and one can take over everything without much work. If the program were massive, it wouldn't be impressive. There are 64 shades of gray; however, there are versions that use various color palettes, and each one fits in 64 bytes or less. There is even mouse control, and one can see the results in the video below. https://youtu.be/hEmK64CKpP0 (Fig. 8.102).

If one gets the urge to do some MS-DOS programming, you can use gcc although you will almost surely get bigger executables. If you are just nostalgic for old games and software, you can run those in your browser. https://www.pouet.net/prod.php?which=78044.

8.6.3 A Ray Tracer for Bare Metal x86

x86-ray-tracer is a ray tracer written in x86 assembler (with usage of SSE/SSE2 extensions) as a proof of concept raymarcher for bare metal x86_64 with an UEFI firmware. It is full of rough edges but should render a sphere at 800 × 600 pixels using a PBR shader (Fig. 8.103).

If you want to run it on real hardware, download the.efi and start it with the UEFI shell or a bootloader of your choice. It is possible that your UEFI does not support the requested video mode, in which case you have to build it by yourself. That is required because the ray tracer does not use dynamic memory allocation. https://github.com/mmha/efiraytracer.

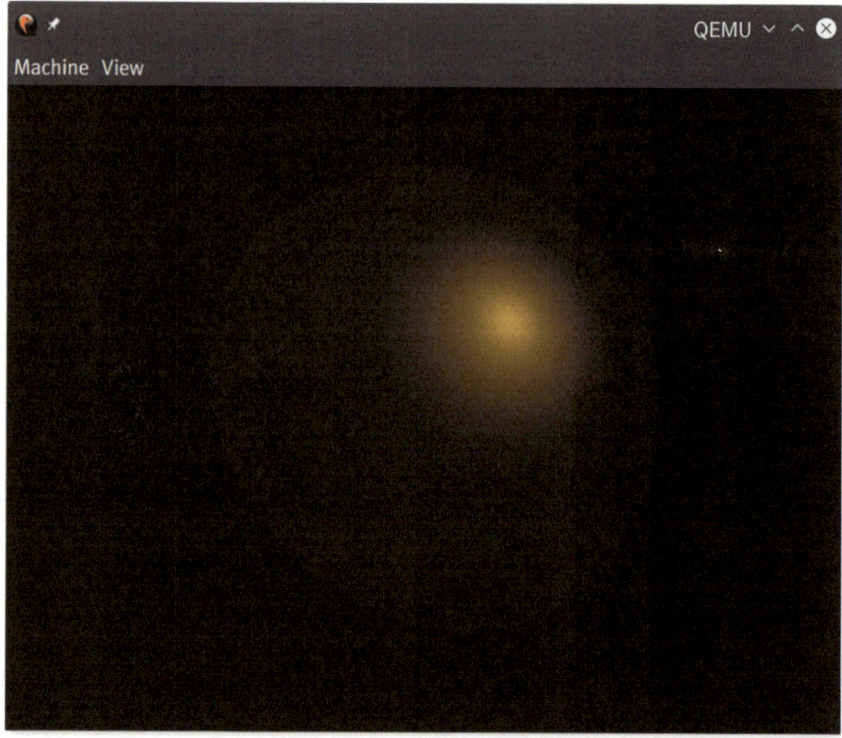

Fig. 8.103 Bare metal x86 ray tracer

One needs Linux with a x86_64-w64-mingw32-g++ cross-compiler, GNU efilib, and CMake. The build system will produce an EFI executable.

8.6.4   Tiny Metaball Ray Tracer in x86/x87 Assembly

This is a size-coding experiment. The author said, … "to see if I could write a 3D metaball ray tracer in 256 bytes (spoilers: I can't, it ended up around 1k)". It runs in 16-bit real mode under DOS, although exit is the only DOS system call used, and the program is compiled as a 16 bit flat binary, so DOS is used just for the convenience of loading and running it.

This program runs in 320 × 200 16 bpp using VESA (VBE) 1.2, which should work on most graphics AIBs. You can download the code from here: https://github.com/jtsiomb/tinyblobray (Fig. 8.104)

There is a video of the ray tracer here: http://imgur.com/2XGEzZ8.

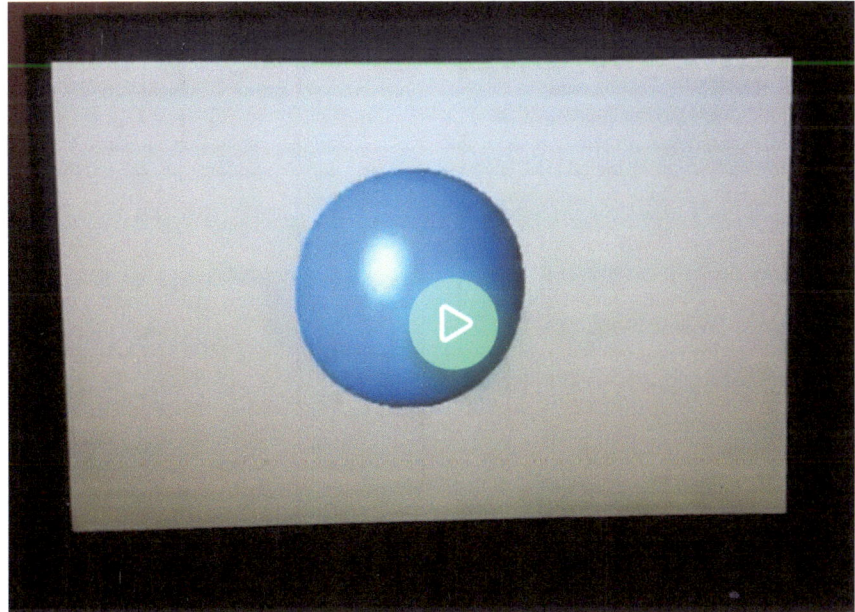

Fig. 8.104 Meatball ray tracer

References

Arvo J, Kirk D (1987) Fast ray tracing by ray classification. Comput Graph 21(4)

Bigler J, Stephens A, Parker SG (2006) Design for parallel interactive ray tracing systems. In: proceedings of the IEEE Symposium on Interactive Ray Tracing

Buck J (2019) The ray tracer challenge: a test-driven guide to your first 3D renderer, 1st edn. Pragmatic Bookshelf, Raleigh. ISBN-13: 978-1680502718

Fascione L, Hanika J, Leone M, Droske M, Schwarzhaupt J, Davidovič T, Weidlich A, Meng J (2018) Manuka: a batch-shading architecture for spectral path tracing in movie production. ACM Trans Graph 37(3), Article 31

Harada T (2017) Radeon-ProRender-and-Radeon-Rays-in-a-gaming-rendering-workflow, GDC2017. https://gpuopen.com/gdc2017-radeon-prorender-and-radeon-rays-in-a-gaming-rendering-workflow/

Mottle J (2018) Architectural visualization rendering engine survey—results. In: CGarchitect, 24 Feb 2018. http://www.cgarchitect.com/2018/02/2018-architectural-visualization-rendering-engine-survey

Nichols C (2017) V-Ray next: experiments with the Nvidia Optix Denoiser, Dec 2017. https://www.chaosgroup.com/blog/experiments-with-v-ray-next-using-the-nvidia-optix-denoiser

Nichols C (2018) V-Ray next: Denoising in production, June 2018. https://www.chaosgroup.com/blog/v-ray-next-denoising-in-production

Seymour M (2016) V-Ray's practical stochastic rendering of 'spec-y' things. Fxguide, Oct 2016. https://www.fxguide.com/quicktakes/v-rays-practical-stochastic-rendering-of-spec-y-things/

Shirley P (2018) Ray tracing in one weekend. http://www.realtimerendering.com/raytracing/Ray%20Tracing%20in%20a%20Weekend.pdf

Starr M (2014) New mo-cap tech renders CG in real-time, Apr 2014. https://www.cnet.com/news/new-mo-cap-tech-renders-cg-in-real-time/

Stéphane G, Cyril S (2004) Graphics gems revisited. ACM Trans Graph (Proceedings of the SIGGRAPH conference—2004). http://maverick.inria.fr/Publications/2004/GS04/GraphicsGemsRevisited.letter.pdf

Stephens A, Boulos S, Bigler J, Wald I, Parker SG (2006) An application of scalable massive model interaction using shared memory systems. In: Proceedings of the Eurographics Symposium on Parallel Graphics and Visualization

Suarez J (2009) V-Ray on the GPU. In: SIGGRAPH 2009. https://www.youtube.com/watch?v=DJLCpS107jg

Wald I, Johnson GP, Amstutz J, Brownlee C, Knoll A, Jeffers J, Günther J, Navratil P (2017) OSPRay—a CPU ray tracing framework for scientific visualization. IEEE Trans Vis Comput Graph 23(1), pp 931–940 (2017)

Ward GJ (1992) Measuring and modeling anisotropic reflection. In: Proceedings of SIGGRAPH, pp 265–272. https://doi.org/10.1145/133994.134078

Wilkie A, Nawaz S, Droske M, Weidlich A, Hanika J (2014) Hero wavelength spectral sampling. In: Eurographics Symposium on Rendering 2014, vol 33, Number 4. https://cgg.mff.cuni.cz/~wilkie/Website/EGSR_14_files/WNDWH14HWSS.pdf

Appendix A

In this section, you will find miscellaneous and related information and reference material supporting various sections of the book.

The next page contains a sample of the view of all the ray tracing programs. The accompanying spreadsheet is an in-depth database of those programs.

A.1. Ray-Tracing Programs and Plug-Ins

See Table A.1.

A.2. Early Photorealism—Who Invented Ray Tracing

Long before computers, and even before cameras, artists sought to create a photorealistic image. One artist, Albrecht Dürer rendered with almost photographic accuracy, *A Young Hare*. In addition to being a fine artist, Dürer wrote two books that discussed geometry. In chapters of his books, he provides instructions for the construction of perspective projections (also with lights and shadows). The methods, as they were described in his *Underweysung der messung*, book can be, according to Georg Rainer Hofmann, clearly identified as "object scanning" and "ray tracing." Hofmann therefore concludes that the great Renaissance artist, mathematician, and painter, Albrecht Dürer, who was responsible for two important books published in Nuremberg, Germany, is the father of ray tracing.[1]

---

[1]Hofmann (1990).

© Springer Nature Switzerland AG 2019
J. Peddie, *Ray Tracing: A Tool for All*,
https://doi.org/10.1007/978-3-030-17490-3

Table A.1 Ray tracing plug-in programs

Product	Int.	Stand-alone	Plug-in	Biased	License	Win	OS X	Linux	Other	GPU	Org.
Blender Cycles	Yes	Yes	Yes	No	Apache 2.0	Yes	Yes	Yes	No	Yes	Blender Foundation
Bryce	Yes				Proprietary	Yes	Yes	No	No		DAZ 3D (Daz Productions)
Dimension CC	Yes				Proprietary	Yes	Yes			Yes	Adobe
FinalRender	Yes		Yes	No	Subscription	Yes				YES	Cebas
Form-Z 8.5	Yes				Proprietary						AutoDesSys
NxtRender	Yes		Yes	Yes/No	EULA	Yes					RenderPlus
Octane Render	Yes				Proprietary	Yes	Yes	Yes	No	Yes	OTOY / Refractive Software
Raytracer	Yes			No		Yes				No	Autodesk
Redshift	Yes		Yes	Yes	Floating	Yes	Yes	Yes		Y	Redshift Rendering Technologies
3Delight		Yes	Yes		Proprietary	Yes	Yes	Yes	No		DNA Research subsidiary of Taarna Studios.
Appleseed		Yes	yes		MIT License						Appleseed
Arion		Yes	Yes	No	Proprietary	Yes	No	No		Yes	Random Control
Corona Render		Yes	Yes	No	Floating	Yes	Yes			No	Render Legion s.a.., - Chaos Software (parent)
Flamingo nXt		Yes	Yes	Yes	EULA	Yes					McNeel & Associates (Tim, Inc.)
FluidRay RT		Yes	Yes	No	Proprietary	Yes	Yes				Fluidray (Fluid Interactive)
FryRender		Yes	Yes							No	RandomControl
Houdini - Mantra		Yes	Yes	Yes	Proprietary	Yes	Yes	Yes	No	Yes	Side Effects Software
Indigo Renderer		Yes	Yes	No	Proprietary	Yes	Yes	Yes		Yes	Glare Technologies
Iray		Yes	Yes	No	Floating	Yes		Yes		Yes	Nvidia
KeyShot	Yes	Yes	Yes		Floating	Yes	Yes			YES	Luxion
Maxwell Render		Yes	Yes		Proprietary	Yes	Yes	Yes	No	Yes	Next Limit Technologies
Moskito Render		Yes	Yes	No	subscription	Yes				Yes	Cebas
OneRender		Yes	Yes								Prefixa
Poser FireFly		Yes	Yes	Yes	Trialware	Yes	Yes				SmithMicro
POV-Ray		Yes	Yes	Exporter	AGPLv3	Yes		Yes			Persistence of Vision Raytracer Pty. Ltd
Renditoner Pro		Yes	Yes			Yes		Yes			IMSI Design (Turbo CAD)
Visualize		Yes	Yes	Yes	Term & Network	Yes	No	No		Yes	SolidWorks/Dassault-Systems
V-Ray		Yes	Yes		Proprietary	Yes	Yes	Yes	No	Yes	Chaos Group
Air 14		Yes			Proprietary						Sitex Graphics
Arnold		Yes									Autodesk (Solid Angle)
Art of Illusion		Yes			GPL	Yes	Yes	Yes	No		Peter Eastman
Artlantis 6		Yes			Proprietary						Abvent
BIGrender 3.0		Yes			Proprietary						Tomas Cayuela / hydragrafix
Cheetah3D		Yes		No	Proprietary	No	Yes	No	No		Dr. Martin Wengenmayer
Clarisse FX		Yes			Proprietary						Isotropix
Click-VR Visualizer		Yes									Code Blend
Fujiyama		Yes			MIT License						Hiroshi Tsubokawa
Guerilla Render		Yes			Proprietary						Mercenaries-engineering
Infinity 3D		Yes			free						Infinity3D
LightWave 3D		Yes			Proprietary	Yes	Yes	No	Amiga		NewTek, Inc
LumionRT		Yes			Proprietary						Act-3D
Manta		Yes			MIT	No	Yes	Yes	No		Univserity Utah
Mitsuba		Yes				Yes	Yes	Yes	No	No	Wenzel Jakob
MODO		Yes			Proprietary	Yes	Yes	No	No		The Foundry / Luxology
Nebula Renderer		Yes	No		Freeware	Yes			No	Yes	Nebula Render
NOX		Yes	No		Proprietary						Evermotion
NuGraf		Yes			Proprietary						Okino
OSPray		Yes			Apache	Yes				No	Intel
Picogen		Yes			GPLv3	Yes	No	Yes	No		Sebastian Mach
Pixie		Yes			GPL	Yes	Yes	Yes	No		Okan Arikan
Radeon ProRender		Yes	No		MIT License	Yes				Yes	AMD
Radiance		Yes			BSD	Yes	Yes	Yes	No		Greg Ward
RenderDotC		Yes			Proprietary						Dot C Software
RenderMan		Yes			Proprietary	Yes	Yes	Yes	No		Pixar
Tachyon		Yes			GPL	No	Yes	Yes	No		University of Illinois at Urbana–Champaign
Visionaray		Yes			MIT	Yes	Yes	Yes	No	Yes	Universität zu Koln
Bloom			Yes		Proprietary						Bloom Unit
Brighter 3D			Yes	No							Brighter 3D
Caravaggio			Yes								Caravaggio DevGroup
CentiLeo			Yes								CentiLeo
Enscape			Yes		Proprietary	Yes	No	No		Yes	Enscape3D
Kerkythea			Yes		Proprietary	Yes	Yes	Yes	No		Solid Iris Technologies (Parent Altair Engineering)
Kray			Yes								MindBerries
LocalRay			Yes		Proprietary				Android		Adshir Ltd.
LuxRender			Yes		Apache v2.0	Yes	Yes	Yes	No		LuxRender
Raylectron			Yes		Proprietary						Softbyte Labs
Shaderlight			Yes		Proprietary	Yes					Artvps
SU Podium 2.5			Yes		Proprietary						Cadalog Inc.
Thea			Yes	Yes						Yes	Altair Company (Parent) / Solid Iris Technologies
Twilight 2			Yes		Proprietary						Twilight Redner
Visualizer			Yes								Imagination technologies
Vue			Yes		Proprietary	Yes	Yes	No	No		E-On Software, Inc. (Bentley Systems)
YafaRay			Yes		LGPL	Yes	Yes	Yes	No		YafaRay developers

A.2.1. Young Hare

A Young Hare (German: Feldhase) is a 1502 watercolor and body color painting by Albrecht Dürer. Painted in 1502 in his workshop, it is acknowledged as a masterpiece of observational art alongside his Great Piece of Turf from the following year. The subject is rendered with almost photographic accuracy, and although the piece is normally given the title, "Young Hare," the portrait is sufficiently detailed for the hare to be identified as a mature specimen—the German title translates as "Field Hare" and the work is often referred to in English as the Hare or Wild Hare (Fig. A.1).

The subject was particularly challenging: The hare's fur lay in different directions and the animal was mottled with lighter and darker patches all over, Dürer had

Fig. A.1 A young Hare but Albrecht Dürer, 1502. *Source* Wikipedia

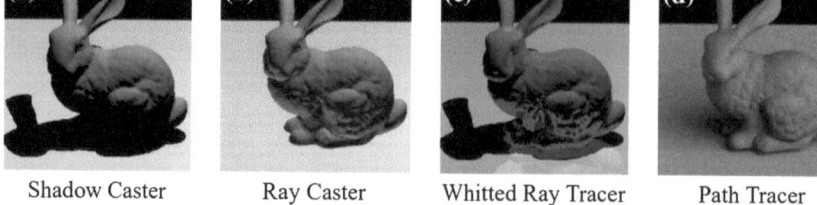

| Shadow Caster | Ray Caster | Whitted Ray Tracer | Path Tracer |

Fig. A.2 Rendering examples using a hare: **a** shadow casting, **b** ray casting, **c** Whitted ray tracing, and **d** Path Tracing. *Source* Ray Tracing on Programmable Graphics Hardware (Purcell et al. 2002)

to adapt the standard conventions of shading to indicate the outline of the subject by the fall of light across the figure. Despite the technical challenges presented in rendering the appearance of light with a multi-colored, multi-textured subject, Dürer not only managed to create a detailed, almost scientific, study of the animal but also infuses the picture with a warm golden light that hits the hare from the left, highlighting the ears and the run of hair along the body, giving a spark of life to the eye, and casting a strange shadow to the right.

This then should be the gold standard of realized photorealistic rendering, not a chrome teapot (Fig. A.2).

It is ironic, and perhaps no coincidence that a young hare has been used as a rendering model by several researchers.

A.2.2. Varieties of Realism; Geometries of Representational Art

Margaret A. Hagen's "Varieties of Realism"[2] argues that it is not possible to represent the layout of objects and surfaces in space outside the dictates of formal visual geometry, the geometry of natural perspective. The book examines most of the world's coherent representational art styles, both in terms of the geometry of their creation and in terms of their perceptual effects on the viewer. A lucid exposition of modern geometrical principles and relations, accessible to the non-mathematical reader, is followed by an analysis of all known styles as variants of natural perspective, as true varieties of realism. Delineating the physical and mechanical constraints that determine the act of visual representation in painting and drawing, the author traces the intimate relations among seemingly distant styles and considers the kind of perceptual information about the world each can carry. Margaret Hagen is a perceptual psychologist with an ecological point of view. Her rigorous but readable presentation of visual theory and research offers provocative new insights into the connections among vision, geometry, and art.

---

[2]http://www.amazon.com/Varieties-Realism-Geometries-Representational-Cambridge/dp/0521313295.

A.2.2.1. More About Bunnies Than You Probably Wanted to Know

The Stanford Bunny is one of the most commonly used test models in computer graphics. It is a collection of 69,451 triangles, and it was assembled from range images of a clay bunny that is roughly 7.5 in. high. Figure A.2 is a synthetic rendering of the model, courtesy of Peter Lindstrom. This Web page describes where the model came from, tells why it was created in the first place, discusses the relative merits of using it as a test model in graphics research, and shows some example images (https://www.cc.gatech.edu/~turk/bunny/bunny.html).

Durer was discovering linear perspective. Newton traced rays in Optiks, and Feinman mentions a job opportunity he passed up ray tracing for a lens company in, "Surely You're Joking." But to name anyone other than Turner as the Father of Ray Tracing really diminishes one of the main contributions of computer graphics to all of the sciences.

A.3. Biased Versus Unbiased Rendering

In computer graphics, unbiased rendering refers to a rendering technique that does not introduce any systematic error, or bias, into the radiance approximation. Because of this, it is often used to generate the reference image to which other rendering techniques are compared. It is important to note that an unbiased technique may not consider all possible paths. Path Tracing cannot consistently handle caustics generated from a point light source, as it is highly unlikely to randomly generate the path that directly reflects into the point.

Unbiased renderers are usually physically based and photorealistic renderer which simulates the physics of light to achieve near-perfect image realism. With an advanced Physical Camera model, a super-realistic materials system and the ability to simulate complex lighting situations through Metropolis Light Transport, Indigo Renderer is capable of producing the highest levels of realism demanded by architectural and product visualization.

A biased rendering method is not necessarily wrong, and it can still converge to the correct answer if the estimator is consistent. It does, however, introduce a certain bias error, usually in the form of a blur.

A.4. Technical Papers and Books on Ray Tracing

Looking at just the leading technical journals from ACM and IEEE, I found over 700 technical papers on ray tracing have been published since 1982 (Table A.2).

Table A.2 Technical papers on ray tracing published since 1982

Year	SIGGRAPH	SIGGRAPH Asia	Eurograph	IEEE
1982	1			1
1983	2			2
1984	6		2	5
1985	3		3	3
1986	3		3	6
1987	5		4	6
1988	4		4	5
1989	6		6	7
1990	8		6	11
1991	2		2	12
1992	3		8	4
1993	2		2	6
1994	3		5	6
1995	3		3	6
1996	1			3
1997	3		1	3
1998	4		1	4
1999	4		3	6
2000	1			3
2001	1		7	7
2002	7		5	4
2003	2		6	8
2004	8		5	7
2005	21		6	12
2006	13		6	25
2007	18		9	29
2008	12		9	31
2009	10		8	15
2010	10	2	9	17
2011	14	3	6	17
2012	7	1	8	15
2013	15	3	10	20
2014	6	4	6	16
2015	7	3	7	12
2016	8	2	10	7
2017	9	2	10	4
2018	6		1	2
Total	238	20	181	347

A.4.1. Books on ray tracing

See Table A.3.

Table A.3 Books on ray tracing

Last, first name	Title	Publisher	Date	Description
Glassner, Andrew S.	*An Introduction to Ray Tracing*	Academic Press	1989	The first book on ray tracing, from 1989, is now free to download http://www.realtimerendering.com/raytracing/An-Introduction-to-Ray-Tracing-The-Morgan-Kaufmann-Series-in-Computer-Graphics-.pdf
Shirley, Peter Mr. Morley, R. Keith Mr.	*Realistic Ray Tracing*	A K Peters, Ltd.	19-Dec-08	Concentrating on the "nuts and bolts" of writing ray tracing programs, this book emphasizes on practical and implementation issues. It also takes the reader through all the details needed to write a modern rendering system. It also adds many C++ code segments and adds new details to provide the reader with a better intuitive understanding of ray tracing algorithms
Suffern, Kevin Dr.	*Ray Tracing from the Ground Up*	CRC Press	09-Mar-2016	This book takes readers through the whole process of building a modern ray tracer from scratch in C++. All concepts and processes are explained in detail with the aid of various diagrams, ray-traced images, and sample codes
Tracy, E. R. Brizard, A. J. Richardson A. S.	*Ray Tracing and Beyond: Phase Space Methods in Plasma Wave Theory*	Cambridge University Press	27-Dec-14	This book is a complete introduction to the use of modern ray tracing techniques in plasma physics. It describes the powerful mathematical methods generally applicable to vector wave equations in non-uniform media and clearly demonstrates the application of these methods to simplify and solve important problems in plasma wave theory. It also covers variational principles, covariant formulations, caustics, tunneling, mode conversion, weak dissipation, wave emission from coherent sources, incoherent wave fields, and collective wave absorption and emission, all within an accessible framework using standard plasma physics notation
Choudhury, Balamati Dr. Jha, Rakesh Mohan Mr.	*Refined Ray Tracing inside Single- and Double-Curvatured Concave Surfaces*	Springer	24-Sep-15	This book describes the ray tracing effects inside different quadric surfaces such as right circular cylinder, general paraboloid of revolution (GPOR), GPOR frustum of different shaping parameters and the corresponding visualization of the ray path details. Finally, ray tracing inside a typical space module, which is a hybrid of a finite segment of the right circular cylinder and a frustum of GPOR, is analyzed for practical aerospace applications

(continued)

Table A.3 (continued)

Last, first name	Title	Publisher	Date	Description
Driemeyer, Thomas Mr.	*Rendering with mental ray®*	Springer	21-Dec-13	Mental ray is the leading rendering engine for generating photorealistic images, built into many 3D graphics applications. This book gives a general introduction into rendering with mental ray, as well as step-by-step recipes for creating advanced effects, and tips and tricks for professional users. A comprehensive definition of mental ray's scene description language and the standard shader libraries are included and used as the basis for all examples
Kulungowski, Alexander Ward Mr.	*Ray tracing acceleration techniques using k-d trees*	University of California	2005	Many computer graphics rendering algorithms and techniques use ray tracing for the generation of natural and photorealistic images. The efficiency of the ray tracing algorithms depends, among other techniques, upon the data structures used in the background. kd-trees are some of the most commonly used data structures for accelerating ray tracing algorithms. Data structures using cost optimization techniques based upon surface area heuristics (SAH) are generally considered to be best and of high quality. The book describes various techniques to accelerate ray tracing with the help of Kd-trees
Eric Haines and Tomas Akenine-Möller	*Ray Tracing Gems*	Nvidia	Mar-19	Real-time ray tracing—the holy grail of graphics—is now possible for video games. Thanks to advances in GPU hardware and integration in standards like DirectX, game developers will eagerly add ray tracing to take the next step in visual quality and ease of content creation

References

Hofmann GR (1990) Who invented ray tracing? A historical remark. Vis Comput 6(3):120–124. https://link.springer.com/article/10.1007/BF01911003

Purcell TJ, Buck I, Mark WR, Hanrahan P (2002) Ray tracing on programmable graphics hardware. In: Proceedings of SIGGRAPH 2002. ACM Trans Graph 21(3):703–712

Glossary

AFIPS The American Federation of Information Processing Societies (AFIPS) was an umbrella organization of professional societies established on May 10, 1961, and dissolved in 1990. Its mission was to advance knowledge in the field of information science and to represent its member societies in international forums. The IEEE-CS joined the ACM to form the Federation on Computing in the United States (FOCUS) in 1991, to take the place of AFIPS as the US' representative in International Federation of Information Processing (IFIP).

AIB (Add-in board) An add-in board, also known as a card, is a board that gets plugged into the PC. When an AIB contains a GPU and memory, it is known as a graphics AIB or graphics card. It plugs into either PCI Express or the older bus AGP.

Albedo Albedo is the base color input, commonly known as a diffuse map. An albedo map defines the color of diffused light. One of the biggest differences between an albedo map in a PBR system and a traditional diffuse map is the lack of directional light or ambient occlusion. Directional light will look incorrect in certain lighting conditions, and ambient occlusion should be added in the separate AO slot. The albedo map will sometimes define more than the diffuse color as well, for instance, when using a metalness map, the albedo map defines the diffuse color for insulators (non-metals) and reflectivity for metallic surfaces.

Alembic An interchange file format for computer graphics used by visual effects and animation. Alembic is used for the interchange of geometry (models) between different groups working on the same shots or the same assets in the same company or different studios working on the same projects. Alembic supports the common geometric representations used in the industry, including polygon meshes, subdivision surface, parametric curves, NURBS patches, and particles.

Ambient occlusion To create realistic shadowing around objects, developers use an effect called ambient occlusion (AO); sometimes called "poor man's ray

© Springer Nature Switzerland AG 2019
J. Peddie, *Ray Tracing: A Tool for All*,
https://doi.org/10.1007/978-3-030-17490-3

tracing." AO can account for the occlusion of light, creating non-uniform shadows that add depth to the scene. Most commonly, games use screen-space ambient occlusion (SSAO) for the rendering of AO effects. There are many variants, though all are based on early AO tech, and as such suffer from a lack of shadow definition and quality, resulting in a minimal increase in image quality (IQ) compared to the same scene without AO.

Anisotropic filtering (AF) A method of enhancing the image quality of textures on the surfaces of computer graphics that are at oblique viewing angles with respect to the camera where the projection of the texture (not the polygon or other primitive on which it is rendered) appears to be non-orthogonal (thus the origin of the word: "an" for not, "iso" for same, and "tropic" from tropism, relating to direction; anisotropic filtering does not filter the same in every direction).

Bidirectional reflectance distribution function (BRDF) A function of four real variables that defines how light is reflected at an opaque surface. It is employed in the optics of real-world light, in computer graphics algorithms, and in computer vision algorithms. The function takes an incoming light direction, and outgoing direction (taken in a coordinate system where the surface normal lies along the z-axis) and returns the ratio of reflected radiance exiting to the irradiance incident on the surface from direction the light source. A BRDF is a simplified BSSRDF, assuming that light enters and leaves at the same point.

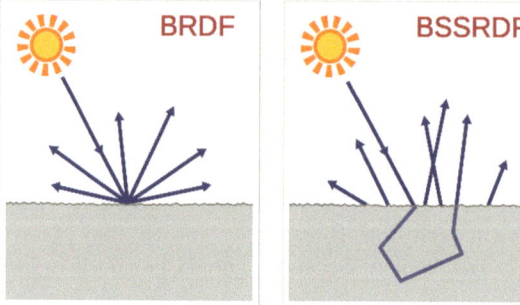

Bidirectional scattering distribution function (BSDF) Introduced in 1980 by Bartell, Dereniak, and Wolfe, it is often used to name the general mathematical function which describes the way in which the light is scattered by a surface. However, in practice, this phenomenon is usually split into the reflected and transmitted components, which are then treated separately as BRDF (bidirectional reflectance distribution function) and BTDF (bidirectional transmittance distribution function). BSDF is a superset and the generalization of the BRDF and BTDF.

Bidirectional scattering-surface reflectance distribution function (BSSRDF) or B surface scattering RDF describes the relation between outgoing radiance and the incident flux, including the phenomena-like subsurface scattering (SSS). The BSSRDF describes how light is transported between any two rays that hit a surface.

Bidirectional texture functions (BTF) Bidirectional texture function is a six-dimensional function depending on planar texture coordinates as well as on view and illumination spherical angles. In practice, this function is obtained as a set of several thousand color images of a material sample taken during different camera and light positions.

Bilinear filtering When a small texture is used as a texture map on a large surface, a stretching will occur, and large block pixels will appear. Bilinear filtering smoothens out this blocky appearance by applying a blur.

Bokeh The aesthetic quality of the blur produced in the out-of-focus parts of an image produced by a lens. Bokeh has been defined as "the way the lens renders out-of-focus points of light." Smartphone cameras have algorithms in their processor that can create artificial bokeh on images when their lenses fail to produce the effect.

Bounding volume hierarchy (BVH) A BVH is a tree structure on a set of geometric objects. All geometric objects are wrapped in bounding volumes that form the leaf nodes of the tree. These nodes are then grouped as small sets and enclosed within larger bounding volumes.

Chrominance Chrominance (chroma or C for short) is the signal used in video systems to convey the color information of the picture, separately from the accompanying luma signal (or Y for short). Chrominance is usually represented as two color difference components: $U = B' - Y'$ (blue − luma) and $V = R' - Y'$ (red − luma). Each of these different components may have scale factors and offsets applied to it, as specified by the applicable video standard.

Complementary metal–oxide–semiconductor (CMOS) sensor A CMOS sensor is an array of active pixel sensors in complementary metal–oxide–semiconductor (CMOS) or N-type metal-oxide-semiconductor (NMOS, Live MOS) technologies.

Color gamut The entire range of colors available on a particular device such as a monitor or printer. A monitor, which displays RGB signals, typically has a greater color gamut than a printer, which uses CMYK inks. Also, see Gamut and wide color gamut.

Color space See color gamut and gamut.

Conservative raster When standard rasterization does not compute, the desired result is shown, where one green and one blue triangle have been rasterized. These triangles overlap geometrically, but the standard rasterization process does not detect this fact.

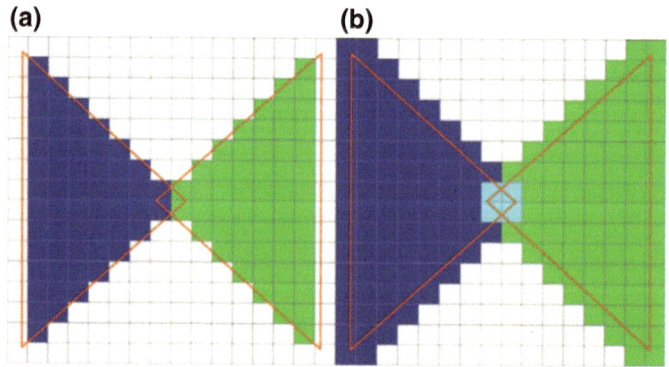

Comparing Standard and conservative rasterization

With conservative rasterization, the overlap is always properly detected, no matter what resolution is used. This property can enable collision detection.

Constant dither A constant dither is the application of a dither value which doesn't change over the course of a set of dithering operations.

Contrast ratio The contrast ratio is a property of a display system, defined as the ratio of the luminance of the brightest color (white) to that of the darkest color (black) that the system is capable of producing. A high contrast ratio is a desired aspect of displays.

CNN (Convolutional neural network) A deep neural network (DNN) that has the connectivity in one or more of its layers arranged so that each node in Layer N is a convolution between a rectangular subset of the nodes in layer $N - 1$ and a convolution kernel whose weights are found by training. The arrangement is designed to mimic the human visual system and has proven to be very successful at image classification as long as very large training datasets are available.

Direct3D Also known as D3D, Direct3D is the 3D graphics API that's part of Microsoft DirectX foundation library for hardware support. Direct3D actually has two APIs, one which calls the other (called Direct3D Retained Mode or D3D RM) and hides the complexity of the lower level API (called Direct3D Immediate Mode or D3D IM). Direct3D is becoming increasingly popular as a method used by games and application developers to create 3D graphics, because it provides a reasonable level of hardware independence, while still supporting a large variety of 3D graphics functionality (see "3D").

Display Port Display Port is a VESA digital display interface standard for a digital audio/video interconnect, between a computer and its display monitor, or a computer and a home theater system. Display Port is designed to replace digital (DVI) and analog component video (VGA) connectors in the computer monitors and video cards.

EDF Emissive Distribution Functions.

Electro-optical transfer function (EOTF) HDR provides a means by which to describe and protect the content creator's intentions via metadata. It contains in essence a language used by the content creator to instruct the decoder. HDR provides metadata about how content was created to a display device in an organized fashion such that the display can maximize its own capabilities. As displays evolve, HDR will allow existing devices to always make the best effort in rendering images rather than running up against unworkable limitations. A formula called the electro-optical transfer function (EOTF) has been introduced to replace the CRT's gamma curve. Some engineers refer to EOTF more simply as perceptual quality or PQ. Whatever the name, it offers a far more granular way of presenting the luminance mapping according to the directions given by the content creator. EOTF is a part of the High-Efficiency Video Coding (HEVC) standard.

Energy conservation The concept of energy conservation states that an object cannot reflect more light than it receives.

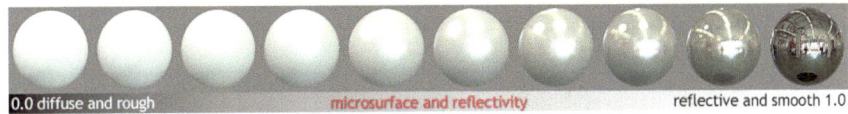

Energy conservation scales

For practical purpose, more diffuse and rough materials will reflect dimmer and wider highlights, while smoother and more reflective materials will reflect brighter and more condensed highlights.

Fragment shader Pixel shaders, also known as fragment shaders, compute color and other attributes of each fragment. The simplest kinds of pixel shaders output one screen pixel as a color value; more complex shaders with multiple inputs/outputs are also possible. Pixel shaders range from always outputting the same color, to applying a lighting value, to doing bump mapping, shadows, specular highlights, translucency, and other phenomena. They can alter the depth of the fragment for z-buffering.

Frame buffer The separate and private local memory for a GPU on a graphics AIB. The term frame buffer is a bit out of date since the GPU's local memory holds much more than just a frame or an image for the display as they did when originally developed. Today the GPU's local memory holds programs (known as shaders) and various textures, as well as partial results from various calculations, and two to three sets of images for the display as well as depth information known as a z-buffer.

Gamma correction Gamma correction, gamma nonlinearity, gamma encoding, or often simply gamma, is the name of a nonlinear operation used to code and decode luminance or tristimulus values in video or still image systems. Gamma correction is, in the simplest cases, defined by the following power-law expression.

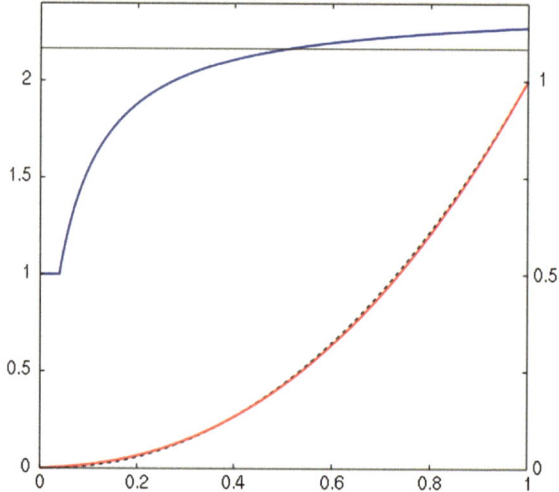

Plot of the sRGB standard gamma-expansion nonlinearity (red),
and its local gamma value, slope in log–log space (blue)

In most computer systems, images are encoded with a gamma of about 0.45 and
decoded with a gamma of 2.2. The sRGB color space standard used with most
cameras, PCs, and printers does not use a simple power-law nonlinearity as above
but has a decoding gamma value near 2.2 over much of its range. Gamma is
sometimes confused and/or improperly used as "Gamut".

Gamut In color reproduction, including computer graphics and photography, the
gamut or color gamut is a certain complete subset of colors. The most common

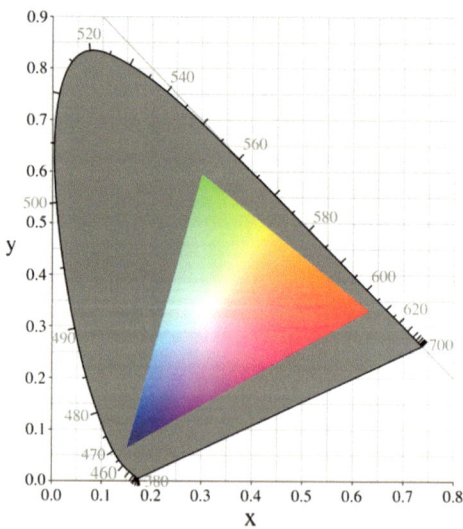

Typical gamut map. The grayed-out horseshoe shape is the entire range
of possible chromaticities, displayed in the CIE 1931 chromaticity diagram format

usage refers to the subset of colors which can be accurately represented in a given circumstance, such as within a given color space or by a certain output device.Also, see Color gamut and wide color gamut.

GDDR An abbreviation for double data rate-type six synchronous graphics random-access memory is a modern type of synchronous graphics random-access memory (SGRAM) with a high-bandwidth ("double data rate") interface designed for use in graphics cards, game consoles, and high-performance computation.

Geometry shaders Geometry shaders, introduced in Direct3D 10 and OpenGL 3.2, generate graphics primitives, such as points, lines, and triangles, from primitives sent to the beginning of the graphics pipeline. Executed after vertex shader geometry, shader programs take as input a whole primitive, possibly with adjacency information. For example, when operating on triangles, the three vertices are the geometry shader's input. The shader can then emit zero or more primitives, which are rasterized, and their fragments ultimately passed to a pixel shader.

Global illumination "Global illumination" (GI) is a term for lighting systems that model this effect. Without indirect lighting, scenes can look harsh and artificial. However, while light received directly is fairly simple to compute, indirect lighting computations are highly complex and computationally heavy.

GPC A graphics processing cluster (GPC) is group, or collection, of specialized processors known as shaders, or simultaneous multiprocessors, or stream processors. Organized as a SIMD processor, they can execute (process) a similar instruction (program or kernel) simultaneously or in parallel. Hence, they are known as a parallel processor (A shader is a computer program that is used to do shading: the production of appropriate levels of color within an image).

GPU (Graphics processing unit) The GPU is the chip that drives the display (monitor) and generates the images on the screen (and has also been called a visual processing unit or VPU). The GPU processes the geometry and lighting effects and transforms objects every time a 3D scene is redrawn—these are mathematically intensive tasks, and hence, the GPU has upwards to hundreds of floating-point processors (also called shaders or stream processors). Because the GPU has so many powerful 32-bit floating-point processors, it has been employed as a special-purpose processor for various scientific calculations other than display ad is referred to as a GPGPU in that case. The GPU has its own private memory on a graphics AIB which is called a frame buffer. When a small (less than five processors) GPU is put inside a northbridge (making it an IGP) the frame buffer is dropped, and the GPU uses system memory. The GPU has to be compatible with several interface standards including software APIs such as OpenGL and Microsoft's DirectX, physical I/O standards within the PC such as Intel's Accelerated Graphics Port (AGP) technology and PCI Express, and output standards known as VGA, DVI, HDMI, and Display Port.

GPU-Compute (GPGPU—General-Purpose Graphics Processor Unit) The term "GPGPU" is a bit misleading in that general-purpose computing such as the type an x86 CPU might perform cannot be done on a GPU. However, because GPUs have so many (hundreds in some cases) powerful (32-bit) floating-point processors, they have been employed in certain applications requiring massive vector operations and mathematical intensive problems in science, finance, and aerospace applications. The application of a GPU can yield several orders of magnitude higher performance than a conventional CPU. These days, there is not much that a GPU can't do. The main missing piece is operating system work (opening files and sockets).

GPU preemption The ability to interrupt or halt an active task (context switch) on a processor and replace it with another task, and then later resume the previous task this is a concept in the era of single-core CPUs preemption was how multitasking was accomplished. Interruption in a GPU, which is designed for streaming processing, is problematic in that it could necessitate a restart of a process and thereby delay a job. Modern GPUs can save state and resume a process as soon as the interruptive job is finished.

Graphics driver A device driver is a software stack that controls computer graphics hardware and supports graphics rendering APIs and is released under a free and open-source software license. Graphics device drivers are written for specific hardware to work within the context of a specific operating system kernel and to support a range of APIs used by applications to access the graphics hardware. They may also control output to the display, if the display driver is part of the graphics hardware.

G-Sync A proprietary adaptive sync technology developed by Nvidia aimed primarily to eliminate screen tearing and the need for software deterrents such as V-sync. G-Sync eliminates screen tearing by forcing a video display to adapt to the frame rate of the outputting device rather than the other way around, which could traditionally be refreshed halfway through the process of a frame being output by the device, resulting in two or more frames being shown at once.

HBAO+ Developed by Nvidia, HBAO+ claims the company, improves upon existing ambient occlusion (AO) techniques and adds richer, more detailed, more realistic shadows around objects that occlude rays of light. Compared to previous techniques, Nvidia claims HBAO+ is faster, more efficient, and significantly better.

HBM (High-Bandwidth Memory) HMB is a high-performance RAM interface for 3D-stacked DRAM from AMD and Hynix. It is to be used in conjunction with high-performance graphics accelerators and network devices. The first devices to use HBM are the AMD Fiji GPUs.

HDMI (High-Definition Multimedia Interface) HDMI is a digital, point-to-point interface for audio and video signals designed as a single-cable solution for home theater and consumer electronics equipment and also supported in graphics AIBs and some PC motherboards. Introduced in 2002 by the HDMI consortium, HDMI is electrically identical to video-only DVI.

Heterogeneous processors Heterogeneous computing refers to systems that use more than one kind of processor or cores. These systems gain performance or energy efficiency not just by adding the same type of processors, but by adding dissimilar coprocessors, usually incorporating specialized processing capabilities to handle particular tasks.

Luminance A photometric measure of the luminous intensity per unit area of light traveling in a given direction. It describes the amount of light that passes through, is emitted or reflected from a particular area, and falls within a given Solid Angle. The SI unit for luminance is candela per square meter (cd/m^2). A non-SI term for the same unit is the "nit." The CGS unit of luminance is the stilb, which is equal to one candela per square centimeter or $10\ kcd/m^2$.

MAGIC Mathematical Applications Group, Inc., code, a program developed for ray tracing by MAGI corporation in 1968.

M&E Media and entertainment.

NURBS Non-uniform rational basis spline (NURBS) is a mathematical model commonly used in computer graphics for generating and representing curves and surfaces. It offers great flexibility and precision for handling both analytic (surfaces defined by common mathematical formulae) and modeled shapes.

OLED (Organic light-emitting diode) A light-emitting diode (LED) in which the emissive electroluminescent layer is a film of organic compound that emits light in response to an electric current. This layer of organic semiconductor is situated between two electrodes; typically, at least one of these electrodes is transparent. OLEDs are used to create digital displays in devices such as television screens, computer monitors, and portable systems such as mobile phones.

Open Graphics Library (OpenGL) A cross-language, cross-platform application programming interface (API) for rendering 2D and 3D vector graphics. The API is typically used to interact with a graphics processing unit (GPU), to achieve hardware-accelerated rendering.

OpenRL A low-level interactive ray tracing API, available for download as an SDK for accelerating ray tracing in both graphics and non-graphics (e.g., physics) applications. OpenRL was developed by the Caustic Professional division of Imagination Technologies.

OpenVDB OpenVDB is an Academy Award-winning open-source C++ library comprising a novel hierarchical data structure and a suite of tools for the efficient storage and manipulation of sparse volumetric data discretized on three-dimensional grids. It was developed by DreamWorks Animation for use in volumetric applications typically encountered in feature film production and is now maintained by the Academy Software Foundation (ASWF). https://github.com/AcademySoftwareFoundation/openvdb.

Penumbra The partially shaded outer region of the shadow cast by an opaque object, such as the shadow cast by the earth or moon over an area experiencing a partial eclipse.

Phong shading Refers to an interpolation technique for surface shading in 3D computer graphics. It is also called Phong interpolation or normal-vector interpolation shading. Specifically, it interpolates surface normals across rasterized polygons and computes pixel colors based on the interpolated normals and a reflection model. Phong shading may also refer to the specific combination of Phong interpolation and the Phong reflection model.

Reflective shadow maps Reflective shadow maps (RSMs) are an extension to a standard shadow map, where every pixel is considered as an indirect light source. The illumination due to these indirect lights is evaluated on the fly using adaptive sampling in a fragment shader. By using screen-space interpolation of the indirect lighting, it is possible to achieve interactive rates, even for complex scenes. Since visualizations and games mainly work in screen space, the additional effort is largely independent of scene complexity. The resulting indirect light is approximate but leads to plausible results and is suited for dynamic scenes.

Relative luminance Relative luminance is formed as a weighted sum of linear RGB components, not gamma-compressed ones. Even so, luma is often erroneously called luminance. SMPTE EG 28 recommends the symbol Y' to denote luma and the symbol Y to denote relative luminance.

Render farm A render farm is a high-performance computer system, e.g., a computer cluster, built to render computer-generated imagery (CGI), typically for film and television visual effects.

Resolution, screen resolution The number of horizontal and vertical pixels on a display screen. The more pixels, the more information is visible without scrolling. Screen resolutions have a pixel count such as 1600×1200, which means 1600 horizontal pixels and 1200 vertical pixels.

RGB Red, Green, and Blue. Color components of a pixel blended to create a specific color on a display monitor. See "Color" for additional details.

ROP ROP stands for Raster Operator; Raster Operators (ROPs) handle several chores near the end of the pixel pipeline. ROPs handle anti-aliasing, Z and color compression, and the actual writing of the pixel to the output buffer.

RT Ray tracer or ray tracing.

SaaS Software as a service.

SAM Served available market.

Scanline rendering An algorithm for visible surface determination, in 3D computer graphics, that works on a row-by-row basis rather than a polygon-by-polygon or pixel-by-pixel basis.

SDK Software development kit.

SECAM Analog TV system used in France and parts of Russia and the Mid-east.

SDR Standard Dynamic Range TV (Rec.601, Rec.709, Rec.2020).

Shaders Shaders is a broadly used term in graphics and can pertain to the processing of specialized programs for geometry (known as vertex shading or transform and lighting) or pixels shading.

SIMD Same Instruction Multiple Data describes computers with multiple processing elements that perform the same operation on multiple data points simultaneously. Such machines exploit data-level parallelism, but not concurrency: there are simultaneous (parallel) computations, but only a single process (instruction) at a given moment. SIMD is particularly applicable to common tasks like such as adjusting the contrast in a digital image.

Subdivision surface Subdivision smooths and adds extra resolution to curves and surfaces at display and/or renders time. The renderer subdivides the surface until it's smooth down to the pixel level. The smooth surface can be calculated from the coarse mesh as the limit of recursive subdivision of each polygonal face into smaller faces that better approximate the smooth surface. This lets one work with efficient low-polygon models and only add the smoothing "on demand" on the graphics card (for display) or in the renderer. The trade-off is that subdivision curves/surfaces take slightly longer to render. However, smoothing low-resolution polylines using curve subdivision is still much faster than working with inherently smooth primitives such as NURBS curves.

Subsurface scattering (SSS) Also known as subsurface light transport (SSLT), is a mechanism of light transport in which light penetrates the surface of a translucent object, is scattered by interacting with the material, and exits the surface at a different point.

Subpixel Morphological Anti-aliasing (SMAA) This filter detects edges in a rendered image and classifies edge crossings into various shapes and shades, in an attempt to make the edges or lines look smoother. Almost every GPU developer has their own version of anti-aliasing.

Super-ray A grouping of rays within and across views, as a key component of a light-field processing pipeline.

TAM Total available market.

Tearing and frame dropping Vsync, where the monitor is synchronized to the powerline frequency, can cause the screen to be refreshed halfway through the process of a frame being output by the GPU, resulting in two or more frames being shown at once.

Texel Acronym for TEXture ELement or TEXture pixEL—the unit of data which makes up each individually addressable part of a texture. A texel is the texture equivalent of a pixel.

Texture mapping The act of applying a texture to a surface during the rendering process. In simple texture mapping, a single texture is used for the entire surface, no matter how visually close or distant the surface is from the viewer. A somewhat more visually appealing form of texture mapping involves using a single texture with bilinear filtering, while an even more advanced form of texture mapping uses multiple textures of the same image but with different levels of detail, also known as mipmapping. See also "Bilinear Filtering," "Level of Detail," "Mipmap," "Mipmapping," and "Trilinear Filtering."

Texture map Same thing as "Texture."

Texture A texture is a special bitmap image, much like a pattern, but which is intended to be applied to a 3D surface in order to quickly and efficiently create a realistic rendering of a 3D image without having to simulate the contents of the image in 3D space. That sounds complicated, but in fact it's very simple. For example, if you have a sphere (a 3D circle) and want to make it look like the planet Earth, you have two options. The first is that you meticulously plot each nuance in the land and sea onto the surface of the sphere. The second option is that you take a picture of the Earth as seen from space, use it as a texture, and apply it to the surface of the sphere. While the first option could take days or months to get right, the second option can be nearly instantaneous. In fact, texture mapping is used broadly in all sorts of real-time 3D programs and their subsequent renderings, because of its speed and efficiency. 3D games are certainly among the biggest beneficiaries of textures, but other 3D applications, such as simulators, virtual reality, and even design tools take advantage of textures too.

Tile-Based Deferred Rendering (TBDR) defers the lighting calculations until all objects have been rendered, and then it shades the whole visible scene in one pass. This is done by rendering information about each object to a set of render targets that contain data about the surface of the object this set of render targets is normally called the G-buffer.

Tiled rendering The process of subdividing a computer graphics image by a regular grid in optical space and rendering each section of the grid, or tile, separately. The advantage of this design is that the amount of memory and bandwidth is reduced compared to immediate mode rendering systems that draw the entire frame at once. This has made tile rendering systems particularly common for low-power handheld device use. Tiled rendering is sometimes known as a "sort middle" architecture, because it performs the sorting of the geometry in the middle of the graphics pipeline instead of near the end.

Tone mapping A technique used in image processing and computer graphics to map one set of colors to another to approximate the appearance of high-dynamic range images in a medium that has a more limited dynamic range.

Trilinear Filtering A combination of bilinear filtering and mipmapping, which enhances the quality of texture mapped surfaces. For each surface that is rendered, the two mipmaps closest to the desired level of detail will be used to compute pixel colors that are the most realistic by bilinearly sampling each mipmap and then using a weighted average between the two results to produce the rendered pixel.

UDIM An enhancement to the UV mapping and texturing workflow that makes UV map generation easier and assigning textures simpler. The term UDIM comes from U-Dimension and design UV ranges. UDIM is an automatic UV offset system that assigns an image onto a specific UV tile, which allows one to use multiple lower resolution texture maps for neighboring surfaces, producing a higher resolution result without having to resort to using a single ultra-high resolution image. UDIM was invented by Richard Addison-Wood and came from Weta Digital (circa 2002).

Voxel A voxel is a value in three-dimensional space. Voxel is a combination of "volume" and "pixel" where pixel is a combination of "picture" and "element." This is analogous to a texel, which represents 2D image data in a bitmap (also referred to as a pixmap). Voxels are used in the visualization and analysis of medical and scientific data (Some volumetric displays use voxels to describe their resolution. For example, a display might be able to show $512 \times 512 \times 512$ voxels). Both ray tracing and ray casting, as well as rasterization, can be applied to voxel data to obtain 2D raster graphics to depict on a monitor.

VPU (Vector Processing Unit) A vector processor or array processor implements an instruction set containing instructions that operate on one-dimensional arrays of data called vectors. Today's CPUs architectures have instructions for a form of vector processing on multiple (vectorized) datasets, typically known as SIMD (single instruction, multiple data). Common examples include Intel x86's MMX, SSE and AVX instructions, AMD's 3DNow! Extensions as well as Arm's Neon and its scalable vector extension (SVE).

VXGI is a new approach to computing a fast, approximate form of global illumination (GI) dynamically in real-time on the GPU. This new GI technology uses a voxel grid to store scene and lighting information and a novel voxel cone tracing process to gather indirect lighting from the voxel grid. The purpose for VXGI is to run in real-time and doing full ray tracing of the scene is too computationally intense, so approximations are required.

VXGI Voxel Global Illumination (VXGI), developed by Nvidia, features one-bounce indirect diffuse, specular light, reflections, and area lights. It is an advancement in realistic lighting, shading, and reflections. VGXI is a three-step process: Voxelization, light injection, and final gathering and is employed in the next-generation games and game engines.

WCG Wide Color Gamut—anything wider than Rec.709, DCI P3, Rec.2020—See wide color gamut.

Wide color gamut High Dynamic Range (HDR) displays a greater difference in light intensity from white to black, Wide Color Gamut (WGC) provides a greater range of colors. The wide-gamut RGB color space (or Adobe Wide Gamut RGB) is an RGB color space developed by Adobe Systems that offers a large gamut by using pure spectral primary colors. It is able to store a wider range of color values than sRGB or Adobe RGB color spaces.Also see HDR, and Color gamut.

Z-buffer A memory buffer used by the GPU that holds the depth of each pixel (Z-axis). When an image is drawn, each (X–Y) pixel is matched against the z-buffer location. If the next pixel in line to be drawn is below the one that is already there, it is ignored.

Index

© Springer Nature Switzerland AG 2019
J. Peddie, *Ray Tracing: A Tool for All*,
https://doi.org/10.1007/978-3-030-17490-3